The Dancing Dead

O|R|S

OXFORD RITUAL STUDIES

Series Editors

Ronald Grimes, Radboud University Nijmegen
Ute Hüsken, University of Oslo
Eric Venbrux, Radboud University Nijmegen

THE PROBLEM OF RITUAL EFFICACY
Edited by William S. Sax, Johannes Quack, and Jan Weinhold

PERFORMING THE REFORMATION
Public Ritual in the City of Luther
Barry Stephenson

RITUAL, MEDIA, AND CONFLICT
Edited by Ronald L. Grimes, Ute Hüsken, Udo Simon, and Eric Venbrux

KNOWING BODY, MOVING MIND
Ritualizing and Learning in Two Buddhist Centers in Toronto
Patricia Q. Campbell

NEGOTIATING RITES
Edited by Ute Hüsken and Frank Neubert

SUBVERSIVE SPIRITUALITIES
How Rituals Enact the World
Frédérique Apffel-Marglin

THE DANCING DEAD
Ritual and Religion among the Kapsiki/Higi of North Cameroon and Northeastern Nigeria
Walter E. A. van Beek

The Dancing Dead

*Ritual and Religion among the
Kapsiki/Higi of North Cameroon
and Northeastern Nigeria*

WALTER E. A. VAN BEEK

OXFORD
UNIVERSITY PRESS

Oxford University Press, Inc., publishes works that further
Oxford University's objective of excellence
in research, scholarship, and education.

Oxford   New York
Auckland   Cape Town   Dar es Salaam   Hong Kong   Karachi
Kuala Lumpur   Madrid   Melbourne   Mexico City   Nairobi
New Delhi   Shanghai   Taipei   Toronto

With offices in
Argentina   Austria   Brazil   Chile   Czech Republic   France   Greece
Guatemala   Hungary   Italy   Japan   Poland   Portugal   Singapore
South Korea   Switzerland   Thailand   Turkey   Ukraine   Vietnam

Copyright © 2012 by Oxford University Press, Inc.

Published by Oxford University Press, Inc.
198 Madison Avenue, New York, New York 10016

www.oup.com

Oxford is a registered trademark of Oxford University Press

All rights reserved. No part of this publication may be reproduced,
stored in a retrieval system, or transmitted, in any form or by any means,
electronic, mechanical, photocopying, recording, or otherwise,
without the prior permission of Oxford University Press.

Library of Congress Cataloging-in-Publication Data
Beek, W. E. A. van.
The dancing dead : ritual and religion among the Kapsiki/Higi of north Cameroon
and northeastern Nigeria / Walter E.A. van Beek.
p. cm. — (Oxford ritual studies)
Includes bibliographical references.
ISBN 978-0-19-985814-9 (hardcover : alk. paper) — ISBN 978-0-19-985816-3 (pbk. : alk. paper)
1. Kamwe (African people)—Rites and ceremonies. 2. Kamwe (African people)—Religion.
3. Kamwe (African people)—Funeral customs and rites. I. Title. II. Series: Oxford ritual studies.
DT571.K36B44 2012
299.37—dc23   2012010953

1 3 5 7 9 8 6 4 2

Printed in the United States of America
on acid-free paper

For Sunu Deli Luc

CONTENTS

Preface and Acknowledgments ix
Language and Orthography xi

PART ONE INTRODUCTION

1. The Funeral of Zra Teri Kwada   3
2. Understanding African Ritual   9
3. Slaves, War, and the Wider World   25

PART TWO RITUALS OF DWELLING

4. At Home in the Mountains   49
5. Sacrifice and the History of Dwelling   74
6. The Other Side of the World   100
7. Rain and the Cycle of Ritual   128

PART THREE RITUALS OF BELONGING

8. Starting Life   159
9. The Song of the Bride   182
10. The Brass Boys: Initiation   207
11. Harvesting Crops, Harvesting People   230

12. The Dancing Dead   249

13. Dynamics of Kapsiki Ritual   281

Appendix   297
    A founding myth of the Kapsiki   297
    Birth order names   302
    Glossary of Kapsiki terms   303
    Kapsiki plant names   309
End Notes   311
References   327
Index   333

PREFACE AND ACKNOWLEDGMENTS

This has been a long-term project, and not really ended, I hope. My involvement with the Kapsiki started with a visit in 1971, some time ago one might say, and still is not finished. The history of my research is part of the text, so I can be brief here. This book results from a lifetime of intermittent, deep immersion in Kapsiki society over four decades; after a first visit in 1971 and a major field stay of 1½ years (1972–73), I have been returning to the field every five years for two decades, and every other year since the mid 1990s. Some of the material of this book has been published in various journals and edited volumes, but the bulk is new, and anyway all earlier publications have been rewritten.

Ritual and religion form the guiding concept here, as in the whole series, and here we are in the realm of what has been called "traditional religion," a concept I will comment upon in the text. It is not about one ritual, but about the whole array of rituals in Kapsiki culture, contextualized within their way of life and with constant reference to their beliefs and conceptions. My focus is on the communal rituals, with the brilliant spectacle of the funeral as the absolute highlight, in fact the iconic Kapsiki ritual. Rites of a more individual nature, usually subsumed under magic and healing, are touched upon only in passing. A subsequent publication will take the smiths as its main vantage point, and there I will dwell at length on these aspects, in a book that can be viewed as a companion volume to this one.

Acknowledgments are due, as always, and a pleasure to do, as always. My institutional support has been constant and unwavering, first from the Department of Anthropology at Utrecht University, later from the African Studies Centre, Leiden (with thanks to Ann Reeves for her language support), and from the Faculty of Humanities at Tilburg University. Additional financial support came, in all these years, from various sides, first of all from WOTRO (Scientific Research in the Tropics) funding W 52-91 plus two travel grants, but also travel grants of the Royal Academy of Sciences (KNAW) and the Hollandse Maatschappij voor de Wetenschappen (Dutch Science Society). I thank Nic David for his screening of the text, Paul Wartena for the permission to use his drawings and Amanda van Beek for her assistance with the pictures.

My first and major debt is to the Kapsiki of Mogode; despite the small services I could provide for the village, the reciprocity is never balanced, and I owe them a deep and lasting gratitude. Many of my first informants are no longer with us, and such a long field involvement generates its own sad nostalgia. On the whole I have been fortunate to work in a society which has not been scourged by famine or war. But the nostalgia is definitely there, as I severely miss several of my good friends. In his series of children's books C. S. Lewis described the fantasy realm of Narnia as a world that runs on different time than ours. That is the feeling that sometimes surges when I return to the Kapsiki area: So much changed, so many people died, time runs differently here.

I am very fortunate to have my assistant still working with me, Luc Sunu, who came into the ethnographic project as an experienced assistant from an earlier linguistic research and quickly took the place of Jean Zra Fama, my first aid, who had to attend secondary school in Mokolo in 1972. Fate has decided that Jean Zra is back in the project now, after a career in agricultural extension, so my first assistant is a retired functionary, serving now as my urban field station. But with Luc Sunu the relation never was broken, even if he has done a stint of work in Ngaoundere. And so it is with his wife, Marie Kwafashè. For my wife and me, a return visit is coming home, to an old and very dear friend and to Marie, with their growing family, Francois, Lade, and the children. My last visit I came alone and was severely rebuked by Luc, as the grandchildren were extremely disappointed that "Wuzha Tizhè," my wife Tini, was not there! Never again am I allowed to come alone, and so it will be, *sɛy Shala ɗepe*. The research has become his life just as it has become mine. Long ago Luc wondered who was the actual researcher, he or Zra Kangacè (my Kapsiki name). So this book is for him, to prove him right.

Zra Kangacè, alias Walter van Beek

LANGUAGE AND ORTHOGRAPHY

The Kapsiki/Higi language cluster is known as Psikiyè in Cameroon and Kamwe in Nigeria, and the two are considered similar. The cluster has in total eleven dialects, four in Cameroon (Psikiyè, Zlenge, Hya, and Wula Karantchi) and seven in Nigeria: Nkafa, Dakwa, Sina, Futu, Tili Pte, Modi, Humsi. The dialects of Fali Kiriya and Fali Mijilu are closely related, but viewing the considerable cultural differences, I do not count them inside this Psikiyè/Kamwe cluster; on the other hand, Gwavar (Kortchi) is considered a different language (of just one village only) but is that closely related culturally that I consider it as part of the Kapsiki conglomerate in this book. The linguistic lineage of Psikiye/Kamwe language cluster is: Afro-Asiatic—Chadic—Biu-Mandara—A—A3 & 4[1].

The term "Psikyè" refers to the process of beer brewing, in particular the sprouting of the seeds (*psekɛ*). The strong dialectization of the Psikiyè/Kamwe language mirrors the proliferation of languages in the area. The greater Mandara Mountain area counts some 65 languages, 22 in Nigeria and 43 in Cameroon.

The Kapsiki language has no standardized orthography yet. For the Psikiyè, the dialect in which I work, I use an adaptation of the orthography of the New Testament, by the Alliance Biblique du Cameroun, Yaounde, 1988.

Specific signs: Examples:

ɛ	mid-central, unrounded	c**a**p
h	voiceless velar fricative	
rh	voiced velar fricative	
c	voiceless alveo-palatal affricate	kit**ch**en
j	voiced alveo-palatal affricate	**G**eorge
g	voiced velar explosive stop	**g**ood
y	voiced alveo-palatal halfvocal	**y**es
ŋ	voiced laryngal halfvocal	lo**ng**
ɗ	voiced alveolar implosive stop	

ɓ	voiced bilabial implosive stop
ʼ	glottal stop
tl	voiceless alveo-lateral fricative
dl	voiced alveo-lateral fricative

The **e** (schwa) adapts to its phonetic environment: after the **w** without other consonants, like in *kwe*, it becomes rounded, like in the English "l**o**ck"; between **w** and another consonant, e.g., in *gwela*, it is lengthened, like in the English "b**oa**t."

For the proper names I use a simplified orthography in order to be consistent with their spelling on maps and in other publications; thus I speak of Mogode, and not *ŋwedʼu*.

All terms in *Psikyè* except names are italicized throughout the book, because quite a few Kapsiki words occur in English as well (with a completely different meaning, of course). Other non-English words except plant names are placed between citation marks.

The Dancing Dead

PART ONE

INTRODUCTION

1

The Funeral of Zra Teri Kwada

"One sends someone to call a non-smith, and he calls a smith," Sunu laughs, gently chiding his fellow digger, who was sent to fetch a digging rod but came back with a hoe. The Kapsiki proverb not only reflects the typical *melu* (non-smith, farmer) disdain toward the smith minority but also indicates that they are doing a smith's job—digging a tomb.[1] As *ksugwe*,[2] the sister's sons of Zra Teri Kwada, the deceased,[3] it is their duty and prerogative to dig his tomb and, indeed, they are being commanded by a smith. Zhinerhu Tizhè, the smith in question, lets the remark pass. He has followed in the footsteps of his late father as master of the tomb, so it is his responsibility to dig a proper tomb[4] and he takes it. Besides, he is used to deprecating remarks about smiths.

However, the diggers do need a digging iron, since the soil is hard and full of rocks. "Why Zra wanted to be buried here, no one knows," one of them sighs. The usual banter among the young *ksugwe* is subdued this time. Zra has died young, just over 30 years of age, much too young in fact, and the village is still wondering what caused this untimely death. His illness was short and he barely had time to express his *mid'imte*, his last words, in which for some reason he chose to be buried here, in a field his lineage abandoned long ago. The diggers view the sunken mounds of earth, the decrepit tombs of almost-forgotten dead. One of Zra's nephews spots a stone slab on a nearby tomb: "Did anyone ever see this person? No? Then we'll take the stone." Since there is no suitable stone in sight to close the tomb, they all agree.

"Who is the big *ksugwe* (mother's brother) of Zra?" Sunu asks. The other diggers do not know, but the smith, Zhinerhu, is better informed: "Fama; Zra married Kuve, Fama's older sister." They all know the dapper little man and feel sorry for him because he has lost his sister's son. The diggers themselves are quite young and are shocked by the sudden death of their "male mother"; seeing their distress, Sunu reflects, using another proverb: "If you have no mothers, no one really loves you" ("mothers" standing for mother's family). Beer is brought by the deceased's younger brother, whose wife brewed it this morning. Along comes the deceased's "little *mekwe*," his wife's younger brother. As usual, he gently scolds the diggers for being slack: "Why are you digging so slowly? You better show the *nasara* (European) what real work is." The youngsters pick up speed with the sweaty job, and the animated banter among the diggers subsides. Yet, when digging they discuss what fields are even harder to dig, where the people from Kamale (the neighboring village they can see from this field) dig their tombs, and why the rest of the nephews have not shown up "the lazy ones who are hiding" (Figure 1.1).

A lot of people come along, curious about the odd choice of cemetery, inspecting the work, and, of course, joining in drinking the beer. A Kapsiki tomb has to be a round underground chamber with the burial mound on top. Therefore the entry should be narrow, just large enough to accommodate the body, and Zra was a big man. To avoid a severe scolding and loss of face, the *ksugwe* took care to make it large enough. The work is completed on time, at noon, because the sun should shine directly into the chamber. Then they all leave to find Zra's in-laws, who have to pay them.

While the diggers are at their job, at Zra's house three other smiths are adorning the corpse. This complicated task has to be done well, since Zra died young, and also was quite important in Mogode, so the mourning crowd should see his worth. Furthermore, with a well-decorated corpse the smiths themselves gain stature. Zra is clothed in two gowns, first a black one and then a white one. Meticulously the smiths clothe and adorn the corpse, specifically the head. It is the head adornment that is full of symbolism, signaling Zra's full identity. (Chapter 12 will go into more detail.) They also give him some eyeglasses, to stress his importance.

Figure 1.1 Conversing with the nephew in the tomb.

Dressing the corpse takes all morning, and gradually a large crowd gathers outside the compound, where the younger smiths have joined in with drums and flutes to direct the dancing. Funerals are smiths' business, and they lead the village during these liminal times; the dance is the highlight for the young smiths, while the older smiths are in charge of the corpse. The smiths quietly do their work, chatting among themselves while they decorate the body, their consummate professionalism contrasting with the deep sorrow and intense mourning of the people outside. In this case, with a young deceased, the smiths are rather subdued since they too regard this as an untimely death, but they do exude a sense of pride, the confidence of craftsmen who feel secure in their calling and destiny. During funeral times, they are the ones who know, who are indispensable, and on whom the others rely.

At noon the work is ready, and the smiths emerge with the "real Zra": large, strong, rich, powerful, master of his own house, a great warrior, a hard worker, and someone who forced luck to be on his side—at least that is what his outfit proclaims. He is put in a chair and the older smiths take a long swig of beer at the place of honor, with the young musicians joining them. In contrast to normal times, they are now masters of the situation. Zra's daughter takes off the top covers of both her father's sleeping hut and his brewing hut, a sign that he is truly dead, while a lineage brother at the side of the house pushes over a part of the wall and puts a mat in the breach, through which the corpse will pass for his final dance.

After drinking, the smiths carry Zra to the wall and put him in the gap. Smith Kwada then hoists Zra on his shoulders, holding him by the sleeves. A frenzy of drumming, wailing, crying and shouting greets the deceased. Poised well above the shouting throng, Zra dominates his kinsmen for the last time. As everyone can see him in his full splendor and he, through his glasses, can see the multitude assembled for his sake. This is his finest hour. Zra's daughter, carrying her iron skirt over her shoulder, follows him through the gap in the wall after their mother's brother has sprinkled some ashes on her back. The dance picks up immediately: everything is in full swing. All throng around the deceased, looking up to him, shouting, brandishing their lances, sticks, hoes, and calabashes. The women strike their iron skirts with their calabashes and the old men start the funeral songs, first a war song, then the real mourning song, the *nhwene gela* (the dirge from the rock):

Zra Teri Kwada
Where is my Zra?
Who opens the bush among men?
Where is my Zra today?
The children drink beer in their family
Who will give me mine?
The girls will eat meat sauce with their people
Who will give me mine?

Zra Teri Kwada
Where is my Zra?
Where is the warrior among men?
Who throws stones at people?
Where is Zra from Kuve?
Family of the viper
Zra of the government
Where is my Zra today?
He is the leopard among men
Where will I drink my sauce?
Leopard among men
Where do I drink my beer?[5]

The smith dances with the corpse toward the largest open space and the funeral dance begins in earnest. The men make grouped charges towards Zra, women circle the smith-cum-corpse, and the young smiths are everywhere with their drums and flutes. Kwada, with the corpse on his shoulders, runs through the crowd, charging the men, dancing in front of the women while moving to the rhythm of the drums. The shouts of the men and the shrieks and ululations of the women mix with the powerful drums of the expert drummers. In the following hours Zra has his last and finest dance, moving constantly, his bearer replaced from time to time by new smiths or occasionally a sister's son who wants to show off (Figure 1.2). It is a hot, sweaty, and smelly job but a wonderful way to stand out among the mourners.

Figure 1.2 The next smith takes Zra on his shoulders.

Here we will leave Zra at his moment of crowning glory, with his full and final identity completely established in the dance with his fellow Kapsiki. Dressed in his spectacular outfit with the symbols of masculinity and belonging adorning his imposing presence and held high on the shoulders of the smith, he is the absolute center of the whirling dance. Each of the dancers expresses his or her special relationship with him, clansmen, in-laws, daughters or wives of the clan, mother's family, all those crucial to him are there, their very adornment part of his existence, his identity. Never in his life was this position so clear, so visible, and so rewarding. It is a pity these will be his last days on earth, as this final and finest dance inevitably leads toward his tomb. And, of course, for him this appreciation came much too early; even part of his identity, so splendidly displayed, was not yet his, assumed but not yet achieved.

This funeral, as is shown by the special care bestowed by the smiths, has been shot through with deep sorrow, a collective mourning for someone gone too soon. Later, during the burial proper, the smiths will take care to leave the option of revenge open: the family may seek revenge against whomever they feel was responsible for this terrible death. So the tale of Zra is by no means finished. In fact, this death has an immediate sequel. Even the great show of her son's importance and the massive support in mourning she has received from her fellow villagers fail to console Zra's mother, who barely danced during the funeral. Three days later she commits suicide, probably by drinking toxic *cene*, African mahogany, oil.[6] The reason why is clear to everybody: with her son dead at a young age and her two other children already buried even younger, she had nothing left to live for. The people of Mogode understand her well and extend no judgment. Anyone who is so sad that life seems to have ended has ample reason to end it: "No children, no millet, no food, what else should she do?" People gently and quietly lament: "Ah, Kwarumba, did you have so little left? Ah, Kwarumba, now we are also alone in the bush." I myself am crushed by this double death just after my return to the village, again feeling the immanent presence of death, just as during the meningitis epidemic several years earlier, so I take pains to assist the smiths in their preparation of this body as well. Afterwards the family thanks me for helping to wash and dress their sister, and I feel honored.

For us here, Zra's burial offers a first glimpse at some of the main themes in this book: a subterranean tomb; a funeral replete with rich symbolism expressed in fervent ritual; death as the end of a long cycle of life transitions; the ambivalent position of the smiths—central and yet so subservient; the structured echelons of village and intra–village organization; and turbulent relations, all set in a long history of wars and slave raiding. But as we have seen in this funeral, two caveats hold. First, there are differences between people, between groups, between villages, and especially between individuals. Funerals to some extent form a good angle into that internal variety: men/women, old/young, insider/outsider, poor/rich, and smith/non-smith. But still, ritual symbolism deals with categories of people, which are not the same as the individual. Even if we have to describe collective action and cultural symbolism, our focus is on how individuals deal with them, use them in their personal lives, and express their own individual identity through ritual and religion.

Second, and even more fundamental: we as scholars tend to define events as religion, ritual, or whatever gloss we may have invented for our understanding and interpretation of what we see and hear. That is why I started out with the burial of an untimely death, two in fact. But religion is basically about human suffering, human joy, emotions, and problems, about the rewarding routine of daily life with its meaningful social interaction, about the joy of feasting, and always about the way people make sense of a bewildering reality. We often have little direct access into these emotions, so we approach them through the collective expression, which gives but a limited angle on human life. Therefore in the descriptive chapters I will include small pastiches of my field experiences in order to retain both this emotional aspect and a view on individual agency and signification. But individual emotion as well still has to find a cultural expression, so what is an angle for us is also a tool for the Kapsiki. The ritual surrounding Zra's death is—albeit partly—a solution to a problem, how to deal with grief. Ritual is the stick to lean on for the bereaved, and although that stick may prove insufficient, it gives insight into how people handle their existential problems. When we explore the way the Kapsiki make sense of their lives, these emotions should never be forgotten.

2

Understanding African Ritual

Into the Mandara Mountains

I fell in love with the Mandara Mountains as a young Ph.D. candidate. When setting out on a reconnaissance trip in 1971, I had noted that among the many options for anthropological fieldwork, the Kapsiki might be promising. "Le Pays Kapsiki" had quite a reputation, since a string of volcanic peaks had made the landscape famous and it had been a major tourist attraction in Cameroon for decades. My French colleagues warned me not to go there because the Kapsiki were "trop pourri par le tourisme" (spoiled by tourism). I considered this an interesting new phenomenon that might be worth studying, and I wanted to see for myself how spoiled the culture really was. Despite the slight disdain that anthropologists showed toward tourists at that time—and I do hope this attitude has now passed—I also realized that tourists never go to an area without a good reason. In this case I had seen some tourist brochures on the Mandara Mountains and saw that the tourists did indeed have a compelling reason to go there: the scenery. One arrives in Kapsiki country from Mokolo, feasting one's eyes on the terraced hillsides of the Mandara Mountains that are dotted with the compact compounds of the Mafa, the northern neighbors of the Kapsiki, with their characteristic narrow huts with pointed roofs. The Kapsiki like to chide their neighbors on their small huts, and the difference is indeed striking: Kapsiki huts are much larger. The scenery becomes more rugged near the first Kapsiki village of Rumsu at the northern end of the plateau. Just outside the village, a round outcropping like a billiard ball stands out. This is Rhu Rumsu, the holy mountain of Rumsu, but I was to learn that much later. The real revelation comes as one turns south from Rumsu. Suddenly the rugged hillside gives way to an undulating yellowish green plain, and then the full glory of the Kapsiki plateau hits the eye: the horizon is covered with strange forms, tall peaks of curious shapes along the rim of the plateau as far as the eye can roam. I vividly remember the thrill my first view gave me: my choice of research area was made! Mogode, the central village on the

Figure 2.1 A view on the Nigerian side of the Rumsiki road.

plateau and also the administrative hub, is surrounded by these old volcanic plugs, towers of basalt that remain a feast for the eye.

But for tourists driving through "le pays Kapsiki," the pinnacle of landscape aesthetics is still to come, which is why they drive straight through Mogode to Rumsiki, the tourist venue par excellence. That drive, of some 15 km, is among the most spectacular in Cameroon. The road skirts the plateau rim, offering a splendid view over to Nigeria: first a deep valley and then spectacular mountain ridges far to the west, the whole countryside dotted with the characteristic volcanic plugs. This stunning landscape has always impressed Europeans and has been compared to various European mountain scenes (the Harz among them) as well as to moonscapes: "un paysage lunaire"[1] (Figure 2.1). For such a landscape, I felt I could easily cope with any irritation tourism might present. This proved to be absolutely true, not only because the mountains have remained a constant delight throughout my years of fieldwork, but also because tourism was a far more interesting subject than I ever dreamed it would be. It was also true because the impact of tourism on a local population is much more superficial than is often surmised.[2] Tourism has in no way hindered my study of Kapsiki culture and in fact has proven a fascinating topic on it own.

Back in the Netherlands I submitted my research application, did my first eighteen-month period of fieldwork from 1972–1973 while living in Mogode, wrote my Ph.D. thesis, and then went back to the region every four or five years for follow up, the last time being in January 2010. This book is the result of a long period of interaction with the Kapsiki and Higi of North Cameroon and

Northeastern Nigeria, almost a professional lifetime from 1972 to the present. Although the lure of the mountains has remained, the people I worked with quickly became central in the tale as well as in my affections, and it is precisely the interaction between landscape and culture, the notion of "dwelling," that grounds my approach.

The Kapsiki/Higi are one of the many groups living in the area south of the Chad Basin along the western edge of the Mandara Mountains on both sides of the border between Cameroon and Nigeria (Maps 1 and 2). In Cameroon they live on a plateau at an altitude of 1,000 m surrounded by mountain ridges rising to 1,300 m. The plateau itself, some 40 km by 50 km, is dotted with those wonderful volcanic outcroppings. On the western side in Nigeria, the Higi, as the group living there is called, cultivate the mountain ridges and the plains to the west extending toward their Marghi neighbors. The Kapsiki and Higi, living on the edge of the small plateau in Cameroon or on top of the mountain ridges in Nigeria, used to cultivate the stony, terraced slopes as did most of the people living in the Mandara area. Before the "pax colonialis" this area offered the best protection against slave raiding while still allowing for subsistence cultivation. After colonial rule was established, people gradually moved down from their hilltops, fanned out onto the plateau, or moved into the lower river valleys, setting themselves up as able farmers and as an emerging group of traders and middlemen.

The Kapsiki/Higi number about 200,000, with the majority living in Nigeria.[3] Population density is between 30 and 60/km,^{2} although this figure is now increasing rapidly. Agricultural practices vary depending on the type of field, mountain, plateau, or plain, but Kapsiki agriculture is generally quite characteristic of the area. Kapsiki cultivation is rain-fed, and sorghum, millet, and maize are grown as staple crops that are intercropped with peanuts, Bambara nuts, beans, and tiger nuts. Lesser crops include sweet potatoes, potatoes, yam, various hibiscus species, tobacco, garlic, peppers, couch grass and occasionally manioc. Fruit trees, pepper bushes, and sugar cane, grown in wetter spots, supplement people's diets. Though most crops are part of subsistence, peanuts, tobacco, and vegetables serve as cash crops as well. Cattle and other livestock such as goats and sheep are an important feature of the agricultural picture and, together with cultivation, form an important aspect of the Kapsiki's value system, including bridewealth, so these feature prominently in their symbolism.

As an old volcanic area, the Mandara Plateau and hillsides are relatively fertile and can be cultivated on a permanent basis by using simple crop rotation and very few inputs. Water holes can be found all over the plateau and slopes, and although the slopes are not overly easy to clear, weeds can be controlled quite effectively. The rains are more dependable in the mountains, which also retain the water better, but the slopes demand more labor investment since they have to be terraced to be really productive. So the mountains are well suited to

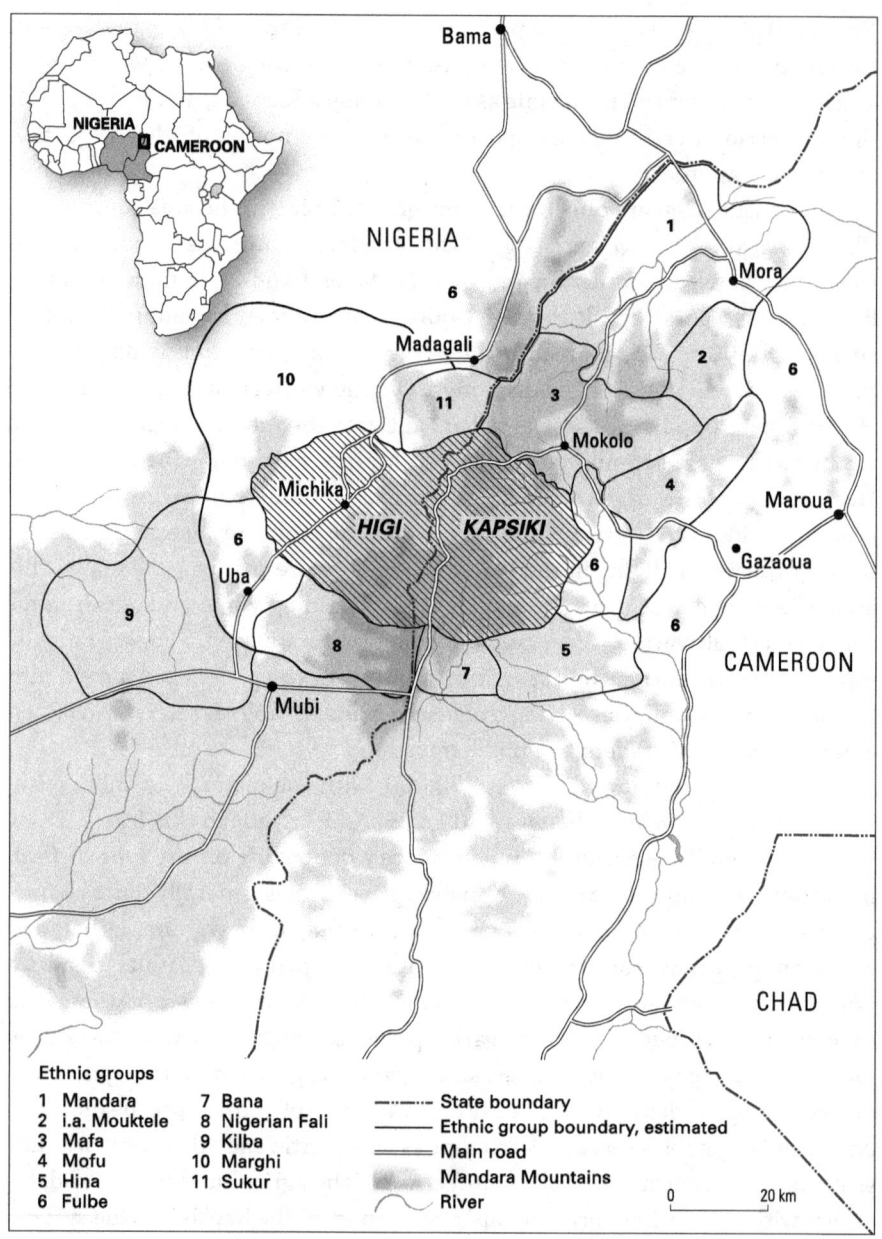

Map 1 The Kapsiki/Higi and their neighbors.[7]

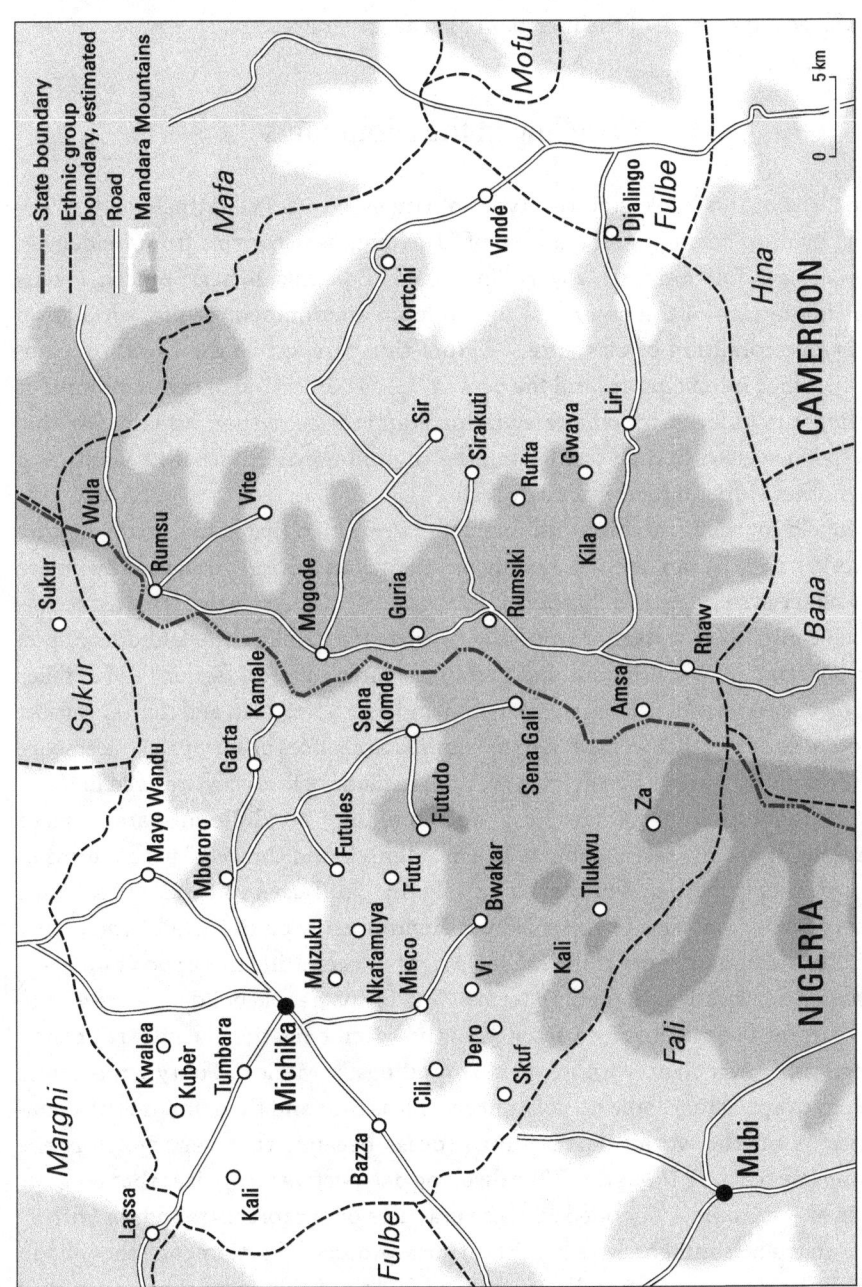

Map 2 Towns and villages in the Kapsiki/Higi area.

labor-intensive horticultural production using relatively simple technology and mixed husbandry, and that is how the Kapsiki make their living. As we shall see, the border area has stimulated commerce and over the years the Kapsiki have produced a fair share of the merchants in the larger area.

Dwelling in the Mountains

The focus of this book is on two types of rituals, which I call rituals of dwelling and rituals of belonging. The notion of "dwelling," which stems from Heidegger, has been put forward forcefully by Tim Ingold.[4] Dwelling, in his approach, means "the immersion of the organism/person in an environment or life world as an escapable condition of existence... From this perspective the world continuously comes into being around the person."[5] Any perception of the environment is the result of interaction between humans and the ecosystem, and the dwelling perspective views human culture and the environment as mutually constituting each other through their interaction.

Ingold contrasts this idea with "building," the notion that man has to construct a world before he can live in it; his environment is an a priori given used by him as raw material to implement his cultural designs. In this perspective "Human beings inhabit discursive worlds of culturally constructed significance, laid down upon the substrate of a continuous and undifferentiated physical terrain."[6] Man takes cognizance of his environment, creates an understanding of it, and then engages it in order to live in that world and to maximize his chances of survival. "The essence of the building perspective [is] that worlds are made before they are lived in."[7]

For Ingold, the terms "dwelling" and "building" are different paradigms of thinking about the relationship between "Mensch und Umwelt," in the terms of Von Uexkühl, the founder of ecology. Like Ingold, I used to think in the usual dichotomy of perceived versus factual environment, or the "emic" versus the "etic" environment, but I think Ingold is right in conflating this opposition in his dwelling perspective. In Ingold's terms: "The forms people build... arise within the current of their involved activity, in the specific relational contexts of their practical engagement with their surroundings."[8] Merleau-Ponty's phenomenology is apt here. People do not conceive ideas first and then impose their conceptions on the world: it is a joint process because that very world is the "homeland of their thoughts."[9] The dwelling perspective recognizes that we grow up in an environment imbued with the practices of our forebears and that fitting into that environment is recreating it in a process of action-cum-thought in which the two are never really separable. We do not think and then act, but we plait our actions and thoughts into our own cultural braid.

For the study of a religion, this perspective enhances the notion of its grounding in a particular culture and society, a notion that has always been a major emphasis in anthropological approaches to religion. Religion does not follow culture nor the reverse, but they mutually constitute each other, resulting in acts and thoughts that can be separated only analytically, not experientially. This view has clear implications for the interpretation of ritual, since these are the actions per se that link man to his environment. Actually, the ritual act finds its meaning through the actor plus the "homeland of his thoughts." Thus, religion and culture nestle in one another, but culture and the physical environment are enmeshed too, the latter offering options, materials, and spaces that come into being only when drawn into the process of dwelling, subject to human signification. Thus, history is one interface where environment and culture-*cum*-religion are intertwined. Just as perceived and acted-upon environment are inseparable, history as "what is told" and history as "what has happened" are indistinguishable. The same holds for ecological and social history: they merge. Kapsiki religion is deeply historical, and the history of the physical and sociopolitical environments forms one integrated backdrop to the present. Thus, dwelling for this religion, as established through its rituals, means its continuous interaction with history, recent as well as distant, with the adaptation of the Kapsiki to the physical environment, with their ways of living in the Mandara Mountains, shaped by and shaping its ecological characteristics and its turbulent history.

I referred to my admiration of the landscape, but the impression the landscape makes on me is different from the way the Kapsiki themselves view their environment. For them it is not the rugged wildness, the unfamiliarity of forms, or the wide views that are fascinating. During my first few months there I commented on the beauty of the scenery, and my assistant's reaction was: "I don't know, I see no houses." As anthropologists have often noted, our informant's appreciation of a landscape seems to be more down-to-earth, reflecting production and survival more than aesthetics: "The crop is standing well, the farms are well kept, the grazing area is nicely green, and, yes this is a beautiful landscape indeed." The difference between my aesthetic view and his practical appreciation is not just a difference in perceptions of the environment, with his perception being closer to the effective environment and mine to a romantic one. There is more to it than that. The mountains are where they live, so what for us is scenery holds different meanings for them. For the Kapsiki the aesthetic can never be an isolated aspect, because they have to live from this scenery. Also the mountains play a role in Kapsiki religion in several ways; they have been guardians of the people against the Fulbe marauders, a safe dwelling in a fiendish political environment. The Kapsiki used to build their homes on the larger, flat-topped outcroppings that served as the ultimate defense against raiders. For Mogode, the central village in this study, this is now their sacred mountain, Rhuŋgedu, home of the village founders. The Kapsiki live not in a romantic landscape but in a personalized territory with historical meaning: they "dwell their mountains."

An important part of dwelling is more social than ecological, and I have characterized the rituals bearing this focus as the "rituals of belonging." Here dwelling in the social environment dominates. In the first part of the book dealing with the more ecological dwelling rituals, sacrifices are central, flanked by all the rituals pertaining to cultivation and harvest. Rites of passage form the core of the second part, which focuses on belonging, and zoom in on births, weddings, initiations, and death, describing how people forge new relationships through ritual pathways. These rituals focus on identity and on entering a new echelon of society, following sociological more than ecological explanations. However, one of the dominant characteristics of Kapsiki rituals is the linking of these two: living in the physical environment as well as in society, as they both come together in the large village festivals described in Chapter 11, in which both the cereal harvest and the harvest of the people are feted as one and the same. No one dwells alone.

Finally, the notion of dwelling as the joint construction of meaning with the implementation of an act might shed some light on the debate between Jonathan Z. Smith and Ronald Grimes about the primacy of ritual over space in the construction of the sacred.[10] Dwelling evidently implies space but never without an act of appropriation and reconstruction, that is, with an action that has generated the attribution of meaning. Anthropologists have stayed out of this debate, since the notion of "the sacred" has received too much attention already, ever since Otto. On the other hand, African shrines now receive increased attention,[11] and in some instances the term "sacred" can have a hermeneutical value. From the vantage point of dwelling, the dichotomy of place versus act dissolves as both are constructs of each other and one cannot contain a meaning without the other. The landscape, for example, does play a role but always an interpreted one, and shrines are often constructed by man for and even during a ritual. Ritual space and ritual history create each other, and we will see what that means for the Kapsiki/Higi.

The Meaning of Ritual

The second major angle followed here in the interpretation of ritual is the cognitive approach to religion, especially modes of religiosity theory, as put forward by Harvey Whitehouse, based on the work of Pascal Boyer and others.[12] This approach focuses on the cognition generated by different types of ritual and is based on the fundamental notion that religious concepts and practices have to be remembered. A major distinction is made between low and high frequency in rituals and between low and high arousal through the ritual, with the high-arousal rituals tending to be low in frequency and vice versa. This distinction leads to two clusters of religious characteristics, imagistic and doctrinal. The first combines low-frequency/high-intensity rituals that base themselves on episodic memory (what did we do first?), set in a social environment with little religious leadership, no orthodoxy, and no exegetic control. The other, the doctrinal mode, capitalizes on frequent rituals, exegetic authority and control, and semantic memory (things we learned consciously), often leading to religious centralization. In itself this division reads as the classic distinction between oral and written religions, or between a traditional religion and a typical church-based one, but the theory highlights the causal connections between the bundles of ritual features and the transmission of the religion.[13] Thus it is not a typology but a logical pathway in which the features are connected and co-generated.

Kapsiki religion is a typical traditional religion, in which the features of the imagistic mode abound. However, the theory addresses not types but modes of religiosity, and both modes occur in any religion, at least to some extent. In the Kapsiki case, there is very little religious authority, not even much ritual authority—which indicates how a ritual should be done—but some features may indicate a refinement of the imagistic model. For instance, quite a few rituals are not high arousal but are quite frequent and low key in terms of emotions. I argue that these rituals, mainly sacrifices, have a more mixed form. To understand them, the notion of minimal counterintuitivity is productive, a concept developed by Boyer[14] for conceptions about the "other world." Minimally counterintuitivity implies that a concept about the supernatural world is based upon a fundamental category of thought, like "man," "plant," or "animal" and then a crucial detail is changed. Just a single aspect in the category is different, which results in a type of concept well known in religions. For instance, a spirit is human–yet–invisible, but for the rest it acts and reacts as we would surmise and predict from the category of man. In religious concepts this kind of minimal transformation results in cognitively optimal concepts, which are easy to learn, easy to transmit, and hard to forget, like spirits, gods, witches, and the like.

In my view, this is a very productive concept. My refinement of the modes theory is to use this distinction not only for concepts but also for rituals. As has often been pointed out, ritual acts are very much like normal everyday interaction,[15] but with one key difference. Rituals are full of acts people know well from daily life and so are easy to reproduce. So my premise within the modes theory is that rituals can be cognitively optimal as well. At least some are. Other rituals, which we will encounter in the rites of belonging, are less self-evident, have to be taught and learned, and demand some specialization, religious authority, and surely memory; these are cognitively costly. The initiation rites and funeral proceedings in particular show such costly characteristics. So the contrast as well as interaction between cognitively optimal and cognitively costly rituals characterizes the rituals dynamics in this religion.

This leads us into the question of the meaning of ritual. The dwelling perspective already hints at the experiential construction of meaning in ritual. In Religious Studies this discussion was fired by the work of Frits Staal[16] on the Veda fire ritual, and was commented on by hosts of scholars.[17] His main thesis is that, in principle, rituals have no proper, intrinsic meaning. In anthropology, it is the work of Wallace (who predates Staal), Rappaport, Bloch, and Boyer that concentrates on this problem, on the whole supporting Staal in his premise but with important modifications and refinements.[18] As I have argued elsewhere, the question is no longer whether ritual has any intrinsic communicative content, since that has been clearly answered now: in principle it has none. The fundamental reason is that the acts making up the ritual have been emptied of their habitual meaning. A more productive question is: "If a ritual act does not have intrinsic meaning, why do people all over the world attach a lot of meaning to those very acts, and to their proper, correct performance?"[19]

To solve this puzzle, I rely on Rappaport's distinction between self-referential meaning and canonical (or exegetical) meaning or, in my terms, between *message* and *meaning*. The notion of message implies the information content of the ritual, which Wallace defined as zero ("ritual is zero communication") but which Rappaport defined as self-referential. This is an important concept, pointing at the fact that the ritual has at least one important message: the simple and undisputable subtext that this act is a ritual. It is not a normal act, but ritual, recognizable within a culture as well as cross-culturally. So the first level, the message of a rite, is that we are here in a different domain, in a virtual world called ritual, that we all have our roles to play in the ritual act and that we surrender to the ritual format. So the ritual self referentially points at itself, and that is what people do recognize across cultural borders. Even in different cultural settings humans are very quick in spotting ritual, one reason that I do not try to define "ritual" any further than the rather tongue-in-cheek definition I use in the next paragraph.

The second level, meaning, is what participants construct during their participation in a ritual, either as spontaneous exegetical reflection or using a more or less official discourse. This exegetical—or in Rappaport's terms—canonical meaning is produced in interaction between participant and act, not as an intrinsic meaning of the act but as an almost inevitable result of the proclivity of man to attribute meaning; after all, "Homo sapiens" is "Homo significans." The trigger to attributing meaning is precisely the notion of minimally counterintuitive actions: the small change in normal daily procedure renders the act itself semantically void and thereby invites the attribution of meaning. For instance, the most fundamental rite—sacrifice—for the Kapsiki is a meal, but with an invisible guest, while for the rest it is almost a standard meal. And that "almost" generates a semantic vacuum that triggers exegesis.

"Symbols Having Sex"

Rituals offer clues for their own interpretation and most of these clues reside in the symbols, the acts themselves, and the language used in the acts, and so through objects and bodily or verbal expressions. Kapsiki religion is not overly verbal compared with other African religions (like the Mande religions) but it does use a wide array of symbols, especially in the rituals of belonging. In fact, rituals are a systematic interaction between actors and symbols, with the actors taking on new roles through the appropriate symbols, and the symbols accruing meaning through acts. Or, as Victor Turner put it, defining it in the inverse direction: "A symbol is the smallest rituals unit bearing the character of ritual."[20] Without symbols in interaction, no meaning would be produced. To put it briefly, ritual is symbols having sex.

Throughout my research I have been careful not to over-construct or over-interpret, trying to base myself on my informants' voluntary exegesis. Often the latter was not forthcoming at all and some gentle prodding was called for. In such cases I tried to use my return visits to check on my interpretations. Sometimes my informants corrected me, told me that I could think whatever I liked, but they thought asking for a meaning of a ritual or symbol was, in the words of my assistant Luc Sunu, "une question stupide." Most of the time, though, they readily agreed with my interpretation, sometimes wondering why it had taken me so long to work it out. Kapsiki culture has very little courtesy bias! On the whole I tended to err on the safe side and thus I feel confident about not only the descriptions but also my interpretations. The Kapsiki are far more interested in a correct and factual description of their rituals than in a deep and moving interpretation of them. Their children and grandchildren should be able to read what to do in a ritual, which is a typical reaction in the imagistic mode.

In this interpretation of symbolic images, the work of Victor Turner has been crucial. The example above, asking for the informants' explanation, is what Turner calls exegetical meaning, the interpretation the informants offer; in the "modes" theory this is indicated as exegetical reflection, spontaneous or systematic. We shall see that this exegesis is usually quite limited, and the reaction "stupid question" should be borne in mind. But sometimes informants do give clues, important ones, and these are integrated in the descriptions. Part of this interpretation stems from the circumstance of the ritual itself: people know why a ritual is being held, in the sense of in-order-to-what, and are aware of general purposes. As we shall see throughout Kapsiki/Higi rituals, references are made to crops, women, health, and children. That is still general and, as behooves an imagistic religion, the exegesis does not usually go much further than this and leaves a host of questions unanswered, but it gives direction to interpretation.

But there are more pointers to meaning; Turner insists that symbols should be viewed from a matrix of contexts. Crucial for interpretation is operational meaning, the place of symbols within ritual, what people do, who performs the symbolic acts, and what emotions are involved. In short, what does the symbol "do"? So here we look at the liturgy or the sequential arrangement of symbolic elements in the larger ritual framework. Symbolic elements stick together; as we shall see in the initiation rituals, where the various symbols—the dress, the weapons, the ornaments—match the acts required of the initiates. Throughout the in-depth descriptions in the chapters, this operational meaning will be our main clue for the interpretation of the rituals.

The third clue is the semantic range and the ordering of the symbols among themselves; symbols as such constitute their own field and derive their meaning from their position in that field. Symbols accentuate contrasts and do so often in pairs or in small fields of similar items. For instance, we shall see the difference between boys' initiation and girls' weddings expressed in brass versus iron. Both metals in their opposition are used to signal different role expectations to the new generation of adults. Similar symbolic fields are found in food, colors, animals, and plants. In the final chapter we will look into these domains.

An example of this threefold interpretation is the two plants used in decorating Zra's head, *safa* and *haze*, as seen in Figure 2.2.[21] What do these plants signify? As we shall see, informants have some exegetical ideas about this, but

Figure 2.2 Putting symbols on Zra's head. Mogode 1979.

also we encounter the same plants as crucial symbols operating in several different rituals and not in others, and finally the two have a specific position within the whole domain of plants that serve as symbols.

In the interpretation I combine the notion of minimal counterintuitivity with this Turnerian matrix; also a symbolic act or object can be cognitively optimal and thus invite signification. Many of the symbols themselves have a clear relationship with everyday life, often a historical one. The ancient grindstone is one of these, a useful object for grinding and for watering goats but a very suitable symbol as well.

Thus, a ritual is constructed by symbols interacting in clusters, in preformed pathways of action, sometimes guided by myth (although not usually so in Kapsiki), and routinely referring to those daily acts from which they derive. Rituals are indeed "symbols having sex," but in their productive interaction they follow rules in order to be able to stimulate the production of meaning. I prefer this view of symbols as open, productive interaction to the idea that symbols should be addressed as a language, with symbols as words, liturgy as the sentence, and positional meaning as a semantic field. Though any angle is only as productive as it generates insight—after all, it is a heuristic device—the language analogy obscures more than it reveals, because it sees symbols as a form of cryptology. Thus it reduces the openness of interpretation and hides the fundamental agency of the actors—and analysts—as the ones constructing meaning.

Just as not all rituals are cognitively optimal, not all symbols are straightforward in their associations. Some are obscure and unclear and may defy interpretation. For instance, strips of *peha* leaf (a palm[22]) are an important symbol for twins and initiated boys. The reason becomes clear only when these are considered with other symbols used on the same occasion, such as cowry shells, which are less veiled as an expression of riches. The links between clusters of symbols and ritual acts direct the exegesis, but they are clusters, not systems. Symbols, like rituals, do not form coherent, integrated systems but show a loose grouping of elements that have some rhyme and reason to them, but only to a limited extent.

Dynamics of an Imagistic Religion

Rituals heavily interact with emotions. Anthropologists have developed concepts to analyze rituals but may feel empty-handed when facing emotions. Death rituals in particular are ways for people to cope with their grief, but other rituals also have to do with a variety of emotions, like joy, pride, or a sense of achievement. As Grimes states: "In scholarly literature love is *never* what weddings are about. In popular literature weddings are *only* about love."[23] I have tried to highlight this aspect of rituals in "thick descriptions", as Geertz calls them, to set the rituals inside human life. Each chapter starts with a vignette that describes an event in which I participated. Chapter 1 serves as an introduction to the whole book, showing the highly emotional final farewell of someone I knew well. Any funeral is emotionally charged, but Zra was still young and this fact increased its poignancy for me too, since he lived nearby and I had worked extensively with him: anthropologists *are* their field. In mourning a death, the funeral ritual is at least one way to come to terms with our grief. At such difficult times in life, ritual is the way we communicate our emotions to our fellow men, encapsulating the communication of emotions, but of a socially constructed and approved kind. Most other rituals are less emotional but generate emotion in their performance. The rites of belonging are often happy occasions, with people rejoicing at the birth of a child, a wedding, or the initiation of a boy, which is a moment of particular pride for a family. So ritual and emotion have a cybernetic connection, steering each other, but judging one from the other is difficult: "We should be cautious about inferring either feelings or the lack of feelings from ritual performances."[24]

Concentrating as I do on rituals of dwelling and belonging, other smaller rites are left in the shade. For instance, the more private kinds of rites, such as performing a curse, using ritual objects to retrieve property or claim outstanding debts, and the many healing rituals fall outside this definition. They are definitely part of the ritual repertoire of the Kapsiki but show different dynamics and thus are treated elsewhere.[25] The same holds true for the special class of Kapsiki who are closely associated with these kinds of private rites, namely the smiths. As was said in the preface, the smiths, with all their medicinal, ritual, and musical specializations, will be the topic of a companion volume to this book since their situation in Kapsiki merits separate treatment. Of course they are frequently mentioned in this volume (esp. Chapter 4) but only in passing, since much has already been published on them.[26]

All rituals change, and so do those of the Kapsiki. My long interaction with the Kapsiki has meant that I have seen rituals come and go. When describing rituals, one has to concentrate on one timeframe, and because my first main fieldwork was in 1972–1973, many of the descriptions included here start from that date. However, there are comments in all the chapters on the rate of change of a particular type of ritual so as to assess its dynamics. What does emerge is that some rituals have changed more than others. As we shall see, wedding rites have changed significantly and have displayed a great openness to new influences. Other rituals, such as the initiation of boys, have been much more resistant to change, a fact that also calls for an explanation.

I do refer to Kapsiki religion as being "traditional," partly because this term is common in the literature. African Traditional Religion is sometimes seen as a unifying kind of shared "africanité," as if all traditional religions in Africa were more or less the same. This is evidently not true and the Kapsiki are a good example. For instance, ancestor veneration is seen as being pan-African but ancestors do not feature in Kapsiki religion. There is no such thing as one singular "African Traditional Religion," but we can well speak about "traditional religions" in the plural, and there is a good reason to use the word "traditional." Rituals are always changing and Kapsiki religion, as we shall see, has a definite historical side, reflecting the past events and deeds of men more than those of supernatural beings. The notion of tradition does point to the past, invoking an unbroken chain of cultural transmission, but that is a discourse more than actual fact. My point here is that tradition is much more than just a repetition of the past. Tradition is a way of referring to the past in order to ratify the present, a discourse on why things are done. Even if the notion of tradition does seem to hark back to times of old, in fact it refers to what happened "yesterday." This insight was brought home to me when I participated in a crop protection ritual and one official, a clan representative, did not show up. A man from another clan replaced him and the blacksmith performing the ritual remarked that from then onward the new clan would participate in this ritual. The following year, when we did it again, the new one was there and the smith was happy, since everything was according to "tradition," indeed following the changes introduced last year, but not earlier than that. Tradition is above all an "argumentum ad autoritatem." Referring to tradition is sufficient validation for the act; though conjuring an image from deep history, tradition refers to any point in history; even yesterday's events may establish the ultimate ritual validity. It is in order to highlight this dynamic and discursive aspect of tradition, that I prefer to use it over a parallel concept like "indigenous religion."

This seemingly historical validation has several consequences. Such a discourse on tradition almost precludes exegesis; after all, ritual has been done *rhala heshi* (since the grandfathers) and that fact is sufficient as explanation. It would be presumptuous to surmise why the people of old performed rituals in a particular way; they were wiser, more powerful, and stronger than we are now, so invoking their authority is more than enough. A discourse on tradition, then, is one more reason why exegetical reflection on rituals is minimal in imagistic religions and is limited just to the general litany: "We do this in order to have women, children, health, and crops." Oral transmission has everything to do with it as well, because this is also characterized by referring to a past and to the unassailable authority of the forefathers (who can be just fathers). The other consequence is that in these religions rituals change in a drifting kind of way. Elements disappear within functioning rituals, are gradually replaced, and the whole ritual drifts in time. New rituals do emerge, often elsewhere, and are then adopted while others fade away. I saw a new village feast tested in Rumsiki that has since disappeared while others are catching on and replacing older ritual formats, with the new wedding rituals as the most spectacular example. These new rituals are still "traditional."

These internal changes, like the whole Kapsiki/Higi religion, have to be set against the backdrop of the growing hold of Christianity and Islam. In the course of my research I saw the number of Christians (of whatever persuasion) increase from just a few to about a third of the Kaspiki/Higi population, and nearly a fifth of the population is now Muslim, though this percentage has varied over time with the ebb and flow of national politics. We shall see why the imagistic religion is fragile in the face of these newcomers. The religion of dwelling will eventually give way to the religion of building, to the world religions that are more in the doctrinal mode and that build their sacred places before using them rather than the reverse. Religions of building start with a blueprint of society—if only from the colonizing society—and then try to implement it on the spot. The history reflected in the religions of building is a foreign one, not the local Kapsiki/Higi history with its village-based sacred places and its remembrance of the great deeds of kinsmen. However, the creativity of the people guarantees some unexpected incursions of local history into the imposed sacred history of the world religions.

> An observation. In January 2009 the non-Kapsiki preacher at the local branch of the Église Évangelique du Cameroun in Mogode stressed the grace of God through Jesus, as Jesus saved all of us without being kinsmen. His translator then became overenthusiastic and translated this as: "We, as people from Mogode, are all the descendants of *Hwempetla*" [the Kapsiki culture hero, see Chapter 6] whom he immediately transformed into a prophet very close to Jesus, "actually a disciple," so "we are all kin after all." It took the preacher some time to understand what happened, and some more time to get his derailed sermon back on track.

In any event, the Kapsiki and Higi are now becoming more a part of either Cameroon or Nigeria, and their links with the Mandara Mountains and its particular history, even if still strong, are fading. At present they seem to opt for a more global religious inclusion, but probably this will not be the end of the mountain cultures. While the construction of ethnicity is the process of the moment and globalization is giving rise to a wide variety of local responses, the Kapsiki and Higi are finding ways to include elements of their cultural heritage in this new era too, so that they can remain dwelling in the Mandara Mountains in their own innovative manner.

3

Slaves, War, and the Wider World

During a ceremonial beer party, the men from Jivu ward in Mogode start talking about the last war, the one with Sirakuti (about 1960). And a glorious war it was, with one dead on their side and no fewer than six on the enemy's side. Teri Puwe, a gifted speaker, describes how Teri Sha, sitting next to him, was hit by an arrow: "*Ptash*," the arrow went into his flesh, and "*ieieieie*" shrieked Teri Sha. With a wealth of idiophones, broad gestures and vivid mimics, Teri brings the moment of war alive again, with the cries of the wounded, the hissing arrows and the screaming women. The enraptured audience roars with laughter when Teri Sha jumps up and limps away, just like he did at the time, now 20 years ago. "War is like a woman, it never grows stale."[1]

War is what this chapter is about, war and slavery. They have dominated the area's past and are still deeply engrained in the collective memory, part of the Kapsiki's way of "dwelling" in the environment. And a dangerous environment it was, with the continuous threat of war and enslavement, so the people's view of their mountainous habitat long focused on the threatening presence of slave raiders just over the horizon. This fear still reverberates in the religion. For instance, when Kapsiki youngsters are initiated into manhood in the *gwela* rites (see Chapter 10), they are symbolically dressed and trained as warriors with bows and arrows, and clubs and knives, also decked out with ornaments that symbolize the dangers of the untamed wilderness. War has been a constant presence in Kapsiki history, both internal warfare between villages and—more important—war against slave raiders, which was a major threat and a source of insecurity for the whole Mandara region.

The area's prehistory shows that the Mandara Mountains were inhabited long before the onset of intensive slave raiding,[2] as is evidenced by many Neolithic remains. For instance, the Kapsiki use small polished stone axes in their communal sacrifices as "stones of the village" (Chapter 5) or in rain rituals, and the sacred mountain of Mogode has been inhabited since the early seventeenth century at least.[3] The deep grindstones and grinding hollows that are found everywhere in the Mandara Mountains also attest to an ancient history and offer a viable lead into the remote past.[4] Each Kapsiki and Higi village has its own oral history, which points to migratory origins long before the historical jihadist waves of Muslim state formation. Together, oral histories attest to a varied provenance of the villages, from the east as well from the west and south, all in rather small-scale migrations.[5]

So when the long series of Fulbe jihads that have dominated the political history of West Africa since the seventeenth century hit the area in the nineteenth century, they found the ancestors of present-day Kapsiki/Higi already in their mountains.[6] Several Muslim emirates have impacted the area, such as Bornu, Baguirmi, and especially Wandala or Mandara, just north of the Mandara Mountains, but it was the large Sokoto realm that most affected the Kapsiki. Like all Muslim polities of the age, this was a slave-hungry expansionist empire, resulting from a jihad, that of Usman dan Fodio from 1804. From Sokoto the local emirs were sent out with their jihadist flags, to conquer as well as to govern. The Fulbe built an administration, with sharia law, with functioning courts, and of course with the necessary payments in tribute, which in their turn led to inevitable slave raiding. And the Adamawa emirate of this realm found a large reservoir of potential slaves at its very doorstep, in the Mandara Mountains. After all, Muslim orthodoxy held that slave raiding could be done only among non-Muslim "pagans." When the nineteenth-century wave of slave raiding swept over the West African savanna, the inaccessibility of the mountains served the inhabitants well. Razzias in the mountains were not without their risks for the cavalry as the poisoned arrows of the defenders scored many victims, and sometimes even a victory when the raiders were repulsed.

In order to gain insight into the dynamics of these turbulent times, I will focus on one pivotal figure in the slave raiding of this era: the Fulbe chief Hamman Yaji. He was the fiercest raider of all and is still remembered with fear and trepidation, with awe, hate, and ambivalent admiration by the local populations in the western part of the Mandara Mountains. And he left a diary! After discussing him, we will turn to the results of colonization and the processes of ethnic formation of the Kapsiki and the Higi, but first we turn to the earliest reports on the Mandara Mountains.

Early Travelers and Slavery

The first contact Europeans had with the Mandara area was in slave raids, and it was Major Denham who was the first *nasara* (white man[7]) to see the Mandara Mountains in 1823.

> We continued to approach a noble chain of hills, which were now in full view, of considerable height and extent with numerous trees growing on the steep and rugged sides.[8]

He was traveling from Bornu to the Mandara area on his way to the sultan of Wandala[9] in a mixed expedition that was "as much a result of internal politics at the court of Bornu as it was a slaving expedition."[10] In the Wandala capital he saw a "Kirdi"[11] (pagan) tribe give 200 slaves to the sultan as tribute in order to buy off a raid.[12] He estimated that about a thousand slaves a year were captured in the hills and sold in the slave markets of Mora, the capital. The Wandala Sultanate had built Mora, just north of the mountains, as its third capital near the mountains under pressure from the Bornu Emirate,[13] the major political force in the area over the previous centuries. MacEachern rightly remarks that the large Arab-Kanuri expedition Denham was traveling with must have intensified reactions from both the Mandara and the mountain peoples concerned.[14] Buying off raids is not a phenomenon often recorded in other sources, and the Kapsiki/Higi vehemently deny ever having resorted to these despised tactics. But slave raids were very much part of reality, as is testified by Denham's Arab escort:

> The Arabs were all eagerness; they eyed the *Kirdy* huts, which were now visible on the sides of the mountains before us, with longing eyes, and contrasting their ragged and almost naked state with the appearance of the sultan of Wandala's people in their silk robes, not only thought but said: "If Boo-Khaloom [their leader] pleased, they would go no further; this would do." . . . Boo-Khaloom was, as usual, very sanguine; he said he would make the sultan handsome presents and that he was sure a town full of people would be given to him to plunder.[15]

However, the sultan had his own agenda and used the large Kanuri force against the Fulbe town of Musfeia (Marua),[16] where he needed the Arabs' assistance against this new and more threatening enemy. The Wandala let the Arabs, Kanuri, and Europeans take the lead in that attack, and Denham escaped by the skin of his teeth. Boo-Khaloom was killed. Thus the Wandala sultan killed two birds with one stone, damaging the Fulbe and safeguarding the slave monopoly. In fact, as Denham also remarked, relations between Wandala and the "montagnards" were sometimes nonviolent, the latter serving as soldiers in the armies of the sultan while freed slaves engaged in trade between the plains and the mountains.

The famous German explorer Heinrich Barth witnessed slave trading in the Bornu capital in the middle of the nineteenth century. When he saw the mountain area (the second European to do so), it was during a slave raid against the Musgum, though it had begun as a punitive expedition against the Wandala.[17] This raid also failed, at least for the raiders.[18] However Barth was the first to mention places in the Kapsiki/Higi area, such as Bazza, Kamalle, Metchika, and Sugur (Baza, Kamale, Michika, and Sukur respectively, though the latter is not a Kapsiki/Higi village).[19] He identified them as Marghi, the name of the western neighbors of the Higi/Kapsiki. However, the Kapsiki identify themselves as Marghi in contrast to the Fulbe, so the term is also a more general one covering the various groups in the mountains. Curiously, the terms Mergi and Mandera appear on a world map drawn by Fra Mauro, an Italian monk, around 1445![20] Europe would only really learn about them five hundred years later.

However, the external threat was by no means the only one for the Kapsiki/Higi. Throughout remembered history, villages have fought each other and war was one of the structuring principles of Kapsiki sociopolitical organization.[21] In principle, all villages waged war with each other, neighbors with neighbors. Some villages claim a common descent and either did not fight each other or did not capture slaves or fight with poison. Mogode, for one, had such a relationship with Garta and Ngkala: they avoided fighting people from these villages, and if conflict did arise, they used the weapons of intravillage fighting only, that is, just clubs. The same held for Mbororo, but that village was too far away to reach anyway. In the *mpa te mpa* (the real war) all the men in the village confronted the enemy on a designated field on the border between the two villages. Fighting was at its most intense in this kind of war, which usually lasted two days or until someone was killed, and people went all out, using all the weapons they had, especially poisoned arrows.[22] Between villages ambushes occurred in early-morning attacks on unsuspecting men or women going out for water. These were intended primarily to catch slaves or to steal special objects, like those for ritual protection. Slave raiding also meant slave trading, and most captors let the enemy village pay a ransom to free their kinsmen. Usually they could get a higher price through a ransom in the village than at the slave markets of Mora or Gawar, and ransom negotiations meant a moment of absolute glory for them. However, captives did get sold to the slave markets beyond the confines of the Mandara Mountains, so slave raiding was still a very serious threat.

The number of pitched battles between villages was limited, each village experiencing about four or five from the turn of the twentieth century onward. In the whole of the Kapsiki/Higi conglomerate, there were some 28 village conflicts during the last century, each lasting one or two days. Though slaves caught in these wars constituted just a fraction of the number caught by the Fulbe, the conflicts posed a constant threat, a "condition of Warre" in Hobbesian terms.

Warriors also had their ritual preparation, magic, and amulets for protection.

> Of all Kapsiki amulets, those for war are the best known, eagerly sought after. The best are those that have been used and sacrificed upon for a long time, worn by a *katsala* (real warrior). One has to steal it from him—by force if possible. But how does one steal something from a strong *katsala*? Zra Mpa, the son of a famous *katsala*—hence his name meaning "war"—recounts how his father Vandu obtained a "protection

against iron." In a former battle against Sir, he had spotted someone with a huge, complicated amulet which he always wore. Someone from Sir told him that the amulet had a name and was famous in the village. In the following weeks Vandu set out very early for Sir to spot the man. Finally, when the man was bathing in one of the pools on the plateau, he took off his amulet. Vandu burst from the bushes, snatched the amulet, and ran like hell back to Mogode. Afterwards he wore it in battle, also in the last one against Sirakuti.

War was serious business but it was also a major diversion, a way a youngster could distinguish himself. The Kapsiki see themselves as warriors, their initiation reflecting the warlike character of their former existence. Few titles honor the owner as much as the above-mentioned *katsala*, and those who deserved it were known throughout the neighboring villages. Even today, when men gather and beer flows, war, the exploits of warriors, and the hits scored on either side form the most fascinating topic possible.

The above-mentioned last war with Sirakuti started when during a funeral the people of Mogode ventured deep into Sirakuti territory to get the *safa* and *haze* they needed to adorn the corpse.[23] Some men from Sirakuti caught them cutting the plants and immediately warned their brothers. No one wants to see their "luck" disappear to neighbors, so they attacked and killed one of them. But the retaliation, as the Mogodians were proud to point out, was terrible: six dead!

So the threat of war was always present. Individuals or families working together in the fields had to watch out for raiders from nearby villages trying to revenge an earlier killing or hoping to catch a slave who could be ransomed for cattle. This threat was the main reason for living in a densely populated settlement. Raiding, ambush, war, and sudden conflicts all played a role in the human relations between families, clans, wards, and villages but also between men and women. Most of the wars and skirmishes started over women, such as wives running away to another husband or another village: more than half of the conflicts started with a "woman question." In fact, the whole system of secondary marriages in Kapsiki is based on hostile intervillage relations; a woman's consecutive husbands are defined as enemy.[24]

The complex of external slavery, internal wars, fighting and unstable marriages made for a "frontier of violence," an area where insecurity reigned and the other was in principle the enemy. Imperial expansion, the succession of emirates and governments, the reactions to these expansions and incursions, plus the violent reactions within the mountain communities generated an ethos of violence, continuous self-defense, the glory of war, and distrust of neighbors, an ethos that not only marked the social relations within and between villages but is also an essential key to interpreting and understanding Kapsiki religion.

The Scourge of the Mountains

Slave-hungry emirates dominated much of the nineteenth century but came to an end in the generation after Barth, when a new major player entered the arena, namely the European colonizer. In the remote area where the Kapsiki/Higi live, colonization came slowly and in its early phase caused slave raiding to increase instead of decrease. The European colonies created an administrative vacuum as military conquest preceded effective administration for a considerable period. At the level of empire, Europeans took over the existing structures but at the grass roots level there was a gap since their control over the bush was much less effective. This void was exacerbated by the frequent turnover of colonial powers in the border region, creating a splendid opportunity for enterprising Fulbe chiefs to intensify their hold on the population:

> The arrival of the German colonizer hardly changed the colonial structures. The relations between Habbe [pagans] and Fulbe remained, vassals paying tribute to the feudal overlords, with the proviso that the European military might was at the disposal of the ruling autochthonous authorities, thus in favor of the Fulbe chiefs. Actually, the German officers relied on the Lamibe [chiefs], just as they tended to confirm officially the Fulbe authority over the very pagans who had rejected this and who had been beyond its reach since time immemorial.[25]

An early German colonist remarked on the state of mountain peoples in 1888, even if he complained more about economic loss than human suffering:

> It is a sorry sight how our German back country is depopulated by these slave raids. All prisoners are transported over the Benue to the North as slaves to Yola, and are from there used as tribute payment to Sokoto, or sold to Hausa merchants, who in turn bring them to the markets of Sokoto, Kuka or Kano as well. It is urgent to support these wretched people, together with the English, specifically with the Royal Niger Company.[26]

It is in this incipient colony that we are confronted with the most-feared slave hunter of all times, Hamman Yaji, the Fulbe chief of Madagali, just to the west of the Mandara Mountains. The oral history of the Kapsiki starts here with tall tales about remembered history. Yaji is at the center of these tales The following is from one of the masters of oral history in Kapsiki, Vandu Zra Tè from Mogode.[27]

Hamman Yaji came from Madagali, he was born there. He wanted to be chief of Madagali, but he did not succeed, as his father was not old yet.
"You are still small, you cannot be chief."
"Says who?"
His father answered: "Zubeiru has said that you cannot be chief."
Hamman Yaji went to Zubeiru: "Make me chief."
"Never, you would never be able to do it."
"Of course I can; what do I have to do?"
"If you can, you operate on your father; you take his heart and his liver and you eat those. If you can do this, you can become chief."
Hamman Yaji went out and—*behu*—killed his father,—*praw praw*[28]—he took his liver and his heart and ate them. So people gave him the chieftaincy.

Hamman Yaji, the Fulbe chief of Madagali, more than anyone else in the wider region still embodies the threats of slave raiding, war, and torture. Vandu Zra Tè, one of the oldest men in Mogodé, with gusto spins his tale about this great enemy, depicting him larger than life, feared but also admired, ruthless but himself without fear, whose profession was raiding, whose coin was captive slaves, and whose trade was unmitigated violence. Yaji raided the western Mandara Mountains in the early days of the colonial presence. Never before—and hopefully never afterwards—have these mountains seen such an intensive slave raiding, such fierce wars, and so much human suffering. As can be expected, the historical account of his succession differs slightly from the almost mythical rendering of Vandu Zra Tè.

Hamman's father, Bakari, was Fulbe chief at Madagali, under the nominal tutelage of the Emir of Yola, Zubeiru, who in turn belonged to the Sokoto Caliphate. Zubeiru had had a long and convoluted history with the three colonial forces—German, French, and British. He was caught in an intercolonial rivalry while he also had to cope with Mahdist insurrections. Gradually he became, in the British eyes, the main obstacle to colonisation, and the ambivalent relationship of the 1880s developed into warfare.[29] Following the British capture of Yola in 1901, the Emir fled to Marua (another Fulbe stronghold, now in Cameroon), and after his subsequent defeat by the Germans in 1902 (the "Marua massacre"[30]), he fled to Madagali and eventually was killed by the Lala people.[31] When Bakari saw that the Germans considered him to be an associate of Zubeiru, he fled as well but he was caught, and the German commander[32] ordered him to abdicate in favor of his son. After his return to Madagali, Bakari told the Germans that Hamman Yaji was not acceptable as chief and fled. However, the German commander sought him out from his mountain refuge and forced him to return to Madagali, promising to spare his life.[33] One version of Bakari's end, with the heroic details characteristic of oral tradition, has been preserved by Kirk-Greene, a later assistant district officer in the region:

Ardo Bakari asked what day it was. On being told it was Tuesday, he replied with characteristic Muslim resignation: "It has been foretold that on a Tuesday I shall die, let us return to Madagali." As his cavalcade reached the District Head's compound, where the German troops were drawn up, Dumnuki gave the order to open fire. In the panic that ensued Bakari quietly dismounted and prostrated himself in silent prayer, alone save for his algaita [a horn] player, Mbico, who refused to join the general flight: if his master died, he said, there would be nobody left he could play for. Bakari was shot in cold blood and then apparently beheaded, for when the townspeople returned in the evening the head was found severed from the body. He was buried at the foot of the bald, black rock to the south of the town.[34]

The way Oberleutnant Dominik tells the story is less detailed and much less romantic. On the hunt for Zubeiru, Dominik hears that the Emir has found refuge at Bakari's and pursues him there, also punishing the Madagali Lamido for his "disobedience." The Oberleutnant at some length relates the end of Bakari.[35] The German column approached Madagali cautiously during a storm, then tried to encircle the town: with some men Dominik climbed a hill opposite the compound entrance, and from their high positions his men fired into the compound of Bakari. They were spotted by the Fulbe, but before the battle was really engaged, his second in command called Dominik to stop firing since Bakari was dead, one bullet in his shoulder and one in his head. Hamman Yaji[36] sent a boy to the Germans, with the ring Dominik had given him in an earlier encounter in Dikoa, to confirm that his father had fallen and to talk with the Germans. Yaji told Dominik that Zubeiru that very night had received fresh horses from his father and had doubled back into the mountains.

> As usual with Fulani, the Yerima (prince) was not very sad about the death of his father. After all, he was Lamido now and thought he had waited long enough. From the court of the Lamido seat, a loud wailing came up. The women stood around the body, rubbed themselves in ashes, heaved their hands to heaven and shrieked with wild grief.[37]

For a fleeting moment Dominik is moved when he sees the "thickheaded old man" dead on the ground, with two of his officials ("Groszleute"), but then he reflects that this was a good thing: "Whatever our sentiments, the important thing was to establish German rule here, like a bronze rock."[38]

The next day Hamman Yaji, aged 35, was installed as chief. This was to be the start of:

a quarter century of unbelievable tyranny and cruelty, of slave-raiding and oppression, that continued untrammelled throughout the tenuous German control and the shadowy French administration of the Great War, right down [to] and after the arrival of the British in 1922.[39]

Oral history has its own rendering of the succession itself, as recounted by an old Mafa man from Mokolo, the regional center of the Mandara Mountains:

> The day he was enthroned Lamido [chief], the German officer led him before the bleeding corpse of his father Lamido Bakari, of which they chopped off the head, and they asked Hamman Yaji: "Are you ready to become Lamido instead of your father, knowing you will undergo the same treatment if you do not obey the authority of the German?" Without blinking an eye he answered: "Yes, I am ready."[40]

In Dominik's account, the Germans had already left to pursue Zubeiru.[41] I have gone into some detail in this story because it still reverberates not only in the area but also in historic literature.

Some ten years after his enthronement, Yaji started recording his daily exploits: he had a slave keep a diary for him, and this document has been preserved and published, a treasure trove of surprising and unique insights in the exploits of a regional slave raider.[42] Yaji, now an almost mythical—at least nightmarish—figure in the area, started his diary on September 16, 1912, and until August 25, 1927, he kept a succinct record of his "administration." Some entries regarding Higi/Kapsiki villages:[43]

> 6-7-1913 On Saturday the 3rd of Mairordu Sumaye I sent my people to Sina and they captured 30 cattle and 6 slave girls. [A week later the same "pagans from Sina" would drive his "soldiers" off; later some of the captives were returned.]
> Between 2 and 27-2-1915 I raided Humumzi [a Higi village in Nigeria] and captured 4 slave girls and 20 cattle.
> 29-9-1918 On Sunday 22nd of Laihadji Fadhl al Nar raided Futu in the morning and captured 23 cattle, 22 gowns, 3 red fezzes and 15 goats.
> 7-5-1919 On Wednesday the 6th of Wirardu Sumaye I raided Sir with Lawan Aji of Gaur and we captured 8 slaves, 122 cattle and 200 sheep.
> 30-12-1919 I raided Wula and we captured 20 slaves
> 15-5-1920 On Saturday the 25th of Wairordu Sumaye I sent Jauro Soji to raid the pagans of Gumasi. They took from them 70 slaves, 48 cattle and 90 goats.

In Mogode, 80 years later, Vandu Zra Tè (Figure 3.1) relates the following, his voice still both indignant and slightly admiring:

> He used people as money, Hamman Yaji. He asked a Fulbe woman for a pounding stick and paid with a slave. He bought a mat, and paid with a slave. He sold them to poor people from his own village, which did not have many slaves. Even to buy a calabash, or some gumbo, he paid with people. Even a jar with *shikwed'i* [a crop for the sauce] he paid with a slave. That is what he did.

Throughout his rule, at least during the period of his record keeping, Yaji was in view of the various colonial powers: from 1884 to 1916, the region was under German control, from 1916 to 1922 it was French, and from 1922 to 1961 it was under the British, as part of the Northern Cameroon.[44] At independence it would go to Nigeria. From 1902 until Yaji's dismissed in 1927 he had to adapt to three colonial regimes, all of them quite different in their general policy but with one common denominator: administration and control were marginal, the local rulers were left in place, and the mountain people were a background worry to the administrators. The first report on Yaji was not that negative. Captain Zimmerman led a military mission against what he called, "Heidenexcesse" ("pagan excesses"), the attacks on Hausa merchants on the roads to Madagali. He seems to have been quite taken in by Hamman Yaji:

Figure 3.1 Vandu Zra Tè, oral history expert.

After a rest day, in the morning of 5/1 [1906] I took my leave of Hama Jádi, who accompanied me for a stretch of the road, with the heartfelt wish: may Allah grant him long life. His 12 year old son, who resides in Bungel, near Demea, luckily seems to take after his father.[45]

Later the opinions changed considerably. A report from a British colonial officer in 1914 states: "The chiefs are indulging in a orgy of oppression and confiscation."[46] But they had in fact no other option but to extend a mandate to the Fulbe rulers, also in their "control" over the "Kirdi," as the mountain people were called. It is only after the 1920s that a similitude of control was established. For the most part Yaji did as he wished: up to 1920 he raided the mountain peoples for slaves and cattle, tortured, lopped off heads, and stole cattle wherever he could. In his diary he recorded some 100 raids, in which a total of 2,016 captives were taken or killed (at least those counted) and a far greater number of cattle stolen.[47] Sukur, the mountain chiefdom north of Madagali and the Higi, was to bear the terrible brunt of his horrors,[48] through both the capture of slaves and his meddling in the internal politics of this important "chefferie" in his immediate vicinity:

> On one raid Hamman Yaji's soldiers cut off the heads of dead pagans in front of the Llidi's [chief's] house, threw them into a hole in the ground, set them alight and cooked their food over the flames. Another time he forced the wives of the dead Sukur men to come forward and collect their husbands' heads in a calabash; on yet another occasion, to take all the heads down to Madagali for the Fulani to see. One witness told me how he had seen children have a coil of wire hammered through their ears and jaws by the soldiers, while another related how, when Hamman Yaji learned of the great significance attached to the Sukur burial rites, he ordered his troops to cut up the bodies of the dead so that they could not be given a decent burial.[49]

Similar tales of horror resound among the Marghi, just as close to Madagali.[50] For Yaji himself, this was simply the way of life of a Fulbe chief: "Hamman Yaji's values were those of nineteenth-century Muslim Fulbe society, which had established suzerainty over the pagans of the area in complex arrangement with the much larger emirate of Adamawa."[51] A callous dismissal of pagan lives sharply contrasts with personal concern for his domestic slaves; the routine theft of cattle contrasts with the meticulous bookkeeping of gifts exchanged with other chiefs. He took considerable care that cattle rustling and slave raiding took place only on his "own" territory, in those villages which constituted his fief. Also, when the British made it clear on December 25, 1920, that there could be no more slave raiding, raiding was finished. At least, no more reports on raids would enter his diary from that date on. In short, he kept to the law— his law and that of his superiors. This was not the real end of slavery or even slave trading, as the internal wars in the region[52] kept providing him with slaves to sell abroad. Sometimes accusations of witchcraft or theft in the villages generated slaves for the market:

> 7-11-1922 On Tuesday the 17th of Haram Petel the pagans of Sina brought a woman of theirs to me, who they say stole from the people.
> 24-11-1925 On Tuesday the 8th of Banjaru Tumbindu the pagans of Kamale accused one of their men of being a "witch" and they caught him and brought him to me. They wanted too to reap his corn, so I sent my horsemen to them.

Selling a "witch"[53] is one thing, stealing his harvest is quite another.

Yaji's relation with the Mogode of Zra Tè is quite ambivalent, though. One of his many field compounds was at Rafa, a ward of Mogode, just a mile from the present center of the village, a place he called Nyiburi. Though he did raid extensively the surrounding villages of Kamale, Sena, Garta, and especially Sukur, he never really raided Mogode, though his people might on occasion capture some animals:

> 21-3-1919 On the 18th of Banjaru Sakitindu I went down to my house in the direction of Mugudi and sent my soldiers to the pagans of Moda in order to bury their dead.
> 18-7-1919 Yerim Abba returned from the Captains celebrations. He brought two horses belonging to the pagans of Mugudi, which he had captured from them.

In fact the people from Mogode were doing more or less the same:

> 29-3-1920 On Monday the 8th of Sumatendu Waube the pagans of Mugudi raided the Kamale pagans and killed one and wounded two. Then the Kamale pagans fought them and killed two and wounded two.

They even got back to Hamman Yaji himself:

> 19-3-1921 On Saturday the 8th of Sumatendu Waube I heard that the pagans of Mugudi had stolen a cow from my home in Nyiburi.

There is no entry about retribution. One of the reasons he spared Mogode may have been his arrangements with other Fulbe chiefs, respecting their "hunting grounds":

> 9-7-1919 . . . I stopped at my house in Tongo and the Lieutenant stopped in Mugudi on the other side of the boundary between me and the Emir of Marua.

Though he mentioned only pagans, according to local tradition Mogode was housing a minor Fulbe chief,[54] dependent on Gawar,[55] part of the Marua lamidate, a colleague Yaji respected.

In other Kapsiki villages the tales about Yaji have an almost apocalyptic character: for instance, in Sirakuti people still tell about a conflict with Hamman Yaji which led to a massacre on the Veke hill, just inside Nigeria. The story goes that that particular ward send a tribute in ash instead of honey to the Fulbe chief, an insult for which he retaliated fiercely.[56]

Also Yaji's end has become part of the local Kapsiki lore, again told by Vandu Zra Tè:

> The people of Mogode have burnt down his house twice; Hamman Yaji then recruited men from the villages around and came to Mogode. It was in the days that Kweji Miyi was chief. Hamman Yaji came with all these people to beat Mogode. He came from Ldaka, in the bush, and from there to Rhwemetla [a central mountain in Mogode], over there on his way to the North. Suddenly the *mazavɛ*—birds[57] descended upon him, and he lost his red fez. He was carried through the village by four people [like a corpse], and exclaimed: "Now I, Hamman Yaji, are close to my death, as I am on the territory of Mogode, and the *mazavɛ* has dropped my hat on the soil of Mogode." Later he went back to Madagali. That was the rainy season the white men got him.

Religion did have something to do with his demise, at least according to the written history. A devout Muslim, Hamman started to follow the Mahdi faith propagated by the warlord Rabeh, who had come over from the Mahdist Sudan and scourged the area until 1900:

> 15-5-1915 On Saturday the 30th of Banjaru Sakitindu I took on the devotional practices of the Mahdist sect under Malam Muhammad's instruction.
> 8-8-1922 On Tuesday the 14th of Dhu al Hijjah I renounced the practice of praying to God for things of this world, and adopted the practice of praying for things of the world to come.

This brush with Mahdism would in the end cost him dearly. More than the brutal slave raiding—which seems to have been ended by then—it was the threat of a Mahdist insurrection that convinced the colonial British government to get rid of Hamman Yaji, in 1927.[58]

In Kapsiki/Higi even his arrest became mythical. Vandu Zra Tè again:

> The white man looked for him, in Madagali. Plenty people, but where was Hamman Yaji? One of the soldiers of Yaji told the white people: "He is in the earth. He has a hole in the earth, where his bed is, inside his compound."
> "Can you show it to us?"
> "Yes, I can show it to you."
> The white man gave money to the soldier, and they went to the tomb: "Hamman Yaji, you are finished now." Yaji came out, totally naked. They put him on a horse, drove off and never has Hamman Yaji been seen again."

Of course, the people in Mogode were happy not to see him any more, as were the Sukur. Judy Sterner noted a splendid story in Sukur:[59]

> He was stopped by the Europeans who captured him and poisoned him. When he died he fell spread-eagled with his arms outstretched. When you go down to the town [Madagali] you see wooden crosses that the Europeans have put up in memory of his death.

The British written sources tell a slightly different story, but also an exciting one. The British colonial authorities wanted to get rid of Yaji, for various reasons, one of them Mahdism. However, their control of the region was weak and they counted on an intense resistance from Yaji's people. Kirk-Greene relates an intensive correspondence between Yola, the center of the Adamawa administration, and their colonial superiors in Kaduna and Lagos. They decided on a cautious strategy: separated military columns would depart from Yola with varying marching orders, as if they were reinforcing the Maiduguri garrison. In Madagali they would meet "by chance." This was done with great caution, but in the end a police detachment of 30 men was sufficient to make the arrest[60] and the rest of the 300 men were kept behind. Yaji, in typical fashion, thought to receive guests but then was apprehended with his son Bello and his chief slave Ajia. It was then that the diary was found.[61] There was to be no insurrection and Yaji was transported to Yola on August 26, 1927. However, his reputation did not fade that quickly, and after a quick trial he was put on a steamer to Sokoto. In the colonial office in Kaduna this arrest was hailed as an important victory over Mahdism, though it was in effect a rebuttal of Lugard's doctrine of indirect rule. Mahdism—and thus Yaji—was still considered too dangerous in Sokoto, too close to French colonial territory (Yaji's brother was Lamido of Mokolo in Cameroon[62]) so he was transferred to Kaduna, where he soon died of an infection of the renal ducts.

The end of Yaji and the abolition of slave raiding and trading were, of course, not the same as the abolition of slavery itself. Slavery in the area was officially abolished in 1937 but in fact died out much later. Until the late 1960s the institution of the "serviteur non payé" was still present in the courts of the Fulbe Lamibe and reminders of slavery are still present everywhere, even today.[63]

Colonial Powers and Reluctant Ethnicity

Throughout their long dwelling history in the area, the villages that are now called Kapsiki or Higi never were under one united polity, and in fact never considered themselves as belonging to any unit larger than a loose conglomerate of villages with a tradition of common origin. The distinction between Higi and Kapsiki as two groups was first made by the German "Hauptmann" Karl Strümpell, on the basis of tales of origin and some agricultural practices.[64] However, these ethnic labels stem either from a traditional enemy (*hegi* means locust in Higi) or indicate just three villages of the whole conglomerate (Kapsiki originally meant just Mogode, Guria, and Kamale), and the people themselves never used these terms, just the village name. As for provenance, at both sides of the border the villages originate from east as well as west of the mountains, and their histories are completely intertwined, just as are their marriage patterns and many other cultural practices.[65] Therefore colonization, in creating tribal unity, created two "tribes."

Effective colonization came late for the Kapsiki and Higi, as for all of the groups in the mountains.[66] After Denham in 1823 and Barth in 1852, who skimmed the mountains, the Mandara Mountains were traversed only by one German column prior to World War I. This expedition was led in 1905 and 1906 by Kapitän Zimmerman, the predecessor of Herr Dominik, and on this journey Zimmerman became enchanted with the Kapsiki:

> Their farms are masterpieces, their houses real showcases, and wherever one goes, one encounters the love of home and order, the sense of coziness and beauty; in this beehive of similar dwellings really lives a bee-people.[67]

Not until 1930 was some sort of pacification achieved and only after World War II can one speak of a "pax colonialis." Skirmishes between Kapsiki villages lasted throughout the 1950s, when establishment of the nation-state was under way.

The Germans were the first to bring pacification to the area. It was, however, a spurious pacification and the main recollection the Kapsiki have of the Germans is of fierce fighters and cruel commanders. Older Kapsiki in the 1970s could still remember them, and they speak with enthusiasm and fascination about the war they called *kwarhweredlɛahweredlɛa*, an idiophone for automatic gunfire. As warriors, they admired the ruthless way the Germans went to war, an admiration shared by other mountain groups as well, such as the neighboring Mofu Diamare.⁶⁸ The prestige of the Germans led the mountain people to actively support them against the French during World War I. When the French won in 1916 and the colony was assigned to France, old hostilities between the "Kirdi" and Fulbe resumed, meaning the montagnards retaliated against Fulbe oppression, which had been supported by the Germans, and attacked the Fulbe, stealing their cattle and killing merchants. The Muslims struck back as hard and brutally as they could, and the area had to be pacified once again. In 1922 the Higi part was mandated to Great Britain as northern Cameroon and the first expeditions ventured into the mountains from the western side. Though the instructions were that "the pagans that have never been subjugated, such as those living in the Mandara hills, are to be left untouched for the moment"; a skirmish between the Kirdi and the colonial forces ensued at Bazza. This was the Higi's first encounter with the British colonial force. Shortly afterwards some degree of administration was set up, but even well into the 1930s this did not amount to much. One colonial British officer remarked:

> [these] are the most lawless, ill-governed places I have seen in Nigeria since the early years of the Northern Nigerian Protectorate. Slave dealing and slave raiding are rampant . . . chiefs of minor importance were given rifles with which they were encouraged to attack the wretched pagans [who are] hiding like frightened monkeys on inaccessible hilltops . . . of course everyone goes about fully armed: spears, shields, bows and arrows, clubs etc.⁶⁹

In 1930 the mountain people resisted the new colonizer and tax collecting but a plague of locusts aggravated matters further.⁷⁰ Slowly the two halves of the Kapsiki/Higi area, the *hedi feranse* and the *hedi aŋgele* (French earth, English earth) fell quiet. Slave raiding and slave dealing went first and internal fighting finally died out after World War II. After the collapse of the League of Nations in 1942, the British part became a British Trust Territory until, with independence approaching in 1960, it chose to be part of Nigeria.⁷¹ It was therefore only during the 1950s, in the last days of the British and French colonial rule, that the mountains were drawn into a system of administration. A certain level of infrastructure was needed to ensure this system and all-weather roads were built into and through the area.⁷²

The last skirmishes and wars between villages in the Kapsiki/Higi area took place in the early 1950s, such as the war between Kamale and Garta and the one already mentioned between Mogode and Sirakuti. Total pacification came later. In 1972, during my first stay in the area, one village (Kortchi) raided a neighboring village (Hinde Gawar), abducting a woman and burning down a number of huts.

I vividly remember the delight with which my informants told me about it. The Kortchi raid had been shouted through the village, even though Kortchi is 20 km from Mogode. The fighting, the burning down of houses, and especially the stolen woman really fired up their imagination. "Like the people of old" they said, "like savages"; but their eyes and eagerness betrayed something of their ambivalence: savages, of course, but what a thing to do, even now!

Evidently, the Cameroonian government took a dimmer view of the proceedings, sending in troops who burned down houses in Kortchi, liberated the woman, and put a few perpetrators in prison.

Despite continuing fascination with fighting, pacification was viewed well by the Kapsiki and their neighbors. The Europeans, called *nasara* after the Arabic word for Christian (Nazarene), brought peace and safety, and their presence and contribution were much appreciated. Even after a generation, this appreciation still lives on.

> My first encounter with the Chief of Wula, in the north of the Kapsiki area, was revealing. Inexperienced as I was, I took a seat—a stone—next to him. Immediately he rose and sat himself on a large boulder, about a meter above me, his notables following him to the spot, selecting a stone slightly lower than his. I had, without knowing, made a small social gaffe: I should have sat lower than the *maze Wula*.[73] But the chief never mentioned it because he had a quite different axe to grind with me. Looking me straight in the eyes, he asked: "Why have you, white people, left here? Why did you not stay?" I tried to explain that independence had been forced on the colonizers but he cut me short: "You have let the brown man [Fulbe] betray you. The brown man tricked you into leaving. You should have stayed." So much for colonial guilt.[74]

After being liberated from the Fulbe of Hamman Yaji—who did not make any distinction between the various pagan groups—the Kapsiki/Higi finally became an ethnic group and faced two processes of identity formation. First, they were now treated as an ethnic group, as a more or less homogeneous cluster of villages with a clear boundary and a common culture. This setup was new to them. Their borders with other ethnic groups in the area were never very clear, and to some extent that still is the case. In the south their Bana neighbors are quite similar in culture and might have been included in the Kapsiki cluster if not for linguistic reasons. Their eastern side exhibits a clearer boundary, since a Fulbe-dominated valley separates them from the Mofu, who have a very different political organization.[75] In the Nigerian west their Marghi neighbors share the self-definition (*margi*, meaning "black") but are culturally and linguistically different.[76] The north shows a fragmented border, with a range of micro-ethnic units between the Kapsiki and the Mafa, the most important one being Sukur (Chapter 7).[77]

Second, with the very same processes uniting them above village level, they were divided as well, falling into two groups, the Kapsiki and the Higi. The line of division had little to do with cultural or social rationales but simply followed the edge of the Kapsiki Plateau. A village like Mogode has closer social and marital relations with the nearby Nigerian villages of Kamale and Garta than with Rufta, Guria, or Sirakuti, its Cameroonian neighbors. So at the very moment when history threw them together, they were divided again by the international border.[78]

One major factor was the frontier itself. Any international border changes the relationship between neighbors. In principle, after the demise of the German colonial administration, the two halves—Kapsiki and Higi—were in different territories after 1922. In theory the colonial policies of the French and the British were very different, with indirect rule being the British hallmark while the French favored much more direct colonial involvement. However, there were few actual differences in administration in the Mandara Mountains, since before World War II the British and the French had hardly penetrated the mountains at all, so all colonial administration was in fact very indirect rule through the Fulbe overlords on both sides of the border. In late colonial times, differences began to emerge and then disaster struck in Nigeria in the form of the 1967–1970 Biafra War. The Higi area, with Michika as the administrative hub of the Cubunawa District, is a remote area in Nigeria and was not very involved, but the war did have its impact on the economy. Prices rose: food, commodities, and fuel became much more expensive on the Anglophone side, and a lucrative commerce developed ranging from fully legal transactions to outright smuggling. In the Mandara Mountains the Kapsiki/Higi were ideally situated between the two countries. All the border villages from Rufta to Rumsiki had footpaths leading down to their Nigerian twin villages, but it was Mogode that quickly developed into a center of commerce, since its partner village, Kamale, was at the end of an all-season road from Michika. Through its Fulanized core of officials and traders, Mogode became a smuggling hub and profited enormously from it. Enterprising Kapsiki earned large incomes, invested in cattle, and after Islamization went on to trade on a larger scale and in a few cases even went on pilgrimage to ensure full respectability.

After the Biafra War the newly established trading pattern continued in both the Ahidjo and the Biya periods, the first two Cameroonian presidents since independence in 1960. The name Kapsiki became associated with the region, and large- and small-scale trading and smuggling continued even though the government had installed a customs post in Mogode. With the many small, meandering goat tracks running down the hills and in-laws and kinsmen living in the other village, border traffic was and is hard to monitor and control. Other ethnic groups, such as the Mafa, joined in and profited from the situation, and for them "going to Mogode" was tantamount to performing a round of nightly smuggling, a welcome and rewarding adventure for women from Mokolo.

The differences in economic development in the two countries remained marked. Cheap Nigerian commodities like cloth, enamelware, glass, household paraphernalia, and cheap petrol were exchanged for Cameroonian food and beer. Though not as lucrative as during the war, people still earn money from this trade on both sides of the border. The two governments have tried to curb this traffic, just as they have attempted to limit another kind of mobility, that of women. Extremely high marriage rates (a better expression than marriage instability in the Kapsiki case) were exacerbated by the presence of the border. Dissatisfied wives could not only run away to another village, as was quite customary, but even flee to another country, rendering informal action by the husband hazardous and legal action impossible. From the 1980s onward the local governments in Mubi and Michika in Nigeria as well as in Mokolo and Mogode in Cameroon have implemented policies to curb this female mobility. Now it has become possible to claim back runaway wives from across the border and to receive compensation payments from villages in the other country. What women think of these measures is another matter, but both governments have unreservedly opted for strengthening marital bonds by curbing female mobility. Women's low expectations of marriage have drawbacks[79] but so do these government measures, for when women lose the option to vote with their feet, they also lose bargaining power within their marriage. Yet the stabilization of marriages on the whole seems to be appreciated.

So the contingencies of history created separate nationalities and different names, Kapsiki in Cameroon and Higi in Nigeria, masking the fact that neither culture nor language warrants two distinct groups. Culturally the villages on both sides recognize their similarity and, as we saw in the Preface, the linguistic situation shows eleven dialects of similar stature, whose boundaries do not coincide with the international border.[80] However, the political situation and the missionaries' activities might in the end act as a kind of self-fulfilling prophecy: one Kapsiki language and orthography and another Higi version are developing. Conflicts over the border area and lingering disputes are still going on and tend to reinforce this cleavage. Whether the 2006 decision on this border issue by the International Court of Justice in The Hague is final remains to be seen, but for the moment everyday life for those Kapsiki living near the border (and this involves quite a few villages) is still the same and the ruling does not change much.

The Catholic and various Protestant missions have been part of this process. When the Christian missions arrived in the 1950s, the Catholics took up residence in the westernmost Higi village of Baza and in Sir on the eastern Kapsiki flank, while the Protestants were more central in Mbororo in the Higi region and in Mogode in the Kapsiki area, just after World War II. Recently the Sir station was transferred to Mogode as well. From the start, schooling was part of the missionaries' goal, either through formal education or literacy campaigns. On both sides of the border this educational work and the need for Bible translations called for a description of the language, for a standardized orthography, and finally for the translation of the Bible and other religious texts into the vernacular. The processes of orthography and translation reduced the number of written dialects to two, one on each side of the border. Both the Catholics and the Protestants developed their own orthography (the Kapsiki one mediated by the anthropologist), while in Higi the Summer Institute of Linguistics was instrumental in describing and writing the Michika Higi dialect[81] and in Bible translation. The New Testament in Higi appeared in 1986, the Kapsiki one in 1988. The vernacular has been made official but in a colonial way: unified, sanitized, and divided between the political realities.

Missionary activities met with varied success, though. The Mbororo mission on the Nigerian side of the border had a steady trickle of converts, as did the one in Baza. In Sir, the Catholics opened a dispensary that still serves the Kapsiki area well. But eventually Christianity did take a firm hold, and now a majority of the Kapsiki and Higi are Christian or Muslim. The last decennia have seen the rise of Nigerian and Cameroonian Christian churches, like the Église Évangélique du Cameroun, with congregations that match the older mission churches. Figure 3.2 shows the new religious generation.

These processes of ethnic formation and reluctant entry into a larger society are embedded in a situation of increasing state control on the one hand,

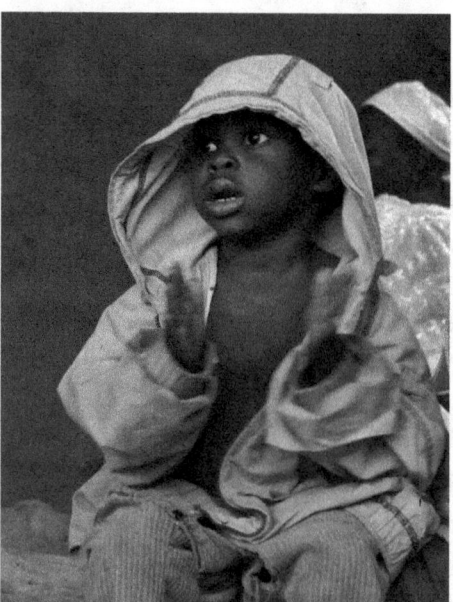

Figure 3.2 Zra Dementsu, the grandson of my assistant Sunu. Mogode 2003.

and Islamization on the other. During Ahidjo's reign in the first decades after independence, official power and Islam went hand in hand. In the Muslim north, urban life not only was Muslim but also was based on Fulbe culture. To become modern was to become Muslim, renounce local traditions, and take up a way of life deemed Fulbe. This process of Fulbeization or Fulanization recorded among the Mafa in the same period[82] was evident in Kapsiki villages, especially in Mogode with its Lamido living in the middle of town. Between 1960 and 1980 its Fulanized core grew until it comprised much of the center of the village. In fact, the Lamido himself, Hamadjoda, was a Fulanized Kapsiki, just as his predecessor and successor were Fulanized locals. With the arrival of Paul Biya as president of Cameroon, this situation has changed. The former president, Ahidjo, a Fulbe of the north, always kept close connections with the north, and his mother-in-law lived in Mokolo. With Paul Biya's arrival, the southerners started to take over and, with them, Christianity, so Islam is no longer expanding. Some Fulanized Kapsiki have reconverted to Christianity, gone back to their traditional religion, or chosen some kind of modernized nonreligion that seems to be on the rise as well in the area. Thus the major religions, even in a politically and economically marginalized area like the Mandara Mountains, wax and wane with political fortunes in the capital.

PART TWO

RITUALS OF DWELLING

4

At Home in the Mountains

The Mountain that "Cuts"

Early in the morning two men arrive at Tizhè Da's compound, each carrying a rooster. Tizhè finishes his morning beverage and joins the men, guiding them through the still-sleepy village toward Rhwemetla, one of the many basalt peaks that dot the Kapsiki plateau. Rhwemetla, a spectacular sheet of basalt, has a peculiar feature as well as a special reputation. It is shot through with holes from volcanic gases that escaped during eruptions long, long ago. For the Kapsiki these holes remind them of their village's founder, Hwempetla, whose heroic deeds—they are convinced—have caused them (see Appendix). Each year at this spot all the girls to be initiated sing their hearts out in a two-day singing contest that is the social high point of their initiation (see Chapter 9). The specific reputation of the mountain is based on its role in judgment, of settling disputes between two equal parties in the village. It is the mountain of the rooster ordeal, in fact not so much because of the mountain, more because of the *mel*ɛ (the sacrificial jar) which is buried at its foot, a jar also called Rhwemetla, "the mountain that cuts," as in "cutting through a knot," i.e. judging.

Having arrived at the spot, the two litigants undress to their underwear, crouch down, and place their roosters between their feet. Tizhè, who is in charge of the jar and the ordeal, settles himself on a boulder and signals the start. Theirs is a conflict about land, as is usual in this ordeal. The first man starts expounding his case, explaining why the particular piece of land that is being contested is his: it was his father's and his father's father's and he has cultivated it since early childhood, a real property. His voice gradually strengthens and he finishes by stating that the *shala* (god) of Rhwemetla has to take him if he is wrong. When he falls silent Tizhè signals the other one. He too tells his story, which starts longer ago, and explains how his own grandfather lent that land to the grandfather of his opponent, stressing that at the start some counter gifts of beer had been given. Indeed nobody just gives land away; it is owned by the clan or lineage and not by the individual. If he can prove the transaction, he has a case here.

However, there are no living witnesses to the loan, and borrowed land is often handed down to the next generation with no information given about its original ownership. This is a typical case: two conflicting claims that cannot be corroborated. Both men touch the ash their mother's brother has put on their forehead, and then put forward the roosters their uncles gave them, to have the god of the mountain speak through the animals. Sometimes the roosters start to fight, but that is not the issue: the one that crows first is the winner; the other rooster has been "caught." The losing rooster then is free game for anyone catching him—one of the two men usually, if they want to—while the winning one is for Tizhè: it is "his" jar—in fact of the *kumbi* lineage of the *makwiyɛ* clan (one of the six major clans of the village)—that is the caretaker of the ordeal.

The ordeal, which used to be recognized by a wide circle of Kapsiki/Higi villages, is now itself at the center of a heated property debate. Kirk-Greene[1] noted the same ordeal in Kamale, Mogode's neighbor downhill in Nigeria, during the last days of the colony. The pot at that time was lodged at the foot of the one of most impressive of all the peaks, Mcirghe, one of the two peaks that characterize Mogode. Mcirghe, the larger one, is the male, and his companion, Rhwemetemale, is the "woman mountain." However, Mcirghe, which Kirk-Greene (1969: 219) called "an awe-inspiring finger-peak that attracts the eye for many miles along the Yedseram valley," may be situated administratively in Mogode but is the sacred mountain of Kamale. The same procedure was used there, even if a lot of tall stories were told about the fate of the bird (one cockerel would kill the other, or the winner would swell up to the size of an ostrich). Reality never matches the tales, but the division of the colonies brought about a division of the ordeal as well. The people from Mogode insist that the ordeal originated on the mountain called Rhwemetla and that the ones responsible for the ordeal got into trouble in their village and moved downhill, taking the jar with them. So when the colonials arrived, they found the ordeal in Kamale and used it accordingly, conforming to the principles of indirect rule. Just after the 1960 independence, and seeing the continuous bickering on national borders, the Lamido of Mogode had enough of his dependence on a Nigerian ordeal, had a new jar made, installed it in its original place, put the original lineage in charge of the ordeal again, and ordered all the Kapsiki villages in Cameroon to use the "new original" one. He incorporated the ordeal within his own jurisdiction and charges the litigants: FCFA 9,000 for the loser, of which FCFA 3,000 ($ 5) go to the winner and FCFA 6,000 ($ 10) to the Lamido. Kamale of course has continued with its own jar, so there are now two, the one in Cameroon more expensive.

Mountains stand as judges but have a much larger presence in Kapsiki life as well. The notion of dwelling, as was pointed out in Chapter 2, implies a multi-stranded relation with the environment, and for the Kapsiki way of dwelling, their mountain habitat means several things. First, each village has its sacred mountain, enveloped in tales of the past that are tied to the people by links of descent that are revived in sacrifices, initiation, and ordeals. In the final phase of their initiation, the boys trek along all the sacred spots in, on, and around the mountains, a smith pointing out all the relevant details (see Chapter 10). Dwelling means transforming scenery into a relationship, imbuing places with history and kinship. For the Kapsiki, sight is transformed into meaning, aesthetics into history, and wildness into kinship. Their eventual transition from their traditional religion, the one that is the main subject of this book, to Islam and Christianity implies a change from dwelling to building, from active signification of a pre-existent landscape to a planned and organized network of links beyond the mountain area. But their own Kapsiki religion, in short, is a *historically rooted, local, people-oriented* religion.

The Mountain Village

The villages of the Kapsiki/Higi, called *meleme*, are clearly recognizable units defined by a demarcated territory, a name, a set of specific patriclans with their migratory histories, and a religiopolitical organization. About 35 villages dot Kapsiki-Higi territory, varying in size from 1,500 to 7,000 inhabitants. Such relatively large villages are common in this part of the Mandara Mountains. The last decades have shown a marked population boom, and many settlements have been expanding correspondingly and have become more recognizable as such. Villages also differ in settlement density, from a highly nucleated settlement such as Rumsiki, to the dispersed ways of living in Sir or Ldiri. In all cases the boundaries of the wards and especially the villages are always clearly marked by boulders, special rock formations, or dry riverbeds. All the villages share a similar social and political structure, as well as an important feeling of togetherness as members of the same settlement. In short, the village is the most important level of social aggregation and identity. Internally it is divided into wards, clans, and lineages, the descent groups usually being scattered over various wards. These groups were important during bouts of fighting within villages in the past, but have relatively little hold over the lives of the members beyond these "high" times. Their functions in resource management and marriage arrangements are limited, but their referential function is much larger. People often refer to their clan in daily discourse, as a constant restatement of identity within the village, and while joint clan membership is not of prime economic relevance, the membership of different clans regulates interaction between people who are fundamentally equals. Especially during the ritual times, clans are cultural ways to make a small difference. The smallest social unit, the compound, inhabited by a monogamous or polygynous family, with the man's parents sometimes living in, is crucial in daily life, bolstered by a pervading sense of privacy and individual autonomy, even if situated inside larger kin groups.

Such a village, like our central example of Mogode, is also a religious unit. The main founding myth of the village is one of common descent from an ancestor who came into the area, settled, and undertook heroic exploits (see Appendix). Usually in those tales, the area was not completely empty but already inhabited, and the ancestor's exploits were aimed at carving out his own niche in the territory. Each of the *meleme* has its own territory with marked boundaries, even marked spots where wars against the neighbors were fought. Each village has its own history, sacred place, and chiefly lineage, its own smiths and smith chief. Characteristically, the clan and lineage system does not transcend the village border: each village in the Kapsiki/Higi village cluster harbors its own set of village-specific clans and lineages. The only commonality between the villages is that each has a clan called *maze*, chief, from which all village chiefs are chosen, often rotating over the lineages of that clan. So, in the social structure of the clan system, the relative isolation of the villages is clear, because in principle villages share few descent ties. Some villages have a tradition of common descent and in kinship idiom they define themselves as brothers, using the terminology of the polygynous family, "child of the same father," that is, half-brother. This link provided a modest degree of peace between the villages, since during the wars of the pre- and early colonial period they did not fight with bows and arrows (i.e. poison), nor did they capture the other villagers as slaves. The wars between related villages—which did indeed occur—were defined as wars between clans within the same village, or in Kapsiki terms, "war of the women," just as co-wives may quarrel. When they did fight, they just used clubs; the Kapsiki knew a segmentary kind of war, in which the use of weapons escalated with the social distance between the parties.[2]

Some villages, notably Rumsu, have a slightly different kinship system, in that the local kin groups trace their main allegiance not through descent, but through residence: one traces one's descent to the ancestor-founder of the particular ward one lives in, whatever the gender of the intervening links. The proper anthropological term for such groups is "ramages," and the difference between the patrilineages of most villages and the Rumsu ramages depends on the residence rule of Kapsiki marriage. Most commonly this tends to be virilocal, so when sons do not move too far away from their father, ramages resemble patrilineages. But neither virilocality nor patri-filial co-residency is an absolute rule, so these ramages are really just that, ramages.

Within the village the clans are usually dispersed: each of the wards houses members of most of the village's clans, because most sons choose not to live close to their father's compound or too close to their brothers, and definitely not next to their half-brother, a classic kinship tension within Kapsiki society. The youngest son is expected to remain in his father's compound and to inherit ("eat," the Kapsiki call it) the compound. Formerly, internal wars and slave raids forced the Kapsiki to live huddled together in a safe place and not to build their homesteads in or near the fields they cultivated, but pacification gave them the opportunity to move to their fields and live out in the bush. Bush wards sprang up, but population growth meant that land had to be cleared further into the bush, so people still have their fields at quite a distance from where they live.

Each village has its own smiths, an endogamous group of specialists who take on most functions that call for specialization. Though the term "smith" derives from their iron working, they might be better called "general specialists" since in addition to working iron, they are the village undertakers, which is in fact their dominant occupation, but they are also musicians, healers, medicine men, and diviners. Their women are the potters of the village, producing both utilitarian and ritual pottery. In fact, the separation between smith and non-smith (*rerhɛ* and *melu* in Kapsiki) is extremely clear in Kapsiki; the *rerhɛ* form a segment of society with specific tasks, their own food taboos, ritual duties, and prerogatives, combined with notions of pollution. This situation is not uncommon in this part of Africa but the Mandara Mountains show this complex in its full force.[3]

Smiths are part of the system of clans and lineages; they thus belong to a *melu* clan and lineage but, being endogamous, have no blood relations with the other members of the lineage. Smiths have to find their marriage partners among their own five percent minority, so have to go far afield to find a suitable partner. Consequently, they are allowed to marry closer kin than are the *melu* (non-smiths); for instance they practice a form of direct sister exchange (which for the *melu* would be, in their words, "marrying death"). Throughout Kapsiki religion we will encounter these smiths, as ritual and medicinal specialists, diviners, and musicians. They are as indispensable in religion as they are in ecological adaptation, being the makers of agricultural implements, or in the olden days fabricating the weapons for war. Their pivotal position in Kapsiki religion is similar in other ethnic groups in the region, and a large part of the Mandara Mountains offers a good example in Africa of the special religious position of these craftsmen.

The village of Mogode has 16 wards, including one Christian settlement and a large Fulanized core. Wards have a loose structure. The ward headman (*mblama*[4]) assists the village chief in matters such as collecting taxes, party dues, and fines, a less than popular endeavor that older men might shirk and that some younger ones covet for a political career. Members of any clan can become a *mblama*. In the last few decades, people from some of the outer wards have moved into Mogode's central ward, resulting in one Christian and two Muslim wards, though the religions are now to be found in other wards as well. Since all the arable land has been claimed, new settlements stay close to available water, as due to its increasing scarcity, people are moving to the few bore holes on the plateau. Mogode is one of the larger Kapsiki villages and the administrative center. It has a primary school and a secondary school that attracts pupils from all over the Kapsiki area. There are plans to build another secondary school as well, this one Catholic.

An Individual Fortress: The Compound

The new compounds are gradually opening up to the world but the classic mountainside Kapsiki compound (*rhε*) was a veritable fortress surrounded by man-high stone walls and a pathway to the forecourt lined with euphorbia, a reminder of the bad old days when these thorny bushes formed a last defense against marauders. Yet the Kapsiki still like to line the access way to their new homes with the picturesque euphorbia or, more recently, with hedges of agaves. And the wall is still important (Figure 4.1).

The man-high stone wall (*yindlu*) is made of carefully arranged stones and is a center of ritual attention (Figure 4.2). The wall separates the inside from the outside, the family from the rest of the society, and kin from nonkin—distinctions that resonate in many variations throughout Kapsiki rituals. Its height precludes any view of the interior or, as the Kapsiki say, it hides their poverty. Toward the narrow entrance, the wall is higher and bears many traces of former sacrifices and libations. The forecourt (*derha*) is a lower structure surrounding the one and only opening in the wall, and it forms the only part of the house outside the wall, serving as the social space of the *rhε*. In the dry season the family eats, drinks, and sleeps here, and guests are received in this space. The *derha* consists

Figure 4.1 The compound from the outside.

mainly of two low stone walls circling the main, high walled, entrance. It holds the piles of firewood of the women; the whole space is protected from the sun by reed mats. The entry path divides the *derha* in two, "female" and "male" sides. Which side is male and which is female depends on the terrain: the higher part is male. On the male side, the fireplace marks the preeminent place of the *derha*, the *pulu ŋeza*. This part of the wall immediately next to the entrance is the place of the master of the house, the place of honor. Some houses have a double *derha*, like the one in Figure 4.2. The house as a whole is oriented more or less north–south, because neither the setting nor the rising sun may shine directly through the opening of the wall, which would be considered unhealthy.

In the dry season most family activities and all public functions of religious life take place in the *derha*. People freely enter the forecourt but neither kinsmen nor friends advance through the wall at the back of the *derha* without good reason and without softly calling out: "Anybody home?" Just behind the opening in the wall is the entrance hut proper, the *dabala*, a round hut with two openings but no doors, where the family cooks and eats in the wet season. The rest of the compound is divided into a male and a female side, corresponding to the *derha*, along the axis of the entrance to the brewery at the end of the compound. The latter is usually built into the wall and is one of the few items of the compound built with communal labor. The male part also consists of sleeping huts for the master of the house and his sons, and the female side has huts for each of the women. If the wives want to have their own kitchen, they have double huts, a kitchen plus a sleeping hut with a granary on top. But in many families the wives share a kitchen and have single sleeping huts. Between the more numerous female huts, the small spaces are covered with reed mats or conical straw roofs, and each woman has her own bath space near the wall, with a small drainage outlet through it. Both the names for the outlet and the roofing frequently figure in personal names, as births often take place here. For the women, the washing place is an important ritual spot, because they bury the umbilical cords and placentas of their children here; for a man it is a place of some danger that he will not readily enter, fearing for his virility.

Figure 4.2 represents a mature compound, with a characteristic structure; it has a male and a female side (the male on the higher ground) and a young–old gradient: inside the house the senior wives are closer to the entrance, their firewood in the *derha* at the male side. A Kapsiki compound waxes and wanes with the family that lives in it and with their fortunes and misfortunes. Thus, the whole cycle of the Kapsiki domestic group can be seen from its compound plans, starting with a simple wall and a few huts, then growing into a fully blown compound like the one illustrated, eventually ending up as a large compound full of

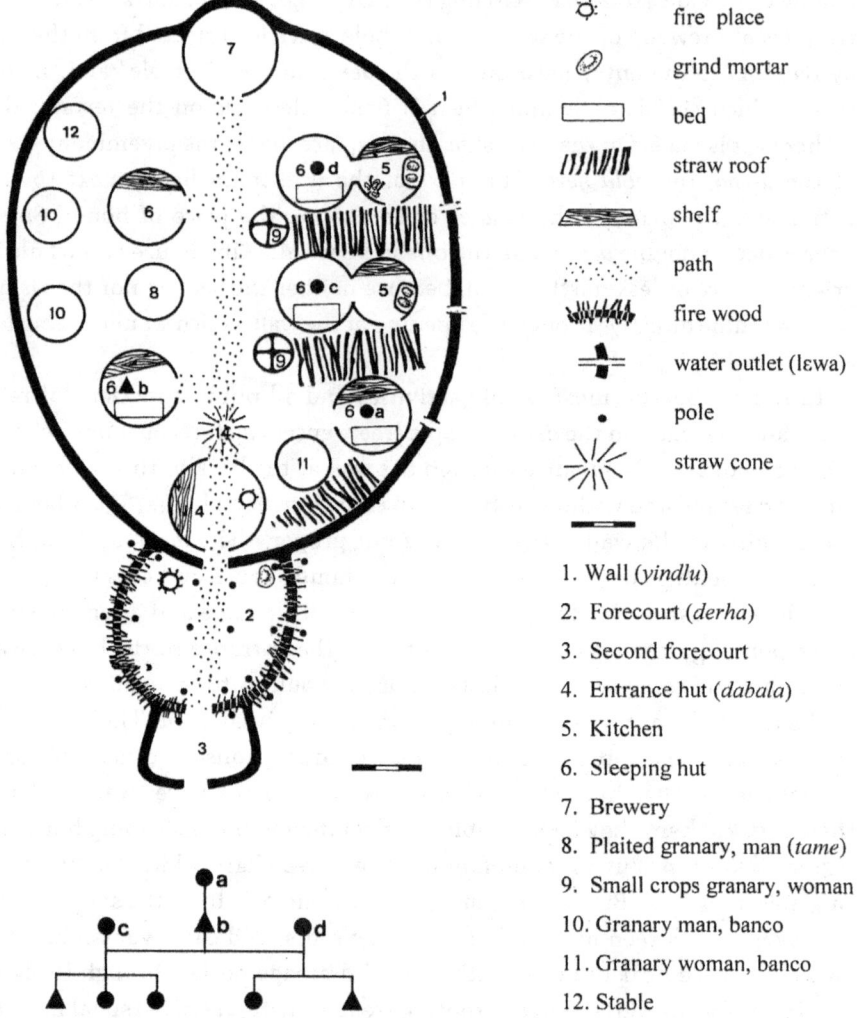

Figure 4.2 Plan of a mature compound.

empty huts when the owner of the house grows old and his wives and children gradually leave him.[5]

Starting a House

The close link between male identity and the house is illustrated when a son leaves his father's compound to build his own *rhe* elsewhere. The son invites an old clansman from his father's ward to help select the site in his new ward and to introduce him to the new ward headman to testify that the young man is not fleeing his ward because of trouble. Usually building work starts just before the rainy season. A hut and the first segment of the wall are the first to be put in place, usually by a small work party.

The young man moves into the new hut with his wife, long before the house is finished, and he holds his first ritual to accompany this move. In his father's house he brews his first ritual beer (tɛ), this time called tɛ kwanteďe rhɛ, beer to leave the house (nteďe means to gather one's things). The men in his father's ward assemble in his father's forecourt and drink, the young man first. With the headman of the old ward, he picks up his own melɛ, sacrificial jar, and together they climb over the wall. The headman heads back to the elders in the forecourt while the young man continues toward his new home, to which he invites the elders of his new ward. The next morning these men assemble in the forecourt of the new, unfinished home to taste his first ritual brew; again the young man drinks first, then hands the beer to the elders, who praise him and wish him well in his new house: "Thank you, son, may your god keep you healthy in your house."[6] The young man then proceeds with construction until the wall is complete.

For the ritual of the *psa pulu* (burn the place of honor), he organizes a work party with his new neighbors. Here is the example of 'Yèngu Baza:

> Early in the morning friends and neighbors assemble at the house of 'Yèngu Baza and divide the workforce up. Thatched roofs have to be put up, but the main job is first to build the low stone wall of the forecourt and then the higher parts of the wall at the entrance, *mɛ pulu*. 'Yèngu's wives are busy brewing white beer while the men finish the low wall of the *derha* and start to build up the wall adjoining the entrance. Very carefully, because any mishap with this entrance would be a very bad omen indeed (the owner of the house would not live very long), the men pile up the stones, finishing one of the house's main sacrificial spots. When it is finished, 'Yèngu brings out a jar of beer and invites Teri Maze, his mother's brother, and Wadawa, his sister's son, to perform the first sacrifice. The latter has brought the rooster and holds it while Teri Maze performs the sacrifice. Instructing Wadawa to stand in the forecourt, Teri Maze cuts the cock's neck while trying to keep his impeccably white gown clean:
> "May he be healthy with his whole *rhɛ, shala shala muhutu* [god, god with a honorific]. Bad things, leave here, that is what we want." Wadawa has gotten some blood on his foot and is putting dirt on it to avoid bad luck. Teri Maze asks: "Did it enter the house?" and indeed the dying rooster ran into the house, as it actually should. The officiator then should take the place of honor near the entrance, at the *pulu ŋeza*, but he refuses since the village chief (a clan member) is already sitting

there. 'Yèngu Baza, the owner, insists: "You have cut the rooster, and someone else would sit there? No, that is not the way. Who slaughters the rooster sits at the *pulu*," and Teri Maze takes his place next to the village chief. [The two are rivals, because Teri Maze just missed being chosen as chief of Mogode a few years earlier.] Then the beer is brought in, and Teri Maze blows beer over the entrance stones for the first time, saying similar words.

After the sacrifice, 'Yèngu Baza will finish the huts, and the ritual inauguration of the house is concluded with the *d'afa kapsa pulu* (the sorghum mush to burn the place of honor). In fact, this is just the final meal for the *psa pulu*.

Two months after the sacrifice the house is again full of neighbors, and 'Yèngu Baza has his wives prepare the mush, some meat, and a special sauce made of field mice, a much appreciated delicacy. At this final inauguration of the house, the whole compound joins in the proceedings. The place of honor at the *pulu* is for the owner of the house, flanked by some elders of the ward, who receive the first food. One of them takes a morsel of mush, dips it in the mouse sauce, and drops it on the floor: "Here, yours, *shala*." Then the other groups eat, and the whole ceremony is quickly over, as there is not too much food. The sauce is eaten by the old men in the forecourt and the sister's sons at the brewery, while 'Yèngu's wives feast their kinswomen on a sauce of their own making from meat they bought themselves. So the mice are for the ritual male officiators, the elders, his sister's sons (*ksugwe*), and himself.

From this moment on the compound is fully functional, though many huts may be added, depending on the marital and familial "career" of the owner.[7] Only one important item will come later as the finishing touch to any house: the plaited straw granary (*tame*). Not only does the granary display Kapsiki plaiting prowess—man-high, strong enough to climb on, and an excellent storage facility for grain with minimal post-harvest loss—it is also the important ritual center of the house that we will return to at the start of Chapter 7. The Kapsiki know three types of granaries (Figure 4.3). The *tame* is the most prestigious and its shape is a model for the others, which are both in mud and are called *mehtembu* if it is for a man, or *dedímu* if for a woman. The third type is the slender *gweru*, internally divided for storing a woman's crops. All the granaries are conical, with an opening at the top which has to be closed against rain and birds with a straw "hat" and, as it is fully covered with a straw mat, the difference between a *tame* and a *mehtembu* is not immediately visible.

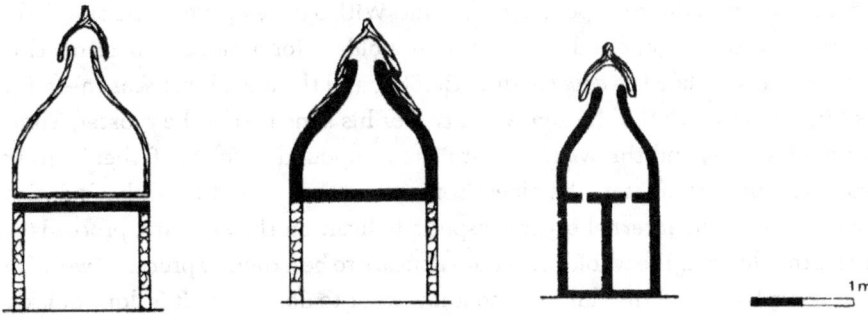

Figure 4.3 Granary types: *tame, mehtembu/dɛdimu and gweru*.

Home Sacrifice

At the request of a close friend of his father's, Tlimu Vandu has consulted the diviner and received clear instructions about holding a *melɛ rhɛ*, a sacrifice in his compound to honor his father, Vandu Zra Tè, who had died two years earlier, as well as a sacrifice on behalf of a friend. In the evening before the sacrifice he buys some red beer, *tɛ*, fills his sacrificial jar with it, and puts it back under the granary. In the early morning, at half past five, he takes the red rooster (red, as he had been instructed, although he had had considerable difficulty finding a red one) he has bought at the market for this purpose. None of the neighbors know what is happening, and since visitors are not welcome, Tlimu closes the compound entrance with a wooden beam: now it is taboo to enter the compound as nonkin. Only a smith could be invited to perform the sacrifice, but that is more usual when slaughtering a goat than a chicken.

Tlimu takes his large *melɛ* from under the *tame*, plucks the rooster's neck—the jar has to taste the first blood—cuts it, and lets the blood drip on the jar. He gently strikes the jar with the dying rooster, saying:

> "My shala, here you have something to eat.[8] Father, here is your friend, he has not forgotten you. I have not seen you for a long time and people have arrived after your burial to honor you with the *tɛ shiŋli* [final mourning rite] in order for the people to be healthy, healthy after your demise."

He throws the rooster on the ground, watching how it dies. It is good if the dying chicken flaps its wings, a sign that *shala* has accepted the sacrifice: "Thank you, *shala*, thank you *shala*."[9] If not, he would be disappointed, but the sacrifice would not have to be repeated. Tlimu then walks around the inside of the wall, counterclockwise, hitting the bloodied neck of the rooster against the wall, an action called *kayisu yindlu* (sprinkle the wall), ending his circle in the entrance hut where some of his children sit in the opening of the hut. With a glowing ember he singes the feathers of the rooster and on an impulse holds it for a moment over his children's heads. Inside the *dabala*—it is October and the end of wet season—a fire is burning to roast the chicken. With two of his sons taking the rooster, Tlimu cuts off its legs and throws them into the compound—"for his father"—to be collected and eaten later. The oldest son, taking over one of his father's duties, puts some of the internal organs, especially liver, on the *mele* and proceeds to roast the chicken. The whole procedure appears to be a routine process, "work" as Tlimu explains, and the children too know what to do. In fact, it is done quickly. At 6.30 am the family is in the *dabala*, waiting for the rooster and some mush to be cooked by one of Tlimu's daughters, but this part of the ritual has to be finished before noon. His whole family cannot be present because he has a spectacularly large one (four wives, 37 children, and numerous grandchildren), but the youngest ones are there. (This particular sacrifice was performed in 1999; at the time of Tlimu's death in 2007 he would have 43 children!) When the animal is roasted, Tlimu takes his *mele* again, picks up a piece of the rooster's liver, some mush, and with his right hand smears it on the *mele*; he then takes a mouthful of beer from the jar and sprinkles his breast, for the *mpisu hwu*, blowing beer on the chest, a rite specifically addressing the bad thoughts in the heart, that is, bad thoughts about other people.

> "Shala, give me health.[10] Take the evil out of my belly, make me healthy, I say. I have to hear the words from outside. Whoever is jealous, I trample under my feet. Our children, who have stayed behind, we should not be jealous. Whatever illness we have should disappear like the wind. May the illness pass because you want it." ["Words from outside" means bad news that should come from another home.]

Then one by one the children come along, and Tlimu smears liver on their chests: "Here, eat." One crying toddler gets some meat in advance, the others simply wait.

Tlimu hands his wives, who are watching the procedure from their hut, some mush which they each put on their own *mele*, a small jar inside their hut. From their side they have been discussing whether the whole family had to be called in, as far as feasible, or whether just the children now present were sufficient for the sacrifice. After some debate they decide that it was not a *mele keshi*, lineage sacrifice, which the central position of their father-in-law might warrant—and which would call for more people—but indeed a *mele rhe*, house sacrifice. His father's friend helps Tlimu pour beer from the *mele* in a standard calabash. (Tlimu does not have the traditional oblong calabash for sacrifices, but it should be a plain, undecorated vessel in any event.) Then as one of the high points of the sacrifice, called *batle mele*, he pours the beer on his *mele* (Figure 4.4):

Figure 4.4 Tlimu sacrifices on his jar.

This is for you, Vandu, because your friendship has to be fresh, everybody has to be fresh after your death. Shala, let the wind take whatever is evil. Please have them return safely to their villages, for them to visit us again.

With shrill ululations a neighboring smith woman comes into the house—as is her right despite the beam—praising Tlimu for his efforts in keeping the house in order. Her presence enhances the status of the ritual, and later also her husband joins Tlimu to drink from the *melɛ*; he has been helping Tlimu with building a hut, and from his daughter's wedding brings Tlimu some rice he wants the family to taste. One child, a young son, drinks first and the family gathers to drink the beer, the men around the *melɛ*, and the women in front of their hut with the smith woman. When the beer in the *melɛ* is almost finished, Tlimu calls some of the men to witness the *mekele melɛ* (lifting the jar), and they watch Tlimu tilting the jar upside down to empty it, the end of the sacrifice proper, the oldest of them drinking first of this last calabash. Finally, Tlimu puts the meat and mush in the vase belonging to the head of the compound and all finish the beer and eat, clapping their hands to thank *shala*.

Now the first part of the sacrifice is over, the beam shutting the entrance is lifted, and neighbors are once more welcome. In the evening the rest of the rooster is cooked as part of the evening meal. Then Tlimu will take another piece of the liver from the cooking pot with some sorghum mush and put the liver and the mush on the jar, which is back at its resting place under the granary: "Here, father some food for you. Give me health take illness away."[11] The family will eat the mush and the rest of the rooster.

Clearly I am the friend of his father Tlimu refers to, the one who instigated the sacrifice. Vandu Zra Tè was the first to invite me to the public part of his home sacrifice, and after his death our long friendship warranted this gentle breach of family privacy. His son Tlimu and I have done this three times before Tlimu himself died, and the last homage I paid to both of them was the *d'afa zhaŋe*, the last salute one gives to a friend or kinsman after the funeral. I feel now that I have made a proper farewell to both: Tlimu, the best raconteur of folk tales, and his father Vandu, the expert in oral history and Kapsiki botany.

There are several types of home sacrifice. This one is, in principle, just for the family, often generated by a problem and indicated by divination. More extensive home sacrifices, as we shall see, involve sacrificing a goat. But sometimes a quicker procedure is used, with a simple mix of sorghum flour with water, a mixture called *rhwempe* in divination and sacrifice (proper *rhwempe* is peanuts ground with sorghum, often serving as ritual food). Most of the mixture is put on the entrance in the wall.

The central object in almost all offerings and sacrifices is the *melɛ*, the sacrificial jar, a piece of pottery that is shaped like a standard beer jar but bears a few symbols: it has a ring of small appliqué spikes around the neck and a symbolic rendition of either the male or the female sex, depending on the sex of the deceased parent it represents. It is closed with a cow's horn, and its usual resting place is under the pedestal of the granary, although the women tend to keep theirs inside their own huts. Both parents can be represented in the sacrificial jar, and an individual can also have a special *melɛ* necked as circumstances dictate.

One special type is the *gumeze*, a jar with a threefold neck joining in one opening, a trifid necked vessel. A man will have this kind of *melɛ* made (by a smith woman) if he has killed someone in battle or if he has killed a specific kind of bird when hunting. Killing this sort of bird brings bad luck, the death of a child, unless he has such a *gumeze* made. In the case of killing someone in war, two jars are made, one large and one small. The small one is given the name of the victim and is buried in a field, in the wall, or inside the hut, while the larger one is used for sacrifices. The small one is dangerous and in principle is not used; in the *mid'imte*, his last words, the owner of a *gumeze* has to tell his son where the small jar is—often hidden in the bush—so the son can break it when his father dies.

The second kind of sacrificial jar is named after the sun, *veci*, and looks just like a normal jar, without symbols. It often is an exacting jar to own. Anyone who rises very early may see the sun walk like a ram, ascending into heaven at sunrise. The ram signifies the transition from moon to sun, and viewing the ram means that it will probably rain in the morning. In such a case it is very wise to perform divination to ascertain who has to make the jar, who may drink from it, who may definitely not, and whether it has to remain hidden. Such a *veci* has a proud owner but it demands many sacrifices, which can be a source of pride in itself, if one is able to perform them all. It is also a risk for other people: Deli Teri said that his father had one and asked him to get some tobacco from under the granary. However, the *veci* was there as well and Deli got a severe headache. Such an affliction is easy to cure by keeping some water in the jar overnight and then washing the patient. Deli at least was cured quickly this way. The use of any type of *mele* involving the shedding of blood has to be specified or checked by divination.

A *mele* proper, with the spikes plus the genital decoration, is only for one son, if possible the Tizhè, the oldest first-born son (see Appendix) of one of the deceased's wives, if possible his *makwa*, for whom he was her first husband. Other children, including first-born sons of other wives (also called Tizhè, followed by their mother's name) have a *veci* made, and so have the younger brothers, and such a *veci* is just a small jar. They "did not see the sun," so their *veci* is without the danger. When they sacrifice on it, they will call not so much on "father" but upon *shala*, since the connection with their father is through the proper *mele* only. If there is no son, the oldest daughter, if possible a first-born Kuve, will take the *mele*.

A sacrificial jar is made at the death of a parent; before that time one has another type of *mele*, usually a flint stone or quartz the size of a fist, or small jars. Boys get their stone from their fathers, girls from their mothers, and during initiation the boys get a proper *mele* (see Chapter 10) while the girls use the largest of the small jars presented during their first wedding as their *mele* (see Chapter 9), jars her new groom has given her. As with all pottery, smith women make the *mele* as well. A son orders one after the death of his father, giving some specifications. The potter gets a fistful of sorghum flour, mixes it with water, and pours the mix on the jar with the words: "Let everyone be healthy," in a rite also called *batle mele*, and so a small sacrifice in itself. Later the son has to give a large bowl of millet flour to the smith woman; if he forgets, she will harass him at his home, claiming that she is "so very hungry"; she also should be invited at the first use of the jar, at the end of the funeral rites, when it is inaugurated as a sacrificial jar, that is as the representation of the parent.

During the sacrifice, as we have seen, the *mele* is addressed as "father" or "mother." The jars serve only the direct descendants, because one's personal *mele* is destroyed during one's funeral rites. Some special jars function as collective points of reference in the ward's or the village's sacrifice and for the rooster ordeal. Though sacrifices also address other spots in the house, such as the wall, it is always the *mele* that gets the first taste of the sacrifice. The jar may be used as regular beer jar when beer is brewed for consumption only—which is increasingly the case now that women have taken up brewing red beer for the market. However, only people from the compound or close friends can drink from the *mele*.

Other types of sacrifice are classified according to the group in the social echelons of the village: a lineage sacrifice (*mele keshi*), a ward sacrifice (*mele keluŋu*) and the most important one, the village sacrifice (*mele meleme*). Any sacrifice consists of four elements:

- slaughtering the animal (*tla wusu te mele*)
- spraying the belly (*mpisu hwu*)
- pouring upon the jar (*batle mele*)
- putting food on the jar (*ŋa mele*).

Though divination might give directions for the sacrifice, the variation rests in the details: who is allowed to be present, the color of the sacrificial animal, whether or not a smith performs the ritual, and any special words that need to be said. The format is fixed and can be found in sacrifices at any social level. Often dreams trigger sacrifices, but the Kapsiki stress that usually dreams are unclear and need interpretation through divination. One common element in all the sacrifices is the chasing away of "bad things" or "bad thoughts," which in themselves are not defined in any greater detail but are ever present. Evil has to leave, has to go elsewhere; it has to be somewhere but not here. Evil is inevitable, so someone has to suffer, preferably someone else.

The home sacrifice has also a larger variant, with a social side beyond the confines of the compound. When the reason for the sacrifice is more substantial, especially when relational problems call for a sacrifice, a goat has to be slaughtered. If so, the man has to brew *te*, the ritual beer of the Kapsiki,[12] which has its proper rhythm and provides the time frame for the major rituals. Though the beer does make a difference, the animal is important too.[13] Killing a goat is not the same as killing a chicken; after all, people live with their goats. When an old billy goat has had a long and reproductive life in the home and when his day has finally come, a small sacrifice will be made before it is slaughtered. Only then can the animal figure in a home sacrifice, for which a large crowd is invited afterwards.

The recipe for beer is much the same the world over. One soaks sorghum grains in water for a day and leaves them to dry and sprout into the *te njinu*, which in Kapsiki must not remain exposed to the air too long lest "the beer is for one's own burial."[14] The brewing process requires a long cooking period, a day and a night, and then the beer is decanted from the large cooking vat into beer jars, including the *mele*. For ritual beer, yeast is not added but one simply waits three days for the beer to ferment on its own. After the second day the beer is just starting to ferment and that is the moment it will be used for sacrifice.[15] The sacrifice follows the same format as the sacrifice of a chicken, though spraying beer on the belly and putting ground millet on the *mele* is done only when the diviner has specifically indicated the need to do so.

In this goat sacrifice the man and his son keep the goat's neck above the jar, and the father stabs the animal in the throat and has the first drops of blood fall on the *mele*; everybody remains silent and listens to the man praying: "*Shala*, let us all be healthy, here is something to eat." The man then cuts the throat of the goat, the rest of the blood is collected in a pot, and all those who live in the compound put some of the blood on their own *mele*. With the goat dead, the first beer is poured in to a special oblong calabash; the owner pours first, asking for health, children, and good feelings in the house and the ward. While his son gives all the wives and children some beer for their personal *mele*, the man pours blood and beer on the entrance of the wall, putting some every few meters along the inside of the wall before finally pouring blood and beer into the *tsu*, the old grindstone at the lower end of the forecourt. Then it is his turn to drink, and his wives and children follow him, spraying beer on their bellies and putting food on their bellies too, as in the sacrifice of a chicken. Later the goat is skinned, butchered, and cooked, while life in the compound resumes its normal daily rhythm; in the evening the goat is cooked as part of the sauce. The owner then takes the broiled liver from the pot and, with both hands, puts a few morsels and some of the goat's cud on the *mele*, and his family does the same, using phrases similar to those in the chicken sacrifice.

Inviting one's sister's son as a special guest is looked upon favorably, but it has to be the "real" one, son of the proper sister, not a classificatory one. While he performs the actual slaughter on normal occasions, he does not do so for sacrifice, but his presence will add to the general well-being of the proceedings. The link between mother's brother and sister's son in Kapsiki, both reciprocally called *ksugwe*, is close and affectionate. When the boy is asked to slaughter non-ritually, he will get a substantial amount of meat—the neck, liver, first stomach (omasum), and a piece of a hind leg—all of which he will bring home proudly, to eat with his family.

The main difference with a chicken sacrifice can be seen early the next morning when some close kinsmen and invited neighbors assemble for the last phase of the ritual, drinking the sacrificial beer. The beer has its optimal level of fermentation now. In such a ritual drinking bout, the owner first carefully distributes a number of beer jars, one for the old men around the fire place, one for some other guests, with the *mele* itself remaining in the house for the immediate kin. He then explains the reason for the sacrifice and, in true Kapsiki fashion, is extremely vague, even elliptical: "I was at somebody's who dreamed that I had to do a sacrifice, a few nights ago. I have put some grains in the water and on the *mele*. I have something left and invited a few people to drink together with me." No problems are indicated, just the fact that he "dreamed," that is, consulted the diviner and prepared beer. But, being as close as they are, the neighbors probably know the reasons anyway; after all, such a sacrifice is aimed at "normal problems" like illness or infertility, and it is held at fairly regular intervals to keep the house healthy when things are going well.

The owner himself drinks first, then his family drinks inside the house from the *mele* itself. The old men applaud the owner, and the oldest or the village chief makes a speech. The chief is an acknowledged master of the favored Kapsiki style oratory, in which a lot is said with as little clarity as possible. Hyperbole, hidden references to things of the past, and scraps of stories are mixed into a discourse which is real "inside speak." The owner had used the same type of figure of speech, for "some grains in the water" is a severe understatement when 80 to 120 liters of beer is standard, and this social feasting of the ritual takes all morning.

A house owner may invite a smith, either at his own volition or because a diviner has told him to. The smith then sits at the side, softly clapping his hands; only if the sacrifice is done in the evening—at the express instruction of the diviner—will the smith perform the sacrifice, but it will be something small, like a chicken. For some serious issues, the sacrifice itself will take place outside home such as at a special spot in the bush. In that case a smith has to do it; it would simply be too dangerous to do it oneself. For such a sacrifice the color of the goat is clearly indicated, often black, and the animal is left in the bush; sometimes just its feet are broken and it is then left behind. In a few cases the smith is allowed to take some of the immolated beast to his house, depending on the divination. Reasons for such intense sacrifices are, for example, a child's death or prolonged infertility.

Divination

In principle no sacrifice is performed without divination specifying its particular details: to sacrifice well is to sacrifice correctly. So in Kapsiki rituals, divination is a continuous background presence, the "ritual of rituals" as Werbner calls it.[16] Though itinerant diviners occasionally come with their own techniques, the Mandara Mountains are home to a wide variety of local cultures with many forms of divination that are not restricted to one group. Of these techniques the crab is the most widely known.[17] The Kapsiki have two other divination techniques, using cowry shells and stones which have their own inter-ethnic distribution.

The standard form of divination in Kapsiki uses a crab (*dlera*), and all types of divination are called by the generic name *dlera*. Thus, consulting a diviner in Kapsiki is called "hearing the crab," while any diviner regardless of his technique "builds the crab" (*kaŋa*[18] *dlera*) (Figure 4.5).

The animal in question is the fresh water crab that lives in small pools on the Kapsiki Plateau. The crab is not seen as a direct representation of the supernatural world nor does it figure in rituals or sacrifices; it is just an animal whose tracks say something about hidden things. Each crab "knows," the diviners say, but some are quicker than others in speaking, and the slow "speakers" have to be

Figure 4.5 Smith Cewuve consults the crab for Deli Rhwazha. Mogode 1973.

replaced by faster specimens. Each crab lasts but a few months in the divination pot and is fed a few grains of sorghum every day. Some stories, in the sphere of folktales, center on the animal:

> In the olden days the crab spoke differently, not in the compound but in the bush. The diviner went out and spoke to a crab after sunset, as people speak to each other. On the edge of a stream, the diviner communicated with this single crab and could ask anything he wanted. Then disaster struck: a woman took the crab and ate it. Since that time diviners have taken crabs from the bush and kept them at home, and the crab only speaks with its feet. At first, only the direct descendants of that diviner could perform the *dlera*, but nowadays anyone who wishes to do so can learn the trade.

Diviners are usually smiths, since they perform the main ritual functions. Though not exclusively theirs, most of the techniques of divination are firmly tied to their craft, because theirs is the authority to uncover the hidden background of anything under the sun.

The standard procedure is as follows: a client comes to the smith early in the morning and asks for the crab. The smith gets his paraphernalia out: a large

(40–50 cm in diameter) bowl filled with sand, a broken pot for a cover, a pot with one or more crabs, and a bag with sticks and calabash shards of several sorts and with varying decorations. He pours lukewarm water into the large pot, puts straws upright in the sand along its rim in small bundles with a calabash marker in front of them. These straws represent the client, his family and the various buildings in his compound, the persons he is asking about, the ward, and the village. In the middle of the pot he buries a small round *kwakweme* fruit (*Strychnos inocuwa*), and behind another calabash marker a small cord. He then loosely places five round and six oblong pieces of calabash on the wet sand, each decorated differently. Finally, the smith takes out a crab from a smaller pot that he keeps in his smithy. Holding the crab in his hand, he explains to it the matter at hand and what is expected. The crab is put in the pot, with the lid on top, and the client and the diviner wait patiently, chatting amicably. After a quarter of an hour the smith looks to see how the crab has rearranged the loose pieces of calabash, interprets this as a first answer, then asks a more precise question, puts the pieces back in the original order, and positions the crab for another go. An entire session involves asking five or six questions and lasts a few hours. The final answer usually offers an analysis of the problem and a means of solving it, often a sacrifice of some sort.

To end the ceremony, the smith puts the crab back in its pot, feeding it some grains of sorghum, pours some water from the divination jar over the feet of the client, and empties the rest of the jar in the four cardinal directions. The diviner takes the loose pieces out of the jar and the client takes the straws that represent himself and his kin from the rim of the jar. The diviner receives his fee, about FCFA 100, and the client goes home to perform the sacrifice that has been suggested. Finally the diviner rubs some *rhwɛ jivu* on the crab, a medication to prevent any bad luck that could stem from interacting with people who are cheating each other though at present this problem has disappeared.

Reasons for divination vary. One major reason is illness and misfortune, and there the diviner can indicate a large variety of small rituals to perform. Sometimes these rites aim at redressing something that went wrong in the past, such as a reburial after a burial full of mistakes, a sacrifice in the bush after a taboo infringement, a small offering at the crossroads for a relationship gone sour. The second reason is an upcoming festival such as the initiation of boys and girls. Here the details are informed by divination, not the general liturgy of the feast. For instance, the crab may indicate the color of the rooster or goat to be sacrificed, some specific words, the presence or absence of other people at the proceeding, or the type of dance to be held. A third reason is inquiry into general well-being, like the risks in a journey, an exam, sowing a new field, or the first harvest. In these cases, the crab usually indicates more general gestures, such as a *tɛ derha* (social beer, see Chapter 6) or gifts to the elders or smiths.

Crab divination is quite iconic, starting with a map of social relations along the rim of the pot, represented by the straws, but always centered on an individual. Other types of divination, with cowries or with pebbles, share this individual orientation in the definition of problems, addressing the tension between an individual and his obligations beyond the compound wall. Essentially, this ritual of rituals is a means of situating oneself in relation to neighbors and kinsmen, house and village, and between *mele* and tomb to reassess one's position in life.

Ritual and Dwelling

Divination steers the sacrifices, but in the details only. The main characteristics of the sacrifices, as the core ritual of Kapsiki life, are more or less given and have their own dynamics. The basic model is the *mele rhe*, and, as we will see, the other echelons of ritual for ward, lineage, and village can be considered extensions of this home sacrifice. Residence practice in Kapsiki implies that married sons live elsewhere, not as next-door neighbors, so nucleated lineages are the exception, not the rule. Kinship is important, but so is co-residence, and the two rules define the household. Participants in a sacrifice are those that live in the house, mainly kin but also lodgers, often distant kinsmen living there for the time being. So sacrifice is a ritual of dwelling: in the house sacrifice the father of the house and his family express their belonging to that house, their dwelling in the social and physical environment. One major characteristic feeds into this concept: the ritual is meant just for the people inside the home, because only the ones who actually dwell there may be present while others are barred. Smiths may be present and often are, as they are "the children of the village" and have a quite different position.

> For me this presented a field problem, since participation in sacrifices of others did not fit into local culture; in fact the presence of "strangers" was taboo and brought mishap to the sacrifice. Also, though I gradually became considered a friend of the smiths, I am not a smith. My own "family" was Christian and no longer sacrificed. I was gradually able to solve this problem in three ways: first, my adopted family showed me how a sacrifice was done; they staged it. Second, the ward and lineage sacrifices were less exclusive and did allow my presence, since my links to the lineage and the ward were by then well established. Of course, I could never participate in the village sacrifice, but then the village chief has been one of my close friends from the start, as was the chief smith, and they were more than willing to inform me in great detail; privacy in Kapsiki is not secrecy. Finally, in the longer term, good friends may be honored in sacrifices, as we saw in the house sacrifice.

If dwelling is a process of inclusion in the environment, it may also exclude others from that same environment. Dwelling is about blending in but also about making a difference, and the texts demonstrate as much. At least once in each sacrifice the officiator addresses "evil," telling it to leave, "all bad things have to go," "bad news has to come from outside."[19] Dwelling is "us" against the rest of the world, and evil things are chased just over the wall, to the neighbors or to whomever, but out. It is here that the *yindlu* (wall) comes into its full symbolic force, as the shield of the home against the threats of the outside. Dwelling in the mountains is a defensive strategy, and the rituals of dwelling continuously reflect that defense. Daily interaction in Kapsiki reflects this idea as well, in the privacy allocated to the individual, a privacy that many African cultures do not grant. When one is inside the house, that is inside the wall, people will not enter unless they really have to. The tall walling at the entrance, the *mɛ pulu*, "mouth of the place of honor," is symbolic and thus a major ritual spot in a house, both during sacrifices and during rites of passage such as initiation and death. At the start of a house we saw that this part of the house was built first, and also when the house expands with it, the *mɛ pulu* remains where it is, and may never be moved. In symbolic farewells one does not leave through the entrance but "through" the wall. We saw the young man leave his father, breaching the wall with an elder; at the end of one's life, during the first two days of the funeral, one's corpse will be carried over the lowered part of the wall, as we saw in Chapter 1. Going or leaving through the entrance is final, while breaching the wall is not really leaving, but a provisional displacement later to be followed by a ritual acknowledgement of the transition.

When complaining about theft, a major focus in beer discourses, the men complain not about losing things but about people entering the compound "over the wall," as surreptitiously climbing over the wall into the compound is evil in itself, more so than taking something. By contrast, when someone steals through direct violent contact, it is not called stealing, but "taking by force," and is spoken about with glee and admiration. Locks were among the first things the Kapsiki took over from the European culture, because every door that could be locked should be locked. "We have lived with theft," my assistant explained to me, but the cases of conflict resolution do not back up his words at all, since most conflicts were about debts and bride prices (especially repayments). But theft is the epitome of privacy invasion, of breaking the wall of security around the home.

I have so far omitted one ritual of dwelling relating to another item inside the house that is symbolically charged: the *tame* (plaited granary). We saw that the sacrificial jar was stored under the *tame* as its proper and fitting storage place, and indeed the *tame* does get ritual attention. Most of that is during the final stage of its fabrication, and here we encounter a different symbolic message, not one of defense but one of plentitude and expansion, of growth and maturation.

The *tame* is the symbol for a successful cultivator, for a homeowner who has succeeded in life. When finished, a *tame* is initiated (see Chapter 7) in a rite resembling the initiation of a boy, which we shall delve into when the main agricultural rites are analyzed (Chapter 7). For the moment, it is good to remember that not all rituals in and around the home are defensive. Dwelling does have an inherent growth element in it, expansion, breaking new ground, and tapping into the untamed riches of the environment.

Sacrifice as an "Optimal" Rite

Sacrifice has received much theoretical attention since the start of religious studies. Here I want to pursue the theoretical stance mentioned in Chapter 2, referring to Boyer and Whitehouse. Sacrifice is the core rite not only in the Kapsiki religion, but also in many of the world's religions, and for a very good reason. Sacrifices come "naturally" in religions; they have been characterized as bribe (E. B. Tylor), as gifts to the gods (M. Mauss), as acts of consensual violence (R. Girard), and throughout as a communion with the sacred. But if anything characterizes the Kapsiki sacrifice as we saw it, it is the notion of a meal; William Robertson Smith would recognize this fact immediately. It is in fact a normal family meal, but for the presence of the unseen, those family members that are dead—father—or defined as being invisible, *shala*. So a sacrifice like the one described above is a cognitively optimal ritual as defined in Chapter 2, one that comes quickly to mind, is easily remembered, and has a liturgy that does not require a good episodic memory, since it is just a normal meal with an extra guest.

The minimal counterintuitive elements are twofold. The unseen presence of both the deceased father and of course *shala*, god, forms a slight but significant departure from the normal meal, plus the presence of the *mele* itself, the jar that represents both of them. Thus the counterintuitive element is not only thought but also embodied, a special object stored in a special place, to be retrieved, filled, and addressed only at this type of occasion. Though some *mele* are recognizable as special pots, many in fact lack any distinctive features, like the one used in our example. A jar is a *mele* because of its history: it was made as a *mele*, has served as such in the rites of farewell for the father, and is simply regarded as special.[20] So there are not only minimally counterintuitive concepts and rituals, but also objects. This complex is what I would call, after Whitehouse, an attractor point: a series of slight changes in the daily routine which lead to a rite in which people can "dwell," feel comfortably at home, do as they are wont to do, and feel connected with the larger world, in short an optimal ritual.

This cognitively optimal aspect is highlighted by, for instance, the absence of formulaic speech, since the spoken texts are quite simple, straightforward, and informal. People just tell *shala* what they want, and what they want are just the basics of life: food, health, fertility, and reasonable relations. And please no evil, not here at least. There is nothing special there, and thus sacrifice is in a way "nothing special," it is just doing what comes naturally.

From this natural ritual stems a series of larger sacrifices that will occupy us in the next chapter, the sacrifices for ward and village, which are in fact an expansion of the home sacrifice, and though these are still cognitively optimal for the most part, some elaboration does set in. In the village ritual, officiators have to know how to do it and certain aspects have to be taught. That is not too much yet in the absence of large oral texts, but aspiring officiators are well aware of the knowledge required, a knowledge that is typically "local": where to undress, where to stand, how to walk to the *mele*, and what to say. That is what truly counts.

Not all Kapsiki rituals are cognitively optimal; some ritual complexes can be characterized as cognitively costly. The Kapsiki rituals for initation, marriage, and especially death are examples of this type of cognitively costly—or maximal—ritual, with complicated liturgies that vary from village to village and that entail a ritual drama with a large array of players who all have to heed the script.

In the case of the home sacrifice described above, we see the family united around a meal, a chicken slaughtered, mush and sauce prepared. What makes the difference is the unseen presence, and that is what is being addressed in a discourse couched in terms of reciprocity: "We give you food, so give us health, or even the reverse, if you do not give us ours, then you can forget about any claims upon us. If you let us suffer, you will suffer as well." Both the visible and the unseen are joined at the hip, interdependent in one fragile universe. That unseen presence—*shala*—has a clear material focus in the sacrificial jar, the *mele*, but also in the wall of the house, so it seems that the unseen is not so invisible after all.[21] In a similar vein, in one of the few gestures that are out the ordinary in the home sacrifice, the children get their first food on their belly instead of inside them. When Tlimu put the stripes of mush on his children's belly, he made the unseen quite visible as well, in an act that in itself was cognitively optimal. Feeding the belly is normal, feeding the belly on the outside is minimally counterintuitive.

Divination, the guiding ritual, has similar characteristics. Kapsiki divination is iconic in visibly sketching social relations and then introducing a randomizer, the crab. Thus divination is just like life, where the well-known social relations are thwarted by the hazards of unexpected events and misfortune. In real life one has to glean meaning out of chance by oneself whereas in a divination seance an expert—the diviner—manages to read the client's problems in such a way that the hazard produces sense in his life. The crab operates with categories well known to the client; the loose calabash shards signal categories of happenings and agents and as such they give a handle to the reading of the client's problematic relations with other people and with his supernatural world. Divination is a cognitively optimal ritual in which the normal meanings and mishaps in life are reformulated as a puzzle, in a quest to uncover a reality behind everyday life. It is the answer to the very familiar and natural assumption: "This must mean something . . .," the premier hypothesis of "Homo sapiens/significans" on his perpetual quest for meaning.

5

Sacrifice and the History of Dwelling

The Price of a Black Goat

In 2008 the sacrifice for the whole village of Mogode was delayed for two years, for three reasons. The first is the death of Kweji Mte, the chief smith, which forces the postponement of the sacrifice by a year, a standard reaction after the death of one of the officiators (in such a case one of the others mounts the hill and just pours some beer and a mixture of ground sorghum and peanuts on the jars). The second problem is the foot infection of the *gwenji* clan representative, Mènkèa. When coming down from the Rhuŋgeɗu, he hurt his foot and it does not heal. So he decided to hand over the *gwenji* task (putting the liver on the village *melɛ*) to a descendant. But to which son? His two eldest sons live in Yaounde and Nigeria, his third son is still young. Though his oldest son is back from Yaounde for the moment to take care of his ailing father—it is not just a question of the foot!—he will have to return to the capital for his business, so the youngest son will have to shoulder the burden. His father now teaches him how to do it, drawing a plan of the sacred mountain and indicating where everything is; the other officiators will naturally help. The *gwenji* role, as he explains to me, is very important because the village chief himself cannot approach the *melɛ* but relies on the *gwenji* representative to put the liver on the jar and, with the chief smith, the beer too.

The final reason for the delay is easier to redress: the village chief is indignant, since the last time a goat was taken for the sacrifice, the owner demanded payment from the chief and, being a Muslim, the man did not care about the sacrifice at all. The chief is angry and wants the full force of misfortune placed upon the man's shoulders because of the omission of the sacrifice. He surely does not want to pay for the goat, not even for a completely black one, which is hard to find. However, his friends convince him that this is not a dignified reaction and is beneath him and his office, especially beneath his long and distinguished track record as village chief. They collect money to buy a black goat to avoid similar problems at the next sacrifice; the number of Christians and Muslims is increasing and one never knows.

A Kapsiki's home is his castle, but dwelling is not something one can do alone, especially not in a landscape, climate, and sociopolitical environment as harsh as the Kapsiki one. In many ways, a Kapsiki village is a segmented society, especially in the internal wars that have characterized sociopolitical life up until the "pax colonialis." Yet some echelons are more important than others, and the village is definitely one of the important units. Rituals mark the boundaries between the social levels. In principle all sacrifices above that of the house are modeled after a home sacrifice, each with its own peculiarities, and can be seen as elaborations upon the home sacrifice. So we will proceed from the home upward through the ward, lineage, and the whole village, ending with a type of sacrifice that has larger regional relevance and links the home to the other echelons, the bull sacrifice.

Ward Sacrifice

Though the ward is an intermediate echelon between the main social units of the house and the village, it is a unit of some social importance. Each ward has at least one *keluŋu*, a cool place in the shadow of a tree with some convenient rock formations where men can sit and rest, take snuff, discuss problems, and play games, and where women spin their cotton or sell their sorghum beer. Hidden under a few rocks lies the *mele keluŋu*, a standard beer jar, on which after the harvest in January, unless divination indicates otherwise, a sacrifice is offered. Everybody living in the vicinity of the *keluŋu* brings a calabash or hat full of grain to the person brewing for the *mele*. Brewing is a rotating job. When the beer is ready, the brewer fills a jar, and selects a chicken with the appropriate colors. His wives grind flour, and the meal is cooked at the *keluŋu*. An old man from the ward performs the sacrifice, just like the home one, assisted by the brewer, who is usually also the person who consulted the diviner. "Let misfortune pass us by, let the people in the ward marry many women. Everyone who wants to harm us has to be the first to die. Let us all be healthy here." While the chicken is being cooked, they drink the beer: "Give us health, *shala*, give us much to eat, give us a good hunt and protect us from harm." When the chicken is well boiled, the liver and some morsels of mush are put on the jar, and everyone eats, the old men from the sacrificial chicken, the younger men savoring the sauce their own wives cooked, if possible made of field mice (a delicacy) or fish. When it is finished, they all walk to the brewer's house since most of the beer is still there.

Such a sacrifice is a splendid occasion to strengthen social bonds and discuss the problems in the ward. Our example comes from Dlaka ward, January 1973. The ward headman Kweji starts the discourse:

> We pray to *shala* and thank him and we thank also Tara (the brewer) and Deli Nkara (the oldest man of the ward). One man has not come,

and we are angry at him. *Shala* has meant well with us; people used to say that *shala* sometimes was white, and now we have a white man in our midst, which means that *shala* has accepted our sacrifice.

An old lady, Kwadaheru:

Thank you Kweji. In the past my children died young and I do not want the women of this ward to give birth to dead children. Their world must be different. If *shala* listens to me, they have to bring forth living and healthy children.

Deli (an elder):

That is what I want as well, and I hope that you will feed me many more times in the future (as the eldest). I am also angry at our absentee, as we have to be well together. I want the whole village to do this. Why would we have *besheŋu* [magic for evil purposes]? If you hated me, I would not come, but you are content. Be good, cultivate a lot and hold the hoe in your hand.

Kweji then joins in again:

We are together because we are glad, happy among ourselves. We are brothers here, all our clans [he lists them all] came from Sirak, and we found only the *mava* [one of the Mogode clans, literally. "slaves"] here in the field. But we are all brothers here, and also the *mava* are our children. We were all one in the war, even the *mava* were with us [in the skirmishes within the village the *mava* would normally side with the other half of the village]. But there is no war any longer and we want to keep it that way. I am the smallest here but the village chief and the canton chief have put me as headman. Now you are all my children, and I have to take care of you.

After the euphoria of this opening discourse, the discussion settles on a common theme, black magic, *besheŋu*. Kwada Tè, the leader of the ritual rain hunt in the village, explains the reasons for a sacrifice such as this:

We perform our *mele keluŋu* to cultivate sorghum, to marry wives and get children. Whoever has stuff to kill people let him die on the road. May *shala* give us all, all that is good. Thank you for brewing.

A fierce discussion erupts on *besheŋu*, in which all vehemently denounce its practice and everybody present fervently denies ever having touched it. Finally the ward headman concludes:

Thank you all, my people. This did not start today, but with our ancestors (*keshi*). They have left us this place and this jar. Some people just want to do their home *melɛ* and pretend to do it for the whole village. They say the home *mele* is sufficient on its own but when they crouch behind their granary, they send the evil things to their neighbors; they just keep their own house clean. Is that why we sacrifice? We all sacrifice to be equal; if the news comes to go out to the bush for a war, may *shala* prohibit that for everyone, my people.

His audience applauds: "Lion, lion."

Thus, as we see in this example, the ward sacrifice and the social drinking after the sacrifice serve as a balance against an egocentric attitude inherent in home sacrifices, in fact against the general ethos of individual autarchy in Kapsiki society. Throughout Kapsiki rituals the balancing act between the more communal values of village harmony and the strong preference for individual autarchy is expressed in both rites and discussions. The main focus of a Kapsiki is on his *rhɛ*, and group orientation does not come easily. Sharing is a great value but most try to limit the group with which they share. The discourse on *beshɛŋu*, as in this particular ward sacrifice, is typical, since this kind of magic is antisocial and easy to denounce while, as some informants stated after this sacrifice, the people who most fiercely denounced the practice "walk with the stuff in their pocket."[1] *Beshɛŋu* as evil poison is a ward matter, where people interact often. This holds both for the "bad" and the "good poison," though. In former days, when war still existed, one elder of the ward kept a huge quiver with war arrows in his entrance hut with a fire constantly simmering under it to keep the arrow poison fresh and active. The ward smith was responsible for keeping the poison in good shape during the peaceful intervals.

The Lineage Sacrifice

A similar sacrifice is held annually for the lineages, *mele keshi*. The Kapsiki clans are divided into lineages and sublineages, all called *kayita* (those of one father). At the higher echelons, the clan and the lineage level, sacrifices are not performed, since these groupings are dispersed across the village, have few corporate functions, are too large to congregate, and are not sufficiently structured for sacrifice by representation. Anyway, most clans have their sacrifice as part of the village sacrifice. Usually there is a *mele* at sublineage level—all descendants of an ancestor of about five or six generations ago—that is used only if there is a serious reason and if the group is not too large. Our example is the lineage sacrifice of the *jewu* lineage, a part of the *makwajɛ* clan. The lineage of this clan is seen in Figure 5.1.

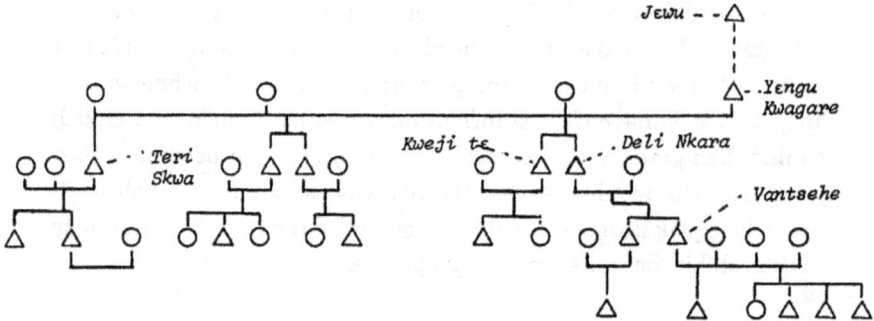

Figure 5.1 Genealogy of the *jewu* lineage.

The jar used for this sacrifice is the personal *mele* of the oldest descendant of 'Yèngu Kwagaru. In Kapsiki burial, one's personal *mele* is routinely pierced at one's son's funeral, but in this case 'Yèngu had so many children that they decided to keep that *mele* intact to serve as their *mele keshi*. There is no set date for this kind of sacrifice; it is usually performed when a problem arises in the larger family or when the crab indicates a *mele keshi*, which is usually about the same. This particular sacrifice had been indicated by the diviner twice already, but during the preparations both goats died due to an epidemic. But on a day in March 1973 all lineage members assembled at seven in the morning at Deli Nkara's house—the men and boys in the brewery, the women and girls in the entrance hut. Deli's son Vantsehe, an important man in the village, has to perform the immolation, assisted by Teri Skwa, the headman of the neighboring ward.

As usual, Vantsehe stabs the goat in its throat and lets the first drops of blood fall on the jar. "We have come here to ask for health. Please accept your food, *shala*, pour good things out over us and prohibit evil." His brother Sunu Derha pours some beer from the *mele* into a calabash and makes the libation on the jar: "Let us be healthy I say." While the two men skin and cut up the goat, everybody takes a sip of the beer from the jar, and Vantsehe puts some cud on the *mele* which is a large standard jar. When the cooking is finished, with both hands Deli Nkara puts a piece of mush and some liver on the *mele* four times: "We have to be healthy, in all our homes, and have many wives and many children."

The women serve the mush with the meat sauce and a general feast concludes the proceedings. There is plenty of beer, eight large jars for the men, six smaller ones for the women. Sunu Derha fills the calabashes again, and all the men and women take a sip of the beer from the *mele* again and then proceed with some serious drinking from the other jars. The whole feast lasts until two in the afternoon, during which time nobody leaves the premises and no stranger (non-kin) ventures through the door, since everybody in the neighborhood knows what is happening. There is no need to bar the door. This is another sacrifice that I could attend, in this case as a "son-in-law": my wife was an adopted *makwamte* clan daughter. And this ritual is less exclusive anyway.

In the evening the neighbors from the ward visit Deli Nkara to congratulate him and partake of the remainder of the beer. He has kept two jars apart for this occasion and offers a speech with the usual understatements: "It is nothing; I still have some residue left. I have dreamed and after two mishaps we could do it." He drinks first, then the visitors. Outside, some men wait their turn but are reticent to enter because they do not want to appear greedy, especially if people from their compound are already inside. They have to wait because it would be shameful if too many from their house were present at the same drinking party.

This sacrifice can vary according to the divination: some people may have to be sprayed with beer (a common blessing in Kapsiki), color and sex of the animal may be specified, and some minor additional offerings can be indicated: some of the beer dregs on the *melɛ*, or some on the wall entrance, and also it is indicated whether not just *shala* but also the ancestor has to be addressed directly (which was not the case here).

The Village Sacrifice: *Melɛ Meleme*

Just as the house sacrifice is off limits for foreigners (non-residents), participation in the village sacrifice is strictly limited to a chosen few, to the representatives of the village's major clans. It is not a secret procedure; people in general are aware of the way the sacrifice is performed, and the participants talk openly about it. In essence, it is the house sacrifice of the original family on the sacred mountain, and as such it follows the general liturgy of the home sacrifices. The *melɛ meleme* consists of two elements, the sacrifice on *melɛ Rhuŋgeɗu* and that on *shala*, the first on the mountain, the latter at a special place near a stream. Like most Kapsiki rituals, this village sacrifice is part of the annual cycle of general rituals. I started the chapter with the struggle of the chief to have this sacrifice acknowledged and respected by everyone in the village, so I will now follow his account of the ritual itself, staying very close to his actual description of what happens on the sacred mountain.

Five people climb the mountain for the sacrifice. They are never mentioned by name, only by clan: the clans *ŋgacɛ*, *maze* (the village chief), *gwenji*, and *zeremba* plus the chief smith. This means that the other clans (*makwamte*, *makwajɛ*, and *makwiyɛ*) are not represented, though the *makwamte* do have their role to play in the proceedings. One immigrant clan has its own *melɛ*, sacrificed after the main one.

The sacrifice on the mountain Rhuŋgeɗu is performed during the month of "moon seven," which used to be the harvest period for the oldest sorghum variety (yellow sorghum), November. Nowadays maize is harvested much earlier and also the red sorghum variety, but the sacrifice should still take place before the harvest of the yellow cultivar, with the intention of thanking *shala* for having provided a good harvest, not after harvesting but before. The moon of the sacrifice is followed by the moon of the harvest, and that concludes the Kapsiki's wet season. It is the village chief who fixes the date for the sacrifice by consulting a diviner. If the response is favorable, he warns the other four officiators to make their preparations. At nightfall he walks through the village, announcing that the next day no one is allowed in the fields. In his own words:

> Before the people make the ascent on Rhuŋgeɗu, we choose a hunter to catch the goat. If the crab (divination) tells us the day, the chief, the smith, and the hunter go out into the fields the day before, and when they see a goat, the hunter catches it.

The hunter has to be from the *makwamte* clan, and his role is important enough for the ritual to be postponed if he is absent. It is not much of a hunt, though, as he picks the first black goat he spots in a herd. But it has to be a black one, at least partly black, and it should not belong to someone from the *ŋacɛ* clan, since the *ŋacɛ* representative is the main officiator and should not sacrifice his "own" goat. If, by chance, the goat later appears to be from that clan after all, they just leave it that way. The goat's owner should not protest lest the evil of the sacrifice befall him (see the opening case). The sensible—and normal—reaction is one of pride and acknowledgement that his goat serves the general well-being. The owner does not gain a special place in the proceedings and is not invited to drink beer afterwards, for "everything is owned by *shala* anyway, all people and all things."

That evening all the participants grind sorghum and salt, and fetch water from the central well in Mogode. Early next morning they set out from the house of the *ŋacɛ* representative, who has the title of *mnzefɛ*, "priest"[2]; the *gwenji* carries a jar of water, the representative of the *zeremba* clan brings the goat, the others follow with their flour, salt and firewood, and all bring their bows and arrows. They leave at sunrise and nobody should see them follow the tracks the mythical hero and village founder Hwempetla made on the ancestral mountain. Before climbing the mountain, which is just a granite outcropping, they rest at an old grindstone that also features in their rain rituals. There they undress, leaving their daily clothes behind, and don the traditional goat skins of old. A short climb brings them to Hwempetla's old compound, at the southern edge of the mountain. A large heap of broken pots, catches the eye, shielding the real village *melɛ* from sight, two small pots, 30 cm in diameter, plus an old, broken one and a new one. They used to fill them with beer but the ritual has changed, and now they do not take beer up the mountain any more. But the jars have to lie with their mouths toward the village; otherwise no game would come to the village. In the words of the chief:

> When we arrive, we sit down. "Come on," we say to *mnzefɛ* and the chief smith. The latter takes the goat and the former his knife. Both hold the goat still over the *melɛ*, *ŋacɛ* slits the animal's throat, and the blood pours on the *melɛ*. The *mnzefɛ* pours some water in an old cup and puts water in the goat's ears; then and only then does the goat die.

No words are spoken, no prayer intoned. The two officiators skin the goat and cut it into pieces. The *mnzefɛ* gets the breast and the skin, the smith the head, and the rest of the meat will be cooked before being divided up. The blood, as always, is caught in a cup. With the water and wood they brought with them (there is practically no vegetation on the mountain), they cook the goat, and make some mush from the flour. When finished, *gwenji* takes some mush and cooked liver in both hands, and while all crouch around the *melɛ*, puts the food on the jar:

> *Shala*, we come to greet you. Here is some food. We brought you some food today. Give us all the good things, so we will be good in your wake, and we shall be able to bring you food again, greeting you again like we do now. If there are evil things, keep these from us, and let only good things happen. We do this now as it has been done of old.

Saying this, he puts mush and liver on the outside of the *melɛ* four times. The others mumble with him and softly clap their hands. The *gwenji* then gives the other clan representatives (but not the smith) a piece of mush and liver with both hands, each of them saying: "Let us be in good health and let the *melɛ* be good," and they put the food in their mouths—the liver and mush all at once. Finally the *gwenji* puts some *safa* (Combretum) leaves on the jar.

The main sacrifice over, the *zeremba* takes the remainder of the mush and the meat from the pot and divides it up; now the smith also gets a portion in his special coiled basketry cap, the *dzakwa*, and all eat at their ease. The goat's legs are distributed among the four non-smiths and the smith gets the neck; he, in turn, hands a leaf with some goat blood and cud to the three clansmen for the *melɛ* of their own clan ancestors. The village chief explained to me:

> Each of us has his own *melɛ*, at a different place. Each takes the mixture of blood and cud on the leaf to the *melɛ*: "*Shala, shala pelɛ rhweme* [god, god in heaven] I want to be healthy," and puts it on the *melɛ*.

From the goat's third stomach, the smith takes some half-digested food and all the men smear it on their breast over the heart. The chief, the *ŋacɛ*, and the *gwenji* each have their own *mele*, but the *zeremba* has not, and he and the smith wait for the others to finish. The *mele* of the *gwenji* is a *gumeze* (Figure 5.2), a trifid necked jar with three necks and one mouth,[3] quite new and recently replaced because the old one was broken. *Maze* sacrifices in a standard jar, some 100 m from the others, hidden in the long grass. The jar stands upright and he puts the offering inside the jar, not on it. The *ŋace mele* is special: not a jar but an opening in the mountain, a small gas hole about 20 cm in diameter that leads deep into the rock. He drops the offering in and on his *tereme ta shala* ("horn of god") makes a high, shrill tone to accompany his "Thank you *shala*, thank you *shala*." The *tereme* is a small earthenware instrument with tiny bellows which produces a high, shrill sound, and is used only by the *ŋace*.

This brings the sacrifice to an end and the five take a break, scouring the mountain for some grasses, for six *berumu* and six *haze* (*Cymbopogon*) stalks. Each takes his bow and lists the enemy villages: "This one for Sena, for Rumsiki, for Sir, for Sirakuti, for Kamale, for Rumsu." With each name, a stalk is fired off, one towards each of the villages, "in order to shame them." Then they chide their enemies, the village chief exclaiming "Ah, that man is dead, thank you my child. Sing a song of rejoicing, we say as amusement."

After this small theater of war, mimicking the killing of an enemy, they make their way down. The *mnzefe* takes the goat's breast, skin, and leg in his bag, the smith the head, neck, and hoofs; the others each have a goat's leg. At the grindstone where they left their clothes, they dress again. *Mnzefe* then fills the grindstone with water: "Oh, we are thirsty, we are thirsty. Take your water, *shala*, and give us

Figure 5.2 The *gwenji* sacrificial jar, a *gumeze* with trifid sprout.

our water." They then continue down and each of them heads home carrying some food to give to a small boy, but not to a daughter, "for they will leave, and in that case would mean nothing in their own village." This sacrificial food is tricky: it is healthy for those who are entitled to it and dangerous for everybody else, because they would get sick. All sons of the officiators should be home for this reason.

About a month passes before the men prepare the second part of the *mele meleme*, the sacrifice at the place called *shala*. This special distinction falls to the burial place of the culture hero Hwempetla, also an important stop in the ambulatory rain ritual at the start of the rainy season (see Chapter 7). Again the chief consults the crab diviner, and, when the date is given, makes his preparations. This part of the ritual is like the *te mele* of the home sacrifice. Because the whole village should participate, the village chief visits the ten compounds of all the clan elders to collect sorghum from each of them. The *mnzefe* uses this to brew the beer for the ritual, which takes about a week. When the brewing is finished, *mnzefe* warns the chief smith that the beer "has descended from the fire: the people should be ready to come and drink in two days. Tomorrow will be the day for the sacrifice, when the beer is still sweet." In fact, the beer is already older, but people want to ensure that the fermentation is up to standard.

The next evening the five officiators assemble in the house of the *mnzefe* and set out for the bush. Again, the itinerary is marked by a few specific spots: at a tree on the stream called *Rhwamerhe* (chief's stream) they undress and put on their goat skins. Two kilometers away two tombs are hidden in a small stand of trees. Hwempetla's is the higher one, and the lower one belongs to his wife. The men carefully cover the two mounds with branches: no stone may remain in sight; in fact they replace the old branches with fresh ones, as has been done in the rain ritual earlier this year (see Chapter 7). The tomb is reported to contain the *mele* of Hwempetla and his stone whistle, but though informants state that these were used in the sacrifice in the past, this is no longer done, but they do put some *haze* on the tomb, meant for the hero's *mele*.

The concluding ritual is straightforward, as in the home sacrifice: *mnzefe* pours beer over both tombs and fills two grindstones with beer: "Let us be healthy, *shala*. We have given you food to eat; we gave you enough, now you give us enough to eat." (The idea of food in return for beer is quite common.) The five conclude the liturgy by drinking themselves, the four non-smiths from a calabash, and the smith from his coiled cap. Returning with some beer, they find their clothes at the tree and collect some *safa* leaves (*Combretum*). At the stream, the smith collects some mud and puts it on the *safa* leaves, and everyone puts some mud on his chest. Another old grindstone near the tree is washed and filled with *te*. Fully dressed, they dance on the way home, singing the songs of funeral, marriage, and initiation, and when they arrive home they put the mud on the wall at their compound entrances.

As in the home sacrifice, the next morning sees the termination of this phase, in a drinking feast at the *mnzefɛ*'s house. A large crowd gathers in the early morning, the young men at the lower end and the old men at the higher male side of the forecourt. Kezha, the *mnzefɛ*, gets two jars of beer, one for the elders, one for the youngsters, and explains what all know already: "Our business has been done. As the sorghum is gathered, so are we here, as always. Even if the beer is not very good, we drink anyhow." The men softly applaud: "Thank you, Thank you" and then the first beer is poured by a young clan brother of Kezha (pouring beer from the jar and distributing it is called fetching water and is an important distinction at such an official function). Every drinker pours a little into the smith's cap by the jar, so all the clans give to the smith. When the two jars are finished, Kezha brings out his own *melɛ*, also full of fermented beer, and the old men continue drinking. In this session of the village sacrifice, called the *tɛ ba* (beer of the epidemic), the young *ŋacɛ* fetching the beer uses not a calabash spoon but a coiled bowl, like the smith's, which belongs to the *mnzefɛ*'s paraphernalia and is used only at this *tɛ ba*. The *mnzefɛ* gets the first bowl of beer, then the leader of the ritual hunt, the chief, and the other clan representatives at the sacrifice, with the chief smith served last (Figure 5.3). Only then do the others dare to drink. The youngsters abstain, because ritual beer is always tricky; foreigners, that is, people from other villages, will never dare to drink from a foreign *melɛ*, and this particular beer is called the beer of the epidemic, so people are wary.

This particular bowl has been coiled by the chief smith, long ago. At that time the *mnzefɛ*, before pouring into it, sprays it with beer: "Keep my compound and the village well in case of war; this bowl has to protect all people going out into the bush."[4]

At the *tɛ ba* ritual, drinking calls for speeches, and an old man starts:

> Thank you, *mnzefɛ*, thank you. It is fast! When the right time is there, one has to honor *shala* and not delay. At the start of the dry season, the *tɛ* has to be drunk, quickly. Why wait? We always have to think of *shala*, so why wait for his sacrifice? Now *shala* will say: "My people have thought of me, I shall give them all they want." Thank you.

Of course everyone agrees.

In December a similar sacrifice is held on Miyi, another outcropping next to Rhuŋgedu, by two representatives of lineages whose ancestors long ago settled there. They sacrifice *tɛ* plus meat including the ear of a cow—if possible of the indigenous breed—on a deep grindstone with an upper grindstone inside. In this case the beer as well as the meat can be bought at the market, neither is the village as such informed of the ritual. People consider it as the *melɛ keluŋu* of old, of the ward living at this mountain, but it is now part of the ritual sequence for the whole village. Also, when the rain hunt does not produce rain, this grindstone on Miyi is washed with beer as one of the last resorts to get rain.

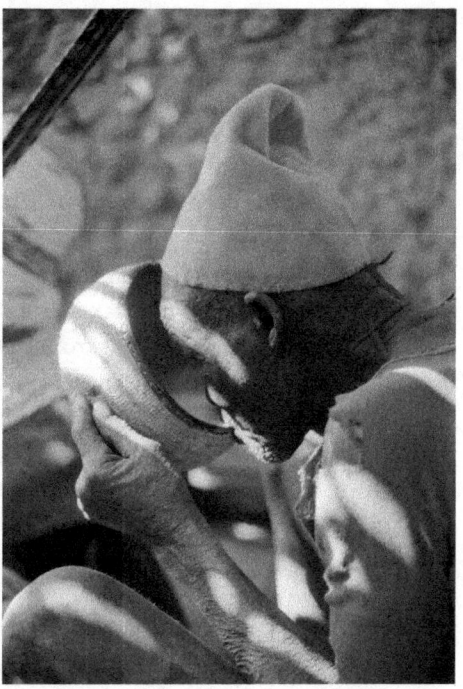

Figure 5.3 Smith Kwada drinking from his cap.

Rituals such as these with a fixed representation of the constitutive clans of the village are subject to the contingencies of history, even if the discourse is always about how they did it as they "found" it. The *makajɛ* clan is notable by its absence, and the chief assured me that in the past this clan was indeed represented at the sacrifice. However, two generations ago the obvious *makwajɛ* representative refused to go with the others, for reasons which have evaporated in the mist of history. Since then, the clan is no longer represented and so will it remain.

One possible reason for a refusal is the risk involved in participation in this ritual. A few times in history some misfortune befell officiators on their return from the mountain.

> One Deli 'Yengu had been assigned the job, though his father never did it. But right the first time he performed the ritual, on the way down he slipped and died. A very old member of the *gwenji* clan met a similar fate, and he was new on the job as well. People interpret this misfortune as the result of the wrong choice of participant. Similarly, the *ŋacɛ* that has to do the rain ritual on the mountain used to be Deli Newekè, and his replacement, Vasekwa, does not dare to try the ascent.

So nowadays if an officiator dies, people wait a considerable time before choosing his replacement; for a few years four people can do the sacrifice rather than risk another mishap. *Maze* and the other elders take great care to choose from the brothers and sons of former officiators. And even an assigned officiator can be changed: the chief indicated that he wanted to replace someone because he quarreled too much and the sacrifice should be done in harmony, so it was better to take his brother. Sometimes an officiator resigns; even the central figure of the *mnzefɛ* himself has been known to do so.

> Deli Kwageze, the official *mnzefɛ*, hurts from an insult: the government had forced him to pay his taxes and the Lamido (district chief) had had the effrontery to take a goat from Deli as payment. As *mnzefɛ*, he is one of the notables, and that duty should be waived for him. So he refuses to go up the mountain for the sacrifice, at least for this year, and asks his brother Kezha to replace him. The chief complies, considering Deli's state of mind. However, for drinking this was cumbersome, since Kezha lives way out in the bush. Therefore the beer described above was actually drunk at the house of a clan brother.

These contingencies render the village sacrifice, which is after all the central rite in the ritual calendar of the village, vulnerable. The same holds for the sacrifice on Miyi, which has been discontinued for several years. After the death of one of the officiators, a new representative was sent up the mountain, just to see whether he would return safe and sound. The young man in question developed an itch over his whole body, so the sacrifice was halted.

The various villages have quite similar ways of doing their central sacrifice. In some villages, however, this "standard" sacrifice is joined by a different kind of sacrifice, a typical scapegoat ritual. For instance, in Rumsiki the two officiators, one of them the *mnzefɛ*, consult the diviner and mount the sacred mountain with a—usually male and black—goat and a large pot. The whole village has been warned by the village chief himself, for this is a high-risk sacrifice: "Cursed is he who touches his hoe handle!" At the high point of the hill, the two take off their clothes, and just in their goatskins spit into the direction they came from (to stop evil from following them) and lead the goat to the ruins of the granary inside the old ancestral compound. They make the animal kneel, put the pot over it, and *mnzefɛ* prays *shala* (*hyile* in Rumsiki dialect) to keep the village healthy and have the goat take away all evil. The other then shatters the pot, and both descend the mountain without looking back. At the home of the *mnzefɛ* the village chief waits for them with other elders, and they drink the ritual *tɛ*, praising the two for keeping the village well. The goat in question is never killed and has to die a natural death. Nobody touches it, but since it often joins another goat herd, people report on its whereabouts. As soon as it dies, the officiators skin it, prepare the meat, and eat it. In the next year a new scapegoat will be dedicated, since the village cannot last more than a year without one.

Of course, the likeness to the Old Testament scapegoat is striking, but for the Kapsiki the difference between a goat that is sacrificed and eaten immediately and this one, which is eaten after a natural death, is not very marked at all: both are against evil, for the health of the village, and both are eventually eaten by the people responsible for the ritual.

Sacrificing a Bull

Thus far we have seen the home sacrifice gradually expand, from house to ward or lineage, and then to the whole village. The main characteristics were preserved throughout: a ritual just for those concerned, to be respected by all who live around the home or are kinsmen, a sacrifice on a jar representing the kindred dead, involving an immolation, beer, and a meal. The social extension of the sacrifice afterwards is restricted but important, the wide sharing of beer ratifying the sacrifice. In short, Kapsiki sacrifices are quite private rituals with a limited social extension at the end. By contrast, the last ritual described in this chapter is the reverse. It is the largest sacrifice, at least in terms of the animal slaughtered, namely a bull. This sacrifice is eminently social: it is done only with a large crowd present and is accompanied by a great show of the sacrificial victim to the whole village, representing also a form of conspicuous consumption that in itself is not alien to Kapsiki culture, but that does make this sacrifice a foreign element in the Kapsiki sacrificial repertoire.

Of course, the people in Wula and Rumsu emphatically state that they have "always" done this: "It is tradition," but this ritual is not specifically Kapsiki at all; rather it is widely found in the Mandara Mountains: the bull sacrifice (*henetla* in Kapsiki, *maray* in Mafa). Throughout the northern part of the mountains, people feed a bull at stable for years to sacrifice it during one big festival, as a major presentation of an individual household toward the whole village. The most thorough description is by Von Graffenried,[5] and although fragmentation is huge in the mountains, this is one of the rituals that serve as a link between various groups, a part of a symbolic reservoir of the area.[6] Only two Kapsiki villages participate in this ritual system, the two most northerly ones, and they have a direct link with the Mafa or Mafa-like groups of the north. This ritual reminds us that ethnic units are historic and cognitive constructs with a limited explanatory value.

Every other year, alternating with the ritual for chasing death (*ba*), this bull sacrifice is done in the months of March and April, on separate days for each celebrant. Sacrificing a bull is optional but is destined to bring luck and fertility for the family, and it generates huge prestige in the village. The procedure described below is from Rumsu, whereas the ritual in Wula is slightly different and more like Sukur, according to my informants.

The sun has just risen and the day is still cool when we arrive at the chief's compound in Rumsu, and we are welcomed as in-laws: his daughter married my classificatory brother in Mogode and I helped with the bridewealth. So I am welcome but I do have to behave as an in-law: sit at the low end of the *derha*, take my shoes off, and suppress any bodily noises. Luckily I am allowed to take notes; I am still white. The chief, Ndewuva, appears to be at the smith's; in any feast the chief and the chief smith have to walk together with some adjuncts of the chief. A chief never walks alone and the smith is his ritual companion. So we go over to the smith's compound and find it full: several people are buying pottery, made by his three wives, who sell their wares from small straw huts next to the entrance. His son is quite busy as well; he recently killed a leopard (it must have been one of the very last!), which is a sign of power but also a risk for anyone he touches. So he has ground up its frontal bone and puts small stripes of the resulting powder on the forehead of any passing woman or child to ward off harm.

As part of the chief's retinue, we stroll through the village, heading for a compound marked by a straw hut on top of a hangar. This is where the bull's meat will be kept, and the proud owner, Tlakema, insists that I take a picture. All assemble in his forecourt. He brings a jar of beer and the oldest person present takes out a calabash and pours some on the road: "*Shala*, give us a good feast today, with health in the village." Tlakema fills the calabash again, and the old man twice pours some beer on the floor of the forecourt: "Let us all be healthy." Then another, larger calabash is filled to the brim and handed over to the chief—called "the measure of the chief." Tlakema gives a short speech with the characteristic restraint that befits the occasion: "I have some beer. It is not for sale, but for drinking, and all has to be finished today." He never mentions the bull. When halfway through the jar, two old men walk through the *dabala*, to a low opening in the wall which leads into a small sunken stable that is enclosed and roofed. For about a year a bull has been stabled here and fed by the women of the house. It is this bull that is the center of ritual and gastronomic attention, today and in the next weeks. With a sickle, the two old men scratch three lines near the feeding hole, one for each of Tlakema's children (all daughters) and hand a shard with ocher to the people in the forecourt. Anyone planning to sacrifice a bull the next year puts a stripe of ocher on his temples. The first of the two men then addresses the bull: "I am going to eat all of you." From the exit at the other side of the stable, the second old man pours some water over the bull: "Here, here, I am going to eat all of you," and gives the boy who has been in charge of the bull a compliment: "Well done, the bull looks great." They rejoin the crowd in the forecourt, where Tlakema has brought another two jars, the "jars of the stable" (tɛ dlema). The "chief's jar," still with some beer in it, is put near the stable and anyone passing can take a sip. The owner will remove it tomorrow.

When this part of the ritual is finished, the whole crowd goes to the next compound that sports a straw hut on high, and the procedure is repeated.

Gradually the conversation starts about who has the largest bull, meaning who has kept his bull inside for the longest. According to the chief, one man has stable-fed his bull almost five years, but that seems improbably long to the other drinkers. They continue their rounds until well past noon. In the afternoon everyone assembles on the dancing ground of Rumsu ward, for the cattle show. Each of the bull owners now has his bull brought out, if possible by the *gwela* of that year, the boys who have been initiated and just danced their final dances in the year festival (see Chapter 11). Before bringing it out, the man's initiation mother puts some flour on the bull's back and two boys drag the beast outside, cords around its neck and a hind leg. This is always a tricky affair: the bull is out for the first time in about a year and is wild and threatens to charge anyone nearby (Figure 5.4).

Wearing cowry bands and holding sorghum stalks, the owners' families dance and sing before their homes and await their bull's return. Tlakema gives the two boys a calabash of beer and sends them home; they should never "see" the bull again. Bulls are slaughtered inside the house between the huts, directly under the straw storage hut. This is not just any killing but the largest ritual sacrifice the Kapsiki know, so it should be done properly: even the beer is heavier than usual and the sorghum sprouts should not be kept on the roof for too long lest it become the beer for one's funeral. A story has it that mice take some sprouts to the bulls to warn them of their death and most bulls refuse to eat it. All the owners have consulted the crab before the feast to know of the dangers. Sometimes the crab indicates that the sacrifice is "hard" and then the owner will not taste the meat first, in which case it will be dried and the first piece given to an unsuspecting stranger to take away the bad luck. Or a piece is left for the vultures. The man in question will then slaughter a goat and eat that meat first. When someone performs *henetla* for the first time, he will not sleep at home but at the home of someone who has performed this ritual before. In the case described above, the old man had received a small bull from his son, who wanted to celebrate *henetla*, but he could not do it before his father had slaughtered a bull.

When the bull is brought inside again, Tlakema is in his hut and all his wives are in their own huts, each with her children, and none should wear red. The helpers make the bull kneel down, its head toward Tlakema's hut and its tail toward the first wife's hut. A few sisters' sons hold its head while Tlakema's older brother (sometimes a Fulbe is asked to do this in order to make the meat acceptable to Muslims) puts some beer in the bull's ears. It shakes its head as it should do, indicating that the killing can proceed. If it does not shake its head, the person is "not good with cattle" and another butcher should be chosen. The butcher first stabs the neck of the beast in the artery (the Kapsiki way of killing) and then slits its throat in Fulbe fashion (for the above-mentioned reason) and puts the knife on the sorghum flour on the bull's back. The mentrix (initiation mother) of Tlakema (or her daughter) puts two brooms (one for each of the bull's years), a calabash, and a grindstone with the knife, "the things to show the way." Then Tlakema emerges from his hut with a hoe handle in his hand and asks, "Who has killed my bull?" Nobody answers. He goes back into his hut and comes out again: "Who has killed my bull?" A hidden brother answers, "Your bull has been killed because he has eaten the millet of the chief of Sukur." Tlakema then beats the dead bull twice with his hoe handle: "Then it is your own fault that you have been killed; you asked for your own death. People, let us eat with joy; it provoked its own end. What made him eat that millet? May everyone now be healthy, may *shala* keep illness far from us."

The first blood is caught in two shards by Tlakema, who will later pour it out on the crossing of the paths "to keep everyone healthy," because killing something male inside the house is tricky and precautions should be taken. Then the serious job of skinning and dividing the bull up gets under way, work for the sisters' sons under the guidance of the older brother. In principle, all the meat is cut into pieces and put in the straw hut; the division of the meat will come later—only the liver, as the best part, is taken out to be used on the *melε*—but the Kapsiki feel no hurry to keep the meat fresh. When all the meat is up in the straw hut, one piece is thrown on the spot below. The mentrix then cleans up the area of slaughter and takes that piece of meat. The two nephews climb down with pieces of the bull's tongue. With everything finished, these nephews and the butchers stand with their backs to each other, first making the movement of throwing the meat over their shoulders and the second time actually throwing it, separating themselves from their handiwork.

Meanwhile, people are gathering in the dancing place, where the dance gradually evolves into a "ladies-excuse-me" dance, a favorite dance with the youth because it gives ample opportunity to meet other youngsters from other villages. We will encounter this type of dance later at the funeral. Later in the day the girls of the lineage—clothed only in their cache-sexe as befits a traditional sacrifice—will come in with ritual food gifts. They stay for two nights and feast on the meat, the part with the windpipe is especially for them. They are sent home with another gift of meat.

Later in the evening, when all the guests have left, us included, Tlakema will finish the sacrifice in the usual way, as a home sacrifice: putting liver on his *melε* and on those of his wives and older children, and eating the roasted liver. What remains is the division of the meat, the social crux of the whole ritual. One of the nephews remains in the straw hut until the bulk of the division is done. He is not supposed to eat, although a friendly kinswoman will probably roast a piece of meat for him to chew on. The division is as follows:

- a hind leg and the testes for the mentrix of Tlakema
- one large piece (of any kind) for the wife who fed the bull

- the upper vertebrae with meat for the nephews who did the killing
- a front leg and the kidneys for the mother's brother
- an ear plus a piece of meat for his assistant
- the skin and any attached meat for the owner's other wives; they will feed their brothers with it, receiving millet in return
- the lips are cut off and will be eaten months later when the owner sows his first field of the season
- the head will be enclosed in dung, cooked after five days, and with old mush eaten by the old men of the ward
- dried strips of meat are given to clan brothers, ward members, and their wives
- the bones are for the small *ksugwe* who did the actual butchering. They will keep them in a large pot for two weeks and then call the women in the ward for a party. Together they beat the bones and marrow to pulp to be used in preserving the rest of the meat. The intestines are put in pots, with hot bone pulp poured over it and then this pot is closed with beeswax. Such a preserve is kept for months, and it is finally eaten or sold.

This is a ritual that has changed, as so many have. In Rumsu in 1973 during the 13 days of *henetla* no fewer than 69 bulls were slaughtered; in 2008 just seven bulls died even though Rumsu had doubled in size. This decrease is undoubtedly due to the area's increasing Christianization and Islamization and also to a reduced need to invest in social capital in Kapsiki society. Whoever slaughters a bull for *henetla* these days simply buys one at the market for the ritual. But the bull is still called *mere*, like the Mafa *maray* for a bull that has been stall-fed and, whatever its provenance, the bull is loudly praised for its tender flesh and skin.

Wula is the other village where the *henetla* is held and, since much of the ritual is similar, I will just highlight the differences; this is, as said, one of the rituals that link the larger region. On the first day in Wula, all the clan elders plus the chief smith visit the homes of the lineage and clan elders, and the smith greets the *shala* in each house, drumming in the forecourt of the house. Finally, everyone gathers in the home of Tlake, the *mnzefe* (the village priest), where the *henetla* always starts, but this year he is slaughtering as well. His daughter is in attendance, wearing cowry shells around her loins to honor her father's sacrifice. Each guest takes off his shoes, touches the ground with two fingers, and claps his hands in greeting, a submissive gesture in Kapsiki. For this kind of sacrifice, beer is given only to the guests "who deserve it," that is, those who sacrifice will get some first and then those who have sacrificed recently. When circulating the beer, the calabash is passed behind anybody who has not cultivated; they will have to wait and see whether any beer is left. Luckily they consider my writing as work.

Figure 5.4 Showing the bull just before sacrifice. Rumsu 1973.

But no beer is given at this first sacrifice of the year, so the elders head straight for the space between two huts where the sacrifice will be done. Other guests—the house is filled to capacity—are seated in a second entrance hut, the youngest in the first (the house has two entrance huts) and in the forecourt, farthest from the action. The assistant of the *mnzefɛ*, an old man from a clan different from the one of the officiator, takes a calabash of beer and approaches the climbing pole between the huts that reaches upto the straw hut on top of the hangar. The beer is diluted with a lot of water, characteristic of *henetla* in Wula. The old man pretends to pour beer on the pole but holds back first and then pours, saying:

> These are the things of my ancestors, the things of my father; this year a bull, next year a cow. Next year we will sacrifice again and eat the belly. Chief of Dlengu [another name for Wula], this is your village. You have to crush all bad things under your feet, and all evil has to leave for Tlukwu. There is the path it should take.

He pours against one side of the pole only, because it would be taboo to do it to both sides, and the rest of the beer he pours outside, saying, *Kadzi Tlukwu na* (go to Tlukwu), the village Death is chased to at the *ba* ritual, (see Chapter 7), plus the same injunction as inside. Another elder comes out with some straw from the stable and throws it out: "Death should not remain here; this feast has to be celebrated in good health." This done, the men inside start the *gwagwa* chant, a song of joy, with all singing more or less together, huddled in a very small space and accompanied by two smiths on a large drum and an hour-glass drum:

> Joy of dancing, joy of the cow. The Marghi do not kill a bull, the pig is their thing. Please, please Father Mountain, protect me.[7]

An elder puts a large beer jar against the pole and drinking starts, just for the people inside. After the beer is drunk, the men come out, chat a bit, and then go inside to sing again and repeat this one more time. The owner sits in the shade outside his home with his two adjuncts. At all the following sacrifices, the singers stay inside for the whole singing time.

Here too, the *gwela* comes to take out the bull to show it to the village. They will do this the following day in all the wards of Wula. At noon they assemble in the forecourt, clothed in goatskins decorated with iron, brass, and glass beads, their heads shaven but for a tuft of hair at the crown (like the chief's hair). They put their bush knives or throwing knives at the entrance and greet the master of the house by clapping their hands. The smiths come out with their drums and start the dance, the old men first and then the *gwela*, all in one line, performing complicated moves, but not all have totally mastered them yet, to the amusement of the crowd. Finally *mnzefɛ* Tlake performs a round of dancing, clothed in three large gowns, and the bull's part of the show starts. The *gwela* gets the bull out of the stable, all the women shriek, the owner dances around his bull—at a respectful distance—and the boys take the bull back into the house to be sacrificed.

This first day, after the showing, only Tlake sacrifices; the other bulls are slaughtered two days later. Two brothers and two of the nephews do the butchering under the pole; one of them sits in the hut above, the other kills the bull by slitting its throat. The butcher puts the knife on the bull's back, with the sorghum flour and, as in Rumsu, the mentrix or her daughter puts two brooms, a calabash, and a grindstone next to the knife.

> In the later sacrifices, the *gwela* kill the animal, and the bull's head is tied to the roof, looking toward the owner's hut. Two *gwela* each take some millet flour, two upper grindstones, and two brooms. Flanking the animal, each boy takes some flour from the other's calabash and smears it on the animal's side from back to front, at the side of the other *gwela*, and the second one does likewise. The first does the same with the two grindstones and then hits the victim's head with the stones, and finally puts knives, stones, flour, and brooms on the bull's back.

Then Tlake comes in. Since it is his first bull, he takes some grass and a hoe handle and asks three times: "Why is my bull dead?" After the third time he gets an answer: "It has eaten in the field of the chief." (Not Sukur!) Tlake then puts the grass on its head and hits it with the handle, saying, "It's your fault." The meat is dried and later distributed to everyone except those who have sacrificed bulls themselves. The nephews get the ears with some meat and the sister who has anointed the man's penis when he was initiated (see Chapter 10), gets meat from the belly with the sexual organs. Tlake's wife gets a large chunk that she will keep, and the rest is put in pots, just like in Rumsu. After this first day, the following days are spent showing and slaughtering bulls, and over the next two weeks there will be one slaughter a day in a different ward. In Wula the village chief has to sacrifice each season, and the villagers will help him out financially, because it is quite a burden, even if the ritual alternates with the chasing away of disease (see Chapter 7).

Imagistics of Dwelling: Shrines and Identity

The symbolic complex of the bull sacrifice is less clear-cut than the home sacrifice with its many echelons. More than the meal-oriented symbolism of the sacrifice, the *henetla* points to life and death but uses many agricultural signs. The symbols of the *henetla* pertain to cultivation, more precisely to food: the flour, the broom, the hoe handle, and the grindstones. On the other hand, the *gwela* and the owner's mentrix play an important role, while the smiths definitely take second place, thus tying the ritual in with the initiation complex. In more than one way, the bull sacrifice integrates the rites of passage with the yearly cyclical rites, the rites of dwelling with the rituals of belonging, and this conjunction forms a dominant theme in the Kapsiki ritual cycle, as we shall explore further in Chapter 11. As has been said, the *henetla* is part of a regional ritual complex, found throughout the Northern Mandara Mountains, but even if the sacrifice as a whole has the air of a "Fremdkörper" inside the Kapsiki ritual complex, the specific symbolism inside the *henetla*, both in Rumsu and Wula, definitely bears Kapsiki characteristics.

The reference in the bull sacrifice to Sukur is curious and, as an indication of the status of Sukur,[8] reminds us that history is being replayed in communal sacrifices. History may not be as dominant as in Mafa ritual,[9] but at ward, lineage, and especially village sacrifices history is reflected in the ritual, the history of Kapsiki dwelling. Sacrifice has been at the core of religious theory since the nineteenth century, and most of the approaches have been largely a-historical, including to some extent the "modes" approach. Here I want to touch on its historical dimension. The Kapsiki "ways of the beer" stage the local histories of settlement, clans, lineages, and intervillage relations, redefining communal identities in a continuous interaction with history, thus highlighting the historical contingencies of dwelling and the cultural view of their own local history. Sacrifice in Kapsiki unites the present group with the constructed past, rebooting the present in the past, not in order to relive the past, but to build the present on the authority of the past. This is the essence of tradition, in my view, and this is what the Kapsiki value in their sacrifices, a dynamic interchange between then and now. But, as this chapter's introductory case shows, reconstructing the past is never easy, is never a given, and comes under pressure with change.

History shows also in shrines,[10] in Africa as well as elsewhere. Major shrines are not easy to recognize in Kapsiki and Higi rituals, but in the village ritual the original mountain with its places of sacrifice is definitely a shrine, that is, Rhuŋgedʼu or the ancestral mountains of other villages. However it is not a shrine *for* a specific supernatural agent, but a shrine *of* people, of a specific ancestral family, and it can become such a shrine only if that family has descendants. These shrines refer to people first of all, to their ritual presence of old, and to their lives and deaths—the latter in the case of Hwempetla. The notion of "the sacred", so readily used in other cultural areas, such as Europe and especially in the context of the world religions, is not easy to apply here. If Hwempetla's tomb could be called sacred, it is not so because the supernatural meets this world of men there, but because it remembers a great human exploit, and then of someone who had an abundant progeny: he has to be productive as well as reproductive. So the sacred has a historical connection first of all, something we later will see in boys' initiation ceremonies. Not only is any notion of the sacred primarily historical, it also depends on the occasion, since only during the ritual is the place really special. As Grimes has argued, it is usually the ritual that sacralizes the place,[11] both in its inception and in daily life. Though few people climb Rhuŋgedʼu of their own accord, it is out of bounds because of the rituals, though in fact mainly during a ritual.

> When I climbed the mountain for the first time, I took care to check with the chief and then climbed very early, before sunrise. Of course I was spotted anyway, but the commentary was revealing: there was no problem, as I was of the *ŋacɛ* clan, who commanded the mountain, the *mnzefɛ* being of our clan.

Even the spot where Hwempetla flew through the mountain (see Appendix) is special only during wedding rituals once a year (Chapter 9) or during the rooster ordeal, but for the rest of the time it is just a forgotten backwater.

One quintessential shrine in Kapsiki, as in the rest of Mandara,[12] is primarily the *melɛ*, the jar. All through the mountains, jars are the sacrificial spots par excellence, but they are essentially fleeting shrines, relating to individual histories of families and lineages, prone to be forgotten after the next generations. In Mafa and Bulahay culture, as David et al. stress, pots are icons for people, which is why they are decorated in the way they are.[13] In Kapsiki/Higi culture this identity is less stressed—we saw the *mele* differ only slightly from the usual ones—but they do refer to people. Some jars are more important than others because some people are more important than others, and again here the main referent is not the supernatural world, but the social historical one. Even the large Gudur shrine against locusts is couched in historical terms, not in those of an "other world."

The other typical shrine is the ancient grindstone, important in many rituals, not so much in sacrifices but more in the rites of belonging.[14] While used for watering the goats in any compound, the old grindstones are the dwelling remains that link the Kapsiki to their past, with rain, with their mythical hero, in fact with their collective history. So Kapsiki shrines are very much "diesseitig," and very little "jenseitig." Shrines dwell in the landscape of history as well as in the history of the social landscape, being part of the Kapsiki's deep link with their ecological and sociopolitical environment. This very human side of their sacred spots ties in well with the main characteristics of Kaspiki notions about the "other" world, since that world is very close, as we shall see in the next chapter. In the imagistic dynamics of the Kapsiki ritual, these grindstones are self-evident relics from the past that do not evoke exegesis. Their function in daily life evolves with the age of the stone. First used for grinding, they gradually become too deep and then serve as a basin for watering the goats at the entrance of the forecourt. When the house is abandoned, they remain on the spot, because only the construction wood is carried to a next habitat. So, there they are, the last visible remnants of a long habitation, their position at the fringe of the old *rhe* making them a visible icon of long habitation. And that is one meaning they have in ritual as well, deep history. The other signification is just as straightforward—as we shall see in the next chapters—the association with water: watering the goats becomes the symbol for watering the village. This is classic imagistic symbolism, easy to interpret, hard to forget and no need to explain. And in a fundamental difference from shrines in more doctrinal religions, these shrines "dwell," are part of the Kapsiki interaction with the environment. Quite iconically, the only imprint the Kapsiki can make on the rocks is through grinding, since the volcanic stones are too hard to cut. The walls are put together as a puzzle, and only the long wear and tear of grinding is a rocky reminder of human habitation, so what better symbol for historical dwelling than these ancient grindstones.[15]

The first three descriptions in this chapter essentially involve house sacrifices, but then there is an additional counterintuitive element, because the house itself does not exist any longer. The discourse on the large African family may easily collapse large kinship groups such as clans into an idiom of "brothers and sisters" and of "one family," but that view is in itself a distortion of reality. The village no longer is one family, it is an imagined one. The images and icons of close unity abound in the ritual, but the imagistic wholeness is continuously breached by the actual discourse during or after the ritual itself. The chief uses the ritual as a religiopolitical instrument; in the ward and lineage sacrifice people speak about evil-doers and an epidemic among goats. The optimal rite of the home sacrifice that rests on the daily interaction between the participants here gives way to a more complicated version, with several counterintuitive elements. First, the house has to be conceived—since it cannot be perceived—then the addressees, *shala*, rain, and the cultural hero Hwempetla as well. That is why history is crucial here: these more complex constructions make sense only through a historical tale, and that is why the ritual on the mountain has to be set in the images of the past—officiators in old dress, staging the old war, using the old and varied *mele*. Here exegesis is already important, both to highlight its occurrence ("nobody touches his hoe") and as an integral part of the ritual itself. Exegesis implies authority, and the struggle for the *mele meleme* is a struggle over authority. Only the officiators speak about the ritual. So with the higher social echelons involved, the optimal rite accrues some doctrinal elements, and the encounter with Christianity and Islam not only creates the ritual arena, but also provides a doctrinal model. The face-off with the written religions generates a discussion and, inevitably, further exegetical reflection and formulation.

Imagistic and doctrinal modes inform identity construction and politics in their own way, the first by highlighting the existing functioning group, the second by creating a new bond between unrelated people. In Kapsiki sacrifice identity shows in the tension between inclusion versus exclusion. Presence at any sacrifice is severely circumscribed, since this ritual is accessible only for the relevant people belonging to the in-group. The only exception is the smith, but as the quintessential outsider he belongs in any group as "child of the village." The house sacrifice of chapter 4 sets off the house against all other compounds, the ward and lineage *mele* against all evil-doers, while the village ritual not only militates against other villages but also differentiates between the various clans, effectively excluding half of the village. The less clear the in-group, the stronger the doctrinal aspect. The bull sacrifice shows a similar tension between inclusion and exclusion, as the individual sacrificer stresses his belonging to the village while at the same time highlighting his eminence vis-à-vis nonsacrificers. The sacrifice constructs an "other" as the enemy,

This dynamic may well be illustrated by the notion of evil. All sacrifices at some time chase away "bad things." In the village sacrifice other villages are the enemy, bad things are thrown over the wall in the home *mele*, and in the bull sacrifice the epidemic—the epitome of public evil—is sent to a faraway village. This chasing away of evil highlights the tension between individual and community interests as well as between communities, wards, clans, and villages, and it finds its clearest expression in the Rumsiki "scapegoat" ritual.

According to René Girard this scapegoat function is essential in sacrifice, but actually the ritual violence does not generate consensus. In my view, theoreticians such as Girard have made too much of the violent act of killing;[16] as I have argued, a ritual sacrifice—be it home, ward, or village—is no more violent than any major meal, even much less than any large feast.[17] The bull sacrifice might seem an exception in this respect. The bull ritual does construct an excuse for the killing ("your own fault"), a type of discourse that is well known from cattle-keeping people, since one should not kill an important animal like a bull without good reason. Such an excuse is not offered to goats or sheep, and nobody excuses himself to a chicken. Yet it is not the shock of killing a bull, but the joy in having abundant meat that dominates. After all, any market day witnesses slaughter on a larger scale.

For Kapsiki ritual the scapegoat story illustrates notions of evil. Evil has its symbols, such as the color black, but mainly by association with the epidemic, *ba*, as in the *tɛ ba* after the village sacrifice in Mogode, and the chasing away of death (Chapter 7). Anthropologists usually feel uncomfortable with a notion like "evil," considering it an essentialist concept, but David Parkin has shown[18] that in many cases it reflects local images, and here it does as well: *ndrimike*, "bad things." It is seen as a presence, a reality that is not primarily relational, but something has to be somewhere, a substance that has to reside at a certain place. Thus any sacrifice sends it "away," over the wall or to the other village, which means that one's sacrificial strengthening of identity is a slight threat to the other. This notion of evil as a "limited good" implies that communal sacrifices do not generate general communion but rather highlight one identity over another, in a competitive system more than a communal one, at least one that stresses hierarchy over belonging and rootedness. The basic model remains the home, which effectively excludes most other homes. The *melɛ meleme* is a reunion of the first family, and though it is for the whole village, its specific attention is only for part of the clans, not for all and definitely not for those lineages that have immigrated.

> During a *tɛ ksugwe* (a drinking bout, part of the marriage proceedings) chief Wusuhwahwele points out all participants in the ceremony, specifying for each his autochthonous status, and his belonging to the first or second group of clans in Mogode.

This attention to autochthony is not foreign to African religion, or to African village politics for that matter;[19] it forms a constant undercurrent in Kapsiki rituals. It is interpreted by Kopytoff as a remnant of the internal African frontier. The difference between first-comers and latecomers is sometimes seen as a way to order social relations through the application of rules of hospitality and reciprocity,[20] but on the other hand it can easily serve as a means of exclusion over inclusion, of hardening distinctions between people. Mobility came late to the Mandara area, and the sacrificial discourse does not embrace unrelated outsiders.

Inclusion, we shall see, comes from other rituals, those of belonging, especially of the large rites of passage of marriage, initiation, and the year festival (Chapters 9, 10, and 11). Within the dwelling complex, the ward sacrifice somewhat counterbalances the exclusionary forces of descent-cum-authochthony, since here the notion dominates that cohabitation is a major element in compound composition. The fact that in one village, Rufta, wards function as lineages underscores this importance of co-residence, which we saw already in the home *meleϵ*. But the real feasting of the arrival of new people is done in the setting of the agricultural cycle, in the collective ways of dwelling, which is what we turn to in Chapter 7. But first, we have to zoom in on the Kapsiki ideas of what unseen beings are dwelling with them.

6

The Other Side of the World

The Spirit Walker

At night we go our way with our *shinaŋkwe* [shadow]. For us the night is like the day for you. Our body sleeps and wakes up when we return, and cannot be woken up earlier. The shadows look for us just like normal bodies, we walk as we do during the day. We cannot help it, we cannot avoid it, and we go whether we want or not, no medicine helps against it.

These are the words of Vandu Kwadeva, one of the well-known spirit walkers in Mogode. Called *keleŋu*, these are the men and women whose "shadow" is different from those of others: in their spirit they walk through the night to other villages. They are not witches (see below) but respected people with a very peculiar "night life." In fact they wage a spiritual war against other villages, which is nothing to be ashamed of in Kapsiki. Vandu Kwadeva continues:

We do not go each night, it depends. Yesterday we went to Guria (a neighboring village), there are few *keleŋu* there and they are afraid of us. We fought in the fields: one boy got a stab wound in his chest; he will die soon, within five days. We fight with knives and clubs, not with bow and arrow, against all villages except Kortchi because they are too strong and too numerous. Women and children join us though they stay in the background, yelling and throwing stones. We also fight with the people of Sir and the Nigerian villages close to Mogode. Also one of the Catholic fathers is a *keleŋu*: he always watches the fight but then we chase him away.

Early in the night we call upon each other in each ward. There are eight of us in our ward, in this ward just three. As soon as they can walk, at the age of one or two, they join us. Even if you try to forbid them, they come anyway. Their father can prohibit them by sacrificing a totally white chicken and sprinkling a collar of blood around their neck. When they are older, that does not work any longer. Often we try to steal sorghum when it is a meter high: we take the stalks with us and plant them between our own sorghum. During the day no one sees the difference, but at threshing time his sorghum does not produce anything, while ours does, a lot. Thorns help against theft because when we come, the sorghum escapes between the thorns: all the stalks run in front of us and as we do not want to hurt ourselves, we let them go. Normally we do not fight in the village, but if anyone wants to steal my sorghum, I will prohibit it. Anyway, I can see whether my sorghum will yield a large harvest or not.

I never know beforehand when we are going, it depends on the fields. In the years of little sorghum we are fat, as we do not tire ourselves in nightly excursions. When sorghum is plentiful, we are thin, as we go out each night. In fact, one could better not be *keleŋu*, for we work during the day and steal at night. I have no rest: if it were calm for a month, I would be fat and shiny.

We also know beforehand who is going to die; we see it from his *shinaŋkwe* (shadow). But if we warn someone, we have to take his place and die ourselves. What we can do is indicate what sacrifice he has to make, but of course I do that only with my family and my best friends, not just anybody. That is about the only future we know, we cannot predict rain. We do see a lot of *gutuli* [spirits, see below] in all sizes and forms, large, small, black, and brown; they are everywhere. Just a month ago a colleague of mine said to his neighbor: "Do not pass over there." The man did it anyway and got bitten by a snake [later the neighbor confirms the story]. Well, maybe it is after all nice to be *keleŋu*, if only for the sorghum. It is like having a star or a crystal [medicine for wealth], only those come and go, but this stays.

In the literature, these spirit walkers are sometimes dubbed "clairvoyants" and with some reason, since they know something of the future. They illustrate that people are complex and that the world beyond the visible is just as complex, while the two are very closely linked in Kapsiki. We turn now to the collective representations of the invisible agencies, as well as to the Kapsiki theories of what visible and invisible aspects constitute a person.

The "Other Side": *Shala* and the Individual

The term "supernatural" is not very apt for an understanding of the invisible beings in Kapsiki world view. When speaking with some informants, they came up with a different model of "the other world," or more accurately the other side of the world. One of them compared the relationship between this world and the "other" as two sides of a piece of paper: one can see only one side, but the other side is always there. But seeing both sides at the same time is impossible, even if sometimes the print on the other side vaguely shines through. Evidently this is typically a model generated by the research itself, maybe even by the presence of my notebook, but the other people present readily agreed that it was a good analogy. Therefore I will speak about the "other side" and shun the notion of the supernatural. As we shall see, some verticality is implied in Kapsiki concepts of the other side, but completely different from the classic heaven/earth distinction.

Shala is the key term in Kapsiki cosmology; though translated as "God" in Bible translations, it is in no way a real monotheistic notion. *Shala* is first and foremost one's personal god; in principle there is one for each human being. So *shala* means primarily *shala ta d'a*, my personal god, just mine. But I am not alone; I am part of several large social units, and the notion of *shala* follows the social echelons. Thus "my *shala*" can easily shade into "our *shala*," and any collective entity—like a family, lineage, clan but also an incidental group—has its own *shala* as well. That means that every being or group has his, her, or its *shala*, individual people, groups or the whole village. But also an animal and many objects we would call inanimate, like a river, a house, a piece of bush, or a particular spot, has its *shala*. In all cases *shala* is both a general term and a specific identity, depending on the unity referred to, since these *shala* have no names, other than those of person or group in question.[1]

So each individual being has his or her own *shala*, and each group of people has its *shala*, but these two *shala* are neither very different nor quite equal. The master of a house has his *shala*, and so do his wives and all their children. But there is also a *shala* of the whole compound (*shala ta rhɛ*), just as there is one of the ward, the clan, and the village. Some trees have their own *shala*, but only special species; likewise all the mountains and each outcropping on the plateau definitely has its own *shala*. Is this a well-populated cosmology, or how different are all these *shala*? The preceding would typically be an outsider's question, but when posed—as I did, evidently—most Kapsiki agree that all these *shala* essentially are similar, even the same, and—when pressed—they state they actually are one. But, again, this type of question is normally not posed. The context of speech or ritual act is sufficient to distinguish the relevant *shala*, be it a social group, a place, or an artifact.

> When I sacrifice, I address *shala ta d'a*, my own *shala*. If my other family members were present, I would address *shala ta rhɛ*, the *shala* of the compound; at a lineage ritual we implore *shala ta ɓumu* (our *shala*), which can be used in the case of any group, however composed. The village sacrifice at Rhuŋged'u addresses *shala ta meleme* (the village *shala*), and during the initiation of girls the young voices sing in praise of *shala ta Rhwemetla* (the god of that particular mountain, Rhwemetla). The main issue is that the precise referent in a discourse on *shala* is the actual relationship of the people present at that moment.

Every *shala* is referred to in the first person,² never in the second, and sometimes in the third: "your *shala*" is never heard, since this would be a serious infringement of privacy. Speaking about the *shala* of a third person is possible if he is absent, but doing so is close to gossip. This restriction avoids misunderstandings, since it is always clear who is meant; in fact, the relevant people tend to be present. Context and language make it usually quite clear: *shala ta ɓu* means the *shala* of the two of us, *shala ta ɓumu* is the *shala* of all us here, *shala ta ŋ'yɛ* (exclusive first person plural) describes the *shala* of all of us-but-not-you, that is, the *shala* of the group to which the addressee does not belong. *Shala* is the counter-ego, the "double," of each one of us and, as individual identities blur into a joint one, the various *shala* merge into one major one. In short, *shala* is the other-worldly pendant of the major identity relevant at that particular moment. That, clearly, means *shala* is neither a guardian spirit nor just a high god. Thus, *shala* means the other side of world, as the counter-identity of any living being or group of beings.

The only exception to the first-person usage is *shala pelɛ rhweme*, God in heaven (*rhweme* also means sky or mountain), the encompassing God above. But since all *shala* are deemed to reside "above," *shala pelɛ rhweme* can also be seen as the totality of all *shala* together, or even the indication of someone's personal *shala*. But that situation is rare, since people usually use *shala ta d'a*. *Shala pelɛ rhweme* is used by both Christians and non-Christians (Muslims prefer to speak Fulfulde) and no misunderstanding can ever ensue; after all, everyone is talking about the same thing: "What is the difference between *shala* and *shala*?"³ Thus for Christians and Muslims it is easy to equate *shala* with God or Allah, especially in *shala pelɛ rhweme*. But then, a person who has meant a lot to me and to whom I owe a lot, is my *shala te hed'i*, *shala* on this earth.

So the notion of *shala* has a kind of structural vagueness that in fact is essential for its understanding. As so often in African thought, these notions are first of all more practical than theological. Important in the Kapsiki way of seeing *shala* is the notion of merging identities: the basic *shala* is a personal one and the *shala* of groups, collectivities, or villages up to *shala pelɛ rhweme* is built from individual ones, not the other way around. So it is not a refractive or fissioning concept, as is "Kwoth" in Evans-Pritchard's classic Nuer case. In Kapsiki we have a concept of individual beings, constantly merging and separating, and incidentally making one whole, though never structurally so.

This referential dominance, with its flexibility and structural vagueness, does not detract from the reality of *shala* or from the for everybody self-evident "fact" that *shala* influences people's lives. The main point is that people live in a world full of evidence, they believe, of their personal *shala*.

> "Nobody can say that he does not know *shala*. *Shala* made everything. The sorghum you cultivate is from *shala*, and *shala* gives rain. No man exists if he does not know *shala*. We are here, sitting and talking

together because *shala* wants us to be happy. Who is not here, who does not share the happiness that *shala* gives us, has only himself to blame," an elder explained during a ward sacrifice.

Places and objects may be called *shala* as well. The characteristic volcanic plugs, eminently recognizable in the landscape, all have their *shala*. Places with a lot of water, ponds, springs and pools are close to the *shala*. A special site such as the burial place of the cultural hero Hwempetla (see below) is simply called *shala*, and during sacrifice the officiator invokes *shala ta shala*.

All living beings, such as animals, have their *shala*: cows, sheep, snakes, mice. The context always fixes the specific meaning, the particular *shala* that is indicated, but these notions merge. In Kapsiki cosmology, all these personal *shala* are "up there" anyway, *peleɛ rwheme*, in the sky. Our personal *shala* act just as we do on earth: they do the same, think the same thoughts, walk when we walk, speak when we speak, but with two provisos. First, we are their copy, not the other way around. We follow them, in almost everything.

> "My *shala* and yours," Dliyeɗa, an old *keleŋu*, explains, "do the same as we do. Now they are sitting together. If they sit down, we sit down. If they stand up, so do we. We are the slaves of our *shala*. If my *shala* steals, I steal. If he makes war, I fight. If my *shala* makes a mistake or breaks a taboo, I make a mistake as well. If he dies, I am finished. Is he rich, then I am rich; his courage means my courage; if he is a good hunter, so am I, and if he is wounded, I am hurt too."

Not only are we the "slaves of our *shala*," another informant used the metaphor of the horse and its rider: we are the horses they ride on. We are also, and more importantly, their dead. A *shala* that dies descends from heaven and remains on the rubbish heap. There he or she waits for a chance to enter the belly of his or her prospective mother. This is one reason why rubbish is never burned: the next generation would be killed before birth. Thus a fetus is often called *shala* as well, and many medications aimed at the health of the fetus and the unborn child are called *rhwɛ shala*. So conception is possible only when a dead *shala* from above enters a woman's vagina. However, this can happen only after the vagina has been opened by sexual intercourse.

During pregnancy "another" *shala* counts the months of pregnancy and then opens the uterus after nine months. This "other *shala*" then becomes the personal *shala* of the new individual. In fact it has always been its *shala*. All the *shala* in heaven are deemed to have their *shala* as well, in another, higher heaven. However, no one speaks about the *shala ta mbeli peleɛ rhweme* (*shala* of the people in heaven). Only the *shala* of the living are interesting and relevant. Consequently we are the *shala* of the people down there, in the earth. When we die, our shadow goes down and is reincarnated in a woman on earth in the same way. The living are the *shala* of the people down in the earth.

> Dliyeɗa explains it to me again: "We here, we are the *shala* of the dead. If I die, my shadow descends and enters the belly of a woman, and a new child is born. They live the same way as we do, with the same villages. Sorcerers over there are as strong as they are here, maybe even better. If people die down there, then the shadow descends further, as they are again the *shala* of the people below them."

This explanation evokes the image of a great cascade of life: people start at the top, and the shadow, the remaining essence, in each following life descends one stage, going down the great ladder of life step by step, rung by rung. The beginning is unknown, and so is the end. When questioned about the end, the Kapsiki use the expression: "It ends in the *tlidi*," in the grass, but that notion has no specific symbolic connotation. Questions after the first beginning and the ultimate ending are not posed, nor do they evoke myths of origin or endings. The mythical corpus barely speaks about beginnings, let alone endings, and the etiological function of the tales is not dominant. This is a religion of relationships, just as *shala* is the ultimate expression of a relationship more than a being. Yet

Figure 6.1 A tomb with a sacrificial jar.

no westerner can resist the temptation to prod, to ask demanding questions which for the Kapsiki are clearly as unanswerable as they are uninteresting. My prodding provoked a suitable reaction, when an informant responded with the counter question: "Where is yesterday's wind?," a beautiful expression of the vanity of this theological search. What counts is today's wind and the rest is an intellectual exercise that never brings any certainty and is highly irrelevant anyway.

So the image of a stepped cascade (or a high rise in which people live each life as directed by the neighbor above, while being the director of their neighbor below) is overly systematic. The notion is ours, not our informants'. The implication would be, for example, that no death is alone: if I die, my *shala* above me and below me, as well as their *shala*, would die as well, and a whole column of related individuals would descend one step in the cascade of existence. No Kapsiki thinks that way, or at least never expresses the idea that way. The only interesting thing is the relationship between me and my *shala* up there, even the dependent down there is only mildly interesting at best. The only clear-cut notion is the idea that the seasons are in reverse: the next world, directly above and under, have their rains during our dry season and vice versa, which implies that they have a lot more rain up and down there than we do on this earth.

Though the *shala* above are almost never seen, our "dependents" below are sometimes in view; these *mbeli kwa hedi*, people in the earth, can be seen in dreams, especially by people with a special gift for spiritual viewing, like the *keleŋu*, as well as in some spots. A few places in the fields around the village have just a thin layer between us and the people down under; sometimes if a hoe is put in the earth at these places, the world down below can be seen. Several informants told us about people who have seen the other world and then inevitably run away, scared to death.

So it is not the system that is relevant but the relationship. Informants disagree about various things or have different views on the matter, but they never argue about it. Some think the *shala* and people in heaven, which are usually equated, may not be the same. Maybe there is a layer between our *shala* and us, peopled with the other people in heaven, and only the latter die and are incarnated here on earth. Maybe the same holds true regarding us and the people under the earth. Who knows? Again, it is not discussed, nor is it a source of argument. What is very clear, though, is that the relationship with *shala* is not one of kinship: he is no ancestor, and any lasting relation with the father, as we have seen in the sacrifice, is sharply distinguished from the relation with *shala*.

The nature of the dependence between an individual and his or her *shala* is open to various interpretations. The main question—which does invoke some discussion, mainly upon prodding—is our accountability for our actions. "Doing the same as our *shala*" is a shared notion, but what does it imply? Where is one's guilt if one does the same as *shala* up there? How responsible is the "slave" for his or her own actions? The general consensus is that whatever our dependence on the other world, the mistakes, transgressions, and faults are ours. Some people try to make their *shala* account for their transgressions ("it is not my fault, my *shala* made me do so") but that excuse is not taken very seriously. A mistake is one's own mistake; of course, *shala* made us stupid enough to make mistakes, but the consequences are ours. If *shala* had wanted it differently, *shala* should have made another type of horse that did not throw its rider (*shala*). Another informant: "I am what I am thanks to *shala*, he has given me all. What I do is my own, with my own *ntsehwele* (intelligence), my physical force, and my will and agency. I cannot refuse what *shala* gives me, but it does not determine my actions and my life." In Kapsiki, theology never supersedes practical reason, and a "system of thought" never impinges on personal responsibility, a situation typical of a religion in the "imagistic mode,"[4] without professional religious specialists. Kapsiki religion is a way to live in the here and now—to "dwell"—to cope with "disturbances of normalcy" and to make sense out of the relative chaos of practical life.

So basically a person with his or her *shala* is in a dual but unequal relationship. Dependence is the norm: *shala menete* (god did it) or *tsarha wusu* or *tsarha nza* (such is life) are expressions of resignation, *shala kelete* (god has taken) in the case of an untimely death, "god did it" in general mishap. But *shala* is just as much thanked for favors and blessings, and resignation as well as joy is an appropriate emotion to be shown toward *shala*. An unjust treatment by others calls for "god will see, god will judge." *Shala* has his hand in everything, good and bad, blessings and disasters. *Shala* takes lives but also helps people to overcome illness. If a child dies after a drawn-out illness, the father says "*shala* has worked," meaning he has kept death at bay and has prevented a quick death. In itself death is a normal happening, but an early one or a long illness calls for an explanation: "god has taken." Thus *shala* is always tied into emotions, be it joy, grief, resignation, or dependency; in all moments in life when emotions engulf one's perception of the world, *shala* plays a dominant role, as unpredictable and ambivalent as life itself.

When reflection sets in, our dependence on *shala* explains the perennial "Why?" *Shala* may have been punishing us for a breach of one of the many taboos. Any infringement upon a taboo can bring mishap: a bad harvest, sickness, a dead child, dead cattle, all signs of being out of harmony with *shala*, but these are definite post hoc interpretations, often revealed by divination. Whether a disaster implies active involvement of *shala* or is the self-evident outcome of a breach of taboo is often an open question. An individual can fall out of grace with his/her personal god in many ways, a part of which may be defined as taboos. A fair number of actions are taboo, from forbidden sexual relations to slaughtering a pregnant goat or having a cock crow on one's granary. Not all of these can be prevented, but even if there is no *fete*, personal guilt, they still call for reparation. What is important is that infringement brings about a disturbed relationship, which turns the tables of fortune. Without reparation, several unfortunate things can happen: illness, infertility, bad luck in trading or in cultivation among them. No specific threat is associated with *shala*. Protection as such is not possible and careful living is called for. If mishaps occur, divination should indicate the source of the trouble.

Despite this constant reminder, the relationship with one's personal *shala* is close enough for the Kapsiki to surmise that ultimately their interest and that of their *shala* will run parallel. Yet, dealing with someone else's *shala* remains quite ambivalent. One can trust one's own *shala* to be on the right side but never completely so and never unconditionally. "Il y a des accommodements avec le ciel," Molière wrote, and that holds for the Kapsiki as well. One's relationship with *shala* is reciprocal but unbalanced, inescapable but open for negotiation, ever present but most of the time as a residual discourse.

Finally, the instances when people speak of *shala* are often mediated by either other people or objects. *Shala* is frequently mentioned in greetings to other people or expressions of resignation toward others; the discourse on *shala* is a mediated one. Special people, like smiths or clairvoyants, are the other party in such a discourse on *shala*. Usually, speaking of one's *shala* is most relevant in a situation where someone else is present; the relationship between *shala* and oneself is a triangle, as the other person—with his own *shala*—is the obvious referent in the discourse. Objects may serve as well as intermediaries but mainly to focus the discourse in the bilateral relationship ego-*shala*. During sacrifices, in the public celebration of a sacrifice, in the elaborate burial proceedings, and most clearly in divination, an array of specific objects may focus communication with one's *shala*. The essential object in the cult is the sacrificial jar, *melɛ* (Figure 6.1), but a piece of quartz, a specific tree, the entrance to the compound, a grindstone, or a variety of small objects may serve as well. When speaking to the jar, the officiator reflects on his (mis)fortunes, ponders his past deeds, and reflects on his way into the future.

Other Unseen Beings

Shala is not the only being—if "being" is the word at all—other unseen beings populate the Kapsiki universe as well, some of them dangerous: An ambivalent aspect of *shala* is the concept of *gutuli*. The term implies primarily a very localized *shala* that might be the *shala* of a house, or spot in the bush, distinct from but not overly different from *shala*. In the sacrificial invocations the term *shala* is used, but toward a third person one may speak of the *gutuli* of the house. Also, the *shala* belonging to specific places in the bush, especially permanent places, are called *gutuli* or *shala teŋkwa* (*shala* of that place). There seems to be a continuum: for the more local reference points the term *gutuli* is dominant, for the more "elevated" ones *shala*. The sky and mountains (the same word in Kaspiki) are always *shala*, never *gutuli*, the *shala* of a house can be addressed with *gutuli* also, unless there is a snake involved, as we shall see below, in which case it is always *shala*. The tomb of the village cultural hero in the bush is *shala*, not *gutuli*. In the home sacrifice, one may invoke *gutuli* as well as *shala*. So the distinction is not hard and fast: *shala* is more general and more benign, and *gutuli* more localized and dangerous—but they do form a continuum.

These *gutuli* are usually associated more with the bush than with the village; one can find *gutuli* in any place with a lot of water, in warm places, in ants' nests, and at the center of the small whirlwinds that accompany the transition from the dry to the wet season. They are most often described as small black creatures, about a meter in length. The men have long black beards, and they are often very dirty. According to some informants, these are the children of *shala* who did not understand *shala* and were therefore let loose in the bush. Normally they are invisible, but special people can see them with their medicine, or they show themselves when they want to. They live in houses "just like white people," nicely made of pottery, like inverted beer vats.

> Kuve Dɛtɛ, a *keleŋu* woman, talks about the harvest festival some years ago. She sat on a rock near the dancing place and saw a group of *gutuli* trying to take the shadows of the dancing people to the bush, also her own. They did not succeed, though Kuve herself was tempted to go with them, but the path she would have had to take was too dirty.

Danger is always present, since *gutuli* may possess a person, which can lead to serious psychic disturbance. Against these dangers, special medicine, known only to very few specialists, must be taken. The Kapsiki distinguish several kinds of possession: some *gutuli* inspire the one they possess to behave dangerously, others make him play without stopping or send him out to steal. They can also possess animals: any beast that behaves abnormally, escapes the wrong way, or keeps biting is considered to be possessed. Each has its own kind of *gutuli*: humans, cows, and chickens.

Since *gutuli* have their own organization, with clans, chiefs, and the like, they also differ among themselves. Some try to help people, and appear when a human is in need of special assistance:

> 'Yèngu Nza recounts a month-long illness. Weird things happened: he saw chickens and goats nobody else could see. A *gutuli* came to his bedside, an old black man with a beard half a meter long, who told him that he was not going to die. He took 'Yèngu's hand, put it in the fire four times and then back on his heart, and put a large bundle of medicines around his neck. No one else could see these. The *gutuli* told him to keep those medicines hidden from others, which was not very difficult, and

that he, 'Yèngu, would heal when his wife died. Indeed soon afterward his wife died, and 'Yèngu got better. Later the old *gutuli* came along for his medicines and told him a prescription for this kind of illness: something with a *kwelemede*[5] tree, was all he could remember.

Some trees are indeed closely associated with *gutuli*, like the *wumbela* (*Tamarindus indica*), *vemɛ* (*Erythrina stanoidea*), *hwemeke* (*Boswellia*), *heyintsu* (*Diospyros mespiliformis*), and *lekeleke* (*Isoberlinia doka*). Though these trees are used for wood, building, and firewood, they have some scary aspects too, especially the tamarind. If a man falls from that kind of tree, all his wives will die young. Consequently he will find no one to marry, unless he cuts the tree down, digs out all the roots, and buries the whole tree, roots and all, in the ground. No one will ever lie down under one of those trees for a nap, because the *gutuli* are in full force in its shade. Some oaths are specifically sworn under these trees, especially the heavy ones, since the *gutuli* will "follow" the oath and punish with illness anyone who breaks it.

Any stand of trees on a wet spot may be the *wufe shala*, or bush of the *gutuli*; if a *mazala* tree (*Ficus*) is among them, the tree itself is addressed as *shala*, since it is considered the chief of the *gutuli* trees. Often this tree is planted inside a compound wall or a new compound is constructed around an existing *mazala*, since its presence is highly propitious, and then the sacrifices for the house are performed on the tree itself.[6]

Some animals have their own association with either *shala* or *gutuli*, especially fat snakes. A snake in a tree indicates the *shala* of that tree and no branches will be cut off it. Instead, one consults a diviner to find out what to do about it. One particular snake may live in one of the huts of the compound, feeding off mice and rats, often in the beer hut, and will be addressed as *shala*.[7] People will be very circumspect with the snake, not out of fear of being bitten but out of respect, since chasing that snake away would be unfortunate. Sacrifices are not offered to the snake, but still it is the *shala* of the house. Such a snake, however, is in fact the visible replica of the "real" *shala*-snake, the *mendereleke*. This mythical being is invisible, a huge snake that selects a human to its liking and then settles inside the compound wall, encircling the whole house with its body, head and tail on either side of the entrance. Nobody but the owner of the house can see it, and then not always. People with such a "snake" are happy family men: they will have a lot of children, both sons and daughters, and are fortunate in their business dealings. Sometimes the *mendereleke* leaves the wall to glide through the fields, an informant told me, and then he is so long that when resting he has to roll himself up in three places; otherwise the coil would be too high. The serpent is reputed to have human-like eyes, with eyelashes.

Though propitious, a *mendereleke* has to be approached with great respect. When someone spots one in the fields—which is sometimes reported to happen—usually at a damp place in the bush whose *shala* it is, he will immediately consult a diviner. A sacrifice is then called for to avoid the dangers of seeing this *shala*, one of which is possession. Crab divination might indicate that the serpent wants to become the *shala* of the client's house. The latter then returns to the spot, searches for the head of the serpent—if it appears again—and takes a handful of sand from under its head and its tail. The snake will follow him to his house, become invisible during the walk, and enter the wall. The owner then prepares the first proper sacrifice for the new *shala* of the house, a chicken and some sorghum flour on the wall. He starts brewing red beer and prepares for a big home sacrifice to which all the neighbors will be invited. After that, one is safe in the home and the house will certainly never burn down. The *mendereleke* will leave only when the owner dies. One inconvenience is that no fire can be lit in the compound at night, since the *mendereleke* does not like fire. The owner of the house, his wives, and children are the only ones who can see the serpent, but neighbors will suspect it is there and will hesitate to enter through the compound wall, a prerogative of close friends and neighbors anyway. Even for the family, though, the serpent is risky: if one son sees it often, one of his brothers will die.

In Kapsiki life, good and evil are—at least should be—balanced and the good is always limited. One downside of the serpent is that the owner will not grow old; during his days he will have to have a double sleeping hut plus straw-roofed open shelter because sometimes at night the *mendereleke* will require sleeping huts to rest, and the man will have to sleep under the straw roof. The association of the serpent with the wall is direct: often the snake is longer than the existing wall, which means that the house will grow in size, until the wall is the same length as the snake. Ultimately, my informants assure me, there is no real difference between *shala, gutuli,* and the snake; they are one and the same.

Other animals that behave strangely may have a brief association with *shala*: a duiker or rabbit running into the compound is addressed as the *shala* of the house, but for a short moment only, as they tend to leave quickly. One other animal, this time visible to everyone and representing *shala*, is the large spider called *tamtamba gwecε*[8] in Kapsiki, which is considered *shala* of the whole village. It is a rare apparition in these mountains and anyone who encounters such a spider in the bush or even in the house will be lucky and have a lot of children. People are very aware of its toxic qualities, and no sacrifices are offered to it. Sometimes they are put inside the quiver to poison their arrows, hence its name (*gwecε* meaning "quiver").

Not only are animals, however mystical they may be, part of the representations of *shala*, other unseen beings are closely related as well. The most important ones, *Va*, the personification of the rain, and *Veci*, the sun, can be encountered in person, and this calls for a sacrifice. These beings are relevant in special situations only, such as during a drought, and then are dealt with collectively either in a rain sacrifice or in communal rituals. Rain is a being which is sometimes portrayed as a ram, invisible to everybody but the rain maker. Some villages have their resident rain maker who not only performs the rituals to procure rain but can also see Rain. Most of the time however, *Va* is of human stature and armed with his "knife," lightning. Cakereɗa, Guria's rain maker explains:

> There are two persons, *Va*, both tall, with white skins and long blond hair, male and female. Both hold a white stick in their hand. If anyone takes an oath on the knife of Rain ("If I am wrong, may the knife of *Va* strike me"), the *Va* couple will follow that oath; if the oath is broken, they will strike the culprit with their stick, which marks the way for a bolt of lightning to strike. Both *Va* roam the earth, and if it has to rain the male *Va* shakes himself like a porcupine and then rain will fall. Husband and wife *Va* are together only when they have to kill someone; normally the man is alone. Whenever *Va* goes out to kill someone, he first appears as a ram in the house of the victim, his loins tied with a goatskin, his wife with a cache-sexe. Those who spot him call out "let him go, let him go" (*pelakɛ, pelakɛ*). Sometimes they renounce their plans, throw off their clothing, and go.

According to informants, someone who has been hit by lightning is not immediately dead: others have to dance around him and whip him with *kwantereza* branches (*Cassia singuena* Del.). Teri Puwe describes how one of Teri Baja's children was once struck by lightning; its mother wanted to pick it up, but bystanders kept her away, shouted "let it go, let it go," and struck the child with the branches until it regained consciousness. The rain maker told me that the rain couple lives in heaven like *shala*, wearing just their long white hair. Any rain maker, who has the rain jar in his care, is respected by *Va* as long as the rain maker respects *Va* and asks politely with a proper sacrifice. When *Va* is resting in the dry season, he is not to be bothered by any sacrifice and the rain maker has to respect that rest (for the relevant ritual, see Chapter 7). The direct family of someone killed by lightning—his children and siblings—tie on special mourning bands just before the first rains arrive, plaiting twigs of a tree[9] around their left wrist to avoid being taken by Rain as well.

Other beings are darker and even more threatening than Rain—Death, Smallpox, and Measles, all beings on their own. *Mte* (Death) is the most feared and features in a large number of traditional stories. He chases people who try to hide from him but—at least in the folk tales—he is fooled by the wily ground squirrel. Sometimes his wife features in the stories too. *Mte* is portrayed as a one-legged black man (a frequent image in Africa[10]), but there are few details about his looks. The only thing that is absolutely certain is that nobody can hide from him for long: everybody is eventually found. The village cultural hero Hwempetla is the model in this case, since even he, with all his powers, could not escape Death. But *Mte* is less active for anyone who follows the rules and who heeds his obligations toward his fellow men. An annual ritual is performed to chase Death from the village, a ritual that in fact links the Kapsiki with their northern neighbors.[11] This ritual addresses Death in its most threatening form, as the instantaneous collective death, that is the epidemic (*ba*), and this has to be chased away at the heart of the rainy season (see next chapter). In the bull sacrifice we saw this ritual foreshadowed when, at the end of the sacrifice, the officiator chased death away to Tlukwu (see Chapter 5).

Two types of epidemic are personified, smallpox and measles. They are like *gutuli*, feared as no other. The most important is *Damara* (smallpox), which is particularly feared by the Kapsiki even though of course the last epidemic was a long time ago. *Damara* knows the good and evil of any person, and kills transgressors. Those who do no wrong will not be infected, so anyone who has the symptoms will confess publicly and then withdraw into the bush to await death. All those infected will assemble in the bush, trying to survive and trying to avoid contact with the village. They will bury their own dead without help and without smiths. Medication against *Damara* is possible but extremely difficult and tricky.

> Teri Puwe recounts a smallpox epidemic a long time ago. Someone from Nigeria (Higi) came over to heal; he stayed over there with Depeɗa and treated the whole village. People collected *kwantereza* leaves (*Cassia singuena* Del.) and he mixed them with his own *hwєɓє* (*Crinum* sp, an onion). It was a miracle: he kept cutting pieces and more and more came off: a whole heap. Only when one turned around it disappeared! He soaked the mixture, took his knife, and cut into the air. A terrible yell sounded, as *Damara*, attracted by the mixture, had approached and been stabbed in the belly. All the patients brought a goat and were washed together with that goat. Then the goats were slaughtered and the water with the smallpox got in the goat's stomach. The medicine man told the people that only one would die, and so it was. The village gave him a lot of presents, especially his host Depeɗa, and people think that he has now a piece of that onion.[12]

Actually, each village has its own stories and "recipes." For instance, Rumsiki has "small pox stones": the healer washes the *hwєɓє damara* in water in which these stones have been soaking. *Shasha* (Measles) is a similar being, an epidemic that takes a huge toll on children's lives. The illness is sometimes called the nephew of smallpox but he does not look for transgressions. Confession does not help, but there are similar medications against him, as against *Damara*. Measles is still very much present in the area. During my first research period a measles epidemic killed most of the children in an orphanage in Mokolo.

Seen and Unseen Sides of Personhood

With the relationship between an individual and his or her *shala* being crucial, then what constitutes a person? As we saw, a Kapsiki can surmise with some confidence that ultimately his interests and those of his *shala* will run parallel, even if at a given moment he cannot be sure of the *shala*'s positive influence. Throughout, what happens to a person has a reason, either through his *shala*, his own conduct, or that of others. The question as to whether it is deserved or not, whether misfortune is unjust or not, effectively does not arise. Though notions of "being right" and "whose fault" are important (especially the latter, *fete*, is important), these are resolved on a casuistic basis, case by case. Any judgment is called *meha rhwu* (light the fire) or *katla fete* (cut the mistakes). The relationship is always two-sided, but on the whole *shala* is accountable for large issues while the individual is in charge of his own details.

A person has one asset with which to balance the influences and obligations in life to preserve his own agency versus his *shala* and his fellow men, and that is his *ntsehwele*. This concept has a broad connotation including cunning and cleverness, even trickery and deceit. *Ntsehwele* is a way to circumvent the agency of a third party, mainly human but also non-human, such as *shala* and the other invisibles. In folk tales it is the wily ground squirrel who in his exploits against the leopard is always the weaker one but overcomes his weakness by being clever: he always tricks his strong-but-dumb opponent. In other African groups, the spider and the hare enjoy a similar position. Lack of agency is a normal feature of life, since ordinary people have a limited amount of power plus their dependence on their *shala*, and this limitation has to be compensated for by *ntsehwele*.[13]

However, people are more than cunning schemers and have personalities that are complex and layered. Life itself is called *mpi* (breath) and everyone has just one *mpi*, only for this life, only for this world, however the visible body houses several characteristics. With the birth of an individual, *shala* creates his *mehele*, his thoughts, his attitudes, his feelings, everything he is born with and which dies with him. To some extent *shala* leads these thoughts and feelings but only up to a certain point, because man is accountable for his own thoughts as well. If anywhere, the *mehele* is thought to reside in the head and to house the *ntsehwele*, but also notions of morality and general character. The more social characteristics, riches, courage, and success are called *ŋki*. These are not exclusively individual as they can be transferred. At the end of each funeral, the son or daughter of the deceased can choose to take over these properties by rubbing the corpse's right thumb. More than *mehele*, *ŋki* is an achieved property, the result of one's own work and endeavor.

A crucial part of the personhood is the shadow, *shinaŋkwe*. Objects have a shadow but each person has two *shinaŋkwe*, a white and a black one. To illustrate the difference between white and black shadows, informants point to the difference between a full shadow and a half shadow, generated by two light sources. One dreams with the black shadow, and it is the black *shinaŋkwe* of the deceased that is sometimes seen as a ghost, and that shadow leaves for the world below after the funeral. The black shadow belongs to the living body, while the white shadow is seen as the shadow of the corpse, and the white *shinaŋkwe* will stay in the grave with the body. The black shadow looks like the living being and can sometimes move independently of its "owner." This is true especially in the case of witches, spirit walkers, and certain illnesses.

> Dègu recounts that a few years ago he saw his neighbor Yite walking in the fields while they knew that he was severely ill at home. So it must have been his shadow, though at a distance the difference could not be seen. When they came to his house, he had indeed not moved, and they interpreted the vision as his *shinaŋkwe* who went to inspect the place of his future tomb. And of course, Yite died that very same day.

Based on the different characteristics of humans, several special types of persons can be discerned. People with a different shadow have a more ambivalent position in the social and conceptual life of the Kapsiki. Two evil types of *shinaŋkwe* define *mete* and *hweteru* respectively. The first, *mete*, is more or less the classic definition of a witch. Their shadows (or something that looks like their shadow—there is no real consensus on this) resides in their belly and leaves their sleeping body through the anus. Red as fire and with a tail like a bush cat, it sneaks through the night, often flying to eat the—shadow of—the heart of sleeping victims, usually children. A victim whose heart is eaten will become sick, asthmatic, weak, and listless. If the *mete* does not relinquish the heart, the victim will eventually die.

Any *mete* activity is somewhat voluntary, the shadow operating partly on a person's own wish and will, partly from habit and partly by force of the matter in the belly. Some *mete* claim that they have become inactive in this realm: "I am *mete*, but I do not eat anyone. It is in my belly, but it does not come out," one informant claimed. He, in fact, compared the *mete* characteristic with a magical object, something that wanders on its own initiative. Usually people know who is *mete* and who is not, since it is inhererited through the matriline in a predominantly patrilineal society. The Kapsiki have their own social recognition of the (restricted) matriline, *hwelefwe te ma*, so this is also called *hwelefe mete*. In principle, anyone who has a *mete* mother will be *mete* him-/herself, though informants are adamant that more women than men are *mete*. Female *mete* are deemed more active than male ones, and more often they target children, the most vulnerable victims. Male *mete* like to eat the hearts of older men but these usually are well protected. In short, the classic idea that women may be witches and men sorcerers holds for the Kapsiki.

Figure 6.2 Honoring *shala* of the home in the house entrance.

Women who have a *mete* reputation are avoided as marriage partners but usually manage to marry anyway as a second wife; since these tend to come from outside the village so their reputation is unknown. If it does become known, the other men chide the *mete*'s spouse, because he has to become somewhat *mete* himself in order to live with her, and, in the intimacy of the hut, a returning shadow can easily make a mistake and enter through the wrong anus. Thus, children considered *mete* always sleep alone.

Though witchcraft is "something in the belly," a postmortem cannot reveal the true nature of the *mete*; in any event culpability in witchcraft cases is beyond the reach of Kapsiki divination. Divination may indicate that a sick child is suffering from a witch attack, after which the child's father or mother ensures that all known witches are represented in the crab's pot for divination, but even then the diviner's verdict will be vague and can be interpreted in many ways. The crab may tell who is a witch, but never what witch is responsible for a particular misfortune. Before the government forbade witchcraft accusations, parents could bring the affected child to the suspected person, saying: "Here it is, now eat all of it and cook it well." The *mete* was then forced to return the heart's shadow. If this did not happen, after the death of the child one ear of the *mete* would be cut off and s/he was chased out of the village. Things have now changed but what can be made is a general accusation. Just before sunset, the parent picks up the child and cries out loudly: "Let it go, let it go, let go of its heart." According to informants, this action should be enough to frighten the *mete*, who is supposed to be afraid of disclosure and retribution. No names are ever mentioned and the whole exposure remains anonymous. From the 1980s Cameroonian courts started to define witchcraft accusations as admissable in court,[14] but these administrative measures have had no discernible effect in Kapsiki society, since there is no divinatory means of establishing individual guilt. "Who has seen the witch eat the heart in actual fact anyway?" informants ask. At present, the Lamido who serves as a traditional judge is extremely reticent about following up on charges of witchcraft, and if it happens, he will collect the whole maternal family through the accused mother's brother, interview them, and then accept their opinion of themselves as final evidence.

> Ritual means against *mete* are just as anonymous. A healer cooks a special millet mush, stirs it with his right hand, and feeds it to the sick victim in the presence of the bound *mete*, who has to witness the whole procedure. If the *mete* does not return the heart, the *mete* will die. Another way is more mystical: sometimes a wild dog in the bush is spotted with a horn on its head. Whenever one sounds such a *tereme ta shala* (horn of God), all the witches will flee into the bush and die.

In fact, only one ordeal is deemed to give certainty in witchcraft accusations: the rooster ordeal of Rhwemetla (Chapter 4). The god of this mountain holds judgment on all witches: any witch coming in its vicinity will be kept immobile and chained to the ground. Though a gift of some iron beads and a goat would set her free, the whole village would know for sure. Chapter 9 discusses how this ordeal may affect participation in bridal initiation rites, which are held on the same mountain.

> When a half-sister of Teri Puwe (different mother!) approached Rhwemetla, she sang: "If I am a *mete*, the lightning has to strike me and burn away the *mete*." However she was reputedly a witch, and on her way to the mountain a bolt of lightning struck her down: her belly was full of blood but she lived and was no longer a witch.

All in all, Kapsiki is not a witchcraft-ridden society. Though some informants maintain that today's world is full of witches because nobody any longer takes any action against them—a common complaint in Africa[15]—accusations are few and far between, in fact rarely voiced. One reason is that only a few afflictions are attributed to *mete*, and then only in strict combinations: fever, frequent urination, diarrhea without blood, and throbbing veins all combined might raise the suspicion of *mete*. The protection required to combat a *mete* attack, also among children, is common knowledge; though a *mete* affliction can be cured only through the culprit witch self, everybody has *hweɓe* and *haŋgedle* (the two major types of medicinal plants, *Crinum* sp. and *Cissus quadrangularis* respectively) that protect against *mete* risk.

Most of the accusations are directed at people within the ward or the house. Jealousy is thought to trigger the *mete* power in a witch, so culprits are sought among those who exhibit such characteristics, among co-wives, wives of brothers, and half-siblings from the mother's co-wives. In contrast, a lot of stories recount how women from other villages turn out to be witches, serving meat that bystanders cannot see. Other *mete* are told to avoid attacking people by entering the anus of a cow. In addition, there is a whole class of *rhena heca*, folk tales, in which a wife from elsewhere is exposed as being a witch by the youngest of three brothers. But throughout, these stories serve more as amusement than as cautionary tale.

Some people have a different shadow, the *hweteru*; in fact they are another sort of witch that is best translated as "evil eye." They suck blood from their victims, be they humans or animals, and as a consequence these "spoil" and become weak and unproductive. If *hweteru* look at millet it will not ripen, chicken they covet will not lay eggs, and children that arouse their jealousy will not grow up properly. Though death is not the result, there is no cure against these illnesses, only prevention, though luckily this is not hard to find. Anyone can obtain *hweβ ntsu* as a preventive, but since the *hweteru* are triggered only by jealousy, the best remedy is to put any object that arouses greed out of sight. This type of shadow follows the matriline as well but less clearly, and people are not as sure who is *hweteru* and who is not.

At the start of this chapter the spirit walker spoke about himself, an example of the complexity of man. These *keleŋu* have a shadow that leaves them at night through the mouth when their body is sleeping, and joins the shadow of colleagues to wage war on neighboring villages and steal their sorghum. This capacity is inherited patrilineally, but only by one or two sons from each *keleŋu*-father are *keleŋu* themselves. Rumor has it that in two villages on the edge of the Kapsiki area, Kortchi and Tlukwu, inheritance of this trait is bilineal, so all people there must be *keleŋu* or witches, but these kinds of tales abound about any faraway place. People from Kortchi, at least, vehemently deny it.

People know precisely who are *keleŋu* in the villages. It is not a secret, since the category bears no stigma, but it is a private matter, spoken about in the relative privacy of the home and not in public. Most non-smiths who divine with the crab are *keleŋu*, but among the smiths there are none, just as there are no witches or *hweteru* among them. One reason for the *keleŋu* being diviners is that they can indeed see into the future: they note what happens to the shadows of people they see in the bush, and the flesh will then follow the shadow. People have great confidence in their predictions, and whenever a *keleŋu* indicates a sacrifice, it will be performed without delay. The world of the spirit walkers is a replica of the visible world: they have a chief, either male or female.

In Mogode the chief *keleŋu* is a woman, Kuve Dεtε. Any sacrifice she indicates has to be performed. Whenever her own home sacrifice is due, the regular village chief has to perform it, and it is he who shouts out at night warning the village folk not to go out in the fields. And whenever she has her own home sacrifice, nobody may touch hoe, axe, or sickle. That day nobody leaves the village or sleeps in. She sacrifices a black billy goat, with the chief and the chief smith waiting in the forecourt of her compound. After the sacrifice, the village chief lends her the iron staff that represents the village, which she holds while receiving people.

The most important spirit endeavor is stealing sorghum from another village. Of course, they just steal the *shinaŋkwe* of the sorghum, and that comes to the fore only when the bereaved ones try to thresh their harvest. Though the ears appear full to the eye, after threshing, hardly anything remains, it withers away. The little that does enter the granary disappears quickly "as if it is cursed." It is impossible to ascertain which *keleŋu* is responsible, so prevention is the only way. People encircle their sorghum fields with specific *hwεβε* (*Crinum* sp.) and *haŋgedle* (*Cissus quadrangularis*), plant a protective black sorghum variety along the perimeter of the field, and encircle it with thorn bushes, which is effective against goats too. Any *keleŋu* thief of sorghum experiences the opposite: his sorghum never runs out, his granary never empties, and he does not have to cultivate much to have enough sorghum.

The spirit walkers (or spirit stealers) are stereotypically thin and always have a drop of white stuff in their eye, which helps them to see others. They explain this as follows: "Whoever takes eye dirt from a dog's eye can see *gutuli*, like a *keleŋu*, for any dog is like a *keleŋu*: it can see Death, see the *gutuli*, that is why it howls at night." Being a spirit walker is not without its risks though, since it involves one in conflicts, and, some *keleŋu* state, there are those of the "day" and those of the "night," meaning that most of them do honorable things, like stealing from another village, but a few just provoke battles. The Sirakuti war mentioned in Chapter 3, was according to the *keleŋu*, started by a *keleŋu* kill during a night raid; at the next funeral the people from Mogode provoked the culprit *keleŋu* from Sirakuti by hunting monkeys on their territory and gathering the funeral symbols near their village. Our opening speaker, Vandu Kwadeva, explains:

> Nobody just dies without a cause. If you do not die from *besheŋu* (magic) then it is because you are *keleŋu* and die in battle or from fever; the serpent or the arrow of the witch can kill you. If you are young, these are the causes of death, at least if you bring your sacrifices to *shala* and do not do evil.

Myth, History, and Hwempetla, the Village Hero

The unseen world, the "other side," is the subject of tales about the distant past, although in fact there are few tales that can easily be classified as myths. A very common story, told in many groups including the Kapsiki, is that of the separation of heaven and earth, but in Kapsiki it is seldom told and bears no relation to any specific ritual.

> Heaven used to be very close to the earth, and people had to bend over continuously. Any food they took was straight from heaven, above them. One day a young girl found sorghum grains on the ground and started to pound them, her pounding stick going straight into the face of heaven. Heaven withdrew, and she kept going till heaven was far away. Now people have to cultivate and eat sorghum.[16]

Müller-Kosack says of the Mafa, the Kapsiki's northern neighbors: "Mythological imagination is more concerned with transformational issues and matters of maintenance and change than cosmological structures."[17] Indeed, the mythical corpus of the Kapsiki does answer "why?" questions, but of a restricted kind. For instance, "why smiths?" is answered in Kapsiki by a tale of how someone acted oddly, ate prohibited meat, and thus was relegated to the category of smith, but that category already exists and no tale explains its origins. The main rituals in Kapsiki are sometimes accompanied by myths, but most are not, and even if they are, the relationship with the ritual is ambivalent. Some tales illustrate encounters with risks such as death, epidemics, periodic drought and rain, but here too the corpus is restricted, as is the scope of the questions posed and answered by the tales.

The Kapsiki distinguish between folk tales and the "history of the village" tales that I call myths. The corpus of the first, called *rhena heca* (old words), runs into the hundreds,[18] just tales and not so much riddles, dilemma tales, or proverbs. Mythical tales are named after the main protagonist and deemed the "history of the village," and they are dominated by the story of the village hero, Hwempetla. His exploits form the main point of reference for several rituals as well as for village identity. The other myths of origin are tales of migration—how people came to the area for the first time. For the Kapsiki, they came from just beyond the confines of the Mandara Mountains, in fact from several points of origin but none very far away, as is told in Chapter 3. Here is the foundation tale of Mogode, characteristic of such tales, told by Teri Puwe:

> The first Kapsiki came from Gudur, from where they moved to Sirak and from there to Mogode. There someone tricked them, as they had grown numerous, with many families. There is a cave there and he told

them: "When you see fire over the Nzambe Mountain, you have to go into the cave." The next morning they saw fire above Nzambe [the sun rising in the east] and said: "That is what the man indicated," and went into the cave. The man in question knew his territory, came with a lot of straw, and set fire to it, fanning the smoke into the opening. A certain Ngweɗu, who was there with his sister, cut open his leather sack and wrapped it around his and his sister's heads. It was very hot but they survived; *shala* saved them, while all the others died. After two days they came out, left the cave, and looked around. No one was in sight. "Sister, let us climb that mountain, we are going nowhere." They went through the *rhwamerhe* [river of the chief] toward Rhuŋgeɗu, which was full of thorns, and cut a way through. On top of the mountain they looked around and saw fire in Guria. "I will go there to get fire, you stay here," Ngweɗu said, "I will get fire." "Do not get caught," his sister said. "If they catch me, you will look for other people" he said and went to the mountain.

"I have come because I saw your fire, and I want to ask you for fire," he told the people of Guria. They said: "Why should we give you fire, because then you would owe us? Where do you live?"

"I live over there on that mountain."

"OK, I will give you the fire but you will remain in my debt. I will not let you die from cold, but from every cow you slaughter, the head is mine. Even if you kill a goat, its head is mine. So take the fire as a loan from me."[19]

Ngweɗu went home and lit a fire. "I have got fire. We'll stay here, on top of the mountain, and we will build our home here." His sister agreed: "Yes, we will stay here." So they built their home and lived there. "You are my wife now, I will not let you go," Ngweɗu said to his sister. She became pregnant and had a son, Teri Dingu, who became Hwempetla's father.

This story outlines the provenance of the village, a relationship of dependence on Guria, and the birth of Hwempetla, the great cultural hero of Mogode. And it is Hwempetla who is the center of the most important tales, so the tale of origin of the village in fact is the preface for the main character, from which most major clans in the village claim descent.

The second and crucial part of the tale is about Hwempetla or Nayekwakeɗɛ. I expected every village to have such a cultural hero but that is not the case. Hwempetla is the hero of most Kapsiki villages but is almost always defined as belonging to the village of Mogode, more in the sphere of a legend than a myth maybe. Only one village, Kortchi, has a similar tale on Nikukuɗ, a variant of Nayekwakeɗɛ in the language of Kortchi. The story of Hwempetla starts with his miraculous birth followed by his exploits in stealing cattle from the neighboring village of Guria and the subsequent war with Guria, which was won by a stranger who joined Hwempetla during the battle. Later on other newcomers also joined him and would become ancestors of other clans. I start the text when he was established as chief (for the complete text see Appendix A) since it is the part most closely associated with rituals.

> Hwempetla became the village chief. He wanted a wife so he tried to steal Rain's daughter, but every time he came near her, Rain started to groan, and he ultimately got tired of the game. "Why do you want to steal my daughter? Maybe you will succeed, but then rain will fall continuously on your little piece of land and drought will reign elsewhere. Your fields will be washed away by the rain. If that is what you want, you would be stupid. You have to go down to the earth, and I will stay up here to go from village to village until the end of the world."
> "So you will not give me your child?"
> "No, I will not give her to you."

Then Rain and Hwempetla made a wager. Rain would grant Hwempetla a favor if he could hide for eight days. Hwempetla left and hid in a beer jar between the sorrel which is kept there, in Rain's very house. Then Rain started his search: he came with enormous winds, tore trees down, and destroyed houses and termite hills. Everywhere he searched, in mouse holes, under stones, everywhere. Exhausted, he returned home after eight days and found Hwempetla, who told him that he was in the sorrel, inside the beer jar.

"You are right," Rain said. "I have ransacked the whole earth and did not find you because you were in my own house. I am for everyone, not for someone particular. If you and your small mountain are thirsty, then you have to tell me so. You tell me: 'I am thirsty,' and then I will come and pour myself out on your mountain. Do not buy rain from someone else but come and ask me for it," Rain told him. And so Hwempetla did.

When Hwempetla was approaching the end of his days he told his people: "I liberated you from our enemies and I will try to liberate you from Death as well. If I do my utmost, I should succeed." So when his time came, he thought: "With my powers I should succeed, I will be too quick for Death." He took his bull's skin and flew through the air. Death chased him, faster and faster, and threatened to overtake him. Hwempetla tried to throw off Death by flying straight through a mountain, but Death still followed him.[20] Then he tried to hide from Death but to no avail. He hid in a thorn bush but Death found him. He hid inside a bundle of roofing straw, but Death found him. He hid inside a termite hill, but his hair stuck out and gave him away. He hid inside a hollow baobab tree, but Death saw him. He then dug himself into the stem of the sorrel and made himself very small. For four days and nights Death searched everywhere—in the straw, in the pool, in a well—but there was no sign of Hwempetla. Then at last Death saw a toe sticking out of the sorrel because the stem was too small. So finally Hwempetla had to admit defeat. "If the sorrel had been larger, I could have beaten Death," he said to his people. "For you, my people, there is no use trying to hide from Death, but prepare yourself for a dignified end, as I will do shortly. Wrap me inside the skin of my bull and during the dance the smith has to carry me on his shoulders and my wife should hold the bull's tail. When you hear a whooshing noise, I will be gone. Then go to a spot in the bush with a lot of flies, above two holes in the ground. Finish my tomb and my wife's tomb there." And so it happened. During the dance, Hwempetla flew off the smith's shoulders, pulling his wife behind him by the tail. People started searching the bush and finally found two holes in the ground, covered with fleas. They made two graves and covered them with leaves.[21]

In some respects this does look like a hero's tale, but then Hwempetla does not leave the village and does no great deeds elsewhere. His only relevance is for the villages themselves, Mogode and Kortchi. In fact a hero such as Hwempetla is quite irresponsible in starting a war with Guria which he would have lost if not for the unplanned arrival of a stranger; and his bet with Rain is just as irregular, and his request is correctly defined as "stupid"; his wise opponent has to transform it into a sensible proposition. Hwempetla's struggle with Death is not successful either, though it does underscore his superhuman abilities—he can fly!—and also highlights his surrender. Even Hwempetla cannot escape his fate, so we all remain mortal.

The myth addresses ritual to a limited extent. In Hwempetla's story, the Kapsiki burial ritual is redefined, and the rain ritual is abolished. At least this particular village is liberated from the ascendancy of rain makers (including the Guria one). This latter element implies full autonomy for the village, as the rain rituals form a special link with the ancestral village of Gudur, the mythical place of origin of many Mandara groups, and Gudur ritual power still touches many villages (see Chapter 7). However, it is not an etiological myth, since the Kapsiki funeral already exists in the tale and the Hwempetla story just highlights one element—the simulacrum of the flight of the corpse on the smith's shoulders from the dancing ground to the grave. Some details of the tale, such as his wife holding on to the bull's tail and the flying, are easy to interpret as the charter for those aspects of Kapsiki burial. After all, the widow dances with the bull's tail, and the smith runs as fast as he can toward the grave with the corpse around his neck, the deceased's gown flapping in the wind. But the Kapsiki never explain this aspect by referring to the tale of Hwempetla. The rain hunt, on the other hand, is explained by the tale but mainly the fact that the rain-hunting party takes care of the graves of Hwempetla and his wife. The main explanation of the myth is why they do not perform a ritual that is well established in the area—rain making. And as we shall see in the next chapter, they do engage in some rain rituals anyway.

The struggle with death tells us nothing about how death came into the world but does tell us why everyone has to succumb to it. It is not the situation in the world that is the explanandum but the submission of mankind to the conditions already prevalent in the world, as well as the way of achieving the best outcome in a difficult situation. The focus is on the human condition and lived reality, and not the virtual reality of history. Telling the tale of Hwempetla is a way of dwelling on the environment, its own history, and bridging the time between then and now. In that way, telling the tale of Hwempetla is in itself a ritual, a "machine à supprimer le temps."

This tale is not specifically told during a ritual or at the time of a burial or initiation. Parts of the story are told for an appreciative audience, usually by a good storyteller like Teri Puwe. The version cited above is well known. The story is remarkably stable and has changed very little: the versions collected in 1972, 1994, and 2009 show almost no differences. The favorite occasion is a gathering of men in which one elder, possibly a ward chief or the village chief, deems it wise to use the story for a particular didactic purpose. Though the performance needs no specific setting, the telling in itself is quite a performance if done well. Because of the extraordinary wealth of idiophones in Kapsiki, a good raconteur makes the story come alive for his audience as any relevant action is accompanied by its idiophone; thus his enraptured audience hears arrows whistle, people running, cattle mooing, and enemies dying.

Some folk tales surround the myth of Hwempetla, having the same story lines, the same themes, and, to some extent, the same characters. The usual hero of the folk tales is the ground squirrel, clever, wily, and full of tricks. His adversary is usually the leopard or the hyena, both dumb, strong, and easy to trick. The Hwempetla theme of trying to outwit Death or Rain is also told with the squirrel as protagonist. In the squirrel version, the ending is different: the squirrel marries Rain's daughter and gives an elephant as bridewealth. To trick his father-in-law, he eats the elephant from the inside, helped by the leopard, and then arranges it so that the angry Rain catches the leopard in "flagrante delicto." The squirrel dallies with Death, giving Death a terrible punishment, centering—again—on the anus.[22] So the difference between the myth and the folk tale is not overly clear and the boundaries become vague. Yet for the Kapsiki, the genres are distinct. For them, the story of Hwempetla is just that, the story of Hwempetla, and it is deemed to be completely historical.

Exegetical Reflection, Agency, and Invisibility

The world invoked, for instance, by the Hwempetla myths is very much the one we know, our daily reality and our direct environment. The tales may tell us why there is a specific hole in the mountain, why the smith has to run with the corpse on his shoulder, stipulating that we have always performed the ritual dances that we do. And even the origins of man mean the origins of the first man and woman in the village or group. The world as a whole is not invoked, nor are the cosmos or the basic facts of life: the existence of death—or Death—is clear, and social categories such as smiths already exist in the oldest tales. The myths indicate that we cannot escape our fate, our "condition humaine", but that we have to live with it. And to live to the full, we have to exert ourselves, to follow the instructions of those that knew and to work at our own lives. It is not the etiology of death that is important here or the cosmo*logy*, and certainly not any cosmo*gony*, but instead it is the existential fact of living, of dwelling in this world.

In fact the notion of *shala* is just that, a very human expression of individuality, with the message that one belongs where one is. One almost stereotypical aspect of an African religion is missing: the notion of ancestors. *Shala* is neither an ancestor, nor a spirit, nor a real high god. The usual categories just do not match.[23] What makes it confusing is the referential domination of the concept, which means that the term *shala* can be used in many expressions, all of which relate to just *shala*. So the core of Kapsiki religion is an almost purely relational concept, part of a human-based social theology. It took me some time to realize that I had never used the notion of "spirit" in my translation of *shala*, and indeed the Kapsiki discourse on *shala* never evoked the notion of what is traditionally called a spirit. After all, a spirit is the supernatural "other," a being that has its own volition and agency, but *shala* is the "supernatural *self*," thus the volition and agency of a person and his *shala* coincide.

Neither is the notion of ancestors applicable. Ancestors in African religions seem almost a must, so why are they absent here?[24] Is Hwempetla an ancestor? Technically, as the progenitor of many clans, yes, but on the other hand he is not the founder of the village. And all villages other than Mogode and Kortchi, do not "own" his exploits, nor do they have such a village hero themselves. The Kapsiki use the term *heshi*, the "grandfathers," those who went before us, but as a very general term, never used in invocations during sacrifice, nor referred to in divination. Also Hwempetla is never addressed for intercession. Even in the rain hunt, when people pray at his grave, they pray to *shala*, without Hwempetla's help, at his tomb, simply because he did have a special relation with rain. Also divination never pinpoints the kindred dead as instigators of mishaps or bad luck, and the sacrifices are not directed to the ancestors. To the father, yes, and sometimes a grandfather, if recently dead, but that is where the buck stops.

The point here is that Kapsiki religion, because of the specific notion of *shala* as a "supernatural" double, in fact has no cognitive space for an intermediary between man and god. The relations in Kapsiki religion are direct and short, just to the dead father, just to the personal *shala*, one's double-up-there, no second layer, no intermediaries or go-betweens.[25] The notion of *shala* is so completely relational that the type of exegesis in which I have engaged is not done unless some anthropologist—or missionary—starts prodding. Whitehouse characterizes imagistic concepts as prone to spontaneous exegetical reflection but a restricted one, and that is exactly what happens here. There is a definite gap between discourse on *shala* and any kind of systematization of a cosmology or theology on *shala*. The clearest indication of the vagueness of *shala*, is the notion of *gutuli*: on the one hand *gutuli* is the expression of the ambivalence of *shala*, on the other hand it is the ethical opposite of *shala*. Thus it was cognitively easy to transform this flexible and uncrystalized discourse on *shala* and *gutuli* into the Muslim and Christian notions of a High God and his opposing demons, and that is exactly what has happened. In the course of my research, from 1972 to 2010, a general shift toward more monotheistic notions has been clear, also toward more of the generic names of *shala pelɛ rhweme*, like *Jigelafte*, while the discourse on *gutuli* has diminished.

The question then is raised whether this Kapsiki/Higi notion of a personal *shala*, as an intensely relational concept, is minimally counterintuitive like the notions of spirit, god, or ancestor are considered to be.[26] In one sense, it definitely is. *Shala* is the unseen version of "person," the being that is one echelon higher than oneself and thus looks like the others, an "optimal" concept. Ancestors are such an optimal concept as well—dead relatives who are still around and behave very much like family does, ever present, sometimes helpful but at times quite obnoxious. Spirits, similarly, are optimal ideas: persons, but without a body, who share the characteristics of individuality and character but lack corporeal limitations and advantages. But the notion of *shala* is more complicated, since it shifts with the group in question, with the discourse, and with the environment the speakers are in. The relevant denotation is not fixed, but purely relational. That makes it a rather difficult concept, one that easily shifts either into a simple one-to-one relationship, like a spirit guardian or familiar spirit, or into a high god. Also, for outsiders reporting on the religion, this is a difficult concept; missionaries easily relegate a notion such as *shala* either to the idea of a guardian spirit or to the category of full-blown or incipient high god,[27] focusing either on the personal or the supernatural aspect. I have the impression that a similar dynamic occurs with the Mafa *Jigile* concept.[28]

> When I presented my 1987 book to a meeting of the Higi traditional authorities in Michika, they understood my interest in the traditional religion very well. At my leaving their meeting, one of them—a devout Muslim—assured me: "There is really only one *shala*, please remember, one *shala* only." One folk tale in Kapsiki does precisely this, telling of a Kapsiki who consistently avows that there is one *Shala* only, in heaven, and who becomes very, very pious indeed. This story closely ties in with Islamic discourse, but the main gist is not a refutation of traditional Kapsiki belief, but a precision. The missionaries and the muslim did not introduce a new concept, they just restricted the existing one.

With a complicated-but-vague concept such as *shala*, it is telling indeed that the elders are not the exegetical experts, but the *keleŋu* and the smiths. These are the relative outsiders, the internal "others" who by their position at the rim of society have accrued exegetical authority. Here it is not ritual that stimulates the exegesis, so neither the frequency nor the exuberance of the ritual—the basic distinction in the modes theory—invokes exegesis, but the inherent challenges within the concept itself, based as it is on the complexities of social life. *Shala* is definitely counterintuitive, but no longer minimal.

So the core characteristic of Kapsiki cosmology is not so much the absence of exegesis but the human complexity of the exegesis, the fact that concepts are part of intricate relations between people. The gods are not so much anthropomorphic as anthroposocial: in my words the gods dwell here among us. And "here" is recognizable—"look, that hole in that mountain over there"—and immediate, bringing the scale of the world down to human measurements and standards. Kapsiki religion offers a window on ourselves, our humanity, our fate, our destiny, and on the ways we can make this restricted life into something worthwhile, not everlasting but interesting for the short, fleeting moment that each of us dwells on his own small patch of middle earth.

7

Rain and the Cycle of Ritual

Initiating a Granary

It is January 1989 and the harvest comes in. Vandu Da, from the village of Mogode, is inaugurating his *tame* today, the straw-plaited granary that forms the center of the Kapsiki household. His friends, lineage members, and some neighbors have gathered in his compound and sit in the forecourt, chatting and commenting on the progress of the work. Some have already started drinking. The village chief, the ward chief, and the head of the clan responsible for the village sacrifice are among them, as are some elders of the sublineage involved.

The *tame* itself—a straw cone that is the height of a man and with an opening at the top—offers the best example of Kapsiki plaiting prowess (Figure 7.1).

> Making a straw granary is difficult, and only a few men in the village are good at it. They are invited to supervise the proceedings, though many help gather the grasses and plait the main elements of the *tame*. Each part of the *tame* is plaited from specific grasses. Several layers of straw form an inner cone that is sewn to a double bottom and to a strengthened collar. The first phase is to make the circular bottom, starting with an oval-shaped mat made of *haze* (*Cymbopogon*) which is folded and fastened. Then some *tere* grasses (*Vetiveria zizanoïdes*, Nash. L) are plaited into long sturdy bands that are fastened on a cone shape made of the same grass. The most delicate work is making the collar, the "mouth." With a thin band of *haze*, the plaiter makes a sturdy cylinder, which he gives a round, even finish with small bands of thin *tere*. For the closing cover, another grass is used, and then the whole *tame* gets a cloak of ordinary straw against the rain.

The week before, Viyima, a good plaiter and a close patrilineal kinsman of Vandu, had fastened the double bottom, the most difficult part of the work. The last phase is now in progress and involves sewing the second layer to the cone itself and fixing the collar. Two of Vandu's younger brothers are inside the

Figure 7.1 The *tame* gets its dung decoration.

granary, and two experienced plaiters, one a neighbor and the other a sister's son, sew the last bands to the main cone from the outside with straw rope. One of the helpers is a recent initiate (*gwela*), as should be the case. He makes a mistake and is chastised, but not too harshly since his presence is more essential than his plaiting skills. The men have started early in the morning because the work has to be finished by noon. During its initiation, the sun has to shine straight into the *tame*. Demashi, the other boy inside, comes out because the others have to clean it before it can be used. Teri Sha, Vandu's maternal cousin, wants to help Demashi but others restrain him: "Don't touch the *tame*, Teri. You just sit at the roadside and you never cultivate. Just keep plaiting the cord, and leave the *tame* alone." Teri Sha desists good-humoredly; he does indeed never cultivate and, as a cattle-rich man with no family, can afford a leisurely old age, selling off his cattle one by one. The village chief retorts: "We sit too, and we never touch the *tame*. Does that mean we don't have to cultivate either?" Demashi tells them: "A man should have a *tame*, a real man. Even if you have no sorghum in it, it is better to have an empty *tame* than none at all." "I do have a *tame*," claims Teri Sha, "and it is indeed empty." Lèwa, a lineage elder, teases the popular old man: "You just sit at the roadside; how could your *tame* be anything but empty?" "Do I sit alone?" asks Teri Sha. "Look at the others!" "Indeed, Vasekwa (Vandu's older brother) is always with you." Lèwa readily admits this, enjoying the slight rebuff of his lineage brother, who is strutting around directing the work as if he owns the place.

The conversation turns to the bands of cattle dung which have to be put on the *tame*, as the decoration and "initiation" of the granary. Comparing these with the ocher markings on the *gwela* (a boy initiate, see Chapter 10), Lèwa remarks: "If the *gwela* is not marked with ocher, who will recognize him as a *gwela*?" "Three or four stripes on the *tame*?" someone asks. The men decide that this *tame* has a female form that is round and squat and so it has to be four. If it had been long and slender (male form), it would have to be three. There is barely enough cow dung for the decoration, but the bands at the bottom should be done anyway. Lèwa applies them meticulously, the rest of the men watching intently. Teri Sha brings some thorn bush and a special grass (*haze, Cymbopogon*), which is as essential in the inauguration of the granary as it is in a boy's initiation ceremony. One of the young men remarks that this is the first time he has seen a *tame* "married." "Yes, of course, nowadays the *tame* is usually bought," explains Teri Sha, "then there is no *wume* (marriage, bridewealth, initiation)."

With the dung decoration in place and the mouth of the granary adorned with *haze*, the *tame* is now an initiate, and the final blessing is due. Especially the *haze* is important here, sometimes with another grass instead of *safa*. The village officiator Deli Zra throws in two pebbles, imitating sheep bleating and cattle mooing: "*Mèè, mèè, wuwu, wuwu*." The ritual part is now in progress but some of the younger ones have only partial knowledge of it. The sons of Vandu bring sesame in indigenous vinegar, but the older men explain that it is used only when the *tame* is filled for the first time; then you put it on the rim, saying: "*keleŋeleŋu na* (be healthy)." The neighborhood women watch from a distance, since this is a man's job. Deli Zra then gets some sorghum mush with sauce, puts two bits on the "mouth" of the granary, and addresses it: "The man has to fill you with sorghum and get goats. You have to pay a lot of things; you must be filled; please keep us cool." He then calls Vandu, the owner, from the edge of the compound and makes him stand next to the *tame*. "Here, take it; I have to feed you and do not chew. Just swallow it." Deli throws some pebbles and goat dung into the *tame*, again imitating goats bleating and cattle mooing. The pebbles in question are called "sorghum stones."

Afterwards, the men try to estimate the capacity of the *tame*. Teri Sha thinks it will hold about 19–20 baskets at first harvest and after the granary has been filled a few times, up to 25 baskets: it is a good *tame*. But then, as most realize, the amount put into the *tame* is not always the same as the amount coming out. Some *tame*, they explain to me, eat their own sorghum: "You can put in 30 but only 20 will come out. A good *tame* takes 20 and gives 30, but then you have to have good magic."

As with all Kapsiki rituals, this one ends with a communal meal and drinking. The workers get a special place in the entrance hut. Deli Zra calls them to eat with him: "I'll eat the neck of the mouse, the rest is for you." All of them join in the special meal, as field mice—a delicacy—have been cooked specially for this truly festive sauce. Banter arises about someone who did not work but is eating mice all the same: a lazy one. The workers all take two helpings. Teri Sha crunches a mouse's head loudly and clearly. The other guests have other meat and stress the importance of the mice: "Sauce made with mice is not to be slighted. Catching them is dangerous" (because serpents live in their holes). Someone asks for the meat and, pointing to two nephews vying for the rest of it, Teri Sha remarks: "Look, this is what we want. This is why we say that you have to work. But you youngsters, you want just to stroll about. Can you eat without cultivating? Can that man build a *tame* without cultivating? You may mock me now, but I have grown old with the Fulbe. In the past, we cultivated, we married. Now, with your father alive, you wander through the village, you frequent the Fulbe quarter, and your father suffers at home. He sees you return empty-handed. Did you ever see the Fulbe become like us black people? Who has ever tied the antelope skin to a Fulbe [sign of initiation]?"

These habitual admonitions and challenges to the younger generation go on for some time until the beer is brought in. Then conversation is quenched in some serious drinking and less serious exchanges.

Dwelling is about coping with a risky environment, about collective risks for agriculture and for life itself. Risk here is collective, risk for the crops, and risk for health. In this chapter we will consider rain, locusts, and epidemics, the boons of and threats to existence, in short the risks that are part of the larger fabric of Mandara ecology. Life is risky, living alone is even riskier.

Preparation for the agricultural season is done individually as each cultivator consults the crab to know exactly how to start the first agricultural activities: what kind of sowing should be done, what sacrifices should be held. An example of a diviner's advice: "Put a bowl of beer dregs on the field that you are going to start with one night. Then sow the first sorghum in the bush. After that sow a little next to the house, and finally some in the field. Then you take the bowl home and eat the dregs."

The seed grains from the previous season have been stored hanging either from trees in the case of maize or, in the case of millet and sorghum, kept on top of the granary. On the morning of the first sowing, the father of the house pours some beer on his *mele*, sows the whole day long, and then invites the elders of the ward for the next morning. He then explains that "he has put some grains in water" (i.e. brewed some beer) and the assembled group voices its consent and also its hope that the sorghum will grow well. The actual date of sowing depends on various factors, the principal one being the onset of the rains. People sow after an early rain, and if the first rains are late, they use as a signal for sowing the arrival of the *yara*, a small long-beaked bird with a green breast that comes from the east.[1] Without rain, the soil is so dry that no seeds will ever germinate. After sowing, several dangers threaten the crop. First, rain has to fall in the right amount and at the right time; in April 2009 a sudden heavy shower surprised people, confusing some of them into sowing, but in vain. Second, parasites may attack the young crop, and third, a ripening harvest can be stolen from the fields; that problem can be addressed by rituals. There is no ritual to stimulate growth, since that happens naturally and ritual in Kapsiki is aimed at preventing unnatural barriers to natural processes. "Do not disturb" is the main motto in the growing season: do not disturb the growing process by shouting too loudly, wailing, or playing certain types of music such as flutes that summon the wind. The closer the harvest is, the stronger the taboos. Before the sacrifice on *shala*, any festive dance is absolutely taboo.

Hunting Rain

As so often in Africa, rain is a major focus of ritual attention. Many Kapsiki villages have a rain maker, a *melu* (non-smith) claiming direct descent from Gudur, the mythical place of origin of the Kapsiki (and of many groups in the region).[2] On demand and for payment, he will perform rituals to procure rain; hence this ritual is called "buying rain." Mogode does not have its own rain maker, since Hwempetla discouraged his descendants from "buying rain." But the neighboring villages of Guria, Sirakuti, Gwava, Wula, Garta, Kortchi, Tlukwu, and Muzuku do have them, the most famous being those in Tlukwu, Sirakuti, and Muzuku. Some 23 villages "buy rain," while the others, like Mogode, perform a communal ritual to get rain. To "ask for rain," the Mogode variant, is also a ritual, a "rain hunt." Rain rituals are done when a dry spell occurs after the first rains, when the first sowing is at risk. Usually one of the old men takes the initiative and suggests to the village chief that the time has come for the *peli va*, the rain hunt.

In 1989 it is Deli Maze, one of the elders of the *maze* clan, who tells the chief that the time is ripe. That evening the chief shouts everywhere in the village that the next day nobody should "touch his hoe": no one is to cultivate, everyone has to participate in the ritual. Some 50 young men assemble the next day and set out hunting. The course they follow is about the same as the one for the ritual first hunt (see below). The main difference is that this hunt is the scene of a series of small rituals at some sacred spots, the most important being, of course, the graves of Hwempetla and his wife. The first stop is the abandoned house of someone who was, indeed, a *ndemeva* (rain maker) in Mogode in the past. Few people know his name but his clan is well known: he was a *makwiyɛ* clansman. It was he who came with the first migration from Gudur to Mogode, carrying a jar for rain rituals with him, a *melɛ va*. When he fled the village during the Hamman Yaji wars and the jar fell into disuse, the people of Mogode harked back to their Hwempetla tradition, since the old *melɛ* was nowhere to be found.

The ritual action is standard in all cases: the hunting party takes branches with leaves from the bush and runs toward the spot, shouting: *a 'ya ndere 'ya, a 'ya ndere 'ya* (I am thirsty, I am thirsty) and then covers the object in question with leaves. Once it is covered, they dance around it, playing their open reed-flutes, singing *Kwaftɛa Magwed'a* (real Mogodian who cultivates yellow sorghum).[3] The first leg is the ruins of the rain maker's hut, the second is toward the northeast in the ward of Devu where an old grindstone is washed with beer, a recent addition to the ritual. In this ward, a certain Perete started washing this grindstone with beer at the start of the season, "amusing himself," but lo and behold rain followed so his descendant kept up the good work, and it is now part of the program.

The hunt then moves off toward the southeast in the direction of the Nzambe outcropping, where close to the mountain a two-meter-high boulder is split vertically. Chanting and dancing, the party pulls out the old leaves from the crevice, and fills it with fresh leaves, meticulously chasing all the male lizards out of the area (Figure 7.2). It is believed that these lizards can stop rain if they climb on the rock and look in the direction the rain is coming from. One guilty lizard is killed and buried at the foot of the rock.

Just a few hundred meters away a 60 cm oblong granite rock is deemed to have fallen out of the sky; shot through with a small layer of yellow, it looks like sideburns, so it is indeed called *Kwabelɛha* (sideburns) and is now covered with leaves.

Figure 7.2 Looking for a guilty lizard.

The party then turns to the south and southwest toward the empty compound of a certain Mata Kweji Yarhwé, who has no connection with rain but, in the past, reputedly performed a ritual against the parasites that ate sorghum leaves. This particular parasite has become rare and the ritual has been abandoned, but his house has become a stopover in the rain hunt. His personal stone, *geŋa* (see Chapter 12), which still stands in the abandoned forecourt, is the object of attention. Now the party is close to the main goal of the hunt, the tombs of Hwempetla and his wife. These are recognizable as small earth mounds covered with old leaves, surrounded by quite a few ancient grindstones. Now all are washed with beer, the graves are cleaned and covered with fresh leaves, and the singing becomes more intense: "I am thirsty, I am thirsty." Some people have taken the shortcut from the village, so the crowd is much larger here; a flute group has brought their reed flute, *zuvu*, and now play while dancing around the tomb. This main part of the ritual completed, the whole party returns to the village, stopping at Rhuŋgeɗu, the mountain where the village started and Hwempetla lived. After singing and dancing at the foot of the ancestral mountain, the whole group returns to the village just after noon.

This rain hunt is a typical example of the cumulative nature of ritual: the course of the hunt and the ritual spots form an open system into which new elements are easily fitted, either from local history or from other groups. The ritual is not a closed system but an agglutination of ritual elements which may easily come from outside the area. The various elements are added without any conflict, whatever their provenance, resulting in a replay of history, which the hunt embodies, highlighting specific episodes in the village past.

What is characteristic in the rain hunt is not so much the insistence on rain but the elimination of all obstacles against rain: after quelling the wind and avoiding wayward lizards, they finally ask the cultural hero for rain. A lack of rain means that something is blocking the natural cause of things, and the rituals aim to restore the natural order. Religion is a way into normality, not excess, for the Kapsiki. As such, the ritual breathes its ecological and social history on the one hand, and the main social values of the society on the other. When rain does not fall, after an unsuccessful rain hunt the village will wonder who has stopped or "tied up" the rain. People can just as easily be the cause of drought, and quite a few claim to be able to halt rain. Rain makers purportedly are able to do this and often also claim they can construct a rainbow to stop the rain, either because they feel underappreciated or because they have to procure rain in another village. People from one's own village can, however, also pull off this kind of mischief.

> In Mogode in the late 1970s Miɗi from the ward Teki claims to have tied up the rain until he was paid to loosen it again. At first, the village chief is adamantly against paying him, not wanting to give in to this kind of blackmail. But a ward member gives Miɗi three pieces of tobacco and a

chicken, because the miscreant is a good friend of the Wula rain maker and might have picked up knowledge from him. That evening Miɗi goes into the bush and a little rain falls on the village. But the ward chief wants to follow up on this: "If Miɗi is telling the truth, then he has spoiled the village, and if he is lying then he is also spoiling the village." So he has the canton chief, the Fulbeized Kapsiki who is in charge of the Cameroonian Kapsiki villages, summon the accused. However, Miɗi does not show up and the canton chief does not want to pursue the matter: "These are all lies. In each village someone claims to halt the rain and wants to get paid. If someone really has a melɛ for the rain, it might work, but this can never come from one person." The village chief decides to ask Miɗi whether this is true, but the culprit is nowhere to be found. However, the people of the ward are convinced that their actions had procured the desired rain. An old man, in the retinue of the chief, chides them: "In Mogode nobody buys rain from a person. If we do, we will die. Hwempetla told us that repeatedly." And to prove his point and drive home his argument, he then tells the story of Hwempetla and the rain. One of the young men from the Teki ward counters: "But we cannot just let our crops die. It is better to try it out; if he lies, we will see it, and if it is true, we can give him something. Trying does not do any harm." The village chief explains the procedure with the court summons and expresses his own disbelief. In the end Miɗi stays away for another week and comes home only after a heavy shower has sent everyone into the fields; then nobody bothers any longer. However, when Miɗi is struck by lightning in a neighboring village two years later, nobody in Teki or Mogode is in the least surprised!

The apparent contradiction between Mogode historically having a rain maker and the dominant founding myth of Hwempetla never generated any comments among my informants. When confronted with it, they shrugged their shoulders: "History is what it is."

The rain hunt described above is not a great success: the wind is quelled but no rain comes. After a week without rain, the chief asks Lèwa, the *mnzefɛ* (ritual elder of the *ŋacɛ* clan), to wash the grindstone on Rhuŋgeɗu, but Lèwa refuses, afraid of falling down the mountain. In itself this is not a high risk, since the mountain is easy to climb, but he is afraid anyway. Indeed, his father has done this but not he himself, and the mountain is a scary place. Respecting his fear, the chief asks Teri Kuve. The choice seems strange, since Teri is not an autochthonous Mogodian, but his lineage does stem from a rain maker in Wula, so "he has business with Rain," and his ancestors even came from Gudur, the ultimate source of rain. One early morning a week after the hunt Teri Kuve performs the ritual and when indeed rain pours down the next day, Teri walks through the village a very proud man. That is exactly how the story is told to me: anyone who washes the stone will not return home dry. Teri's success here not only means rain at that time but also implies that the next year he and later his descendants will continue this ritual. Ritual authority is as good as one's last project, an illustration of the notion that tradition is about authority and performance, not history.

How to Buy Rain: Rain and Power

Buying rain means paying a rain maker to perform the ritual he is in charge of. The ritual itself is not overly complicated, resembling more than anything else a home sacrifice: a private ritual inside the compound of the rain maker. The example comes from my first fieldwork period in the summer of 1973 and takes place in Guria, the southern neighbor of Mogode. I had already contacted Cakereɗa long before then and knew him well.

Cakereɗa keeps the *mele va* (the jar of the rain) in his home in a separate little hut with a diameter of 70 cm that was made just for the jar, an abode built in a communal work party by the whole village. Its roof is repaired after each rainy season, again by the whole village. This year the first rains were early but then a dry spell set in. Some Guria notables—actually prodded by me—suggest to the village chief that it might be a good idea to sacrifice for the rains, so he warns Cakereɗa that evening to be ready. In the morning the chief brings a chicken, a red one just as the crab has indicated. Cakereɗa makes some objections, one of them being that a stranger is present—me—but eventually he gives in. Making objections is a normal way of stressing one's own importance in Kapsiki, and many tales circulate of rain makers who had to be beaten before doing the job. During the long day together Cakereɗa tells me with some pride how the elders used to have to beat him before he budged. An additional reason for negotiating the ritual is that it might give the rain maker some leeway in choosing a day with more chance of rain, but that is my own interpretation.

The ritual elders in the village, the chief, the *mnzefe*, and the chief smith of Guria assemble at the rain hut. The *ce va* houses a collection of objects which together are indicated as *mele va*, though only one of them is a real jar, a small one in the form of a rugby ball and without decoration. The other objects are a small round bowl, six pieces of clay of indefinite form, plus a few special stones, mostly quartz. The jar is crucial because it stems from the ritual center of Gudur, through the lineage of Cakereɗa, who claims that he is a lineal descendant from the chief of Gudur, the main rain maker in the Mandara Mountains.

All the objects are taken from the small hut and spread out on the ground, one of the clay pieces serving as a seat for the rain maker. At noon the red rooster is sacrificed. The village chief holds its feet while Cakereɗa cuts off its head and makes sure that blood drips on all the objects. "*Shala* in heaven, I suffer from thirst, now I give you food. I ask you now: give us water to cultivate sorghum, do not thrust your knife [lightning] into anyone, I do not want the jealousy."[4]

All the objects are put back in the hut and it is closed. With some sesame twigs and water, the rain maker washes a few grindstones lying next to the rain hut and sprays some water on the cɛva, saying "We are thirsty, we are thirsty," to conclude the ritual part of the morning. All the grindstones are then washed with water and sesame in the presence of the remaining notables. Cakereɗa's compound is close to the market and people flock around the house, busy with the market but much more interested in the—slightly illicit—gambling game that is going on than in the rain ritual. The ritual elders quickly leave the compound to join the market.

Just before sunset, when the women of the house have made mush and cooked the rooster, Cakereɗa and I conclude the *melɛ va*. The rain maker gets all the objects from the hut again and puts some mush, sauce and chicken liver on each of them, first on the *melɛ va*: "*Shala*, I am thirsty, here is food for you, let us be healthy, give us water for the sorghum."[5] As a conclusion he puts some *haŋgedle va* (*Cissus quadrangularis*) on the *melɛ* and then eats the rest of the food himself.

And now for the rain. There had been a little shower in Mogode, just to the north, but not a drop in Guria. The people who had been enjoying themselves at the market without paying any attention to the ritual were confronted on their way home with its results: visitors from Mogode were soaked by the time they arrived in their village because of the heavy rainstorm that swept over Guria. A huge success for the rain maker and a minor for me, as the Guria people later said: "*Shala* has respected the white man in the *melɛ va*; from now on he has to help our *ndemeva*." For Cakereɗa I was henceforth the "son of his father," since I had shown myself to be "family of Rain." My skin helped here because *Va* (rain) is considered to be red as well (Europeans are red in Kapsiki). A year later people invited me for another rain ritual but I was preparing to leave the area, and furthermore my confidence in my own ritual prowess and relationship with Rain was not sufficient to run the risk of failure.

> Cakereɗa told me he could also halt rain, for any reason. The procedure is as follows. He takes a piece of quartz and puts stripes on it of beans, ocher and a rooster's tail feather. This will produce a rainbow which in turn halts the rain. One reason for halting rain could be that rain is too plentiful. Conjuring a rainbow alone will not be enough, however; an additional ritual is called for. He takes all sorts of ashes from his compound, mixes them with melon and millet flour, and puts this mixture on the wall at the entrance to his forecourt. When the time comes and the rains have to

fall, he kills a rooster, mixes its blood with water and ash, and puts this on the *mele va*. Then no rain will fall, surely. To start it again, he simply performs the sacrifice described above.

Both types of rain rituals—hunting and buying rain—indicate that the range of human interference in the normal way of things is limited. First, timing is of the essence, since any rain ritual is done only when and if rain is due: the rituals are not an infraction of the normal processes but a stimulus for things to take their normal course. Second, success depends not only on the recognition of *shala* and Rain—and thus of the position of the officiator—but also on the willingness of the other world to acknowledge the demands as legitimate. The same notion of legitimacy shows in Rhwemetla's rooster ordeal (Chapter 4). The rain ritual has an additional dimension since it has a close association with the area's major ritual places, Sukur and primarily Gudur. Like any "normal" phenomenon, rain is a vulnerable asset, a boon that comes when nothing interferes. Rain makers have to be respected, rituals have to be performed, and individuals should not try to make a profit from unsubstantiated claims or blackmail the village with substantiated ones. The rain situation is thus fraught with vulnerability, with problems or even disasters. Anything other than normal is a problem, and in the Kapsiki definition of the rain situation there is no optimalization, no "bumper year," just "normal." The range of actions open to man is limited; avoiding discord with the other side of the world is the most important, and regressive action is needed to restore normality. The powers that command rain should be left unimpeded. In this vision, man is often the main liability, as someone who works and sometimes even plots against his own evident interests. Group interests may clash here with individual gains, as they often do in Kapsiki culture. Individual gain, be it money or recognition (for example, a rain maker might stop rain, feeling that he is not well enough respected in the village), is perceived as a threat to the long-term common good: rain.

It is, however, the external connection with the quasi-mythical village of Gudur that is crucial in procuring rain; all villages with a residing rain maker proudly claim such a direct link. In fact, Hwempetla's refusal to acknowledge the authority of rain makers (or rain sellers) in other villages is a clear expression of village autonomy. In his earlier exploits, Hwempetla freed Mogode from the suzerainty of neighboring Guria, eventually waging war with that neighbor to free themselves of earlier obligations. "Rebellion" against rain makers is an expression of that same vaunted autonomy. Not buying rain means not bowing to the authority of Gudur, that is, not recognizing the ritual dominance of the ancestral point of origin. So, in many ways, the discourse on rain is a discourse on power and dominance: the center of rain is the center of power. Gudur, as we shall see, is home to the main ritual against the major threat to the crops besides drought, namely locusts, but also controls the most exotic threat of all to human life: leopards.[6] Gudur's power base resides in rain, in locusts, and in leopards—all of which underwrite its importance and might be one reason that so many villages trace their origin to this place—but rain is by far the most important. So rain and power go together, with control of rain implying control of people and vice versa.

But no rule in Kapsiki religion is without its exceptions: the *mele va* in Mogode, mentioned in the rain hunt, is sometimes used in regular rain sacrifices. The *mele* consists this time of a grindstone in the abandoned house of the late Kweji Kwakwene, since the jar has gone. Just before the *peli va*, a representative of Kweji's lineage washes that stone with beer, and later sacrifices a chicken on it. Kweji, so the story goes, had a red stone, which attracted water: wherever one put it on the ground, the soil became soaked. The provenance of that particular stone is not known, and it was lost when Kweji moved to a Nigerian village fleeing Hamman Yaji, but its properties still cling to the grindstone where Kweji had kept it. Another story, reminiscent of Old Testament tales, links Kweji Kwakweme with water as well. Reputedly, he also had a stick that parted the waters: when he struck a river, a throughway appeared in the water, which closed after he had passed. So the authority of Gudur has not been eroded, not even by Hwempetla.

Chasing Death

Sterner[7] refers to two rituals as a link between various ethnic groups in the area. One is the bull sacrifice as performed in the northern half of the Mandara area, in Rumsu and Wula. The other is what is called in Kapsiki *berhe mte* or *berhe ba* (to accompany death or an epidemic). At the heart of the rainy season, people from different ethnic groups perform a ritual in which death or an epidemic is chased out of one village toward the next. How exactly the ritual is done varies by village, as is the case with all major rituals. In some villages red beer is brewed, in others there is no beer in sight. The ritual is more complicated if beer is included. Mogode is one of the villages without beer where the *berhe mte* has become a memory, albeit a recent one; Rumsu, to the north, will serve as its contrast.

Mogode's village chief announced when the ritual was to be held and in the middle of the night walked through the village shouting that no one should light a fire. The following morning nobody goes to his fields and everyone walks around chatting and drinking. The chief smith also makes his rounds, playing his hour glass drum in each compound. About 3 pm, the old women in the village gather behind the smith, naked except for their cache sexes, carrying calabashes full of all kinds of refuse: calabash shards, broken pottery, old hoe handles, old cache sexes, used oil, and so on. Yelling and shouting, they follow the smith to Megeme, a mountain to the south of the village. At the foot of the mountain they throw down their refuse, yelling *Kwidi, kadzi Tlukwu na* (go away, go to Tlukwu), and run home without looking back.

If there is beer present, the picture changes, as the rhythm of the brewing process sets the pace for the ritual: it is much longer and more complicated, as in Rumsu. The chief of Rumsu indicates the date, usually a Sunday. The Friday before, the chief smith and the village chief start brewing their beer; the others follow on Saturday and all kill a goat. Early Sunday evening in the northernmost ward of the village, the chief smith starts shouting and drumming, accompanied by four youngsters playing their *zuvu*, reed flutes. At the smith's signal, the four throw burning straw on the road, shouting: "Go away, go to Tlukwu." In the wards to the south, people do the same, tearing straw from the roof of their personal huts (children take it from the entrance hut) and setting fire to it; they then yell and scream as they run toward the road to throw it away "Go away, go to Tlukwu, Death." When the sun has set, the village elders join the chief in his compound to drink the first beer, and whatever has been butchered is now cooked. After this so-called *ndirhwu* (making fire), people relax and tell jokes in a festive atmosphere.

The next morning sees the young *makwa* (this year's brides) go to their father's home with a gift of mush, returning with a reciprocal gift of meat and unfiltered white beer. People dance to the music of the *zuvu* and drink at each other's homes, although over the years dancing has decreased. In the past the *gwela* could not dance, because this was the dance of death; anyway the youngsters today consider the dancing pointless since "there is no one to watch, so it is a useless dance." On Tuesday the eating and drinking continue, and the festival lasts until everything is finished, the food running out long before the beer, because "What woman will cook when there is plenty of beer." Wednesday is the end of the party. The old women wait in their houses, naked, for the village chief to call them. In the early morning he does call out: "Women, take your things. No woman should stay in her hut." Again, the chief smith leads the women to the road, drumming. The women yell and shriek and throw rubbish on the road to the south: "Go to Tlukwu, Death, go to Tlukwu." The road is strewn with broken objects and utensils, beer and vinegar dregs, melon leaves and seeds, and indigenous cucumbers.

Variations in the ritual depend on the role of the *makwa*, as the *berhe mte* can be combined with various aspects of the *makwa* proceedings (especially in Wula). The crucial aspects of the ritual are setting fire to the straw and throwing it on the road, throwing the refuse down, and sending Death westward, usually to Tlukwu. In fact, the villages wait—or waited—for each other. Gudur started, as well as Sukur, and sent Death to Wula; Wula to Rumsu and in Rumsu the direction was Mogode. Mogode relayed it to Guria and to the southwest to Nigeria and toward the south. Not all the villages mention Tlukwu but simply chase Death westward. Gudur also sends it to Kortchi, which relays it to Ldiri and further west. So the course of Death is to the south, then veering to the west (Figure 7.3).

Why this direction, and why Tlukwu? First, according to the Kapsiki/Higi, Death is chased with the wind, since there is a close association between wind and illness. For instance, when a strong wind clears someone's courtyard, according to an expression it clears the place for one's grave. In traditional tales too, Death travels with the wind, and whirlwinds in particular are closely associated with death, embodying *gutuli* spirits and sometimes sorcerers. During the wet season the wind can upset the rain and brings illness, according to the Kapsiki. Since the much-dreaded epidemic meningitis is carried by dust, this fear is not without justification.

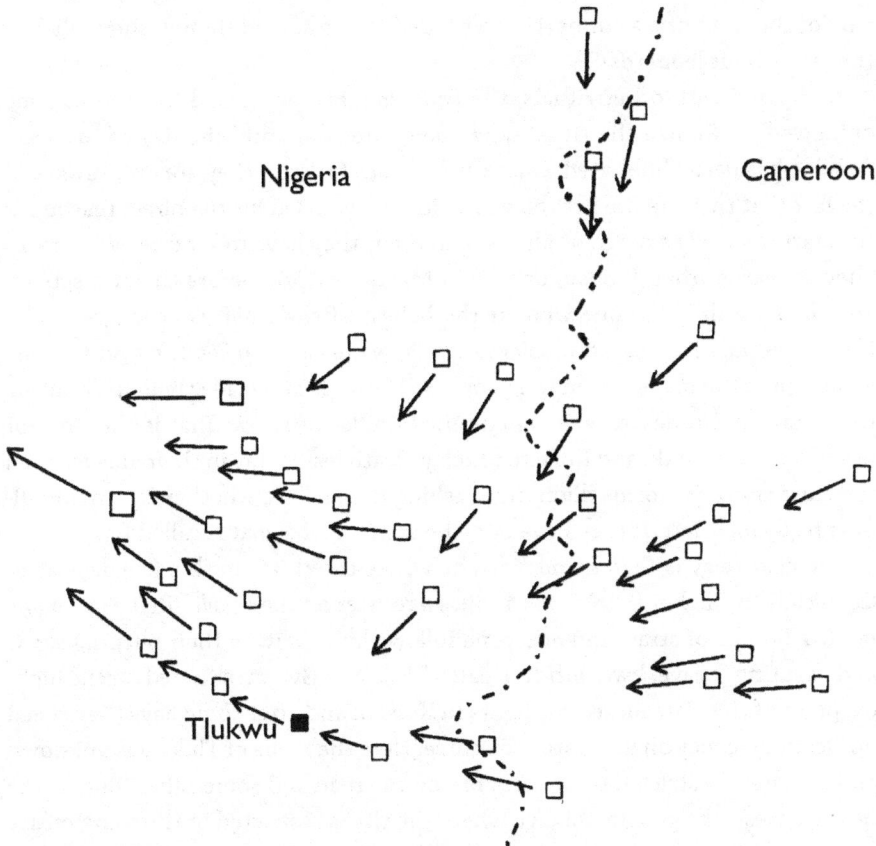

Figure 7.3 Chasing Death, from village to village.

The close association with the wind does not hold for Sukur in the north, which sends the epidemic to Rumsu, south veering to the east, so the association seems specific for the Kapsiki leg of the itinerary. Then the question: Why Tlukwu? Actually, I have not been able to establish any other reason than that: "Tlukwu has always been the village of death," at least for the Cameroonian villages; Tlukwu's neighbors just send Death westward, as does the village itself. The association of Tlukwu with death is, however, wider than just the *berhe mte*. The mother of Vandu Ntsu, one of the village elders and a *keleŋu*, came from Tlukwu. One day when Vandu fell ill, people from Tlukwu came, he told me, in the form of leopards, to mourn him. On their return, they reputedly ate a person in Sena. And when Vandu's mother died, people fled the compound when the howling of leopards came from all sides as the Tlukwu mourned one of their daughters. They are just like *keleŋu*, these Tlukwu people, but stronger since the other clairvoyants cannot see them. So they roam the villages without being seen; their *shala* have given them this gift. They are so strong that no village will wage war with them; even white people do not dare to take them on. In Tlukwu itself, one of the most isolated villages in the Higi part of the territory, a connection with death was denied though they relished the tales about leopards.

Compared with other rituals, the *berhe mte* has withstood the test of time quite well. In Rumsu the ritual now takes three days and the day of "useless" dancing has been eliminated. Gudur is still the start and they are quite aware of the fact that they are the first on a long itinerary. In Gudur the direct reason for the start is usually a death or illness, and then "they have to send away the fear." They are earlier than Rumsu, usually in March or April, before the rain sets in. The chief smith is the one who, at the behest of the chief, is at the center of things: he puts his special medicine in the water, announces the event to the village, puts the medicine on the people's foreheads and leads them in shouting that Death has to leave, waiving flaming bundles of straw. That is the sign for Godala, Cuvuk, Sirak, and Kortchi to relay Death lest it stay in their village. Then the chief smith performs divination, asking the pebbles whether Death and illness really have left. If they have not, the sacrifice of a goat is called for.

The next relay is Cuvuk and Kortchi, where the chief smith a few days after Cuvuk advises all households to sacrifice a rooster on their *melɛ*. That evening he lights a bundle of straw and everyone follows him, waiving their burning straw and shouting "Leave, leave *mtidʼi* (Death)." Kila and Gwava, situated on the highest point of the plateau, see the lights in Kortchi and after some days they speed up Death's journey on its westward course. Here the name of Tlukwu is unknown and the rite is restricted to its core: fire on the road and some ashes. But on the next lap west, the people of Ldiri, where the rite is restricted to throwing refuse on the road, are well aware of Tlukwu as the village of Death. By then Sukur has already started as well, leading the northern villages.

Locusts, Leopards, and Gudur

Once the rains have fallen, the crops face other risks. There are some rituals performed by the smiths against worms, which threaten the crops,[8] but by far the largest threat, demanding all the attention of the Kapsiki, is from locusts, the catastrophic threat to crops in Africa. According to the Kapsiki, these *dzale*, the swarming species—well distinguished from their "own" endogenous *hegi* locusts, which they eat—used to come once in a generation, and although there were no great swarms in the second part of the twentieth century, locust control has been less effective in West Africa in recent decades. Of course plagues are always in a larger region, so measures against locusts need to be just as regional. Gudur is the center for this ritual too, and more than anything else it is his prowess against locusts that gives the chief of Gudur his recognition in the Mandara Mountains. This "great chief" is the one everyone appeals to in times of stress, not only the Kapsiki and Higi villages but also the Mafa, Mofu, and Hina villages, which trace their descent from Gudur too. Not all the Kapsiki/Higi villages are descended from Gudur, and those with a more Western origin, like some of the Nigerian villages, do not participate in this ritual.

What exactly the chief of Gudur does when a swarm hits the area is known only to a few, and the description that follows comes from the Mogode village representatives and some people from Gudur, including the chief himself. The preparations are well known. First the village representatives go to Sukur on the Nigerian side just north of Kapsiki/Higi, with presents of money, goats, and clothes. Wula sends its rain maker, who is kin to Gudur, and the smiths in Sukur forge five irregular-shaped sheets of iron that the delegation takes, with other gifts, to Gudur, where they hand everything over to the chief who "commands" the locusts. Somewhere deep in the mountains belonging to the village is a deep hole in the ground. Legend has it that at the bottom lies a *mele* under an upturned beer vat, serving as the *mele* of the locusts.[9] The Gudur chief now sends an elder of the particular clan that is in charge of this *mele* to perform the sacrifice. He slaughters two cattle, a bull and a cow, over the hole, shuts the opening (reputedly about a meter in diameter) with iron sheets, and then covers the sheets with earth. Informants describe the result as a burial mound. According to the Kapsiki, the hole is the home of the locusts that normally have no wings but once every few decades perform their initiation and then the males develop wings. The others are like termites. During initiation they swarm and eat everything in sight, so they have to be calmed with sacrificial meat. Iron, of course, is used to restrict their movements because it takes locusts "decades to eat through a sheet of solid iron."

This ritual generates a great deal of contradictory information, especially from informants who have no part in it, an indication of the emotional value and almost mythical dimension of Gudur. In the past, people told me that it was a human sacrifice and villages in the mountains were asked to send victims. People assured me it was better to sacrifice a few than have everyone die, and the ones they sent were usually smiths. Even allowing for the usual and well-founded skepticism about these kinds of stories in anthropology, this case might have some historical foundation. The area suffered huge losses of life in the past, as the chapter on slavery testified, and people used to sell their own kinsmen into slavery at times of famine. Sacrificing the odd smith would therefore be a distinct possibility. Anyway, Gudur is a dangerous place for smiths. At the funeral of the Gudur chief, a smith was buried with him, the story goes, although nowadays it is a dog. Not only smiths might have been sacrificed, children can be considered as a commodity too. During a beer party some elders were discussing death and one of them said: "If Death comes, do not ask him why he has come but immediately give him a child, and then he will not take you." Indeed, the old threats still survive in the discourse.

Outside Gudur everyone thinks that the chief of Gudur himself performs the sacrifice and that the chief of Sukur is part of the delegation. A story from Wula underscores the dangers of the ancestral place: "Last time the chief of Sukur did not want to go to Gudur for the sacrifice, when it had to be held. His own people then cuffed him and took him to Wula, the first leg of the journey. From there he went on his own. When he returned, people chose another chief, and the old one died within two years." In Sukur these tall stories were denied vehemently. In any event, the last plague dates from the early 1930s and the chief of Sukur never participated in the delegation.

These tall stories and intense discussions illustrate the high regard and deep awe people hold for Gudur, a place of danger and threat. As much as people disagree about actual events, they do agree on the proper behavioral codes for the delegation: they must be humble, refuse a proper sleeping mat and sleep on the floor, refuse the good mush, take the leftovers and always "be lower" than the chief. Transgression of these rules means death on their return, and the main guardian of this etiquette is an emissary of the chief. On their return journey the delegates are thought to be followed by a leopard "who walks behind them like a dog." At Sukur, the delegation has to offer the animal a goat, which then returns home to Gudur. The delegation brings home a certain amount of beer dregs that are divided among Sukur, Wula and Mabass, the three sister villages, and are buried at their chiefs' houses in the middle of the villages. Then the locusts will leave. Nobody should ever cultivate on the spot where the dregs are buried; otherwise the locusts may come back with a vengeance, bringing leopards with them and a plague of diarrhea.

The chief of Gudur himself is part of the local mythology about the place. People insist that he used to send his emissaries to run through the villages in order to check whether people were sticking to the ancestral ways, with the sending of locusts as the ultimate sanction for not following customs. The people from

Gudur were easy to spot since they walked naked and never spoke to anyone, while the chief himself used to stay out of the sight of strangers. During my days in northern Cameroon, the chief did venture out, though covered by a blanket under which he was reportedly naked.

Visiting Gudur: A Fieldwork Interlude

Visiting Gudur from Mogode is a slightly stressful trip, at least my assistant was quite apprehensive the first time I went in 1973. "What are you going to ask?" he wanted to know. I actually had just a few points, mainly about history and of course about the locusts and leopards. He insisted that I keep quiet and let him do the talking, which I readily agreed to, since the last thing I wanted to do was to make him uncomfortable. He was and still is an excellent guide in Mandara manners. So off we went to Gudur, which proved surprisingly easy to reach; I had expected such a quasi-mythical place to be hard to find, but in fact Gudur is near the main Mokolo–Marua road, and I realized I had often passed it before. Coming into the village, Sunu walked in front, with me dutifully behind, and at the chief's compound we sat down on the floor. His son, a youngster, came out and greeted us. He arranged some mats and insisted we sit on these which, after some polite hesitation by Sunu, we did. The son pulled out a chair and called for his father, while in the meantime some other elders had gathered around us. Everyone rose when the chief arrived but he immediately asked us to sit down, and the small, dapper man remained standing, clothed in a white blanket. Only after some time did he sit down on his chair, making sure that nobody was higher than him. When one elder had to go, the chief immediately rose as well, greeting the stooping elder from on high. Sunu explained our visit and my function in the whole project, stressing the fact that I wanted to know about history so that traditions would not be lost forever. The son translated, since the Psikiyè and Gudur languages are too different to allow easy understanding, so Fulfulde was used as the medium. Sunu concentrated hard and, after the first introduction, hardly referred to me any longer; in fact he did his own research. After all, he was just as curious as I was, having heard the tall stories on Gudur from our Kapsiki villages as well as from Sukur. What "exactly" was the case nowadays? Afterwards he joked that without him I would not have known what to ask, and he was probably right. The chief was open and forthcoming with information, reducing the tales to a life-sized format on the one hand while insisting on his own position of power in the regional religion on the other. The account given above is, for the most part, the result of his disclosures. After we had said farewell, Sunu was both relieved and exuberant: we had been to the chief of Gudur and come out in one piece, and it went so well that he was confident that the chief would not send leopards after us. And indeed he did not.

My second visit to Gudur was 37 years later in January 2009. Collecting information about the spread and dynamics of the initiation in the area, I visited Gudur again but this time with much more information, since Catherine Jouaux had in the meantime done fieldwork there.[10] Sunu and I had both aged (considerably!) so there was no tension this time but instead some excitement about the visit. The scene had changed, since by now much of Gudur has been islamized. The first person we saw was the very same son of the old chief, who himself had died long before. The office of chief of Gudur was divided between him and his older brother, who was not present that day. The administrative part was his responsibility; the ritual part of the traditional chiefdom was his brother's. The son still remembered our first visit! I never fail to be amazed by this phenomenon in Africa: the extraordinary memory Africans have for visits and faces from way back in the past. Sunu felt much more at ease this time and insisted that I take a picture of him. On the first visit he had been very apprehensive when I wanted to take a picture of the chief. I had done so anyway, and could now bring—after a 37-year delay!—a picture of his father (the one in Figure 7.4a) for the new chief, which he appreciated enormously since he had few pictures of this grand old man. But now Sunu knew what he wanted more than anything else—a picture of himself, displaying the correct posture of respect, with the chief of Gudur. I was instructed to ensure that this picture would receive the widest possible distribution and have herewith granted him this wish (Figure 7.4b).

Figure 7.4a The chief of Gudur in 1973.

Figure 7.4b Sunu (left) and the new chief of Gudur, 2009.

Harvest and its Rituals

The various measures taken during the growing season against possible pests do not cost the average cultivator a lot of time, because the rites are done by specialists, and it is only with major plagues that more people become involved. Harvest time, though, is considered the critical moment for everyone. At the start of the wet season people can still be heard whistling and shouting in the fields, whereas just before harvest this conduct is taboo; the sorghum has to thrive, multiply. People with a special ritual status, such as twins and their parents, carry *peha* (palm leaf[11]) strips to indicate their position and remind people of the behavior required toward them. Everybody consults the crab before starting to harvest in order to find out which field should be harvested first and how it should be prepared. Here is an example from 1995:

> You put a calabash with sorghum flour with water in the field, break a few stalks, four nice ones that should bend over, and leave this in the field, covering the calabash. Bind the ears of those broken stalks together. Cover the calabash with grass and let it stand in the field overnight.
> Starting out very early in the morning, the family eats peanut sauce in the field, leaving some in the calabash in the field. The four hanging ears will be cut last and taken home with both calabashes. Their ears will be seed material for the next season. The husband fills the calabash with sorghum and hands it to the wife who has cooked on this first day of the harvest. The rest of the harvest does not call for special measures and people spend the following weeks cutting off the large sorghum stalks. The ears will be separated from the stalks later when threshing starts, the next crucial phase.

Whatever details the crab may indicate, some general rules hold. People will not leave the bones of sacrificed chicken on the field, because these hollow bones will "blow away" the sorghum. That is cited as the reason why the meat for communal work parties will not contain chicken. The Kapsiki believe that the content of the ears depends on the respect people show the crop, including the ritual measures. Inside the ears, the grains have to thrive and, regardless of the state they were in when harvested, the final result can vary considerably. Each transition is vulnerable: sowing, the first harvest, threshing, and storing in the granary. Each process entails risks. During threshing, the main precaution is sexual abstinence for a few nights before the start, and the man will also consult the crab.

Threshing is, however, a women's job, and a gentle gender inversion governs this activity. Dispersed throughout the village one can see flat round surfaces, surrounded by a stone circle. Each ward has a few, and the women from one house work at it together, flailing the ears with large wooden threshing clubs and winnowing in the steady January wind. Their husbands and fathers look on, put the grains into baskets, transport the baskets home, and empty them inside the granary of choice. This is a moment of joy and pride, and the man sings the *geza ha*, the song of the sorghum, as he walks through the ward. As a proud informant told me:

> He who does not cultivate is poor. He covers his ears when people talk to him. Look at me, I can buy a woman with my grain, I can buy a cow if I want to. I drink the best beer, the lazy one only the dregs. The wife of a lazy man is poor, hungry, and has no clothes. My wife is fat from eating and has many clothes. The lazy one says, "Next year I will cultivate," but when the rain comes he has forgotten his hoe. If a woman does not cultivate, who needs her? She is good for nothing. What woman will stay with a man who does not cultivate? A lazy man's wife just cooks a sauce of couch grass seeds (*luku*), mine eats meat. My son marries a *makwa*, let the lazy one die!

The content husband will give his wives a good quantity of grain. Together his women will get about a quarter of the harvest for their granaries, to be used for brewing beer.

This chapter began with the initiation of the granary, and that is what we turn to now, for the last important point is the granary itself. Especially the *tame*, the central granary type, is a focus of ritual attention. "Nobody can tell how much grain a *tame* will contain," an informant told me. "One year it can be ten baskets, the next year just six." A full *tame* stays open for a time, a cone of grain in sight above the rim, and some *haze* (*Cymbopogon*) stuck in the plaited collar. When the collective hunts are held a month later, the *haze* is joined by its usual companion, *safa* (*Combretum*). Then the top cone of grain is set aside as next year's sowing seed and as the basis of the first post-harvest beer, the so-called *tɛ derha* (beer of the forecourt). After a particularly good harvest, irrespective of a new *tame*, the man also invites the neighbors and lineage elders, makes beer from the first sorghum, and immolates a Guinea fowl, rabbit, or the rooster of the house (the *ɲulu rhɛ*, which we will see in Chapter 12). The guests eat the meat first and then drink the new *tɛ*.

Other crops receive much less attention: maize, which is important as the first crop to be harvested, does not call for divination or sacrifice even though its importance has grown considerably in the last decades, as the introduction of machine grinding has made its preparation much easier. People do, however, take ritual precautions against the theft of some labor-intensive crops, such as tobacco and sweet potatoes.

One should not eat the new harvest without ritual preparation. As often in Africa, children are the first to taste new crops, here the crops other than sorghum. To protect the children against risks, notably malaria, the elders of the ward perform the *melɛ hwule* (*hwule*: *Euphorbia* sp.) at the end of the wet season. In one of the *keluŋu* (meeting places in the ward), a jar is hidden under a tree. All the children in the ward come together, each with a bowl of sorghum flour with beans, and a drop of euphorbia latex. The women prepare a mush and peanut sauce, mix the children's foodstuff with it, and cook it. An old woman puts some mud on the jar, plucks neck feathers from a white chicken, and puts them on the *melɛ* as well. Then she cuts the chicken's throat: "Let all children be healthy; do not let Death touch them, let them eat the new food in good health." Finally everyone eats the mix. Thus the *shala* of the child has eaten. If a child cannot participate, his or her mother can do the same sacrifice, using a beer jar that she puts under a euphorbia for the occasion. She does not share the food with other children in the ward; if she does, any illness the others get will attack her child too, and vice versa.

Later the first sorghum is dealt with differently. The first measure taken from a new granary or a newly filled granary should be used for the *tɛ derha*, which resembles the closing rite of the home sacrifice-with-goat (Chapter 4). This time it is mainly a social affair, sharing the new crop with neighbors and kinsmen. The top cone of grain is used to brew red beer and the man invites everyone he has had no problems with, as well as some elders. They come early in the morning; he gives the usual introduction about "having put some grain in the water," and they all drink. No sacrifice is performed, no beer is poured on the *melɛ* because for the owner of the house it is important that he partakes of the new harvest for the first time and lets his "brothers" share it with him. The guests thank him at some length, the ward chief and village chief being among the first to speak. Then they all start the *rhena za* (the men's talk) and all admonish the men to do the same, the village chief adding comments and exhortations as he sees fit. This *tɛ derha* can also be held on other occasions—a new house, a new granary, or to solve a conflict between brothers or neighbors—in fact at any time, although there is usually a clear reason for such a gesture. Sometimes the crab indicates it. A traditional story relates how this tradition started, with the now familiar motif of trying to escape death.

> Once upon a time there were two friends who were inseparable. They were together day and night, eating so much that they grew fat. Being rich, they could eat what they wanted, and nobody was as nicely fat and smooth skinned as they were. One said: "Death cannot reach us, we are so large!" "You are right," the other one said. "People who look like us will not die. Those who die look meager and sick. Have we been ill since we are together? Never, in all those years. But in the three months I have been married now, I haven't seen my wife, so I am going home now."

Death visited the first speaker. "Good evening." "Thank you, who are you?" "I am Death." "What do you want?" "You just said to your friend that you would not die because you look different, the two of you. So I came to claim you."

"If you really are Death, I won't refuse to come along but my wife is three months pregnant. What am I to do? If you come back in three days, I will have paid the chicken [for the delivery] and then I will join you."

Death grants him his wish, and is back in three days. "My wife is right now giving birth, please come back in another week."

[. . . The man keeps procrastinating: he has to kill a goat for a new wife and then hides in a bushel of straw, in a well, in a cavern, and every time Death finds him. Exasperated, the man jumps in the water, where again Death tracks him down . . .]

"Do you drink water because of me?" Death said, "please come out." The man came out. Death chided him: "Your words, those were the things that stung, that you would not die. You die when your days are finished. Stop that nonsense!"

"Does that mean that you let me go?"

"If you stop talking like that, yes I will let you go. You have to go home and raise your children. I will come back when your days are over, when I have counted all of them. Then I'll come to collect you all."

The man went home, brewed beer, and invited all the people from the village. "My brothers, I have said foolish things. I cannot hide from Death, and now I share my things with you." Everyone drank his beer and ate from his goat, and stayed at his *derha*. Then Death suddenly appeared, again. "No, I have not come to collect you," he told the frightened man, "I could have done that at the waterside if I had wanted so. You now have shared your riches with all the others, so I have added another thirty years to your life."

Since that time—assures our raconteur Tlimu—people started to make beer for each other. "If Death is so merciful as to let him live, I had better brew beer as well and have everyone round to drink. Better to brew beer, give presents, and invite people than to die. This is how our ancestors started the tɛ *derha*."

The First Hunt

Though Kapsiki is an agricultural society, hunting still has a special place in this culture. Not only is a hunt used to procure rain, as we have seen, but the first hunt at the start of the dry season is also a ritual. Among the village clans, this time the *makwajɛ* clan is responsible for leading the hunt, and a representative of this clan consults the crab to determine the best date to make the required preparations for avoiding accidents and to establish where to hunt. A day before the hunt the *makwajɛ* places an offering on his *melɛ*, and announces to the village that the first hunt will be held the following day.

The next morning the participants—anyone who wants to go plus the ward elders—gather at his house for some beer. The master of the hunt explains why he has made *tɛ* and gives a calabash to the eldest, who blesses the people present: "May *shala* protect you all, and no animal attack you." People down the beer quickly and are on their way to find the other participants at the gathering place on the east side of the village. The *makwajɛ* leader of the hunt asks a few boys to get some *safa* and *haze* from the bush (*Combretum* and *Cymbopogon*), takes some remains of yesterday's sacrifice, and sprays on his chest: "It is not very important, but we are together here. May *shala* protect us from wounds, and have no quarrel about game [whose is the catch]." He then puts the *safa* and *haze* on some boulders at the gathering place. All hit the stone with their clubs, shouting "*ŋada, ŋada*" (mine, mine) as they shout when hitting an animal, and the party is under way.

This first hunt follows a set course: to the west, then quickly toward the south, then east, and finally to the north, a loop that coincides with the rain hunt. This association with rain is intentional and when the group passes the grave of the rain maker, they divide into two equal parts, "to share the rain equally." Though not about agriculture, the first hunt is clearly the opening of the agricultural season, as the following shows.

> A week before the ritual hunt, Kweji Tè, the master of the hunt, has already announced it in the village. On the morning in question the elders come to drink the *melɛ peli* (hunting beer), but no beer! His wife has gone the way of all wives and left him, taking his beer along to Rumsu, where she sold it! No beer, no hunt, and the people go home empty handed. Later Kweji explains to me that he had concocted this whole story on behalf of the village chief, who thought the weather was too misty and not lucky for a hunt. Since the *tɛ* had been made, the chief suggested that Kweji's wife sell it in Rumsu in order to postpone the hunt, thus blaming the woman again. The point is that mist is considered "rain that goes elsewhere," something quite normal in the wet season but a bad sign at any other time. Not giving the true reason for a change in plans is common, as is blaming a woman.

The hunt consists of some 80 men who move in a large semicircle to catch and kill any animal they encounter. With wooden clubs as their main weapons, the men shout loudly to frighten the game and then kill it together. If an animal runs away, people throw their clubs at it, shouting ŋada, ŋada, even at a bird or cricket. The route leads the men through a much-hunted area close to the village, and very little game comes into sight but nobody cares because this first hunt "has to be done." The eventual catch—and there should be some—in fact consists of a few crickets, not much to show for their efforts but the men have great fun.

The hunt is repeated farther from the village over the next few days, led by the same Kweji Tè but following a different procedure. Kweji goes on his own early in the morning and has a friend tell the others where he has gone and they join him. A hunter who wants to catch something should not bring food from home and will not give his club to anyone who has slept with a woman that he has ever slept with himself. Often this is hard to establish, so people will not willingly lend their clubs. Certain women bring bad luck, and intercourse with them has to be avoided as well. But who they are is unclear. The kill from the first hunt is for the whole group, while in later hunts any game is for the person whose club killed it, though the first to hit the animal will get a front leg.

Two game animals enjoy special attention: a guinea fowl is for one's mother's brother in return for a rooster to sacrifice at the hunter's *mele*. Guinea fowl is a delicacy for the Kapsiki and such a gift is highly valued. An uncle who never gets a guinea fowl from his nephew will stress this negligence by giving him a large rooster: "You will not give me a guinea fowl anyway; you are not a good *ksugwe*." But the most prized game in Kapsiki country is the duiker, and any duiker killed is distributed with great care. Its rump steak is for the master of the hunt, the skin and one leg for one's mother's brother, who reciprocates with two arrows and money. The main part is taken not by the hunter but by the old men in the hunting group, who will cook it and invite their daughters and the ward members to come and enjoy it. The hunter himself gets just one leg; the hoofs and the head will be eaten on the morning of the next hunt when the elders in question come to his house, eat the broth, and put stripes of oil and ocher on the hunter's forehead as a sign that he killed a duiker. And all that for the smallest and slowest of all antelopes, but then the male duiker excels by having huge testicles. One classificatory in-law of mine once came to the house suffering—he felt—from swollen testicles. He and the others explained his condition by the fact that he had knocked down a duiker in such a way that its testicles touched the ground. Killing this animal was likely to result in a similar problem for the hunter, and so it proved.

Coping with Risk and Time

We have seen the ritual handling of several major risks, inherent in dwelling in these mountains: rain, locusts, and animals. But what constitutes a risk for the Kapsiki? Life is risky anyway, but the way of assessing risks, weighing them, is culturally informed.

During my first fieldwork in Mogode a passing car killed a teenage boy. For me this was a tragic event, a traffic accident waiting to happen as the all-weather road runs straight through the village, traffic is on the increase, drivers are not careful, and people are not used to the vehicles. Maybe some road signs could be put up . . . For the people of the village it was a shattering blow: they had never had a traffic accident in the village, so this was a death that came without any warning, without any sign or signal. The child was perfectly happy and healthy one moment and gone the next; it was like in the wars of old, but war was a thing of the past, not of today. Sometimes Rain strikes that way with lightning, but that was not the case here either. The funeral was chaotic as people could not dance—which is the normal way of mourning—and tried haphazard new ways of expressing their grief because they could find no way to attach any meaning to this death. There was talk of revenge magic, of taking court action, but any response drowned in the massive question mark that shone through the grief. The usual rituals of mourning fell short at this time.

So people make a distinction between expected risks and events that defy interpretation; expected, "normal" risk can be addressed through ritual, and in this way it is redefined, in a process called "coping." Coping rituals are aimed at collective risks, that is, normal ones, those defined as occurring with some regularity and that can be interpreted within existing cultural categories. Agriculture faces "normal" risks because crops are vulnerable. The number one risk is rain, or lack of it, but there are also epidemics and locusts to fear. These are the big ones, with epidemics being loosely defined but in practice focusing on a few killers such as meningitis and measles. Actually there are more deaths now from malaria, tetanus and intestinal infections, but the great cultural scare is still smallpox, considered the most dangerous, though the disease has in fact been eradicated.

The rituals addressing environmental risks denote a specific relationship with that environment by redefining its risks as human problems. Rain is couched in terms of power; the vagaries of the weather are brought home as infractions by humans—people who stop the rain—or as a general relationship with external powers such as Hwempetla and *shala*/Rain, or Gudur. The rituals domesticate the risks and thus are part of the dwelling mode of existence. Calendar rituals, says Bell, "impose cultural schemes on the order of nature,"[12] both to control nature and to harmonize the social with the natural. The first goal is dubious. In Kapsiki controlling nature is not the real issue, since even in rain rituals the agency of the other world is stressed throughout. The main gist of the rituals is to eliminate impediments to rain, not to produce it, and certainly not to procure a certain amount of rain. This, incidentally, is one reason why the symbols of the rain rituals barely point at water at all. The most aquatic symbol is washing a grindstone with beer—an indirect iconography at best—but the majority of symbols address the wind as the obstacle to rain.

It is not a question of control, but of discourse. In rituals that stress the insecurity of human life, the discourse is in terms of certainty. The officiators exude a huge self-confidence when performing their rituals, as if the outcome is perfectly clear in advance. Afterwards however, when they talk about the probable effect of the rites, they fully realize that things might turn out differently: "It may help." Rappaport stresses that the ritual act calls for surrender to the terms of that very act, which makes rites fundamentally self-referential[13] and it is this self-referential aspect that generates a discourse of absolute certainty, molding the participants into a way of thinking and acting that for a fleeting moment relieves them of the hazards of life: the problems of drought are over after the hunt, rain will surely fall after the sacrifice, and no epidemic will strike this year. During the ritual, nature itself becomes domesticated and is rendered as (un)predictable as a human being.

Cyclical rituals are not frequent, but neither are they cognitively costly. The harvest rites occur each year and contain little that is counterintuitive: filling the granary, using it for the first time—all ritual actions pertain to daily use of the grain stock. The communal first beer from the harvest is one of the general themes running through all Kapsiki rituals, since all lead to a joint drinking spree. Initiating a *tame* is relatively rare, and here the owner of the new granary had to be instructed by elder kinsmen, and the details of this initiation do rely on episodic memory: how to decorate, what exactly to use and do. Chasing Death involves acts slightly out of the ordinary, but there the specialized knowledge of the chief smith comes in. In both instances the basic symbolism is straightforward: sounds of cattle for riches, trash for death. The rain rituals are different— infrequent and more highly charged with emotion and insecurity—and show a division between specialist ritual and public ritual: buying rain is a specialist job, while the hunt is completely communal. The specialist's authority stems not from his knowledge but from lineal descent. The public ritual has an inbuilt mnemonic device in the route of the hunt; the features on the route point to the small rituals that make up the rain hunt. So here the ritual provides its own learning effect.

The real cognitively costly ritual is indeed the most infrequent one—in Gudur, for example, against locusts. This disaster ritual, which demands both a lot of preparation and know-how in various villages, links various ethnic traditions and generates tall stories. Exegesis is completely dominated by the aim of the ritual: the locusts have to die. The problem at hand directs the exegetic reflection, so conceptualization and explanation of the ritual are done in terms of risk, not in terms of the ritual and symbols themselves.

Cyclical rites often involve the crossing of boundaries, because two opposites have to be mediated: village and bush, rain and wind. What is ritualized is the transition pattern of the crop: from the field to the threshing place, from there to the granary, from the granary to the kitchen for (first) consumption. The grain has to ripen or mature (*wume*), the same term as used for marrying a girl and initiating a boy, as well as for the initiation of the granary described at the beginning of this chapter. The *wume* of the sorghum in the field is followed by the *wume* of the *tame*, then by the riches that will lead to marriage and children, who eventually will become mature members of society. Throughout Kapsiki and Higi rituals, the spheres of human and agricultural production and fertility are linked, forming the warp and woof of survival.

All this is set in a ritual time frame. These calendar rituals not only link one year with the next, and the present to the past and the future, they also link the local community to the larger region and its history. It is through these rare-but-serious threats of locusts and epidemics that villages are no longer isolated but part of a wider Mandara Mountain system, the higher echelons of time correlating with larger regional scales. Lévi-Strauss characterized rituals as "machines à supprimer le temps," and Gell, in his ground-breaking study on the anthropology of time, acknowledges this aspect of what is called "B-series" time.[14] In rituals, time does not produce a date which gradually moves into the past (the "A-series"), but just is related to what went before and what will come afterwards, that is, has a fixed and permanent point in a cycle. Thus time seems to stand still in ritual because the action denies that time has had much influence at all, ignoring its impact on society. However, Kapsiki rituals are still conscious of time, not because they hark back to the ancestors—that is exactly what they do not do—but because they derive their ritual authority from the original migrations and thus from the point of origin, Gudur. How long ago is not relevant (and informants tend to underestimate the depth of history), but the itinerary of old provides a permanent time frame for the present relations. So ritual time in Kapsiki means ritual geography, historical provenance, and the authority of origin, all fixed in the yearly cycle.

PART THREE

RITUALS OF BELONGING

8

Starting Life

The First Appearance

Zra Dabala's wife Kuve has given birth to twins, a highlight in their young marriage and a huge boost for their status in the village. After a series of rituals, both parents are ready to come out (*shave*) with their new treasure, an occasion that is a routine element in any birth but of special weight with twins. Early in the morning Zra Dabala's clansmen flock into his compound, with me among them; after all Zra is my close lineage brother. One important guest, the village chief, is present to advise the young father, who has never conducted such a ceremony before and needs guidance, in fact clearly feels insecure. Zra has brewed twelve jars of *tɛ*, and—having only one wife—has asked his brother's wife to brew the twelve jars of white beer, as the twins are a boy and a girl. The old clansmen take their place of honor in the forecourt and gracefully accept their two jars of *tɛ*. In the usual cryptic explanation the Kapsiki use on such occasions, Zra says: "This is not something common. I have made just two jars, and as you happen to be here, please taste a little bit." The village chief puts him at ease: "No apology is needed for the paucity of the beer. You just do what you can and what you have to do. May *shala* help you and give you health."

When the clan elders have drunk, Zra's father's brother oversees the sacrifice of two sheep, a ram, and a ewe. Two of Zra's nephews perform this ritual duty and, at the signal of the older man, cut the throat of both sheep at the same time, one at Zra's hut, the other at Kuve's. They carefully collect the blood in a bowl, to be used for the sacrifice on the jar, and then, also simultaneously, skin the animals. Their personal rewards are the pancreas, the neck, and the colon; they hand the third stomach, the omasum, to the boy who has herded the animals, while the elders of both the parents' clans get the sheep heads. Zra then kills two chickens for the mother of the twins, a hen and a rooster, as he will have to do henceforth each day. The women of Zra's lineage cook one sheep and the women of Kuve's patrilineage cook the other one at her hut. Meanwhile the sister's sons make carrying slings for the twins from the skins of the animals and, when ready, sew two cowry shells on each of them, the sign of a twin. The nephews carefully cut some strips of skin with hair from the skins since the twins will wear these.

The sun is already high when the preparations are done. By then the sister's sons have eaten, the slings are ready and decorated, and the babies, their mother, her close kin, and the midwife all sport the *mnta*, strips of sheep skin with hair, on their left wrists. The midwife proceeds with the habitual sacrifice at the washing place of the mother, done for each birth. Kuve's lineage gathers in her hut, Zra's lineage in his. With the wives of both lineages in the brewery, the guests from other clans and important elders, such as the village chief, are seated in the entrance hut (it is still the end of the rainy season). Curious visitors are scattered around the rest of the compound, with me among them of course, moving from one group to the other. When Zra Dabala and his matrilateral kinsmen have tied their strips of *peha*[1] palm around their foreheads, the sign of a relation with a twin, people start drinking, the clansmen in Zra's hut from his sacrificial jar.

After drinking and eating, the moment of *shave* is there. Shouting with delight, we as clansmen take our twin-parents on our shoulders, Kuve's clansmen take their kinswoman, and we all carry them out of the compound. The other kinsmen, shouting and yelling too, run out of the compound and dance with the parents for some minutes, then Zra and his wife descend, quietly wait for most of the people to leave and walk back into the house, still wearing their *peha*. The final scene is now set for the women of the ward to help the mother leave the compound with one of her babies; in this case a young sister of Kuve will carry the other child. A crowd of women watches both women walk from Kuve's hut to the opening of the wall and bend over. The midwife rubs oil and ocher over their backs and positions the young baby on the back of Kuve, placing it upside down! A loud chorus of *awu, awu* (no, no!) wells up after this "mistake," so the midwife tries again. Again "No, no," wrong position. Four times the babies are placed the wrong way, but finally the midwife gets it right: "Yes, yes!" Laughing out loud all the women shout their approval (Figure 8.1). Two of the new mother's sisters then put on the baby sling at Kuve: twice wrong " No, no," and then finally the right way—"Yes."

Kuve's sister simply ties the baby on, as she does not have to "relearn" to be a mother. Now for the first time, with the babies upright and well tied up, the new mother and her sister quickly walk through the opening in the wall and through the forecourt. Because there is to be no dancing—on the instructions of the crab—the guests then leave. On the advice of the same crab Kuve will not visit her father for some time.

The Slow Dawn of Kapsiki Personhood

Twins, of course, are not the standard birth, but any birth is surrounded by pre- and proscriptions, taboos, rituals, and symbols. Societies celebrate the birth of

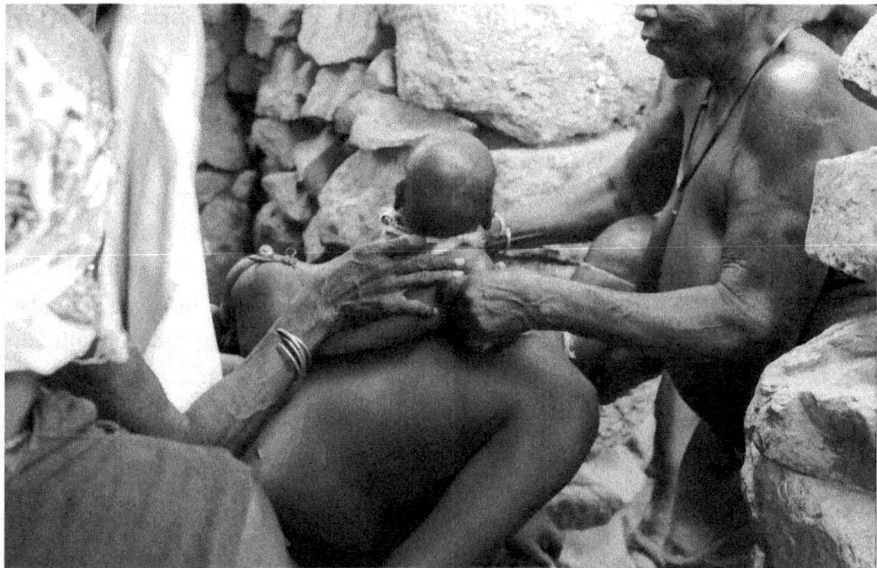

Figure 8.1 At last correct!

an infant as a lease on their future, also the Kapsiki, so birth rituals are the first of a series that gradually lead the new individual toward a full social personhood, a mature identity, defined along established lines in the community. This is what the Kapsiki rites of belonging are about, and they form a relay of rituals from birth until the final dance of death. In this relay rituals increase in scope and intensity, from relatively simple birth rituals to the complex feasting of mature personhood in the year rites and in funerals. This is what I call the "slow dawn of personhood," as a social person will be gradually built during one's life.

Little ritual accompanies a Kapsiki pregnancy. People consider it normal that the mother has different, even bizarre, food cravings, but she will go on working until her delivery. A woman can give birth anywhere as long as it is not in her father's house, since doing that would be a thorough negation of her marriage and, evidently, of his receipt of the bridewealth.

> If she does happen to deliver in or near the walls of his compound, a small ritual has to cleanse her, and especially him. If she happens to be in her father's compound when the birth starts—which is not at all impossible, as she has to come back to her parent's house quite regularly during her first year of marriage—people set her on a flat stone just outside the wall. After giving birth, she is then taken inside, where she will remain for a while, just as she would in her husband's home. On the fourth day after the delivery, the husband brings a goat for his father-in-law to slaughter at the place of birth: "Thank

you, *shala*, thank you, *shala*, that my daughter has given birth, thank you, *shala*."

Usually, however, she delivers at home. When the contractions start, the husband calls an older, experienced woman from the neighborhood to help his wife, not as an official function but as someone who has proven her experience in the past. This "midwife" in fact only looks after the baby and is hardly involved with the mother at all. The latter is seated on a stone outside her hut and has her clothes removed until she is wearing just a cache sexe. Her bracelets are also removed. A man from the neighborhood who has many living children spits on her swollen belly: "*Shala*, give him the way, open the way," and at a later stage gently beats the belly with an indigo stem.

> Problems during delivery are ascribed to the marital problems of the pregnant woman or to problems surrounding the midwife, her children, or her father-in-law. If the delivery is difficult, and if such problems are suspected to be the source, these people are all called into the compound. The husband then takes his sacrificial jar from under the granary, takes some earth from under the jar, and spits on it to make mud, announcing: "*Shala*, I did not make myself, but you have made me. Let the child come quickly." He then puts the mud on the *melε*. All concerned do the same: spit on some earth, say similar words, and put the mud on the jar. If the quarrel is between the woman and her husband's children, the latter have to spit on her belly: "*Shala*, let the child descend quickly."

The woman usually sits on a stone in front of her own hut, where the male neighbor (normally not her own husband) supports her from behind. The midwife crouches between her legs, concerned with one major danger: that the newborn baby will cry either too much or too little. Once the baby is born, the old woman sprinkles the baby with cold water to make it cry a little, but not too much lest the child's blood clots. Then the old woman announces the baby's sex in a loud voice to all present, usually women from the neighborhood. The umbilical cord is left intact until the placenta has been delivered, although another worry is that it will come too quickly. The midwife takes measures against this by putting the stick to stir millet mush in the mouth of the young mother, who must either blow on it twice or whistle. Once the placenta has arrived, the umbilical cord is cut. If the baby is a boy, the midwife uses the edge of the grass used for an arrow shaft, and if it is a girl, the edge of a cut millet stalk. The baby is then washed in cold water and the umbilical cord smeared with a mixture of ocher[2] and mahogany oil.

The subsequent proceedings depend on divination. A number of days before the delivery, the husband has consulted the crab diviner to establish what type of sacrifice would be called for, especially the color and sex of the fowl. Now that the most delicate period is over, the new father plucks the chicken's neck, the midwife holding its feet. At his wife's washing place, he cuts its throat, lets its blood flow onto the floor, and then swings the dying fowl by its legs, sprinkling the doorposts and threshold of his wife's hut, while she looks on from inside: "Let all be healthy, *shala*; do not let evil enter, may I have no evil inside; thank you, *shala*, thank you, *shala*."

The midwife then takes the child into the mother's hut, where the latter has taken off her last garment. The midwife sticks the millet stalk or arrow shaft used for cutting the umbilical cord into the thatched roof of the hut for everybody to see. Outside the hut, a few women from the neighborhood clean up the birth place: they take a broken pot, wrap the placenta in leaves, put it inside, and bury the pot at the washing place, leaving the rim of the pot just above the ground. The father gets hot water and looks for branches of a medicinal plant, *kwantereza* (*Cassia singuena*, Del.), which he gathered in the days before, as they are supposed to give off a healthy smoke for the mother. Hot water is needed, according to the midwife, to "let the blood flow. The bad blood has to come out." At the washing spot the midwife sprinkles the hot water over the young mother and finally pours it over her anus and genitals. The mother then finishes her washing inside the hut.

Meanwhile, the father signals the birth to the village. In the forecourt of his compound he puts a long, slender piece of euphorbia at the male side if it is a boy, and if it is a girl a broad, squat piece on the female side.

> The placenta, as well as the umbilical cord that the baby will lose in about ten days, remain important for the mother, part of her symbolic vulnerability. Anyone wishing her ill might use it for evil magic (*besheŋu*), rendering her barren for the rest of her life. She usually gives the umbilical cord to her mother to take care of, who will bury it at her daughter's washing spot. This is one reason why, after her first child, a woman will not normally leave her husband. She stays at least until her second pregnancy or else may leave after a long stretch of infertility, since she has to wait until she and her baby are less ritually vulnerable.

According to the Kapsiki, a mother's first milk is harmful for her baby, so it is drawn out and thrown away. "Real food," water mixed with a little bit of ocher, is given to the baby by means of a small oblong calabash used only for this purpose. A young woman once explained to me that she never fed her baby at night, meaning that she did not give him water but just the breast.

Number Names

The second day after the birth, the "official" announcement to the village of its newest member is made during the *d'afa mndɛ* ceremony, which is named after the leaves used in the sauce that is served then. The young father slaughters several chickens or a goat and a chicken, according to the baby's sex. About ten o'clock in the morning, when the people from the neighborhood and his lineage brothers are gathered in his forecourt, the father expresses his gratitude in a short speech, and everybody eats. The distribution of the meat, as always among the Kapsiki, marks the occasion: the wings and claws for the new mother, the breast and feet for the baby's father and his father, and the rest for the midwife. The latter is sent home with a substantial food gift of mush, a chicken, beef fat, and salt. Distribution of the goat's meat or the other chickens is less specific: one bowl of meat for the men from the neighborhood gathered in the forecourt (or in the *dabala*, the entrance hut, in the rainy season), three bowls for the women and children in the various kitchens, and one bowl with choice meat (a little bit of everything) for the new mother. As usual, the sister's son distributes the meat.

Just after the *d'afa mndɛ*, the new mother's mother comes to instruct her daughter on how to feed her child and how to sleep without harming the baby. Her son-in-law welcomes her with a huge calabash containing choice fine meats for her daughter. She herself brings a substantial gift of beer and ceremonial food: a mixture of millet, peanuts, and ground sorrel. She is not present at the birth of her daughter's first child but will assist in person in the future. Her husband will not come to his daughter's compound because she first has to present the new baby to him at his house. This grandmother stays until the umbilical cord drops off, usually after about eight days, though the Kapsiki have noted that this may take longer for a boy than for a girl. When it does drop off, certain female family members are alerted: the wives of his father's clan if it is a boy, the women of her mother's clan if it is a girl. After an interval of three or four days they will come with millet mush and a sauce of beans and peanuts. The new father will have bought meat and a large piece of salt which he distributes among the women to eat on the spot.

Until now, the baby has no name. This has to wait for the day that the new mother first leaves the compound. How long she remains within the compound depends on birth order: for her first child and for any type of special child—such as twins and breech births—she will stay in the house longer. In addition, the crab diviner may indicate to the father that she should remain inside for a specific length of time. During the rainy season a lot of work has to be done in the fields, so her stay will be shorter, just one or two weeks, but usually it is at least three weeks before she leaves the enclosing wall of the compound. Her leaving is the most characteristic of the birth rituals: "to take the new mother out of the house" or *shave* (go out), the one we witnessed above, for a pair of twins.

In the morning, members of the ward and lineage of the new father gather in the newborn's compound, not in the forecourt but inside the wall. The father has slaughtered a goat and a chicken, just as for the *d'afa mndɛ*, and follows the same order of distribution. Before anyone starts eating, the midwife takes a bowl of meat and sauce to the spot where the new mother washes herself, and she pours some sauce on the earth, saying: "The child must be healthy, evil must be far away, and *shala* must not send evil things here." She then dips a piece of mush in the sauce and drops it on the earth. She then eats the rest of the mush and meat herself.

After she has finished, the men, women, and children in the compound start eating, each in their respective huts and kitchens. It is during this meal that the young father names his child. The usual Kapsiki names follow birth order; so each Kapsiki man and woman has one name that indicates the order of pregnancy of his or her mother. A woman's first child is called Tizhè if it is a boy, Kuve if a girl. The second child is Zra (for a boy) or Masi (for a girl), regardless of the sex of the first-born. The names have no specific meaning other than their order, but still themselves are not numbers but proper names.[3] Still, they can also be used as nouns in daily speech: "This is my Zra" and "I also have a Deli." People are often referred to by their own name plus that of their father or their mother (both are possible), such as Tizhè Sunu, Deli Zra, or Zra Kwasunu, a kind of identifying genealogy. In practice this system still amounts to a lot of people with the same name and combinations such as Tizhè Zra, Deli Kwanyè, and Zra Deli abound.

So at the naming ceremony, the father gives his child an additional name based on the circumstances at the time of the birth itself: Kwabake (fanned, if people used branches to cool the mother), Kedra (too late), Lèwa (born close to the water outlet under the wall), or, as we saw with the twins' father, Dabala (born in the entrance hut). Something the mother ate just before the birth can also be used; for example, the Mogode village chief is called Wusuhwahwele (thing-in-the-water), because his mother ate a fish just before giving birth. The father of the newborn may express some of his own feelings about the child, about himself, and about his place in society through the name. Names such as Mèkwele (at the mouth of the grave), Fama (does not listen), Mbekewa (where to go), and Cewuve (like a cat in the field) express not so much ideas about the newborn but about the father himself. Fama implies that the other clan members do not listen to him. Still, some pessimism about the newborn's chances is seen in these names; for example, Mèkwele implies both his own imminent death and the chances of his son dying young. The names echo a definite pessimism but also serve as apotropaism, to fend off fate.

All these secondary names are, however, considered fleeting and ephemeral compared with birth-order names. The latter never change and cannot be altered. With the introduction of name registration at the canton offices in the central villages such as Mogode, the baby's name is officially given very early in life, which means that birth-order names are becoming more prominent, and the secondary names are now seen as secondary. One influence of the Christian missions, evidently, is to give Christian secondary names that, like the others, may or may not be accepted socially (usually they are not) and always take second place to birth-order names. Muslim names are adopted later in life, on conversion to Islam, and encounter a similar fate to the Christian ones. Christian names are used only within the church, Muslim names among Muslims; and between religions birth-order names will be used because they give a person's true identity.

After the naming ceremony and with the meal finished, most of the men leave. They should be careful not to wipe their hands on one of the house-poles or to wash them inside the compound, lest they bring bad luck upon the child. The final scene is now set for the women of the ward to help the mother leave the compound with her baby for the first time, the *shave*, a ritual like the coming out of the twins, but with only one baby. We saw the gentle show of putting the baby wrong first, as if the mother has to relearn how to "mother." We pick up the ritual at that point now.

When her baby is well tied on her back, the new mother quickly walks through the opening in the wall and through the forecourt.[4] Into the middle of this forecourt she throws some goat dung and makes cultivating motions with the handle of a hoe that she holds in her right hand. The other women follow her, sprinkling water on the dung and on the mother's buttocks. This is the actual *shave* and as such has its own vulnerability. Only women from the immediate neighborhood or from her husband's lineage may be present, because if too many show up, some of them might be witches and harm the baby. (In the case of the twins described above, the crab had forbidden this ritual.)

When the mother leaves her husband's compound for the first time, she usually heads straight for her father's house. Only in the case of a Kuve or Tizhè (first-born) does she wait one or two months. When she arrives at his compound, she presents him with some mush and a mixture of ground sorghum and peanuts she has prepared. If it is her first child, she also brings some jars of red beer, one for a Tizhè, two for a Kuve. The food is put on her father's usual seat in the forecourt and he welcomes his grandchild and daughter with a fat goat. He slaughters the beast and gives his daughter the four legs as meat. He prepares the animal's skin for a baby sling, rubbing it with oil and ocher to take away the hairs and render it supple, then meticulously fashions the sling that is to carry his grandchild. (This was done by the nephews in the twins case.) Of course, the baby is shown to everyone in that ward, and a smith woman from the neighborhood is called in to shave the baby's head for the first time, since "the hairs of the belly" have to go. Whatever the birth order of the child, the mother stays a few days at her father's compound; her mother may also be there but, because of the frequent marriages within Kapsiki society, this is not always the case and she may have moved elsewhere. For her father, however, his daughter's visit is the definite recognition of this "grandson of the clan." Because her father's clan will remain important for her child throughout his or her life, especially if the baby is a boy, this ceremonial installment of a sister's son is of social importance. She, as its mother, is now recognized as a "daughter of the clan" in the full significance of the term, a woman who has established a productive link between the two patriclans.

An additional significance of this visit, with its official showing of progeny, relates to bridewealth. Kapsiki society is dominated by a marriage-cum-bridewealth problematic. A bride's father gains considerably from his daughter's marriage, especially her first marriage, and so the arrival of a grandchild is more than welcome in many ways, not least because the baby secures the bride wealth as his legitimate and enduring property. Now he will never have to return it, even if his daughter leaves her husband at some later date, as she usually will. In the case of a miscarriage, the woman also makes this ceremonial visit. Though norms are changing, a miscarriage is also supposed to be a "repayment" of the bridewealth, as the traditional ritual means of ensuring repayment does not work after a miscarriage.[5]

According to the Kapsiki, sexual relations may start immediately after the coming out, but with one proviso. The first month after birth the woman is considered especially fertile and people like to avoid such a close second pregnancy. The risk for the first child is well known; it will become a *matini* (a child without milk) when lactation is interrupted too quickly, so the child's health is put in jeopardy. If a *matini* survives, people reckon it will remain small and puny. Still, examples of *matini* growing up well are known, and sexual abstinence in the first month is not total. The curse of such a *matini* is feared, a fact that gives these weak children some power.

> Lactation is crucial, anyway. If a young mother has no milk for her baby, adultery could be the cause; she then has to make a public confession of her affair by crying out on a *keluŋu* while a horn whistle is blown beside her. However, with all the births I attended, I never witnessed such an announcement.

So, from the second month to the time the baby has two upper and two lower teeth, the mother is considered infertile. After that period, some abstinence is called for until the baby is about three years old, always bearing in mind the decreasing risk of *matini*. Any baby that does not grow well will get a necklace made of a tail of a *rhwazha* (a slender lizard) and the name "Rhwazhake" will be added to his or her birth-order name.

One special little ritual later in life is worth mentioning here. During the child's first rainy season, the little toddler acquires its first *leke*, a straw plaited rain cape. However, this cape is first put on the head of a dog, which then runs off, losing the *leke*. Only then is the cape put on the child, for to do otherwise would be an infringement of a taboo and might harm the child.

The small rituals of birth are changing gradually. The goat skin baby sling is giving way to a cloth one made from sturdy cotton, and the *leke* is becoming rare, since generally umbrellas have become very popular among mothers, so also for their babies. If people still use the skin as a baby sling, they take care never to sell it, nor are any of the other items important for the protection of the baby ever sold, such as amulets, used for children who are still considered vulnerable. Still very much in force, though, are the bracelets for the special births, the *matini*, the breech births, and surely for the most important of all special births, and the prime fascination of Africa, twins. Mothers coming out tend still to heed to the little "cultivation" ritual, though more and more as a way of amusement if they have become Christian.

But then, rituals such as the children's ones, as well as most of the others, always have a definite aspect of play. Being used to the seriousness of Western Christian ritual with its clear distinction between the sacred and the profane, I had to become accustomed to the free and easy atmosphere in Kapsiki rituals; people joked, dozed off, visited with each other, and simply had a good time, while still performing the intended ritual. So these kinds of small child-oriented rituals, which are joyous anyway, easily lead to some internal folklorization, to doing playfully what more or less should be done. When things do not go as planned and hoped for, the mothers will heed the old customs more meticulously; for instance, when many of her children die, she will not shave the hair of her youngest baby, but braid a cowry in its hair. When the child is eight years old and has passed the most dangerous period in its life, a smith shaves the child's head with a special large blade, and the child will keep the cowry. Combating actual hazard has changed little; change in ritual occurs for those rituals with a relatively loose connection to danger.

Birth ritual aims at introducing the newborn to the world of the adults, so the first ritual of belonging in this case is one of "becoming," of "starting to belong." The group in question is still small, just the resident family in the house, plus interested neighbors. Very much a woman's matter, birth rituals are small-scale and informal. Neither lineage nor clan is in the picture yet, so in a way birth rituals serve as a bridge between the dwelling rituals—viewing the importance of house and its family—and the larger rituals of belonging pertaining to later phases in life. Actually, that divide is already crossed in the rituals surrounding twins, as these are no longer just a family matter but involve clan and village as well. And this will occupy us in the next section.

Twins

This chapter began with the coming out rituals of twins. The Kapsiki distinguish four kinds of special babies: *dlave*, breech births, *ghi*, and multiple births, that is, twins and the much rarer triplets. The first refers to a child born in the caul, the birth membrane remaining on its head. The Kapsiki compare this with *dlave*, a piece of cloth. The caul will be removed, dried, and put in a medicine container. There are two kinds of *dlave*, one covering the whole head, the other just a strip. The first type of child has to be very careful and carry a medicine vial with some of the *dlave* inside, and may never sleep in a hut other than its own. The second type is the lucky one. These children will be rich and, if male, marry a lot of women, father a great number of children, and earn a lot of money, that is, become rich in both Kapsiki senses, in material goods and in people—but characteristically not in hunting or in health. One can never have everything in Kapsik culture. The curse of people with *dlave* has power, as does the curse of all "special people."

A breech birth is a problem mainly during the difficult birth itself. If the baby survives, it will still present some danger to both its parents, which they can avoid by having a blacksmith make two special bracelets that they will wear for the rest of their lives. Another special bracelet is made when a baby gets its first teeth in its upper jaw instead of in the lower. This latter "peculiarity" threatens the harvest, a risk they may stave off by wearing the smith's product.

A child conceived without any prior menstruation by his mother (*ghi*) forms a hazard as well. Such an almost-twin means the father runs a serious risk of dying before the child is initiated. However, risks are there to be combated, so the father makes a hole in the thatch of his own hut roof, pushes the baby out through it, and then removes part of the child's left earlobe. The risk is now reduced and the father may see his son through initiation or his daughter through marriage. Often the suffix *ghi* is added to the child's name to avoid bad luck.

The attitude of the Kapsiki towards new life and personhood is best seen in its relationship with the last, and highly ambiguous, phenomenon, people who are born together. In this respect Kapsiki culture is almost standard, as twins are Africa's fascination. It is not so much identical twins that fascinate Kapsiki but the fact of being born together of the same mother at the same time. Regardless of whether they are identical or non-identical twins, twins are two people sharing the same social space and time, occupying the same node in the social network. For Kapsiki, twins, *kwalerha*, are highly relevant and quite complicated: they love them and fear them, are proud of them and shun them at the same time. They are, as informants state, "not of this world" and "twins are like *gutuli*, spirits roaming the bush, children of *shala*." They are not easy to live with, taxing those around them to the limit. Twins get angry on the spot, are quick to take offense, and are especially quick to take a liking to some wonderful object. Then they become dangerous, the Kapsiki say. Therefore they should be indulged in any wish: whenever they really like some object, people have to give it to them; if not, a twin will fall into a trance and faint; in Kapsiki parlance he "dies," and, in doing so, heaps curses upon the stingy nongiver. Evidently, this behavior puts tremendous pressure on the twins' parents, especially upon the father. Tlakema, an adult twin, described the situation to me:

> Us twins, we are not normal people, as we are from *shala*. If we "die," the fault lies with the father; the mother has been chosen already by *shala*, but if the father does something wrong, the twin children will know it immediately. The heaviest responsibility is on the father.

More than anything else, red things kindle their desire and push them over the threshold of trance. Like the spirits of the bush, twins have a special liking for the color red, so in their vicinity nobody can wear red[6] clothes with an easy mind.

> During a dance a twin woman, Kwandè, suddenly faints on seeing a small boy with a slightly reddish shirt. People shout "Twin, twin," flock around her, rip the shirt off the boy, put it on her head and start dancing around her: "*Kwalerha* that came to dance, *kwalerha* to dance." The festival was organized for another twin, so that twin's mother searches out some *sesele* (indigo), calls Kwandè by her name: "Stand up, Kwandè, stand up," and beats her with the twigs. After some time Kwandè starts trembling and comes to. People then help her get up, and she slowly opens her eyes. Finally she walks away, unsure, dazed, and on leaden legs.
>
> Kwandè described the event in her own words: "When I see something like that, everything becomes dark around me, and I hear the voices of everybody from very far away. Everything I really like—meat, red necklaces, red clothes, but also white clothes when they are beautiful. I should not look at them. It only happens when I fix my eyes upon it, when I keep on looking, but sometimes I cannot help it. To bring me around, another twin, or the parent of a twin, has to beat me with indigo or vetiver grass (Figure 8.2). Once I did the same to another twin woman who had fainted, I beat her with vetiver grass, but when she regained consciousness, I fainted myself. If something is really beautiful, two twins might faint at the same time."

Not only do twins heap a curse upon people who refuse them something, the thing that is refused will be spoiled as well. So twins will always be the first to taste food; similarly they have to taste the beer first; otherwise it will not ferment properly and food will rot if their presence is not honored with the first bite.

Figure 8.2 Kwandè is brought back to consciousness.

Twins are closely associated with scorpions: they "command the scorpions," meaning they can send the beasts to anyone who thwarts them. The Kapsiki stress that twins do so consciously as well as unconsciously, just as they can harm anyone just by disliking them. A scorpion cannot harm twins since these seem to be immune to its sting. Some twins like to boast a little bit. According to the adult twin Tlakema, "People cannot, truly, keep us twins alive, as each time we want something, we get angry in our hearts. Only *shala* can keep us well, as everything spoils us."

If both twin children stay alive, they remain close to each other, also in marriage, marrying close relatives if they can, and a twin sister will not move to another village if her twin brother is still at home. Marrying a twin is considered tricky: "If a man is married to a *kwalerha*, he cannot even beat her without her dying on him." However, I have found no example of a twin marrying another twin, which would be the obvious solution. If one twin dies, the living one is also carried on the shoulders of a smith during the dance (see Chapter 12). Still, people stipulate that when of the same gender they are not really close friends as they are in continuous competition with each other. But generally, twins live lives like other people, though they are respected and their wishes are seldom crossed; in any event, they always have the weapon of trance.

Thus, parents of twins have to meet a number of challenges. First, they order from a blacksmith two bracelets, *takase kwalerha*, one for each parent, because with these bracelets at their wrists, the twins' powers will not harm them. The beer will be right if the twins taste it, the sorghum will flourish when they touch it first, and sesame will ripen when they look at it. In daily life, twins carry cowry shells and sesame in their pockets and wear a band of *'yanka* grass around their wrists. Of all the crops, their special one is sesame, which they have to eat frequently; actually, they smell it from afar, and no one passes them with sesame without their knowing it.

Twins are close to Rain, which is to be expected with such an "overstatement of fertility." During the birth of twins it should rain, and my informants testified that it does so. I am among these informants myself. The three twin births I witnessed all happened in the rainy season during heavy rainstorms. Fundamentally, twins are not of this earth but of heaven, and this aspect shows in their dreams: they dream of the "other-world"; their "shadow" does not go down when dreaming, like the one of normal people, but soars on high. In the words of Kwandè:

> We, as twins, we dream of heaven. There we drink white water and we find people like here; they are our *shala*. One particular white-haired woman I know very well, she is my *shala*, who has created me. An old woman, her hair all white. If I die, I will know it in advance. After my death, my shadow will not go down into the earth but will return to heaven. When as a twin you do not dream of heaven, you will die. When dreaming in heaven, we see other twins. We do not fight, only the *keleŋu*[7] fight. We do nothing in secret, everything is public. It is our character; *shala* has made us this way.

People stressed that twins occur more in some families than in others; Kwandè's family boasts eight pairs of twins. Also, twin births seldom seem to occur in a first pregnancy. Birth itself is easy and fast, so often outside the house.

> Kwatere, Belama's wife, gave birth in another ward; she was not suspected of carrying twins but both little girls were born healthy. Later her husband consulted the crab diviner, and following instructions, sacrificed two chickens and left indigenous vinegar with some ground millet soaked in water on the spot where she had given birth. He then closed off the spot with thorns and stones, all to prevent the *shala* of the place from following her home.

When the twins are born at home, both umbilical cords have to be cut at the same time with a *haze* grass and immediately afterward their parents have to engage in a mock quarrel. If not, the twins will be angry when their parents quarrel later. The father should have intercourse with the young mother the same day, lest she be not fertile afterward. Both partners hate this requirement, so it is usually done very quickly or they just pretend to have intercourse for the benefit of the many bystanders. Right after the birth, the father orders two small jars from a smith woman, which will be the *mele* for the twins, jars that are also called *mele ha*, sorghum jar, as they are closely associated with harvest. During a working party, people sometimes do not want to be disturbed by rain, so they put such a *mele ha* with beer, ocher, and ashes on it in the field: no rain will fall. Actually, these jars will not serve for sacrifices but just sit in the dark hut. Later the twins will order a real *mele* on which to sacrifice.

Feasting a Twin

Twin names do not follow the normal birth-order names. Boys are called Pimbi, Mara, Tlakema, or Puhu, girls Kwandè or Kwalerha, and these names can be freely chosen but usually follow the instructions of a crab diviner. But before the actual naming ceremony of the *shave*—the one described at the start of this chapter—a lot has to happen.

The first rites for twins are in principle similar to those described above for a single child. For the first ceremony, *d'afa mnde*, the father kills two chickens, the same sex as the twins. He then has the two chickens broiled in identical tripod meat pots, puts the cooked meat in two men's eating vases, and scouts for two identical drinking calabashes, two halves of the same fruit. While word of the birth of twins is shouted through the village, the father warns his clan brothers, who live all over the village, to help him. Early the next morning they assemble in the hut of the father of the twins. All bring chickens and a friend comes with a long band of white cloth which they string up between the huts of the father and mother of the twins. From that moment on the parents start to talk again, having kept silent up until now. The two stay close together for the rest of time, both to be addressed by their new status as "parent of twins." Early the same morning, the twins' father asks the chief smith for some *hweβe kwalerha*, a special medicine (*Crinum* sp.) used to ward off evil from young children. Other measures depend on the instructions of the crab.

At the next rite, the coming-out party, each guest brings chickens, a handful of sesame, and a handful of millet for the father. They present the mother with small coins and quartz pebbles, offering all presents with two hands. The sesame and couch grass grains are cooked as *zhazha* (a ritual dish eaten at the end of funerals, made of sorghum grains and beans but here with couch grass seeds). After eating, dancing and singing, the guests return home, and the father arranges the "interrogation" of his twins. Therefore he asks an adult twin, another Pimbi or Kwalerha, to conduct the interview.

Tlakema Pimbi, a twin of about 45, is the one to interview the twins of Zra Dabala. Before entering the hut of mother Kuve, he asks her to face the wall of the hut. He then enters, greeting the children with "Good afternoon my people." The baby closer to the door cries, and both babies thrash their legs and arms around and turn on their backs.

These movements, according to Tlakema, mean that there would be dancing. He explains that the answers to his questions are given by the crying, thrashing, and heartbeat of the babies. The interview takes a full two hours. Afterwards Tlakema goes straight to Zra Dabala's older clan brother to report the interview, and the twins' father, in turn, gets his instructions from this older brother. In the case of Zra Dabala, the instructions were quite elaborate:

> You take a club and a shield, your wife Kuve takes the little mat she uses for the millet mush and the stick for stirring the mush, and both of you pretend to quarrel, really hard. Someone else should calm and separate you, and after that you two may never quarrel again.
> Once the umbilical cord falls off, you have to sleep with the twins' mother once, lest she become infertile. Then you mix ground yellow and white sorghum in water and have the babies drink it. Do not put red clay on their navels; they do not like that, just a bit of oil is enough.
> From then on, you always have to provide two bowls of sauce, two lumps of mush, two calabashes with water, and two bowls of meat, all of it for their mother. In order to have children again, you apply the sesame I have given you with your left hand to the mother's vulva and with your right hand to your own penis.
> People coming to greet you have to present couch grass grains and sorghum in their two hands. You keep what your clan brings, and your wife keeps what her clan presents her with; if this is not done, then "simple people" (non-twins) cannot enter her hut. Pebbles have to be thrown in front of her door. Everything has to happen in twos—for example, two chickens each day. Your wife has to tie a bell around her wrist to warn the babies each time she is coming into their hut (i.e. her own hut). It is not good to visit twins without warning.
> The cloth between your two huts has to have a little bit of red on it to prevent the twins' asking for red things from other people.
> Now enter, Zra, I have put sesame on their mat. If they are real twins (i.e. if they behave as twins should), then they will have the sesame in their hands.

Zra does find the sesame in the twins' tiny fists and follows the instructions to the letter. As usual in these cases, his wife is too weak for the mock battle, so her sister replaces her. That evening the youngsters of the ward come for the twin dance, singing out loud:

> Our twins, people from the heavens
> Black sesame, Kwandè from heaven
> Twins for the dance, our twins
> Sesame of the heavens
> Who has come down from heaven to dance.
> Why did you come, black sesame?
> Thing of our ancestors; he did not start it.
> There is a lizard hidden, Kwandè
> I saw the house of the rat
> But Kwandè had already seen it.[8]

The singers greet the twins the same way as everybody else, putting handfuls of millet and couch grass grains into a bowl close to the babies. Almost everybody asks the twins: "Why did you come? Did you come to dance or to cry?" (i.e. to live or to die). The twins' father cooks the *zhazha* and serves this ritual dish to the singers, who take just two grains of millet, two beans, and two couch grass seeds.

For the next month, the father of the twins will stroll through the village with the friend who tied the band of cloth, and during this period anyone who wants to speak with him will have to do so through this friend, after first giving him two coins. Adorned with a palm band around his forehead, the father carries his sickle, a gourd, and a sack as signs of his new status. Anyone visiting the mother also hands her presents in pairs until her *shave*, her coming out. The obligations between this first naming and the ritual leaving of the compound weigh heavily on the father. While his wife stays inside the compound, he has to procure two chickens a day for her to eat. Because this period may last up to four months, this can add up to an astonishing number of fowl. If poor, he limits the number, but getting thirty chickens is already a sizable task, even with his clansmen helping him. Zra Dabala, the father of twins referred to at the beginning of the chapter, scours the market during these months, dressed in his finest outfit and wearing a bracelet of wild sugar cane,[9] the same grass his wife wears as a girdle, to indicate his status as twin father, and he asks anybody for a gift, money or a chicken. Working hard, he collects a dozen chickens at the weekly market. Later markets see him begging again, but less successfully, as people start to avoid him: speaking with the father of a twin is expensive. Whenever there is beer to drink, his calabash will be filled first, before the chief's, since any bad thought by the twins' father is a curse on the village. Twins are considered to be like *hweteru* (the evil eye, but more ambivalent in their case) and their parents share that power.

Then the time for the *shave* approaches, two months after a birth in the wet season, four in the (less busy) dry season, and for the twins this is a large feast indeed. Separately, the twins' father and mother consult the crab for the specifics of the feast and for any special sacrifices, arrangements, and taboos. Zra Dabala recounts:

> The crab told me that I should not dance during or after the feast, nor brew too much *tɛ*. My sacrifice is: a cockscomb, some sorghum from a man and some from a woman, and the testicles of a male goat mixed with a few hairs from a small goat. I put all of it on the *melɛ*. The rest I have to throw outside the wall of the compound, with the words: "You children have to be in health and remain healthy." For the twins to remain well, my wife has to grind pieces of female and male goat bones and spray a little of the mixture on the twins and their two small pots and throw the rest away. She must cook porridge from sorghum sprouts and put a pot of it on the road to Ldiri, her native village. The crab warns her not to visit her father's home [contrary to custom].

The *shave* forms the mainstay of the twin rituals, much larger than in the case of a single birth, and as we saw earlier, Zra Dabala did follow these instructions to the letter.

After the *shave*, about a year after the birth, a third and final twins' ritual consists of the first cutting of the hair. Early in the morning the relatives of both parents gather in the compound around the hut of their own kin. All have their heads shaved while sipping the beer Zra has prepared, the *tɛ kwaŋsu rhu* (beer to shave the head). At last the band of cloth linking the huts of the parents is removed. The feast itself is almost a reenactment of the *shave* ritual: two goats, male and female, are killed, skinned, and boiled. People drink, eat, and give blessings. The young girls of the wife's clan take care of cooking the mush. Before the meal, the initiation father of Kuve takes a bowl of sesame sauce prepared by Kuve's mother's sister and sprinkles the sauce over the two babies, who rest in the arms of two sisters: "You have to be healthy, to be healthy, to dance the *la* festival (initiation)." The food and beer are distributed, and people drink and eat. Finally, Zra's mother's brother takes Zra's *melɛ* and pours a calabash of red beer over it: "*Shala, Jigelafte*,[10] everybody must be healthy, all must marry wives and have children to have the family continue. Let him (addressing the boy) marry a good wife who will not run away, but a good wife who stays." He lets the beer flow over the *melɛ*, sprays some on the posts of Zra's hut and on Zra, drinks himself, and then has Zra and the other kinsmen drink.

The next morning the twin parents plant two trees, *menkweda*,[11] in one of their fields. They put a grindstone close to the saplings and water them regularly. Nobody will ever touch these trees, nor will anyone else ever cut their branches for firewood, as they directly represent the twins. If anyone should cut one of their branches, the corresponding twin will become ill, and if the tree were cut down, the twin would die. After the planting, Zra and Kuve head for the blacksmith's to have the twin bracelets made. Only after this rite may the twins be seen anywhere in the village. They remain a little marginal, since the attention of the public is on their mother and father.

> Later, the twins themselves will perform sacrifices on those trees, using them as a second *mele*. When a twin girl marries her first spouse, just before her *makwa* rites, she dresses herself in her straw cape and her iron skirt and wraps a cloth around her body. She takes two jars of *te*, a sheep, and a goat to the trees and cuts a branch off both of them. After slaughtering the animals on the spot, she lets the blood run over the branches. Later she will use these branches to build the straw roof before her hut.

With these rituals, the twins have now been introduced to their their kinsmen, and to their clan and lineage. In all their individual rites, as well as in initiation and first marriage, their bilateral kinsmen have to participate. Twin rituals are much more complicated than those of "normal" people: all sacrifices are made in twos, the special symbols of *peha* palm, ram's hairs and wild sugar cane are used, and there is an abundance of cowry shells and invocations. Also, more kinsmen have to show up, many more: twins never host a group, always a crowd.

The fact that they are twins will continue to color their lives: if they die young—as many do—they will be buried like a small child but not with their hands on their head, as a child is. Instead their hands will be placed under their chin, palms upward: they are people from heaven and have to beg *shala* that way. If they live until their initiation, their father slaughters sheep instead of goats, and they will wear a piece of the animal's skin on their wrist for the rest of their lives. For twin girls the trousseaus have to be exactly the same, because twins are considered to be competitors. The father keeps the two jars made at the twins' birth under his own *tame* granary, not to sacrifice on them but he might use these *mele ha* to halt rain.

The link with sesame will remain strong: a twin can freely take any sesame he sees anywhere, even if he does not specifically cultivate it himself; in fact, it should be cultivated for him. At the end of a twin's life, a special song is sung at his funeral, with a text almost identical to the one used at the coming out: "Twin, twin of the sesame, did you come to dance, do you have anything to hide, dancing twin." However, at his last dance, like everyone, the twin dances not on his own legs but on a smith's shoulders.

For the parents of the twins, their special status continues to entail as many obligations as for twins themselves. For the rest of their lives they will be called "father and mother of twins," and they remain imbued with extra meaning. For instance, at all times they have to wear their bracelets, since without them their grains will disappear from their granary, while with their bracelets at their wrists their mush will fill many stomachs, their crops will ripen into full ears, and their *tame* will always be filled. However, they have to be careful with their grains. When the mother of a twin is threshing and winnowing, the father is there too, but both should remain completely silent, as they were when the babies were born. The father also should transport the grains in complete silence.

> That bracelet is really important. Once, the father of a pair of twins had lost his, so he immediately headed for the blacksmith. At the forge he did not explain anything but just showed his empty wrist to the smith, who then asked, "The third one?" also avoiding mentioning the twins. The father nodded, and waited in the forge until the bracelet was finished.

Symbols of Personhood

In the birth rites in general and in twin rituals in particular, we are in the realm of the low-frequency rituals in which the imagistic mode is dominant. Yet, as we saw with single births, some of these are low-intensity/low-arousal rituals, quite straightforward also in their symbolism. My distinction between cognitively optimal and costly rituals parallels the difference between single and double birth rituals quite well. The basic models for the first type are the communal meal—the omnipresent element in the dwelling rites—and the straightforward act of tying a baby on one's back, which ritual renders counterintuitive by doing it wrong first, plus the mimetics of cultivation, in the forecourt! Optimal rites such as these are easy to remember, and interpretation can stay "close to home": the meal gives the baby a name, the mother accepts her role as a proper mother, and she resumes her daily chores with the addition of a baby on her back.

The *kwalerha* rites are another matter. Zra Dabala had to inquire of the elders how to do them, be careful not to make mistakes, and throughout the festivities the whole clan and village were involved. This is a ritual of specialists, other twins in fact, and here emotions run high. Such cognitively costly rituals ask for some exegesis, which is furnished by twins themselves, thus highlighting their special status. For most Kapsiki the exegesis comes in the various associations of the twins with danger and fertility (scorpions and rain), and with a second layer of association with *shala/gutuli* and heaven. Compared with a single birth this is less about simple rejoicing, for joy and pride are mixed with much apprehension: cognitively costly also means a mix of contradictory emotions. In Kapsiki thought the twin complex leads to questions about the concept of *shala*, which is never simple anyway, but more complicated with twins, and it is from twins, just as from the "spirit walkers," that most of the reflection on this concept stems, reflection that transforms a minimally counterintuitive concept into a complex one.

Bridging the divide between optimal and costly rites, the twin ceremonies also transform the dwelling rites into rituals of belonging. Several rituals of the twins are just a more complicated version of the normal ones, with more people present, everything done in duplicates, and a tenser atmosphere. The larger family and the clans become involved; everybody in the village is aware of the twin births, and most people are actively interested in them. Twins are never the children of just one pair of parents; they belong to all, so from the start twins have more of a personality, more presence in the village than single children, and their "dawn of personhood" is quick, not slow. The question then is what twins belong to. For an answer to that question, we will follow the symbols used in all these birth rituals; after all, I have defined ritual as "symbols having sex," so let us have a look at that (re)productive interaction between symbols.

Rituals define personhood, birth rituals define parenthood. Motherhood symbols are intimately associated with the compound, sprinkling sacrificial blood over the entrance, door posts, and thresholds, and marking the place where the birth took place outside the wall but always with a specific place for the placenta within the wall. This focus on borders and mediations of borders offers one of the few instances of body symbolism in Kapsiki and shows in the placenta, and especially the umbilical cord, as an essential bridge between the mother's body and that of her child. During the birth, the placenta and umbilical cord get almost as much attention as the baby itself, and both are buried very carefully at the mother's washing place and are closely watched in case anyone ritually misuses them. They signify the bond between mother and child, but mainly the mortal, fragile side of this bond, the separation between the two having defined a new human being. The symbol of lasting motherhood, usually milk in other African societies,[12] in Kapsiki is the baby sling that is made for the child by its maternal grandfather (in the case of a non-twin), a sling that links mother and child again; they are two separate persons but close.

Notions of fatherhood operate through the mother, since direct symbols of fatherhood are present only in the case of twins. The father of a "normal" child stresses his relationship with the new baby in several ways: first, by hosting kinsmen and neighbors and accepting their gifts, and, second, by sharing a sacrificial chicken with the midwife. In that ritual he is linked with the midwife through the chicken sacrificed over the place where the placenta and the umbilical cord are buried. He does name the child, but the birth-order names reflect his wife's progeny and not his. His wife's father, in fact, has a more direct link to the child since he is the one who makes the sling for his daughter's child, his grandchild, a very close relationship. For the father, the highlight of his fatherhood will be during the son's initiation or his daughter's wedding, but then the main symbolism is preempted by his stand-in, the initiation or wedding-father.

The child links two clans and two lineages in many ways. Any child does, and most of the symbols aim at the parents, especially the mother, more than the child itself. The new father offers his father-in-law another goat, in fact an addition to the bridewealth he has already furnished. The central moment is when the baby's mother makes her first visit to her father's. Leaving the house, she has first to learn (or relearn) her role as a mother and as a cultivator. Then she goes with gifts of food to her father and puts the ritual food in the place of honor in his house, the *pulu*, in fact just as she did right after her wedding (next chapter). He reciprocates by making her a baby sling, just as he gave her a rain cape before her *makwa* marriage. His token of full acceptance is the shaving of her baby's head; it is the mother's father who cuts the "hairs of the womb." This act has parallels with other rites of passage when the head is also ritually shaved. The grandfather ends the liminal period of the baby and his daughter with the integration of the two into her family of birth.

The food used in birth rituals is used in other rituals as well. Its general significance is one of strength and fertility and general festivity. Couch grass is used in various dishes eaten in rites of passage and in many sacrificial dishes as well. On the whole, the birth ritual food is the same as that used in the sacrifices for compound, lineage, ward and clan, a similarity that underscores the general message of the arrival of the child in the patrilineal system. Gender markers can be seen in several types of symbols but mainly in plants, in the sex of the sacrificial animals, mostly chickens and goats, and in the choice of white or red beer, the latter a very visible gender marker in Kapsiki society.

Symbols for twins breathe a different message; after all twins are notoriously difficult to classify in many cultures.[13] First, rituals for twins engage much larger groups, the whole patrilineage, even the whole clan.[14] Crucial is the central place of the bilateral kin (*hwelefwe*) on, in fact of both *hwelefwe* of the new father and the new mother, though the father's one dominates. This is a complicated group, which includes bilateral kinsmen (*hwelefwe te za*) and a restricted matrilineal group (*hwelefwe te male*).[15] The group lacks a clear boundary and is important mainly in initiation and burial. The implication is that twins belong to the larger patrilineal system as well as to the cognatic stock of both parents. Evidently, this classification links the majority of the village with the *kwalerha*, so it gives twins a much broader identity. Twins do not belong to just one lineage, are not the "sons of our bride," but instead are a force on their own with a separate, powerful identity. Ultimately they depend only on their peers, other twins, to solve the problems they create for themselves. Their rituals concern the well-being of the whole village but remain quite ambivalent. Even while rejoicing in this excess of fertility, there is worry about the viability of the twins. "Will they die or dance?" Will the parents (the father more so than the mother) live up to their responsibilities? Curiously, the *ghi*—the "almost twins," as they are considered in other cultures—meet with a very different attitude: the child is a danger since it has not come into the family in the right way and is neither a single child nor a twin.

But the presence of the *hwelefwe* means more than simply the involvement of a larger circle of kinsmen. Plant symbols may give us clues for a further interpretation of twin rituals. Sesame is "for twins," as are *'yanka* grass and the *peha* palm, which all figure in one other set of rituals: initiation. In Chapter 10 we will see boy initiates dress in their leather loinskins and adorn themselves with brass objects, also marking their identity as liminal warriors by donning strips of *peha* on their forehead and ankles and by *'yanka* bracelets, finishing off their attire with a long necklace of cowry shells. Girl initiates wear the same grasses in their cache sexe as the twins do. An even clearer symbol of liminal adulthood is provided by the *mnta* and the cowries. For twins, the *mnta* are just strips of sheep skin with long hairs, which they will wear with cowries their whole life. However, the word *mnta* also designates the long hairs on a ram's dewlap that at the end of his initiation the boy wears on top of his lance. Cowries point in the same direction; in this part of Africa cowries were never money, and their use as decoration is restricted. Just the *gwela* and the twins adorn themselves with cowry shells as an indication of liminal identity. Sesame, an important ritual food, shares this aspect. *Gwela* cultivate a lot of sesame during the wet season that is part of their liminal period.

So, the positional meaning of twins' symbols is clear: twins are not children, but neither are they adults. They are allotted some maturity during their interrogation, with their interrogator respectfully knocking on the door before entering, and in fact they are always addressed as young adults. The very power and danger of twins preclude ever viewing them as children. All in all, their symbols designate them as young people during initiation, so they "are" *gwela* and *makwa*, initiates. But twins are even more liminal than the initiates themselves. They wear the outfits of liminality during the twin rituals but then continue to wear them throughout their lives, and so to some degree do their parents, who always wear their special bracelets and are always addressed as "parent of twins." From the very beginning twins are surrounded by sesame and cowries. While normal initiates are reintegrated into society as mature individuals, shedding the paraphernalia of their initiation, twins never leave their symbols of initiation behind. They are forever liminal. When they undergo the *gwela* and *makwa* rites, they do not change their outfit, but remain as they are. By defining twins as non-children and not-yet adults, the Kapsiki solve the tenacious problem of the coexistence of two people at the same node of a social network. Thus the *kwalerha* are forever liminals, born eternal initiates, forever in-between, powerful but fragile, a dangerous blessing because they are people from on high and not from down here.

9

The Song of the Bride

The Bridal Skirt

It is time for Kwada to marry and to move from her father's house to that of her bridegroom, Sunu Ba. One day in April, Kwada's father Tizhè invites the wives of his other sons to prepare the *livu*, the bride's iron skirt. Tizhè bought it some weeks ago from a blacksmith across the border in Nigeria, where many things are cheaper, including these iron skirts. The price he paid, namely one goat, is rock bottom, for less than a goat for a bride's central piece of adornment would be stingy. Still, he is happy to have saved the price of one more goat: at the local market he would have paid two. Demand is high and the supply low because in this large village all the girls marry in the same month (the year is 1988), and the smiths of Mogode cannot cope with the demand for bridal skirts. Yesterday his future son-in-law brought four jars of beer and announced that the wives of his clan brothers would come the following morning to prepare the skirt. The women arrive, more than willing to do their part. Theirs is a simple but important job, and well remunerated as there is a lot to drink and the groom will give them presents.

The skirt needs only minor modifications: a rope has to be replaced by a string of cow hide, and the number of small iron shields has to be rendered even, in this case reduced from 15 to 14 (odd is for men, even for women). If possible, the cow hide should be from a "real Kapsiki" cow, the West African dwarf shorthorn (*Bos taurus*) breed that is indigenous in the mountains.[1] Of the six women present, two busy themselves with the task at hand while another makes a bundle of bean fibers that will serve as the bride's intimate cache sexe, the *rhuli*. This is another important symbol of womanhood: it is wearing this particular *rhuli* that transforms a girl into a woman. When finished, the four oldest women, the bride's mother's sister among them, take a large draught of beer and spray it over the *livu* (Figure 9.1). "You must repay the bridewealth quickly, so conceive many children." They then leave for the groom's house to receive their presents (of food) and pester him for more beer. Later they will try the same at the houses of their respective husbands, Sunu's brothers.

The Song of the Bride

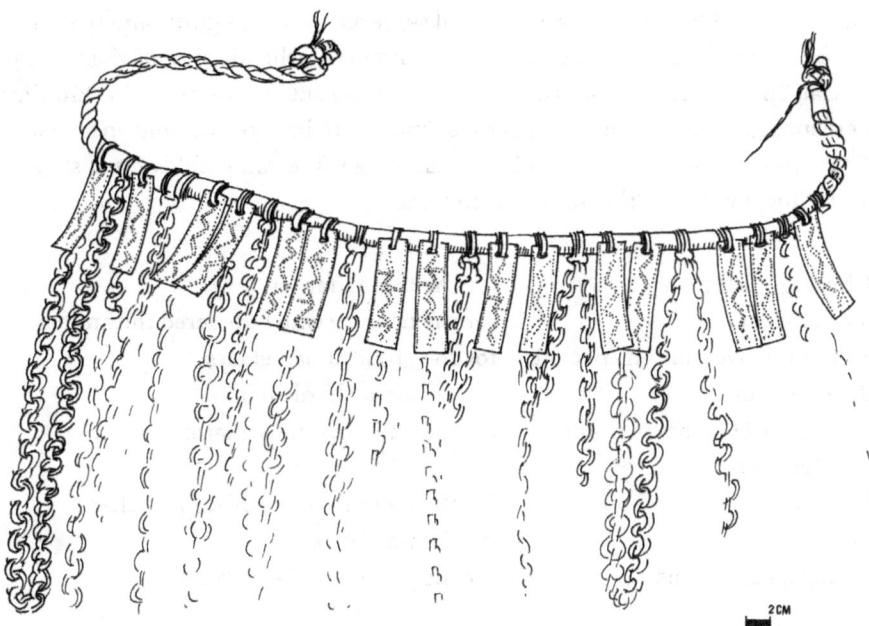

Figure 9.1 The *livu* before the women work on it.

The skirt is not the only piece of iron worn by the bride, called *makwa* in Kapsiki. Iron bracelets adorn her wrists and sometimes her ankles too, and she has iron rings on the fingers of both her hands. Her bridesmaid, *mehteshi*, wears a girdle of iron beads, as does sometimes the *makwa*. Iron beads, according to Kapsiki blacksmiths, are among the most difficult shapes to forge, and as a consequence they are more expensive than brass beads.[2]

The actual wedding, called *kadzembe cɛ* (to enter the hut), starts with the calling of the bride. All weddings for first-time brides (*makwa*) are performed in the same month, around April, and in the subsequent month the boys will be initiated. All grooms will try to choose a day when no one else has his feast, so the month of April is dotted with these *verhe makwa* (wedding feasts). Two weeks before the big day Sunu Ba asks his sister's son to slaughter a bull, if he can afford a bull. Before the killing, the guardian[3] of the bull—usually a friend—takes his farewell from his charge; he puts grass in the animal's mouth: "Bull, you are finished now. It is not your fault because you have been killed by a stronger force." He then tells the groom's brother, who is present during the sacrifice as master of ceremonies: "The bull is yours now. It is no longer with me." And then the nephew slaughters the bull. The blood is collected in a bowl, and the guardian will later sprinkle it in the bull's pen with some of the stomach.

With the groom looking on from a distance, his brother accepts the slaughtered bull on his behalf, and one nephew divides up the animal. From both its sides, a strip of hide is cut away; one will serve as his bride's girdle and the other will be for the bride of a poorer kinsman. As usual, the division of the meat is crucial. The first rule is that the meat around the slits in the animal's skin that were made for carrying it is "dangerous" and has to be eaten by only one person: if two people eat it, they will die the same day. The same holds for a sheep's heart. The division of the meat is as follows:

1 foreleg + 1 hind leg	for the bride's father
the pancreas	for the nephew who butchered the animal
part of the liver and the paunch	for the groom's clan elders
the reticulum	for the actual herdsman
part of the liver, paunch, and intestines	for the bull's (former) guardian
the heart	for the groom's real mother's brother
the neck	for the ward elders
the leg meat + penis	for the groom's oldest sister

In the two weeks that follow, the groom arranges a hut for his bride, in fact using a hut that has housed a wife who has left.[4] Two days before the wedding, the little girls from his ward plaster the walls of the hut with termite earth to make it nice and smooth, and Sunu gives them food and beer residue. That very evening some of his kinswomen bring four jars of red beer to his Tizhè, his father in law.

Figure 9.2 The *makwa* in *livu*, going to crawl to Rhwemetla.

The next morning both parties—the groom and the bride's father—consult a diviner, usually the crab diviner, about the proceedings and the risks of the *verhe makwa* (the bridal feast). That afternoon the *livu* is prepared by the wives of the father-in-law's clansmen (Figure 9.1 & 9.2).

Calling the Bride

While these last preparations for the "calling of the bride" are being made, the bride and groom are each having their heads shaved in the nearest blacksmith's compound. That evening, the last in her father's compound before her marriage, the bride calls in her "bridesmaid" (*mehteshi*) and ties the new *livu* around her waist. Both set out for the well, where the *mehteshi* washes the *livu* on her body; the bride washes too and then, for the first time, puts on her newly cleaned iron skirt.

The *livu* is indeed important, the bride's central piece of adornment. Kwada will wear it when called to her husband's compound that very night and on all festivities in the year to come until the next harvest season. During the *verhe makwa* she will wear nothing else. Sunu Ba's uncles will bless the marriage by spraying red beer over her body and skirt. Later, when visiting her new father-in-law with a ceremonial gift of millet mush, she will wear just the *livu*. On the closing days of the boys' initiation, when all future brides of the village gather on a mountainside for a two-day singing contest their *livu* will again be all they wear.

But this is the first time Kwada will wear her own *livu*, at her own wedding. When the groom's delegation arrives, accompanied by a smith with his guitar or one-stringed violin, she is ready, and so is her father. However, the arrival of the group is met by a massive show of disinterest. The women of Sunu's group start singing. "Mama, give us your child as the rain is near." But no response comes from Tizhè's dark compound. After some time, when the darkness is complete, Sunu's representative hands over a large new calabash containing millet flour, meat, and a chicken to one of their own women, who then heads into the compound of the father-in-law. The groom's party has five small jars the groom has ordered for the festivities (on the orders of the crab divination). One of them is the new *melɛ* (the sacrificial jar for the bride), hidden in the calabash. The other four are filled with beer and brought by the children in the groom's group, who put them in the forecourt, possibly venturing to take a sip. However, almost immediately some of Kwada's little brothers and sisters will come running out of the house to catch the "intruders." If they happen to capture one, the groom is obliged to ransom his kinsman with a large jar of beer. If all escape, the children who live there drink the beer. This practice is called the "amusement" part of the ritual, and the crab indicates whether the auspices are good enough for such joviality. They usually are. If there is to be no play, the woman calling the wife will take the four jars. Also the crab indicates what types of sacrifices need to be performed by both parties in both compounds. If the two divinations contradict each other, the groom's has priority.

Outside, the children of Sunu Ba's party start to sing: "Give us the women, the ones calling her are already under the firewood [which lines the low forecourt walls]." At last there is a reaction. Kwada's aunt comes out of the house and accepts the calabash and the gifts: she will be the *kweperhuli*, an important functionary in the proceedings of both the bride and the boy initiate. She is the one who binds the cache sexe (which is what the name signifies), and as such she will accompany the bride to her new house, together with a small boy from the compound. Tizhè then calls in all the family, plus the *kweperhuli* and the small boy, for the sacrifice at the entrance to his hut, following, again, the directions of the crab.

> Terimcè, the father of another bride, Kuve, learned from the crab that everything had to remain very calm: no quarrels. To arrive at that state, Kuve had to put a ball of white flour on her father's jar, and Terimcè himself had to put a mixture of meat from a female and a male animal, with some white flour, in his brewing hut. The sacrifice is performed while the children outside keep singing: "Mother of the *makwa*, give us the girl because the sun has set." Terimcè has, through an intermediary, contacted his son-in-law to find out if his crab has told him anything about how to dispose of the ritual beer, the *tɛ*.

Despite all the laughter and joking, the moment is tense, and people are careful to follow the crab's instructions to the letter. After the sacrifice, there is no hurry whatsoever and both groups of women—the bride's kinswomen who made the *livu* and Sunu's delegation—start to sing to each other, chiding the other and calling them names, flinging their insults with great gusto. Not only is this fun, they and the bride's father may try to gain some money from their moment of power, however fleeting.

> Zra, the father of a bride called Masi, told the calling party that he was not very pleased about his son-in-law. "He has butchered a bull and I am still waiting for the leg. If he does not come forward, I'll give my daughter a dish of beans when she comes home [instead of the meat dish which is due]. I give him my daughter, and he gives me nothing? I hope that she will get pregnant immediately and then I will show my heart [by giving her to someone else]. Maybe my son-in-law thinks that he has paid her well, but I am not content. And he will have to wait for a long time tonight." [In fact, the bridewealth was paid and the groom had given what was due but he had slaughtered more animals than usual, thus raising expectations.]

Midnight usually arrives before the bride does, but at long last some people appear in the opening of the main wall. Kwada is clothed in her *livu* and *rhuli*, with a plaited straw cape over her head. She kneels in the wall opening, facing inward. From the inside, Tizhè, in the quiet that suddenly reigns, gives her his blessing and advice (Figure 9.3):

> You are stubborn and when I talk to you, you turn the other way. Do not go through the river in this spirit, not to your husband. I never laid a hand on you, but a husband is not a father. There you are not in your father's house and you are not the only one. Many people are there. I want you to become pregnant right away; then I will explain everything to you and maybe give you to someone else. I want you to work hard over there, to have sex with your husband and become pregnant after your first intercourse. That is what I want.

He then takes a mouthful of red beer and sprays it over her. She remains silent throughout, as do all the others present (lest the birds eat her next sorghum harvest). She joins her aunt and the little boy and together they walk toward her husband's group. Before arriving at her new husband's home, she enters the house of one of her father's kinsmen, her *yitiyaberhe*, her "initiation

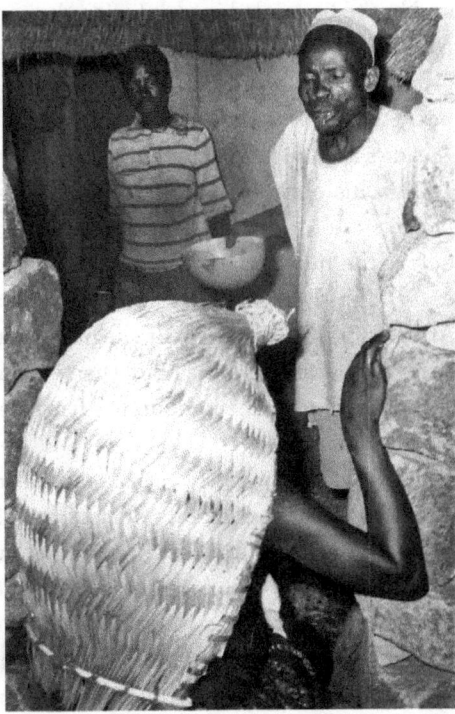

Figure 9.3 Kwada and her father. Mogode 1973.

father," who will watch over her well-being from close by. He has been waiting for her and also blesses Kwada: "Give us two pair of twins and then I will give you to someone else," and then sprays her with beer. Still silent, the girl enters her groom's compound, leaving her aunt and the boy behind. Inside, she participates in the sacrifice that is done on her behalf inside her own new hut. She has brought a chicken from her home for the sacrifice, again following the crab's instructions. Coming out, she throws part of it away, as instructed, and rejoins her party.

> For Kwada's entry, the crab had given the following directions: "Grind as a mix of white sorghum, couch grass seeds and the ear of a goat, and add water." The bride brings a white rooster. The groom cuts its head and lets the blood drip on the wall, then roasts the head and the liver. The *makwa* partakes of the mix, walks out and throws the rooster's comb in the direction she came from. The other women take some of the mix in their mouth, spit it on their stomachs and put the rest on their jar. All the children just dip their fingers in it.

The bride has not really entered her new abode yet; she has to be accompanied if she is to count as *dzembe cɛ* (married, literally: entered the hut). A playfully drawn-out intermezzo now follows, in which the groom's party tries to convince the bride and her people to enter the house. The bride's aunt is the pivotal figure and has to be cajoled into entering the compound. She should never have reason to become angry, which would amount to a curse upon the marriage, so the groom's friend gives her small presents, flatters her, and shows her his empty pockets. Most *kweperhuli* evidently savor the situation and make the most of it. Kwada's aunt gives a running commentary on the groom, on his representative, and on his entire family. Only when the groom's man convinces her that his pockets are completely empty does she give in and enter the compound. Just before the hut of the *makwa* she hesitates again, accepts a last small gift, and enters only after an impassioned plea by the woman who has called the *makwa*. After all, that is the moment she has to act out her title: she ties a red *rhuli*, cache sexe, at the bride's back. But the reticence to hurt any of the bride's family's feelings will last throughout the feast, lest the bride become infertile or leave quickly.

At long last the *makwa* settles in her new hut, takes off her cape, and stays inside the hut for the remainder of the night. She is very busy, grinding grains and sweeping the floor, assisted by her aunt. The latter will again ask for a few coins, to take the flour from the millstone, to remove the dirt or whatever, and the groom's friend has to keep giving her small change. A girl (*mehteshi*) joins her from her husband's family and will assist her in all the rituals to come. One decision is already taken in advance: the bride has consulted the crab in order to know whether men could enter her hut during the feast, and whether they might touch her or not. She heeds that advice, because these are a crucial few days for her (a ban on touching means that guests may enter her hut but may not touch her).

The groom is not in sight. Sunu Ba remains with a friend, especially at his first *makwa*. In the early afternoon of the next day he joins his bride for the final ceremonies. With his subsequent weddings he may be in the house, but not prominently so. Kwada is married because she has entered the new house, not because she has joined her husband. Also later, when the women move on to another husband, as was almost inevitable in the past and is still common today, the entering of the compound of her second husband is the crucial moment. What follows at the time of the first wedding, as described here, is the social and ritual consolidation of the transfer of the bride. Later, after the rainy season, the girls' initiation will be the last phase of their wedding ceremonies.

The Wedding

This wedding day is a feast, *verhe* in Kapsiki, a term uniquely applied to festivals with meals—first the wedding, then a boy's initiation. The term for a nonfood feast is *geske*. This is the day the bull's meat is eaten and this is the day for which the groom has been brewing a huge amount of red beer.

Early in the morning the clan and ward elders gather at the groom's home and take up their rightful position at the place of honor in the forecourt. Here they will be served first, the choicest meat and the first beer, and here they will stay, without moving, for the whole day. Groom Sunu Ba brings a rooster or hen (depending on the crab), one of the elders cuts off its head (usually a chicken's throat is just cut in a sacrifice) over the place of honor, and pushes the knife with the head on it into the straw over his head. The groom's *ksugwe* (sister's sons) pluck, dismember, and disembowel the animal and will later cook it and serve it to the elders. At this moment the chicken's body serves as a gentle oracle on the bride. One of the sister's sons sews its belly shut with bean fibers and puts it on a roof in the sun. The notion is that if the sewing splits open, the bride has slept with someone other than her groom. If the sewing remains intact, she is "socially a virgin," meaning she has slept with her fiancé only. If her "virginity" is in doubt, there is little sanction though she might have some problems with breast feeding her first child—to be remedied with sacrifices. But in practice, the groom makes sure that he is on very good terms with his nephew, and so is Sunu, our groom, who with a handsome gift has ensured that his nephew will use firm stitches to keep the chicken together. At the end of the day, the *ksugwe* will show the chicken to the woman who accompanied the bride and then will give it to the bride's father. The latter will later eat it with some of his brothers, content about his daughter.

Guests at the *verhe* do not come empty-handed. Everyone brings food, millet mush or flour, yam and beer, "to greet the *makwa*." Sunu's clan members in particular excel in gifts of food, since this *verhe* is the pride of their lineage as well. Meanwhile the *makwa* receives her guests in her new hut, taking in their gifts of millet mush and serving them beer that Tizhè gave her early that morning.

Gradually the compound fills to capacity and everywhere there are people drinking, gossiping, serving food, and slowly getting drunk. In the cooking huts, the women of the house prepare sauce and cook more mush. Three groups of men remain seated during the proceedings: the elders in the forecourt, a group of Sunu's uncles near his personal hut, and the *makwa*'s male relatives including her father, who gather outside the compound wall. Kwada's female relatives stay inside her hut. The nephews run around, arranging six jars of beer for the bride's relatives outside and some bowls of ground millet and peanuts. Later, they will make sure that the girls who served this group get a good piece of meat. One of them oils the strip of bull's hide that will serve the bride as a girdle for the rainy season. Together, the small *ksugwe* have to divide up the meat and the food, making sure that nobody goes home hungry; especially the bride's family should be content, that is, supplied with beer, if not with the red variety then at least good-quality white beer. All the gifts of food and beer are hauled over the wall of the compound, since all the beer has to seem to come from the groom; the difference between entering over the wall, discreetly helping out one's kinsmen, and entering through the door, as the bride did, is essential.

The old men in the forecourt ask for more, but, being clansmen, they have to take whatever is given, even dregs, and they may not complain. In fact, they start out with the residue as "family holds back." However the groom's mother's brothers have to get the best quality, and a lot of it. For the other guests, one jar among five will suffice if they brought food. Smiths, who are crucial in other rituals but here are more marginal, are spread out all over the compound, serving as musicians and praise singers for the various groups of guests who put coins on their foreheads in appreciation.

While the women in the groom's family work hard cooking, those on the Kwada's side amuse themselves singing derogatory songs about Sunu Ba's family, exhorting them to greater feats of hospitality: "She will not go without elephant meat, give us beer" or "The groom is poor, has the head of a vulture and the hut is poorly constructed," while praising their own girl: "*Makwa* of the sun, when he beats you, he may only do so with a millet stalk or his cap. Flee into your room" or "This home is not for you to stay in. Give it up, and come back home to us." In fact, Kwada's father Tizhè would be very embarrassed if she followed this advice, since he would have to return the huge bridewealth!

Some women on the groom's side redress the balance with their songs, admonishing the *makwa*: "You beat people in order to get a husband. You think you are the mistress of the house now, but wait . . . You think you sleep on an iron bed but just the floor is enough for you. You had better give us twins." Their commentary on Sunu Ba is much more flattering: "Chief of the sun, lion, thank you. You give the best beer; feed us with sauce of choice meat. Do not run around, everything will be fine today." But the refrain of both groups is the same: "We are thirsty."

About noon the meal is ready: the meat, the sauce, and the new mush. The peanut sauce should be especially plentiful since it is an integral part of all ceremonial meals. The older mush prepared the day before by the groom's kinsmen has to be soaked in water. This time everyone tries to be involved, because the meat will be divided. This wedding feast is too big for a strict ritual division of meat like in other rituals, but the special guests get the first and the best: the groom's oldest sister, the old man who cut up the chicken, the real mother's brother and his companions, and the old men in the forecourt. The *kweperhuli* who brought in the bride receives a calabash with four pieces of mush, two bars of iron, a bowl of peanut sauce, and a bowl of cooked meat. She is accompanied by a son of the groom's sister; he goes with her to Tizhè and, at the same moment, another nephew of Sunu presents the bride with her new bull-hide girdle.

Some important persons refrain from eating: a representative of the groom's clan, including his initiation father and those uncles who will bless the bride, the real mother's brother among them. (In Kapsiki both types of kinsmen are indicated with the same term, *ksugwe*, but the distinction between the mother's brother—the great *ksugwe*—and the sister's son—the small *ksugwe*—is still crucial.) Each of these uncles has a friend with him for the occasion. The groom brings along four jars of the best beer, one of which is his *mele*. He addresses the group, thanking them for their presence and for agreeing to this marriage, assuring them that they will be content and happy. They tell him not to worry and hand over money and iron bars as a sign that they agree to this marriage, some small pieces of iron, which are passed on to the *kweperhuli*, as mentioned above.[5] Being a sizable group of some fifteen persons, they help the groom out with a dozen bars and FCFA 4,000.

The bars were previously an exchange medium and tool blanks: one bar equals a hoe—in fact the term *duburu* means "hoe"—and the bars should come from indigenous smelting, not from scrap iron. The first calabash is for the village chief, who is always among the "uncles." He pours some beer on the ground:

> She has to bear a daughter and then again a daughter. We give to the people who are dead. If there is anyone with evil wishes and thoughts, let him stiffen. Let the groom marry more women and all be healthy.

Sunu pours beer for a second time from his *mele* and passes around the calabash. Everyone present spits in the beer and then the initiation father and a classificatory uncle walk over to *makwa* Kwada, who kneels in her door facing them, clothed in just her girdle, her plaited cape, and her *livu*. The groom's initiation father takes a large mouthful of beer and douses her with it, saying: "You have to be healthy, bear a lot of children, and pay back the bridewealth. Bear children right after one another." Then the *ksugwe* does the same: "Bear children one after each other, fast," and he sprays the beer over her. He then hands the calabash with beer to the *makwa*, who is supposed to drink it all. Since the beer is full of spit, she pretends to do so and lets the beer run over her body. After that, the bride eats, just a little bit, for the first time in her new home. Later that night she will eat well.

> In the early 1990s, some changes occurred in the proceedings as described above. After the eating of the *verhe*, the groom's *ksugwe* still assemble at his granary, at least they do so if they are real *kagwevi* (autochthons). If they are "immigrants" (meaning descended from an immigrant), they remain outside. Nowadays the *makwa* does not pretend to drink the *tɛ* but gives the calabash to a smith woman.

This is her final "ritual intake" into the new family and the ritual high point of the day. The rest is eating, drinking, and taking one's parting gifts. The old men get a sauce with the head of their sacrificial chicken and go home, each with two pieces of mush. They wait for the mother's brothers to depart, who do so as a group, singing. Then the old men eat and go home, singing as well. This ends the *verhe* proper, the feast. Some of the bride's friends remain in the compound eating and drinking while the sister's sons finally get to eat the meat, peanut sauce, and mush that they reserved for themselves. Two of the small *ksugwe* bring four pieces of mush, meat and sauce for Tizhè in his house "to stop him on the path." If he lives far away, they hand it to the bride's second father, who lives close by.

Close friends stay until nightfall. The friend at whose home the groom has slept brings two jars of white beer for the *kwageze rhena*—literally: to say the word, meaning intercourse—and with other friends seats himself on the doorstep of the bride's hut. From inside, the *makwa* throws her iron bracelet toward Sunu Ba "Here are your things." He tosses it back to her and they both throw the bracelet once more and then "start talking," implying verbal and later sexual intercourse. Outside the hut and listening to the proceedings inside, the friends drink beer, happy when they hear muffled sounds coming from the hut. The bracelet will remain with the bride and eventually feature in her burial rites.

Traditionally this is the time the bride has to start her work as a married woman with household chores and sexual intercourse. Officially the groom had to wait until this moment before having intercourse, but actually the couple will have had sex long before then. During the season before her wedding, Kwada stayed overnight with her *mehteshi*, a girl companion, at her future husband's home. Though not officially, this was in fact the acknowledged start of sexual relations between the couple. And of course, each couple has its own history.

A few gifts have to be exchanged after the *verhe*. On the wedding day, Tizhè has sent a gift to his wife's brother, Kwada's uncle, part of the gift he received from the groom. The crab will have indicated the details and, in the case of Kwada these consisted of a goat's leg, millet flour, and red beer. Later, at the end of the *verhe*, Tizhè will send a goat to his brother-in-law who was not present at the wedding. Two little children, a boy and a girl, take it to him and they receive a rooster and a hen respectively. The boy will later help the *makwa* when her family brings her firewood.

During the four days immediately after the wedding, the bride stays within the walls of the compound and then has a friend accompany her to her father's home with four pieces of mush, a large bowl of meat, and peanut sauce. She stays for two nights in her parental home and then returns to her husband with the same gifts of food. In both homes she helps in cooking and other chores, but she has more freedom of movement at her father's, from where she has always ventured out of the compound without restriction. However, after her wedding she always has a little girl from Sunu's lineage at her side. After four days at her husband's, Kwada goes back to her father again, this time with two pieces of yam plus sauce. She stays for two days and her mother (or father's wife) gives her peanuts, couch grass seeds, and sorghum grains. After grinding it, she returns with that flour to her husband and that evening leaves her new home for the first time to venture out in the bush. With some boys and girls from her new neighborhood and her *mehteshi*, she gathers sesame in the bush for sauce and distributes ground peanuts and water to the children. Then Sunu Ba and his mentor collect some more gifts of food: a mixture of ground couch seeds and peanuts for Sunu's father, his mother's brother, and his lineage elders. Kwada brings these food gifts herself, handing them over in silence and recieving a gift of money in return; after that exchange Kwada and her in-laws start a conversation for the first time. Finally, she gives her *mehteshi* a hen, flour, and some money.

One small transaction remains before the initiation phase after the rains. If the ordeal with the chicken on the wedding was all right, her father invites his brothers during the wet season. They feast together, because their daughter behaved well. After the meal they all go into the bush to cut wood, which will be collected a few weeks later by Kwada with a group of women from her new home. The little boy who accompanied the *makwa* on her wedding day walks in front, playing his flute, while the women behind him sing: *a shurhwu zhara zana* (the wood of the daughter of a good man). The boy carries a branch and some sorghum stalks, the *makwa* wears her *livu*, her calabash around her neck. This stack of wood should contain at least four branched sticks, which will be used for her shed during the *la* festival after the rains.

In marriage transactions the groom is the great giver, in addition to the very substantial bridewealth he has furnished. Throughout, the pattern of other gifts around the *makwa* is highly significant. The bride gets her bridal attire from her father (the cape), her father's women (her iron skirt), her mother's sister (a cache sexe), and her husband (her girdle and jar). The many gifts demonstrate the girl's gradual transition from her father's home, and the provenance of her outfit highlights this. The gifts to her husband's kinsmen restore some balance in the gift exchange and highlight the fact that in this transitional period she gains in-laws while "losing" kinsmen. She gradually regains her former mobility, first at her father's, then at her husband's. This slow "social weaning" marks a period of relational transition that will last throughout the agricultural season: she is still liminal, with limited mobility and very circumscribed duties and obligations. Gradually she assumes all the duties of a married woman, the first intercourse semi-public in her own hut, later sexual intercourse but still in her own hut, and only after the concluding *la* festival does she have intercourse in her husband's hut. An illustration of the gradual transition is the number of assistants she has during the marriage proceedings: the *kweperhuli*, two *mehteshi*, one girl, one boy, and later during the final rites another small boy (Chapter 10). Effectively, all these contribute to her change of dwelling, the *kweperhuli* getting her out of her father's compound into her husband's, the various small helpers making sure she does not return to her father's home. As part of this transition, she starts to grind and sweep, gathers leaves for sauces, and later starts cooking for her husband at the time when sexual intercourse commences. A month after her wedding she and the other girls who got married in the same year will perform rites during the boys' initiation. After the harvest, that is, after the concluding rites of the *la* festival, her liminal period is over.

A crucial distinction in Kapsiki marriage is between *makwa*, the bride at her first wedding, and *kwatewume*, which a woman becomes when leaving her first husband for another man. For the latter union a simple ceremony suffices.[6] On the third day of her stay, her new husband slaughters a goat or a sheep (usually done by his sister's son) which is divided among his kinsmen. The abomasum, fourth stomach, of the goat is filled with choice parcels of meat, tied shut with intestines, and cooked as a whole. The *kwatewume* waits in her hut, and a friend of the groom has to persuade her to open the cooked stomach and eat meat for the first time in her new home. This is the *kwe yitu*, the hidden goat, and in all privacy follows the general format of ceremonial meals: the slaughter of a goat by the sister's son and a standard meat distribution to the relevant parties. After eating the filled abomasum, the new wife has to start cooking for her husband.

Later on that first day the friend and nephew of the groom will present the *yitiyaberhe*, the local guardian of his wife: with a gift of three legs, the chest, seven bowls of sorghum (partly ground), and a *duburu*. When the new wife visits him on one of the next few days, the guardian will reciprocate with a gift of food and a large iron bracelet.

Wedding à la Mode

In the various Kapsiki and Higi villages the order of festivities may differ, both for *makwa* and *kwatewume*. Described above is the dominant "liturgy" of the Cameroonian villages on the Nigerian border, with the exception of Rumsiki, where things are done differently. This is not because that village is a tourist spot—that does not change customs much, if at all[7]—but because Rumsiki has a western Higi provenance, having been settled first by people from Sena, who had different traditions. These are reflected in ritual but not in basic social relations. One difference is that in Rumsiki and Sena the *makwa* rites are performed much later, after the bride has had one or two children. The first wedding is marked by the simple rituals such as the *kwatewume* marriage in Mogode. Only after the marriage has proved stable is the *verhe makwa* held as well as the new forms, the *hirdɛ* and the *amalɛa*. In principle, the customs of the groom's village are followed.

> *Mogode 24-2-2003*. Masi, the daughter of the Lutheran pastor of Mogode, Tlimu Maze, marries a man from Rumsiki; in fact she has already had a baby and has been living with him for over a year. Tlimu has chosen a *yitiyaberhe* for his daughter in Rumsiki, in fact his brother, who lives there. Masi stays one night at her parents' with the baby and waits for the people from Rumsiki to fetch her by car. She will spend the next night at her father's brother's house and will be called from there. In this case, half the bridewealth is paid before she moved in, and the other half is being paid gradually, with payments completed after her second child is born.

The way marriages are celebrated has been changing over the last few decades. One important change is an increase in marriage stability. Women still seek new husbands, but not as often as before 1980, and this change—welcomed by men as well as women—has various causes. One major factor is a much lower infant mortality due to better medical services, another is the increased cost of divorce, as the coordinated administrative measures on both sides of the border have shown to be effective, with a heavy fine on men who take runaway wives, and the coordination of these measures across the border. This means that *makwa* ceremonies have become more important, as the first wedding has become more stable. Before 1980 the *makwa* proceedings consisted of the calling of the bride plus the *verhe*, the festive gathering of the groom's kin to celebrate the newly arrived bride, with its insistence both on beer and on iron. In the early 1980s the *hirdɛ* wedding party was gradually introduced to be held after the *verhe*. At the *hirdɛ*, the friends and clients gather in the afternoon in the groom's compound where, clothed in their festive best, they present money to the groom, with a smith acting as speaker. Each gift of money is widely acknowledged, with the speaker greatly exaggerating the amount given: FCFA 1,000, for example, is hailed as FCFA 5,000. This custom, according to my informants, came from the Hausa in Nigeria.

In the late 1990s a new custom, *amalɛa*, arrived on the wedding scene. It is probably also of Hausa origin but in any case came via the Higi part of the Kapsiki area in Nigeria. Here the *hirdɛ* has grown into a full-blown festival, with a ceremonial procession of the bride and groom and their respective friends and kinsmen and an evening-long spectacle in a special enclosure. Drumming, dancing, and gift-giving are the main activities, but the proceedings are quite formal. A secretariat keeps track of the gifts, speakers use a microphone with loud speakers, and a band of musicians, not always smiths, is hired for the whole night. The *amalɛa* draws a huge crowd, though a strict division between the invited and the non-invited is enforced by the use of fences, a gate, and gatekeepers. Only real givers and some guests of honor are welcome.

The evening before, a dance is held to announce the *amalɛa*. A group of young smiths is required with tuners and large speakers, and a table, chairs, and lights are set up inside a fenced-off dancing area. The groom's sister's sons will have made the arrangements, and they also need a few "secretaries" to note down the gifts and who brings food and drink, some organizers to keep out the uninvited, and a smith with a whistle to direct the proceedings. The musicians and singers are paid by the dancers with gifts of money and food.

This preparation, evidently, is just the warming up. The real *amalɛa* starts in the late afternoon on the day after the *verhe*. Two smiths with drums lead a procession of friends, the bride and groom, and some of the bride's friends, dancing slowly out of the house, all dressed splendidly in gowns and dresses but with expressionless faces. On their arrival at the dancing area chairs await them at the place of honor. The smiths return to the house to collect the groom's father and his friends as well as the groom's mother and her retinue. When all have arrived, the smiths present the bride and groom in the first dance. The guests have arrived now and start giving money to the master of ceremonies, who with his microphone directs the session, while secretaries write down the amounts given. Unlike the case in the *hirdɛ*, the exact amount is now written down, because this is an enterprise that should make money for the groom. The cost of the evening is considerable, with between FCFA 20,000 and FCFA 40,000 for the performing smiths, half of which has to be paid in advance. Whether the event will indeed show a profit depends on the number of friends and kinsmen the groom can muster. The bride's group will give money too, but much less.

The audience is divided into the usual groups in Kapsiki ceremonies: the groom's father with his friends, the groom's mother with her friends, and the same on the bride's side. The groom's kin makes a collection with a dish but most people prefer to give their contribution to the master of ceremonies to

Figure 9.4 Girls lining up behind the groom during *amalɛa*. Mogode 2003.

have the amount broadcast over the sound system. The bride's mother and her friends give mainly clothes to the bride. Not only do the different kin groups give as one, they also dance together as one: the groom's lineage and his mother's, and the bride's lineage and her mother's (Figure 9.4). As usual, the village chief takes the microphone to warn anyone with evil intent that no provocation will be tolerated. Most of the money given is in Nairas, because the Nigerian currency looks more generous than the Cameroonian FCFA. FCFA 25 is a coin while the Nigerian equivalent is a five naira bank note.

After this huge festival of conspicuous giving the secretaries count the money, pay the smiths and give them a few presents, such as beer, a bottle of whiskey, a case of Castell beer, and tobacco. On average, an evening like this can make a profit of FCFA 100,000. Both the *hirdɛ* and the *amalɛa* are prime examples of conspicuous giving, a trend that is becoming more common in Kapsiki society. In the "classic" *verhe*, the groom is helped discreetly over the back of the wall to avoid showing off, but showing off is becoming increasingly popular in present-day Kapsiki.

Initiation at the Singing Rock

The wedding completed and the bride integrated into her new family, she and all her co-brides from that season wait for the boys to be initiated. This is the topic of the next chapter but the girls' part in the festivities belong here as the next phase of her "becoming a woman," her initiation. This is done as a group, just as with the boys, and neither their homes nor their family relations play a part of any importance. In these liminal proceedings they are one as newlyweds, all equal and all part of the village.

About a month after her wedding, the girls wait until the initiation rites of the boys are well under way, in order to participate on the last day of the boys' confinement. With their *mehteshi*, all *makwa* head for the chief smith and all go together, because this custom is slightly scary. Their helper takes along mush and meat in a small decorated calabash as a gift for the chief smith, a calabash they will later use to give water to their first child. The food is wrapped in *keyitu* grewia leaves and the *makwa* uses the same kind of leaves in the cache sexe under her *livu*. Her *mehteshi* wears a string of iron beads and at the smith's she takes off four beads which she gives with some of the food as payment to the smith's wife for the operation he is about to perform. First the smith shaves the hair on the *makwa*'s head to leave a helmet-like cover and then makes two vertical incisions in the left lower belly of the *makwa*. Some terrified girls just get a stroke with the back of the knife, the brave ones looking on in some disdain, sure of receiving their family's and husband's admiration later. The small incisions have to become scars. The girls are "operated" on according to their husband's clans, with no distinction between smith and non-smith girls.

Around ten o'clock they have all finished and go to the initiation mountain of Rhwemetla, the one bearing the traces of Hwempetla's flight (see Appendix), also the mountain of the ordeal. At the bottom, an old gas hole has historically been used in girls' initiations. As all the girls cover themselves liberally with ocher and oil, the entrance to the mountain glows a fiery red. The first association is indeed quite feminine, at least according to a female colleague of mine who, on seeing it for the first time, immediately announced: "This is a vulva." Of course she was right, but it had taken me over a year to see the similarity.

The girls assemble 100 meters to the west of the outcropping at some flat boulders and start to eat the food their assistants have brought. They eat kneeling down (not crouching) and again group themselves according to their husbands' clans, following an elderly woman's instructions. This is more than just a quick meal, it is a moment to show off. The food has been prepared by their husbands, and the color indicates whether or not he is pleased with his bride so far. A light-colored mush is favorable, which means rice mush. Other colors, such as mush made of yellow or red sorghum, would indicate displeasure. In practice, all husbands are careful to give rice mush, since they do not want to give their bride a reason to leave. The next phase is crucial. After finishing their food, the girls take off their cache sexe and walk to a flat boulder some 30 meters from the entrance to the cave. Again they kneel down, now in the order of their marriage date, the first wed at the front. Then, clothed in just their girdle and iron skirt, they crawl in single file toward the cave. In one case the first girl to get married refused to go at the front because her wedding had followed slightly different customs (those of Sena, a neighboring village across the Nigerian border). Feeling "out of order," she was afraid to be the first and, after a long discussion, finally convinced the girl behind her to take her place. Rhwemetla is to be feared, not only for the rooster ordeal but also because the mountain's *shala* is reputed to catch witches. If one of the *makwa* turned out to be a witch, Rwemetla would grab her and she would not be able to leave unless she made a substantial offering of iron beads. She would also suffer a severe loss of face in front of the whole village.

The first girl starts singing:

Laliyama
It is the custom of my *Kwenu* [grandfather]
It is the custom of my *Zra* [father]
I did not start it.
It is the things of people long ago, a *laliyama*
I did not start it.
These things are of people from people
The things of the people who cook and rot [*gwenji*, an insult]
The things of people of Rhuŋwedʼu
The things of people with many cows
The things of my mother Kuve
The things of the *shi* [grandparents] of those that make a sacrifice
The things of the people of *Zagwayɛ* [her grandparent]
The things of the people of *Lakwa* [watering place].
Lalɛ [be greeted] rich people
Lalɛ things of those who founded the village
I did not start it.

At a rock close to the entrance, all the girls stand up and run to the cave, each one trying to get a position against the rock wall, and afraid to hesitate lest she be suspected of being a witch.

This ritual approach of Rwemetla is the high point of day, the rest of which is a kind of song contest. The *makwa* will sing and each time one of them improvises a line, the rest repeat it. A crowd of spectators gathers around them to watch and listen, to hear "their" *makwa*. The melody line is simple but the girls are judged on their improvisation. Singing well is important: the mother of a poor singer will sigh, "Who will mourn me when I am dead?" A good singer, on the other hand, receives continuous gifts of money. The husbands, of course, come to listen as well and are happy if they hear praise from their brides, praise for their riches or their generosity; good looks seem to be less important. The husband rewards his wife by putting coins on her forehead, and then he has to give her what she asked for in song. If she sings badly or insults her husband, she can count on red mush the next day. The girls' assistants run to and fro, fetching water for the singers and plaiting cache sexes out of leaves from the bush, but they also have to contend with the boys' *mehteshi*, who try to get their attention and to call them over. The singing continues until about four o'clock in the afternoon, by which time the *makwa* have praised the heroism of their lineage, their ancestors, and their husbands and have insulted other clans, other girls' husbands, neighboring villages, and especially the girls who cannot sing. The whole genre of songs is called *Yayɛ*, with the exclamation coming at the end of each line:

> *Yayɛ* stay calm sister, stay calm, *yayɛ*
> Masi of the chief clan, Masi the famous, *yayɛ*
> Greet me, Masi, *yayɛ*
> Masi, daughter of the chief, say the boys of Douala, *yayɛ*
> People continue to talk about you, Masi Kwarumba, *yayɛ*
> Thank you Masi the famous, daughter of the chief, famous Masumba, *yayɛ*

Here, the singer, Kwatemba Deli, praises her mother, who is famous even in Douala, the main port of Cameroon in the far south, serving here as the icon of the "great city far away." Kwatemba then turns to herself:

> Kwacènè, I go up to my home
> Kwacènè *derha* of the Nigerians
> I am not mistaken, family of the chief
> I am going home.

She calls herself *Kwacɛnɛ derha*, the one who has a mahogany tree (*Khaya senegalensis*) in her forecourt, referring to Sena in Nigeria, which is full of these trees.

After some time insults are appearing:

> As soon as the children of the bush arrive, the talking stops [the girls from the center of Mogode are losing the contest]
> If words could kill, I would no longer be alive
> Keep still, you slaves, and I will speak
> Wait, I will dominate the festival.
> The *makwiyɛ* [her clan] do not make many mistakes
> If nobody of the Teruza [her lineage] is here, there is no village.

Often they react to people in the audience:

> What are you looking at, Kweji Nzama?
> I have been calling you all day, and only now do you show up.

You have to talk to your kinsmen, people say [he is her mother's brother]
Why do you look at me from behind the people?
Why did you not buy me clothes when you came from Mokolo?
The people of my mother are coming!

Remarks about their husband are usually less direct:

There is a letter from me ready to be sent [the implication being that she will leave her husband]

Between these *yayɛ* songs, which are clearly the girls' favorite, they have to sing some ceremonial songs highlighting the ritual occasion. Two songs are important here, the *anteriligu* and the *njanjaga*, songs which reflect two genres of flutes, the *tereme* (antelope's horn) and the *zuvu* (reed, *zuvu ha*, flutes), each of which is played in groups at different times during the growing season.

> *Anteriligu*
> I am a daughter of Deli Kweji and have come to greet you, *kwaraba* [owners of cows]
> (Choir) *Anteriligu*
> I have come, daughter of Deli Masi, to greet you
> *Anteriligu*
> I have come to sing about you, daughter of Deli Kweji
> *Anteriligu*
> I am Kuve of Dele, Kuve of Deli Zra
> *Anteriligu*
> I sing the *anteriligu* as a real Mogode woman.

This song has a fixed structure: the singer delineates her ancestry [only her mother's father is missing] and then sings about the village near the Lakwa well, hinting at Rhuŋwedu, the ancestral mountain.

> *Anteriligu*, real villagers
> *Anteriligu*, I come to greet you, *shala* of Rhuŋwedu
> *Anteriligu*, daughter of Masi
> *Anteriligu*, *shala* of the chief
> *Anteriligu*, *shala* of Rhuŋwedu
> *Anteriligu*, my mother
> *Anteriligu* I have come to greet the *shala* of Rhuŋwedu
> *Anteriligu*, I have come to greet the *shala* of the chief of Mogode
> I have come to greet you, *shala* of the mountain
> God of the people of old of Lakwa

Shala, source of cow-dung ashes.

This song is alternated with a second one.

Njanjaga
A njara taranja [untranslatable]
Most of the people of Sena are blind
Most of the people of Sena do not cultivate
Most of the people of Sena are blind
A njara taranja.

The background to this song is obscure but probably dates from the past when Sena was one of Mogode's main enemies.

At about half past four they stop, put the cache sexe their *mehteshi* has made for them under their iron skirt, and together head for the pool to wash, continuously striking their *livu* with a calabash and still singing insults about those girls who sing badly. The well is named for this ritual—*kwapεdεgwu* (to wash away the youth)—since this is considered the last time they will wash as young girls. Finally they go straight back to their husbands.

The next day is the boys' big day but it is also important for the girls, who partly follow the boys' initiation rituals. These days are the ritual highlight for this middle phase of their liminal time. Their general program is identical to that of the day before: they go to the smith to rework their incisions—this time the daring *mehteshi* may have their own done (paying him in the same way), eating their (white) mush on the rocks facing Rhwemetla, but instead of crawling they dash to the cave opening to get the best spot (Figure 9.5), where they spend most of the rest of the day singing.

The crowd on this day is even bigger, as visitors and kinsmen arrive from neighboring villages and smiths with their guitars and banjos add to the festivities. The boys and their *mehteshi* roam the area and sing their songs while the *makwa* continue their contest under the eyes of a growing crowd. At the end of the day, the *gwela* try to pry the *makwa* out of their cave, asking them to come to Mentsehe, the final initiation which they perform together, *gwela* and *makwa*. The first two times the girls reply that it is still too early and they want to sing for longer. The third time the boys get "angry" and throw stones inside the cave, where there are supposed to be some wasp nests, at least there may have been in the past. The girls run out of the cave, clad in their *livu* and cache sexe and clutching the calabash in which they brought their food. On the way to the small mountain called Mentsehe, they pass a pool, dip their right foot in it, and then run in single file to Mentsehe, with their calabashes against their chest. While the initiation mothers of the *gwela* go to the pool, the *makwa* leave to fetch water to throw into the boys' hut "to be cool." Cool in Kapsiki stands in contrast to hot

Figure 9.5 The girls jostle for the best place. Rhwemetla, Mogode 1973.

and indicates health, just as a cool body has no fever. The initiates fetch water in the girls' calabashes, divide the food they got from their uncles into the calabashes, and each boy presents it to his fiancé: if possible a goat's leg and mush. If he does not have a fiancé, the betrothed of a clan brother gets it. He presents the mush to the *makwa* of his own lineage, who will eat it later with her *mehteshi*, while the *mehteshi* of the *gwela* will get a bag of meat.

The scene is now set for the final ritual for the *makwa*, with the *gwela*. Between Mentsehe and a boulder some 30 meters from the face of the small mountain, the elders clear a running strip and spectators line up on both sides. The *gwela* join the *makwa* at the boulder. In pairs, a *makwa* and a *gwela* from the same lineage or clan run from the boulder to Mentsehe. If numbers do not work out, two boys or two girls can run together, the first three clans first, then the others. They run to Mentsehe, touch the base of the mountain with their right foot, and run back, four times. If someone stumbles, a ritual elder runs toward the pair and makes two cuts with his knife in the underarm of the boy or girl who fell, in order to avoid another accident. When all the runners have finished, the *gwela* run toward Mentsehe, pull themselves up on the protruding rock, touch it with their tongues, ring the brass bells they carry on their belt, and shout: *Za 'ya, za 'ya* (I am a man, I am a man). The *makwa* stay at their boulder and then go home to eat, while the *gwela* finish their rituals.

The Iron Bride: Symbols of Belonging

Here we are in fully imagistic rituals, complex in outfit and liturgy, accompanied by intricate gift exchanges and emotionally charged events. Participating once in her life, a *makwa* has to be guided and coached during the whole period, and the ritual furnishes these guides in quite a number, from the ritual mother and second father down to the *mehteshi* helpers and some small boys. The liturgy is entrenched in the new social positions and relations, the episodic memory stimulated by the many "functionaries" surrounding the *makwa*. All these exchanges with food gifts, different calabashes, and trajectories of crawling, walking, and running, are needed for performance, but also both exchanges and activities breathe the fact of belonging. Nobody can perform all this alone.

Cognitively costly rituals sport a plethora of symbols, and here, truly, "symbols have sex." Symbolism is much less straightforward, much less minimal than in the dwelling rituals, so we have to construct meaning in the Turnerian mode. We started with the *livu*, and we will finish this chapter concentrating on this central symbol too. The *livu* features in all the stages of a wedding, as it will in the *la* feast (see Chapter 11). But the skirt remains important long after a girl's *makwa* days. Her father actually has bought it, earlier, "for the dance," meaning his own funeral dance, and any father who has not given his daughter a *livu* will be chastised after his death in her funeral chants. At her wedding, her husband reimburses his father-in-law with one or two goats for the skirt or, in the past, with iron bars. Any groom who fails to give money or goats for the skirt will hear his father-in-law remember him for this crucial debt. This blacksmith's product has become easier to produce since iron from abandoned cars is abundant now, even though it is still considered a "tour de force" for the sheer amount of work involved. Girls want to have a *livu*, and although they may borrow one, they want their own.

Later in life the woman will take the *livu* out of her chest on festive or ritual occasions, smear it with ochreous mahogany oil, and dance with it. When her son is leaving the seclusion of his initiation period, she will honor him by wearing it. Just as her son is born "from the *livu*," as some Kapsiki women put it, so on his return from the bush he will be greeted with it. The most common reason to dance in her *livu* is the burial of kin. When mourning a deceased clan member (male or female), her husband's clansmen, or a friend's kinsman, she once again ties her iron skirt around her loins. Now the skirt serves as a musical instrument and she follows the rhythm of the drums, scraping the *livu* with a calabash to commemorate the deceased. At her mother's death she will take two shields from her mother's *livu*, tie them onto a leather strip, and wear this until the end of the mourning period. At her own death, her daughter may inherit her *livu*, since she herself will not be buried in it. Rust will set in and her daughter will wear it at the concluding rites of her mother's funeral. If it is not worn out by then, the daughter will use it as a second *livu*, wearing it under her own to dance in at her marriage.

The *livu* has withstood change better than other parts of the ceremonial costume. Brides no longer wear just their iron apron; nowadays they are decked out in their finest "wax" dresses, as is their entourage, and the *leke* (plaited cape) has disappeared. But the *livu* is still there. In the 1980s, brides started to wear their *livu* over their other clothing; after 2000 it was sometimes worn under a dress or even just carried inside a calabash. The groom's *ksugwe* (mother's brothers) still spray beer on the *livu*, even if they no longer douse the bride with beer.

A bride's outfit is symbolic in several other ways. First, the cache sexe is redefined at various points during the wedding, at least in more traditional settings. The Kapsiki term *rhuli* used to encompass a wide array of coverings for the pubic or buttock area, and they symbolize the various phases of a girl's life, from a few iron beads worn at the front, to bundles of various kinds of fibers, to *rhuli* made of empty medicine holders, and for an adult to the brass plaited *shafa*, three bundles of goatskin strings tied together by a brass sheath, a type that has become the quintessential cache sexe for the Kapsiki/Higi.

But it is the *livu* that is the central symbol. The core element is, evidently, iron. A bride is decked out in iron objects: she wears decorated iron bracelets given to her by her future husband, she pays the smith in iron, gets an iron ankle ring from her father and an iron ring from her second father. At the wedding, the *ksugwe* give iron tool blanks when blessing the bride, or small iron points. Her bridesmaid wears a girdle of iron beads, as does the *makwa* too sometimes.

> Later, after she has settled in with Sunu, Kwada (the bride of our opening case) will visit a friend of her father's who lives near her new home. He is her second father (*yitiyaberhe*), who has to shield her from abuse in her new surroundings and protect her from her husband. When she first visits him, he presents her with an iron bracelet to honor the marriage. Later, Kwada will offer him gifts of food and he and his wife will reciprocate with a gift of household utensils. But it is the iron bracelet that seals the bond between them and, after receiving that gift, she will call him *yita* (father). Though women's second marriages follow a very different pattern,[8] this element is the same and women marrying after a divorce will also have a "second father" who will give them an iron bracelet as an expression of this new relationship.

The Kapsiki offer two interpretations for iron. The first is wealth. Though one main expression of Kapsiki wealth is cattle, iron sings the same tune. Some of the women's iron bracelets are just an indication of wealth. Most iron used to come to the Kapsiki area in the form of *duburu*, valuable tool blanks. In the marriage proceedings the flow of iron wealth follows that of the cattle in the bridewealth, which is symbolically represented by the bull of marriage.[9] Marriage presents a new kind of wealth for the groom, namely offspring. Marriage, through the payment of bridewealth, transforms monetary wealth into social wealth (relatives), considered the only stable form.

It is here that the second, more pervading association is located, that of stability and immobilization. Medicine and magic tend to "walk away" if they are not in iron containers, slaves were put in iron clamps, and likewise the *makwa* should be decked out in iron to have her "stay." Iron, in short, is the central symbol of belonging, of the bride belonging in her new social network, the symbolic means of creating stability in this union and transforming fleeting nonhuman wealth into stable human wealth. The two strips of bull hide used in decking out the bride are part of this symbolism. One string of hide is put into the *livu*, and the larger one forms the girdle that the *makwa* wears during the rituals. Symbolically, she wears the link between the two families—her husband's and her father's—through the *livu* and her girdle. This piece of hide is later used as a symbol of mourning and, when her father dies, the former *makwa* wears the hide for a whole year as a mourning band. She is the link between families, and her attire testifies to this fact. Iron means stability, so symbolically, the *makwa* just has to stay.

10

The Brass Boys

Initiation

Boys and Brass

Dègu checks his outfit for his first appearance as *gwela*,[1] as the newest initiate in the village. His older brother Deli assists him since this is an important moment for the whole family: Dègu is *their* gwela. The initiation started about a week ago when Deli early one morning tied a *hweta*, an old goatskin, around his brother's loins in the presence of all this year's other initiates, each with their older brother. More than eight days have now passed and Dègu has to appear in his new splendor for the culminating rites of the initiation to join his *mandala* (initiation mates) in the big festival that concludes the *gwela* just before the rains come.

Dègu's outfit as *gwela* is of high importance. The main item is the *hweta* (goat loinskin), the traditional clothing of men. For the last week, Dègu has worn an old, well-worn goatskin that he borrowed from his father's older brother, who was honored by the request and laboriously anointed the old vestment with mahogany oil and ocher. The initiate will now replace this with an antelope skin, also called *hweta*. It is strongly associated with war, a reminder of the days when life was precarious and vigorous defense against marauders was called for. Dègu sports a band with a double row of cowry shells over his right shoulder and left upper arm and adds other paraphernalia: a piece of a bull's forehead bone on his left hip, some broad brass bracelets on the upper arm, plus a smaller iron bracelet on the other arm. If possible, a *gwela* replaces the bull's forehead bone with a *matlaba* (a brass plaque) but these have become scarce and Dègu will have to make do with a bone one.

He ties a brass triangle on his forehead. Chains of glass beads in many colors, if possible old mosaic beads. Pendants made of old medicine vials set with red berries add a feminine touch to his outfit. With some pride he slips a few shiny brass bracelets over his arms, ties on a cowry belt with a brass bell in front and at the back a brass medicine vial. His head is decorated with plaited *peha* palm strips; his brother ties an inverted U-shaped piece of *peha* with some leather strips to both of the boy's calves.

Dègu then takes his lance and a small shield as the final accompaniment to his outfit. A brass bell is tied with cow hide to the lance, as are some brass medicine vials. The Kapsiki have two types of lances: one has a barbed spearhead and was used in combat, the other is leaf-shaped and comes from their old enemies, the Fulbe. This is the one the *gwela* uses. In their wars, the Kapsiki relied more on bows and poisoned arrows than on spears, but after the Hamman Yaji years they adopted the spear as a weapon and ceremonial object. The shield is special. The *gwela* in most villages use the regular war shields made of buffalo hide that are prized family possessions. In Mogode, a kind of replica shield is often used: it is about a foot high and is made of acacia bark with *wetle* grass (the grass for arrow shafts) tied to it. Dègu's father made it for him, as he should, the day before.

Dègu's outfit proclaims him a real *katsala* (warrior). His *hweta* defines him as an adult, while the cowry shells underline his liminality. The *peha* strip bears a connotation of liminality, as we saw with the twins.

> There is a story that this part of the outfit came from heaven; during an initiation in the days of Hwempetla, people told me, a man fell out of the sky clothed in just cowries and *peha*. He was dead, of course, but since then the Kapsiki added both to their initiation outfit. This curious tale is not common in other villages, where nevertheless the same outfit is used.

His decorations also convey another message. The brass elements of his outfit define Dègu as a wealthy young man. Brass objects signal wealth, success in hunting and war, and chieftainship, and they form an ostentatious presence throughout. Brass contrasts with iron in Kapsiki symbolism. We saw brides adorned with an iron skirt (*livu*) as their most characteristic dress, and the brass decoration for the *gwela* signifies the opposite of iron. Brass is used for objects of status by those who want to distinguish themselves from their peers. It is expensive and is the preferred metal for ornaments for older women, those who are no longer brides and who want to adorn themselves in their own personal way.

However, brass means more than just wealth. It is during the second phase of the initiation that *gwela* start to wear brass. Then they are like bees going everywhere in the bush, and bees are after all essential in the production of brass through the lost wax technique. In fact, most non-smith Kapsiki believe that it is the wax itself that is transformed into metal during the melting and casting process; of course, the caster-smiths know better! So the main association of the *gwela* is with the bush and the wild and uncultivated environment where

Figure 10.1 Gwela Vandu with his girl helper. Mogode 1973.

wild animals roam—or rather *used* to roam, since most have been hunted out—and where enemies lurk(ed). So brass is a bush "matter."[2] Just as bees cannot be domesticated (according to the Kapsiki) but live in and from the bush, bringing its riches home to their hive, likewise the *gwela* will be men of the bush, bringing in the wealth of others. And that is what Dègu is going to do in the next days, when with his agemates he will set out to accost strangers coming into town to ask them for a contribution to the *gwela* beer fund. But for now he has to leave the house for the first time in a week, and doing so demands another ritual, called *shave mbe cɛ* (leave the house). First we will go back to the start of the initiation, and then resume with Dègu at this point.

Toward Manhood: Preparation

The boys' initiation is a yearly highpoint of village life. Differences in the exact liturgy between the various villages are considerable and this description centers on Mogode as one of the central villages; later we will use a comparison with other villages to understand the role of initiation rituals in the identity construction of the Kapsiki. After all, the boys' initiation is a collective ritual, more so than the *makwa* for girls, and the village unites in a series of spectacular rituals.

Initiation rites take place every year at the end of the last moon in the dry season in May, the moon after the *makwa verhe*. For the *gwela* rites the villages follow each other in a fixed order: Rufta, Sirakuti, Sir, Mogode, Guria, Rumsu. The other villages have their own sequences. Rufta starts, the others follow a week later, and Rumsu is last, with its ceremonies lasting into the first rains. Villages are present as spectators at the each other's *gwela* rites.

A father decides when his boy will be a *gwela* and usually does not announce it immediately, but makes him cultivate *luku* (couch grass[3]) with a friendly female neighbor. She will become his initiation mother, called *kweperhuli* like the *makwa* initiation mothers (Figure 10.1). *Luku* is a typical female crop for the Kapsiki and is used in the sauce that the initiation mother will present to her *gwela*. The boy's father also asks a brother or good friend to serve as the *yitiyagwela* (initiation father, mentor), a crucial player in the ritual drama. At the start of the dry season, father and son together build a hut in which the boy will receive his friends, a hut that preferably will be roofed in the ancient way, not with wooden support beams but with a straw roof reinforced with a bundle of lianas. This old type of roof is plaited in one piece and positioned but not fastened yet, because that will be part of the *gwela* proceedings. The boy himself has to cut the long *haze* grasses for the roof, which not only are used for roofing but also serve as an important symbol in many of the Kapsiki rites of passage. The father then organizes a work party with friends and kinsmen to construct the roof, although this part of the proceedings has changed: the new construction with beams has replaced the old style. This new and easier way of building allows for larger huts, and furthermore the really long grasses used in the past are becoming rare as more cattle graze the plateau.

Now it is clear to all that the boy will be initiated, and he is no longer allowed to enter a house where a *makwa* lives, nor eat food cooked for a *makwa* lest he become "soft and slow like a woman." His father makes additional preparations for the feast in order to have enough sorghum for beer, and either has to save up or take out a loan to buy a lot of meat.

The complex ritual has a definite rhythm that is geared also to what the *makwa* do:

Day 1   Tie on the skin, fasten the roof
       2   Shave the head, shut the boy in, first *verhe*
       3–5   The boy is inside during the day but can roam the fields at night
       6   Division of the goat
       7–9   Like days 3–5
       9   Second *verhe*, coming out, assembling outfit
       10   Various tests, the call of *makwa*, the Mentsehe ritual, small *verhe*
       11   Hunting

As we saw in the last chapter, the *makwa* get their scarifications on day 9, sing at Rhwemetla on days 9 and 10, and participate in the same Mentsehe ritual.

The initiation proper starts just before the third new moon, around the end of April: all *gwela* assemble at the village chief's to ask whether the time has come. He tells them to wait another four days, and in the last week before the new moon he orders the start of proceedings. Sometimes the moon count is off and the elders have to discuss whether to start on this moon or the next. They are quite aware that the lunar calendar is at odds with the solar one, and ultimately it is the onset of the rains that is conclusive. Rain should fall right after the initiation rituals and in fact some drops on the last days of the *gwela* are considered propitious.

The boys get up in the middle of the night and look for each other in the pitch darkness, all of them blowing a two-toned wooden flute so that they can find each other easily. During the night the older brother of each *gwela* comes for him, accompanied by a younger brother. The older one carries a bow, a stick, and a quiver of arrows, plus an old well-used goatskin, the traditional male dress. The whole company awaits the rise of the morning star and then heads north toward Rumsu. At a boulder, all the older brothers wait until everyone is present and then suddenly, all at the same time, they grab their younger siblings, undress them by taking off the skins they are wearing, and replace these with the old, mature skin, the skin of men. As was already mentioned, Dègu got his from his uncle. This step is called *kwatlahutu*, to cut the *hwutu*, the leather belt that held the skin that the youngsters used to wear. This belt is now for the *mehteshi*, the little helpers, who tie it onto the pot they use to fetch water for the *gwela* when he is in seclusion during days 3–9.

One of the few changes in the *gwela* ritual today is that now all the boys wear shorts and wear the goatskin over them. But the name has stuck; dressing in the skin forms the main symbol of transition. The *gwela* hand their old skin over to the younger brothers, who take it home. Tying the new skin is also called *kawume gwela* (to initiate the boy), the term in fact being used for the entire initiation process. From this moment onward the boy has in fact performed the initiation. If he were to drop out of the coming rituals, as some Christian boys tend to, he is still considered an initiated *gwela*. Now properly clothed as men, the boys run a short distance, shouting *Za 'ya, za 'ya* (I am a man, I am a man), then walk to a nearby rock where their initiation mothers are waiting for them grouped according to clan. The women put some *hazhaze*, a grass used for a girl's cache sexe, on the back of the new skin. Later the *gwela* will hang this bundle in his hut "to wait for the bride." Right now they head for a row of stones nearby and line up in front of them: the first to step over will be the chief *gwela*. At first they all hesitate, or seem to hesitate, trying to push the other forward over the stones, but then one of them defiantly steps over them, content to be this year's leader and to head the line of *gwela* in the days to come.

Under his guidance, the boys walk over to a hill, shoot an arrow toward the west, and then run home with their brothers trailing them.

Back home, they immediately start to finish their roof, tying the straw roof to the circular wall. The way an initiate does this will decide how he will finish each roof of his personal hut in the future. One *gwela* used old binding straw tying on a new roof hat and will therefore have to do the same in the future. This time the work is done in haste, but this does not mean they will have to hurry in the future as well. The *gwela* plaits a cord from fibers of the *cibeni* tree[4] and his *yitiyagwela* ties the cord around his loins, to be removed only at the end of the initiation process.

That evening the boys gather under a very old acacia tree near the village chief's hut to play a board game that is usually played with two but can also be played with four, as "real men" do, which the *gwela* now are. They play it twice, joined on the playground by their *mehteshi*, the little boys who will be their helpers during the initiation. That evening the little helpers sleep in their *gwela*'s newly finished hut. They are usually chosen by the mentor, who presents the boy with a belt plaited with grasses he got from the *gwela*.

Both the *gwela* and his helper head for the smith the next morning to have their heads shaved. Since this is their last day of mobility for the next week, the initiates use the occasion to pick up from the smith woman the two pots they will need for the ritual that night. When all the *gwela* are present, the smith starts shaving: the first three clans first, the other clans next. He has to use a traditional razor even if razor blades would be easier, and he also shaves their eyebrows. The *mehteshi* are shaved too.

Now fully liminal with their heads shaved, wearing a goatskin and carrying a stick, bow, and arrows, the *gwela* will amuse themselves the following nights with a new sport—stopping and harassing strangers (people from other villages) in order to extract money from them. Because this is the dry season, commerce is lively and visitors are coming to Mogode, a trip which will now cost them an additional coin (FCFA 25 in 1973, FCFA 100 in 2008). Some Muslim merchants may protest but most settle easily, some saying: "This is good, I did something like this. It is from the ancestors, and I will pay." If it rains on the day the skin is tied or later when the *gwela* is brewing, this is a good sign, but in most villages the first rains are still a long way off.

Early in the evening of the second day, a meal of mush is prepared in the *gwela*'s hut. The helper lights a fire in the hut and will ensure that it stays burning for the whole initiation period. He also fetches water in a small pot that the *gwela* has tied around his neck with a string of leather. While the women are busy cooking, the *gwela* entertains visitors and friends and watches his mother's brother plait bracelets for him out of palm leaf strips, an important initiation symbol, as we saw with the twins. The *gwela* now wears his brass bracelets—this being the first occasion where he may wear brass—and will continue to decorate himself throughout this special period.

The meal is called a *verhe*, just like the *makwa* wedding, a public eating party with a lot of visitors and with peanut sauce as the central ceremonial element. It is the first one of three, for the *gwela*. One of his sister's sons divides the meat into five portions: one for the *gwela* and his *mehteshi*, one for the *kweperhuli*, one for the initiation father, one for the elders in the forecourt, and the last for all the women and children in the compound. This meal is the formal introduction of the initiation father and mother but it is also the meal that will shut the *gwela* off from the outside world.

It is a moment of some tension and, as is usual in Kapsiki, everybody tries to get involved, resulting in heated discussions about the distribution of the food, so the sister's son, who is in charge, often has a hard time. But all the food has been distributed by the time the initiation father arrives, though people wait to eat until the ritual is finished. The *gwela* has put a forked ladder against his hut and has driven his lance deep into the ground near his entrance. The initiation father arrives with a cord in hand, takes a wide-rimmed pot and a cord, and while the *gwela* enters his hut the mentor climbs the roof. The wide pot is put upside down over the top of the roof and a rope is tied around it. The *mehteshi* waits outside and hands over a calabash with a mix of water and flour, such as is used in sacrifice (see Chapter 4). The mentor takes a round flint or quartz stone from his pocket, puts it on the top of the upturned pot, pours some of the mixture on the stone, and while everyone falls silent, intones his wishes for the boy:

"Let nobody do any harm to this child. *Shala*, let him just marry, have children, and cultivate sorghum." He then pours more liquid. *Mehteshi* also climbs the ladder, pretends to take the stone twice, and does so the third time, saying: *kamale, kamava, kaha* (women, slaves, sorghum). As soon as the helper arrives safely on the ground with the stone, the women ululate since the sacrifice, as it is called, has been successful: the stone has not been dropped! *Mehteshi* brings the stone to the *gwela*, who will use it from now on as his *melɛ*. To conclude the sacrifice, as usual, people eat, and the mentor puts a new belt on the *gwela* that has been plaited from *wetle* grasses by the *mehteshi*, just after the *gwela* had his loinskin tied on.

For the next eight days the *gwela* has to stay inside his hut during the day. He eats alone, from a special calabash and pot. He should not walk around in daytime and, most important, he should not be touched by the sun. When he has to leave the hut during the day, when nature calls, he covers himself with a meter-wide granary cap, making him look like a walking toadstool. But at night he is free to go out, and after sunset all the *gwela* assemble at the edge of the village to talk, to play, and to accost strangers for money. All the *mehteshi* are there as well, clothed in goatskins, carrying brass ornaments and a lance. It is the helper who keeps track of the eight days that the *gwela* has to stay indoors. During the first four days, when he comes with sand as a toothbrush, the helper brings a shard, and in the second half of the seclusion he brings one grewia fruit each morning, counting the initial day of seclusion and the day of leaving as full days. With a full collection of four shards and four grewia fruit, the *gwela* can leave his hut,

Eating a lot of rich and soft food is crucial during this time, so the *gwela* is fed mush, porridge, sauce, and meat, the latter usually without bones—the Kapsiki normally love to have some bone in their meals and eat chickens bones and all—since he cannot tolerate hard pieces, like a baby who still has to get used to normal adult food. So porridge from peanuts and sweet potatoes is the staple, plus soft meat and not too many intestines. He should grow fat in the seclusion period, a transformation that is eagerly anticipated—even in just seven days! One reason the fire has to be kept burning is that heat will make one grow, and cold, according to the Kapsiki, makes people thin. The boys take pains to keep themselves covered in oil and ocher, since washing will let out the fat. During these days a *gwela* is busy brewing a lot of beer, for the first time without supervision; it is *his* beer. Eating will remain important during the whole following season. A *gwela* whose mother is still around—is alive and has not run away—will get mush with meat each morning to stimulate sperm production; the age of the *gwela* should be such that he has just started to produce sperm. But this is never tested openly.

Thus the association of the *gwela* and fertility is very close in Kapsiki. In one village to the north, Wula, the *gwela*'s penis is anointed by his sister so that he will produce children. In Mogode in the past, boys with a penis without a foreskin were called *rhelaza* (male clitoris) and were fêted from their mother's brother's home, being "like their mother." During the initiation, the other boys would put some mud on such a boy's glans; otherwise the rains would not come. Nowadays with islamization, most of the boys are circumcised and this is no longer done. A boy with only one testicle is considered sterile and is also initiated from his uncle's house: for his father this sterile *gwela* is useless. Some symbolism is related to death: a left-handed *gwela* performs his initiation from his father's house but then his father will die soon afterwards. Left-handedness is considered a social handicap (left-handed children have weights attached to their left wrists to change their awkward habits), but "lefties" are also considered the fiercest and strongest warriors of all.

Halfway through the period, on day 6, a goat or sheep is slaughtered and divided among the *gwela*'s older sisters, one of whom is chosen to be his *kwatlazewe* (the one who cuts the cord). She gets the lion's share of the meat, matched only by the share of the mentrix. Usually the *kwatlazewe* is a wealthy woman and she has to repay the honor by being the first to feast the *gwela* on meat and mush, often in a huge gift of mush long after the initiation. After all, "one does not give a loan to someone who cannot repay it." *Kweperhuli* on her part will present smaller gifts to the *gwela* during the rainy season, like white beer or a chicken and mush. Like any functionary in Kapsiki rituals, these women too have an assistant to help brew red beer and assist in grinding peanuts for sauce, which she will give to the *gwela* and his party at midnight. During the last food gift, *kweperhuli* puts an iron bracelet with the food, as a kind of ritual test. If the *gwela* has had a sexual relationship with a woman (not with a girl!), he is expected to throw up after eating the food but no further sanctions will be taken. He may, evidently, have sex with his own fiancée.

Though they receive a lot of attention and visitors, the *gwela* are supposed to be relatively silent and not speak too much. If they do, birds will eat the sorghum and millet. This stricture does not prevent their brothers, friends, ward members, and other kinsmen from visiting them, generously partaking of the meat and porridge while asking solicitously whether the *gwela* has had enough to eat.

Coming Out

The next high point is the day of coming out, the same day we saw the *makwa* assemble for Rhwemetla. This is the day we started with Dègu in our opening example, working on his outfit. His *kweperhuli* is busy decorating the rim and inside of a calabash with a pattern of burned lines. The *gwela* has received this calabash from his mother for tonight's meal in order to give to his *makwa* on the evening she is called. The Higi have taken this custom of decorating calabashes from the Marghi. In the past, people told me, the *gwela* ate only from undecorated calabashes, as the chief and the *mnzefɛ* still do: they also eat out of pottery and never from enamel bowls. Dègu has given the old goatskin he used at his initiation to his *mehteshi* and this morning he is wearing an antelope skin, an heirloom. If the family had not had one, he would have worn another old black goatskin. The antelope skin is not knotted but tied around the hips with a piece of sorghum stalk called *kwalkwala* (*kwala* means penis, but informants categorically deny any sexual innuendo!). These preperations take an hour or so, and in the meantime the father's sister's sons have brought along the mush and the sauce, dividing it among the following groups: the elders in the forecourt, the initiation father (mentor) plus *kweperhuli*, both with their assistants, the *gwela* and his people, girls of his clan, children, women, and finally the nephews of the clan.

Dègu hosts his initiation father and mother plus their assistants in his hut while the other groups are dispersed over the compound, the brewing hut, the forecourt, or the shelters between the women's huts. After the meal, which is called the second *verhe*, the *gwela* puts on his antelope skin and his full paraphernalia (see beginning of this chapter). A sister's son gets a jar of beer, and the mentor fills a calabash, crouching before the door of the *gwela*. Dègu, freshly shaven and oiled with mahogany oil and red with ocher, wearing his full attire, now comes out in full splendor, lance in hand, crouches in front of his door, and the mentor gives his blessing:

"The child has to marry and cultivate sorghum. He is an orphan and has to take care of himself." [Dègu was called an orphan because his father was in prison; he did have a mother, but she left for another husband two months later.] He then takes a sip and sprays it over Dègu three times, with all the women ululating. The *kweperhuli* then does the same: "You have to marry and father a child, like you were begotten yourself."

All the women in the house shriek and ululate, and the young children throw cow dung over the *gwela* and his helper, who run from the compound to the assembly point. While he was shut away, the *gwela* was bullying the young children at night since his first *verhe*, tying them up, slapping them, and making them eat nasty things, so this is the day of their sweet revenge. This ritual is called *shave mbe cɛ*, the same term that is used for the young mother who leaves her compound for the first time with her baby (see Chapter 8).

Dègu joins his agemates under a huge, gnarled acacia tree, in the village's central ward, where the *gwela* put their lances in two groups, one for the first three clans of Mogode, the other for the second moiety. No distinction is made between smith and non-smith, and any smith *gwela* participate just like the others. The *mehteshi* carry the bag with meat and try to eat it themselves, while the initiates have to take it from them with force (and speed!). That afternoon the *gwela* amuse themselves playing games and demanding money from strangers, and later that evening they take up their lances and head for their uncle's home to spend the night there.

The next day, the second chanting day for the *makwa* in Rhwemetla, is also the ritual high point for the *gwela*. Again they assemble at the usual point, put their lances in two groups together, with shields and bells attached, and check whether their helpers have all the food needed: mush, meat, and sauce with chicken (Figure 10.2). They wait until the girls are at the smith's and then badger their own *mehteshi*. Four *gwela* drive forward the whole group of little helpers, who have to chant while running. Again, as with the *makwa*, the good singers are praised, especially if they sing to honor their *gwela*:

Answer me, answer my song
Oh, rich Kwada, my rich Kwada [his *gwela*]
If we go back to your house covered with iron
Your wife awaits you on your bed
Hit the ones who cannot sing, hit them
This year many cannot sing, *gwela*
What happened with your mouth, what happened?
There is money, money for you
Marry a woman, marry a woman, my Kwada
You are my Paul Biya, my *gwela*, Biya the president[5]
You are the government, my Kwada, the government.

Figure 10.2 *Gwela* with lances and shields, small and large.

If the boys' *mehteshi* can find the *mehteshi* of the *makwa*, they will do the same with them, but usually the young girls are quite good at hiding. The boys' *mehteshi* wear the old goatskin, the *gwela*, as already mentioned, the antelope skin, but for one clan, the *makwiyε*, this custom is taboo and they are thought to get diarrhea from an antelope skin.

When the *makwa* eat their food on the mountain, the *gwela* have their meal too, grouped by clan. Their helpers eat as well. The start of the singing also signals the first test for the initiates: they have to jump over a threshing floor. The floor in question is very old, it has long been in disuse, and the boys are disputing exactly where it is, when an old woman who has sown seeds close to the floor threatens the boys with fire and brimstone if they disturb her field. The boys line up and quickly jump twice over the floor, not a very long jump (2.5 m), and if they do not make it, there is no problem. Flanked by their helpers, they then walk in a single line to Mentsehe, a mountain 400 m to the east of Rhwemetla. At the halfway point the *mehteshi* run toward their *gwela*, hand over the meat, and join the back of the line. Mentsehe is a small rock covered by a larger one, creating an overhang where the *gwela* spend most of the day. An old man points out where to put their lances, grouped by moiety. One by one the *gwela* climb the rock under the shelter, ring their brass bells, and say *Za 'ya, za 'ya* (I am a man), and then face their second test. They have to pull themselves up to a rock and touch it with their tongue. Content with "being a man," they then rest.

If they fail—and some of the smaller ones do—the spectators have fun but, again, no sanctions follow. After everyone has passed the test, the *mehteshi* have to sing again, exhorted by a group of *gwela*. Others try to get money from strangers—there are a lot of them around the singing rock—while some stand at the rock's entrance as guardians for the girls, to make sure they have enough space to sing. The boys' helpers, while running and singing, pester the *mehteshi* of the girls, preventing them from fetching water for the *makwa*.

After a pleasant afternoon, the initiation mothers of the *gwela* bring the evening dish in the newly decorated calabashes at about 5 pm: white sorghum mush, peanut sauce, goat meat—partly cooked, part raw—usually some ribs given by either the initiation mother or the mother of the *gwela*'s fiancée, if he has one. The meal is called the "small *verhe*." The fiancées are normally not among the girls who are initiated at that time, for the *makwa* usually marry older men since the bridewealth is steep and has to be paid in advance. The *mehteshi* return from their singing spree and rush to the food. The *gwela* come to the spot, touch the mountain, calling again *Za 'ya, za 'ya* (I am a man). With sunset approaching, two boys invite the *makwa* to come to Mentsehe but the latter will refuse twice before coming. The third time they do come, leaving the calabashes they came with at the side of the pool. The *gwela* initiation mothers then hurry from Mentsehe to the pool, pick up the boys' calabashes, fill them with water, and put them in the *gwela*'s hut. In the meantime the brothers of the *gwela* have collected the calabashes of the *makwa* of their own clan and divide the food. Each boy gives a goat's leg to his future *makwa*, if she is among the spectators—if she is not, then to one of his clan brothers. He then hands the mush to a *makwa* from his clan, and they eat it with their *mehteshi* while the boys' *mehteshi* finally get a large sack of meat.

Everyone eats except the *gwela* themselves, since they have other things to do first. When this small *verhe* is done, the ritual of the running to Mentsehe is due, as described for the *makwa* in the previous chapter. As clan siblings they run the 30 m between Mentsehe and the boulder and back. After doing the course three or four times, the boys again run to Mentsehe, pull themselves up onto the high rock, touch it with their tongue, and again exclaim, *Za 'ya, za 'ya* (I am a man). The *makwa* eat their food and go home, but a last ritual awaits the *gwela*. Lined up with their lances in hand, they follow an old smith along a series of special spots, to remember the people of old. Hidden in the long grass lie old grindstones and remnants of old houses, and in each of these the *gwela* set their lances and sing the first lines of songs: the *ntereligu* (*makwa* song), *kwanjanja* (song of the *la* feast), *wakedaŋe* (a song about the harvest), and *yamyame* (a burial song).

> *Wakedaŋe*, I am a child for the last time
> Now a famous person will come
> I warn the ones who do not want to perform *gwela*
> Because of the cost of the work party [for hut construction]

> Hear, all you who do not want to do the *gwela*
> Because they stole melons [taboo for *gwela*]
> The arrow will enter their body quickly!
> *Kwanja, kwanja*, small calabash
> To drink water from Lakwa [village well]
> I work without drinking in Lakwa
> I work without drinking in Mwuli [another well]

Their final destination is a sloping rock where the chief *gwela* takes up the highest spot with the others close to him. The rock is called *Kwatladlerevɛ* (the place to chase the dragonfly) and that is exactly what they are going to do. The *gwela* put down their lances, the *mehteshi* make a beeline to the bottom of the mountain and beat the grass with branches to scare the dragonflies. It is hard to see in the dusk but the spectators as well as the *gwela* keep very quiet waiting to see what happens. The first try seldom succeeds but after a few times one dragonfly at least settles on someone's lance: that boy will then marry quickly and have many wives and children. Some years there are plenty of dragonflies, some years none at all. The smith told me that if there are none in sight, after three fruitless attempts he himself will announce the lance the insect has landed on, since by then it is so dark that nobody can see it anyway.

> A story accompanies this ritual. In the past, informants tell me, the *gwela* sent their helpers to this place to scout for enemies or wild animals. Their lances already stood near the mountain. The helpers thought they saw shapes with the lances, something sitting on one of them. Since it is taboo for someone else to touch the lances, they slowly approached and saw a dragonfly on top of it. They called the *gwela* to see the miracle and that year the *gwela* on whose lance the dragonfly had rested was the first to marry. So that is why today it is still done that way.

For the initiates it is eating time now. The mush that remains is brought by the faithful *mehteshi* and eaten by clan, and the smith who has guided them is rewarded with food as well. On their walk home, the smith directs them to two other sacred spots, which they touch, singing the songs mentioned above. One seeming omission is the two mountains where the people lived in olden days; neither Miyi nor Rhuŋgeɗu are part of the initiation itinerary. According to informants, these are omitted because there are many boys whose ancestors have immigrated to Mogode among the initiates, and the sacred spots on these mountains are only for the "real" Mogodians.

The next day the boys go hunting. Assembling at the place of their first jumping trial, they are joined by their *mehteshi*, who now wear the cowry belts of the *gwela*, and everyone eats the food prepared by their friends this time, chicken with a peanut sauce. The boys put their lances together as always, and after the meal they try to prove that they are now real hunters. Armed with clubs, bows, and arrows their *mehteshi* have provided them with, they—sometimes desperately—try to catch something. If they do not succeed, they tell the people waiting for them that they have caught a cricket. In any case, they return from the bush with the leaves that the cache sexes of the *makwa* used to be made of. The *mehteshi* take these leaves from them and run home to put them in the boy's hut: he should marry quickly. Any game they have caught (although there is often none at all) they give to the iniate's mentrix, who joins them at this spot. At last she does the work her title indicates, cutting the cord the *gwela* has worn since the first day of his initiation process. Women from the *gwela*'s compound take the rest of the food home, add mush, beer, and meat, and eat it with friends, giving everyone who has contributed an immediate reward in the form of food. Any old men and children present get their share as well.

Then the last of the gentle tests follows. Near the main well in Mogode, the boys look for a place with some water, not an easy task because it is the end of the dry season, and they select a spot to jump. Most spectators have left by now and the boys are on their own in this last phase. Each *gwela* jumps over the selected spot twice; if he does not make the distance and falls into the water, he will receive inevitable ridicule: "Your father has made you in vain; he wants to keep you." But again it is not the result but the shared experience of jumping that counts. They put their lances by the side of the pool and wash, still wearing their antelope skins. After washing, they let the loose leg ends of the skin dangle at the back. Until then these have been tucked into their waist but now they are worn as a "real skin," since the boys are masters of the bush with proper skins!

The collective ritual over, they head home, where they eat and drink the beer that their initiation mothers have brought in large quantities: white and red beer, mush with meat sauce with peanuts and a special vegetable.[6] The last part of today's small *verhe* follows, an eating party with as many of the ward members present as the compound can hold.

Back now to Dègu. In the evening our *gwela* comes home, where his father's brother Deli is busy arranging everything. The *kweperhuli*, a mother's sister of Dègu, with her assistant, has brought huge amounts of food, and the guests eat their fill. After the meal she gives Dègu his large decorated calabash, which he fills with sorghum from his father's granary. A clan brother brings natron, and Dègu's nephew takes this and an empty jar to the home of the *kweperhuli*, who lives close by and is home now. Deli accompanies the two, praising the amount of food the *kweperhuli* has given, stressing his own poverty: "If he were rich he would bring them much more!" But scores and scores of people have eaten their food and drunk beer endlessly! The atmosphere is jovial, especially when one uncle joins in the fun with a mock battle over a jar of beer and a slurred debate on the number of jars that have been emptied.

The *mehteshi* return home with a first parting gift of a chicken, but the relationship with the *gwela* is by no means at an end. For this entire cultivation season they will spend one night in four with their *gwela* until the concluding *la* festival. The *mehteshi* of the *makwa* will return to their duties just before the *la* feast.

For the boys' *mehteshi* it has been a challenging time. The Rhwemetla days were particularly busy, running, singing, and being chased by the *gwela*. Some of them thought it was great fun but others were not very keen from the start; in their case the *gwela* had asked their father and he agreed, so they were more or less obliged to participate. A few were very enthusiastic and wanted to do it again the following year.

Variations

Different villages, different *gwela* rituals; at least that is what my informants continually told me. We have seen here the Mogode initiation; a brief comparison with those in other villages will show both the differences and commonalities of this Kapsiki/Higi initiation. I will highlight three variations here: two will be only short descriptions of the elements that are different from those in Mogode, and the third one, Wula, will be described in more detail because it shows some relevant dynamics for all Kapsiki initiations.

South of Mogode in Rumsiki, the first part of the *gwela* has another name, *huntere*, and the boys are usually younger. The feast is usually scheduled for the middle of November and should straddle the harvest period. During the weeks before, the young men enjoy a general license to eat or plunder the harvest (in a limited way). The people are thus obliged to take in their harvest as quickly as possible to avoid losses, since no one can blame the boys, who are at the end of their childhood and prone to all the follies of youth.

The boys meticulously dress up, "like a corpse," with a large gown, hat, and ostrich feathers and strips of cloth crossed in bands over their chests. The most specific part of their outfit is the *hweta zheda*, bead skirts that are worn over both shoulders.[7] One of their tests is to run—quite a distance—in full attire without tripping. The boys are accompanied and supported by their brothers in case they fall and ruin the whole ritual. Some of the boys have invited girls from the village or Sena to assist them, and the girls will put water for them at some points along the route. The high point is when they gather at the place called *Rhuntere* (the head of Ntere). After considerable preparations, the boys run toward the hill, *Ntere*, and return walking backwards, assisted by their kinsmen, the boys still "like a corpse."

This rainy season they will cultivate and after the harvest they will perform the second part of the rite, which is called *gwela*. One specific feature in the second part is the *gela kwarafrafe*, a boulder with old grindstone surfaces, also called the "hand of *shala*," a roadside feature near Rumsiki. Here the boys undress, climb the rock naked, and call out: "I lay down my youth, all my young ideas have to leave me now, I am now grown-up, a real man. I will cultivate, I will look for a wife, will marry and have children."

The *gwela* rites in Sir, on the eastern edge of the Kapsiki area, are characterized by a complicated itinerary along the various sacred spots in the village, plus some mock battles between the *gwela* and other boys of the village. Their run through the river is also highly charged. The *gwela* here wear a crown with rooster feathers. Being a *mehteshi* in Sir is a complex task, because when the *gwela* are on their way to the dry riverbed, their helpers line up and run toward them, hit their shield with an iron club, repeating this once more near the stream. All the *gwela* have to run into the water, or at least they have to try to run. The boys have consulted divination the day before and now follow the advice they received, so some walk carefully as instructed. The spot has a bad reputation and the weak ones will sink down into the mud. Everyone reemerges anyway and touches a nearby baobab with the butt of his lance. This is the moment a mock battle ensues between the young boys in the village and the *gwela*. The boys throw pebbles at the *gwela* shields, while the *gwela* try to hit them with the rim of their shields, but all quickly move on. On their way to the baobab they can choose between two routes, a short and a long one. They can take the shorter one only if they have not slept with their uncle's wife; if they did so, they have to take the longer way, otherwise they will become sick and die. They have a joking relationship with their mother's brother that allows them considerable leeway, but sleeping with his wife is a bridge too far, for most. After the baobab they again gather at the side of the stream, singing and dancing. The *mehteshi*, carrying the shields, circle the stand of trees twice and then the *gwela* take the shield and club, leaving the lance standing in the water, and give their cowry bands and bracelets, in fact all of their ornaments, to their helpers to take home.

One peculiar feature about the next day is an unusual form of divination. The *gwela*'s father selects a spot by a nearby stream, digs a small hole and then puts some acacia leaves, cow dung, goat dung, and ants in it. He then covers it with a calabash. The idea is that his son will become rich and have a lot of children. When the *gwela* comes home, he and his father check whether a frog has entered the moist hole. If it has, the *gwela* will certainly become a rich man. Anyway, the *gwela* takes out the leaves and shakes the bundle: if no leaves fall out, the signs are good and people happily beat his shield. If a leaf falls out or if the leaves have turned red, he will get leprosy or may have to marry a "red girl," a Fulbe.

Wula, on the northern edge of the Kapsiki area, has the most spectacular variations. Wula sees itself as belonging to the Kapsiki, but historically the three villages of Sukur, Wula, and Mabas have a tradition of joint descent, in which Sukur was culturally closer to the Marghi, Mabas to the Mafa, and Wula to the

Figure 10.3 A Sir *gwela* being blessed by his initiation father.

Kapsiki.[8] Wula initiation is performed in two festivals, and the mothers of the *gwela* are central in the final feast. Because the seclusion period lasts a month here, they have not seen their own sons for that length of time, and the *gwela*'s homecoming is a time of celebration for the women. We zoom in on a *gwela* homecoming in 1988 in Wula.

> At noon the women assemble at home and start drinking; on this day they control the beer and decide which of the men gets some. The grandmothers of the *gwela* lead them, wearing one cowry shell for each grandson who has performed the initiation, in addition to her many brass ornaments. The mother of the *gwela* proudly shows off her dancing axe, adorned with iron pendants with hollow pouches (for medicine, but empty here), which tinkle as she dances. The women pour some beer on the floor and dance in the smelly mud. Young boys come in and greet the women respectfully, fingers on the ground, clapping their hands. These are women to be respected, as these women are seeing their sons again for the first time in a month, and the women greet each other with songs hailing their courage and their devotion to their boys. One of them sings about the wound her boy has (his eyes were injured), and she is comforted by the fact that he is still alive (at first she thought that he had died). "Do not puncture the eye of the culprit, but wait for the trial!" Another *gwela*'s mother enters with her

entourage proclaiming: "Our house is the house of pride today; let us break the jar and drink!" Her host honors the new arrival by wiping her face, and compares the well-decorated women with an ostrich feather, while she continues to sing: "I am not the daughter of nobody; I am the daughter of someone who can read and write. I am the battery in the machine, when I arrive everything starts to move!" After an hour, when the beer is finished, the party leaves the house to join the others at the dancing place.

Later, at about 4 pm, the whole village dances at the dancing place, waiting for the *gwela* to appear from the bush. At the side of the dancing throng, the *mehteshi* wait for their *gwela* with some food, a lance, an untreated goatskin, and a sickle. Just after 5 pm the boys are spotted in the west, walking slowly toward the waiting throng. The boys are led by their initiation brothers, who kick the fiber cord and the skin they are carrying with their left foot. Behind them the *gwela* are naked, and just before they reach the dancing place, the line splits, with mentors going on one side and the *gwela* on the other. The *mehteshi* hand the skins over to the mentors, and suddenly the *gwela* and the mentors run toward each other. The mentor lifts up his *gwela* and ties on the skin, a huge melée of people all trying to do this at the same time.

The ritual intensifies the next day. The *gwela* roam the village and then come home, where the women of the house sing their welcome: "Thank you *shala* that our son has lived to this day. Help him now to be strong so that he can bury us. He is my first maize" (first harvest) and the visiting women, consisting of the relatives of both parents, praise the initiate's mother: "Here is one who knows how to raise children!"

The *yitiyagwela* then starts the sacrifice at the place of honor in the *derha*. He puts a fiber cord he has just plaited on the floor with the *gwela*'s lance and sickle, takes some mush with *rhedle* sauce and a calebash with beer: "You have to cultivate with two hands. If a *mete* [witch] woman wants you, she has to leave. If a *mete* man looks for you, he has to leave. You have to work the land. Your penis should become tired from the many women." He then pours some mush and sauce on the items on the floor four times, and twice sprays some beer. The father's older brother has witnessed the proceedings from the opening of the wall and calls out: "*Kaha, kamale, kamava*" (sorghum, women, and slaves); the initiation father says the same and adds: "You are alone; you should get a brother, a nephew, and a friend." He takes the cord, the lance, and the sickle, hands them to the *gwela*, ties on the cord, and drinks "à deux" with the *gwela*.

The women start dancing again, joined by other women, again pouring beer on the floor so as to dance in the proper smell, and the *gwela* gives them small presents, usually sweets. Beer is plentiful, over twenty jars of it, and they should be visible. At about 3 pm the women stop dancing, assemble in the house, wipe the floor clean, and prepare ointment for the *gwela*. All the *gwela*'s clan sisters stay and the other women leave, while the *gwela* positions himself at the place where the women were dancing. The mentor ties the cord around the boy's loins, handing him the end of the rope, and then takes away the skin the *gwela* has worn during the day. One young clan sister who stayed in his hut last night takes a bowl of mahogany oil and copiously anoints his penis with it. Smiling and amused, the family watches the proceeding, the girl herself awkward and a little bit self-conscious but enjoying it all the same; the boy shows no sign of self-consciousness as far as I could see. The initiation father covers the penis with a sheep skin, ties on a girdle with brass bells, and then leads the *gwela* twice around the inner court, counterclockwise, while the women sing: "Child of the chief, marry a lot of women, capture slaves, father children." *Gwela*, his mentor, and clan sisters then leave the house to head for the dancing place. The *gwela* and their parties again head for the bush, and the liturgy of two days ago is repeated: the *gwela* come from the bush, eagerly awaited by the village. At the dancing place they are once again lifted up and covered with the goatskin.

The Structure of Initiation

What are the commonalities of the *gwela* rituals? The various elements of the initiation seem to be rearranged between the villages, and the village liturgies of initiation are transformations of each other. Each village makes its own composition of interchangeable elements, adds some specific items, and together these make the ritual in each village unique.

The general structure for the Kapsiki/Higi initiation is clearly tripartite, following the classic Turner definition.[9] The first *gwela* rituals mark the end of the dry season, followed by a liminal period during the cultivation season, to be concluded by the massive homecoming rituals of the *la* festival we will encounter in the next chapter; but also if we look at the first initiation phase, the *gwela* proper, we see a similar structure (Figure 10.4).

Generally speaking, preparations involve cultivation of a specific cultivar, usually sesame and couch grass, so a woman's crop, and building a hut or a roof. The first phase starts with tying on the new skin, followed by actions to do with the hut of the *gwela*. A period of seclusion then follows in which the *gwela* is part of the compound during the day but roams the bush at night. He has to stay out of the sun and, as we have seen, the sun has a definite association with sacrifice, and indeed the boy receives his first own *mele*. This liminal period is best illustrated when he walks under the granary roofcap by day, almost totally covered by a huge straw hat, not overly human and firmly associated with the granary. It is in his coming out that the *gwela* is decorated in his very best finery, as a complete warrior and rich man of the bush. The privacy of the house has finally been

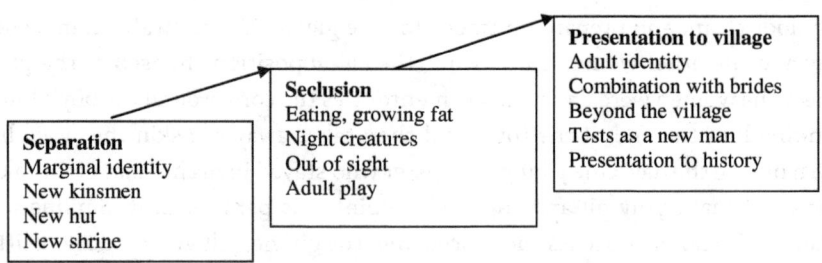

Figure 10.4 The tripartite structure and content of *gwela* initiation.

left behind: now he is *mandala* (age mate) with the other boys as well as with the *makwa*, moving as a group, relating to his clan and becoming part of the history of the village. This is the part of the symbolic tests and is the period of his mobility, with the *gwela* spending nights "abroad" either at the home of one of the village officials or at his initiation father's.

According to Van Gennep the transition of the boy is not so much to actual sexuality as to a "monde sexué," an accepted sexual life,[10] and that is indeed the case here, well attested by the various symbolic tests on virginity—like the *makwa*—with "symbolic" being the operative word. But this is not the only transition for boys, because manhood implies much more than being sexual. They also transit from being a person confined to the house into a man who goes to other villages, someone to be reckoned with, dangerous for foreigners and a pillar of strength for his own clan. Third, the boy changes into a cultivator, someone with his own fields and produce, who can feed his own family as well as others. Rituals, as Bell remarks,[11] are a means of constructing masculinity, and that is clearly the case here. A real Kapsiki man has his own compound, is not dependent, can hold his own in combat but also in disputes with fellow Kapsiki, marries many wives, and fathers a host of children. Such a Kapsiki man is deemed to be quite autarchic and never lets social obligations supersede his individual interests. The Kaspiki model for masculinity implies someone who is both combative and clever but also a loyal friend and a respectful kinsman.[12] This masculine complex is topped by his independent *mele*, as he and his personal *shala* now have their proper dual recognition. So he brews his own beer now. This definition of manhood is highlighted by the extension of kin, by having the *gwela* build, sacrifice, wrestle, and play, by some gentle tests, by the continuous interaction with brides, by becoming a father to his helper, and by his performances in front of the whole village.

So far this is quite a classic case of initiation in which the boys are separated from their old existence, then marginalized in a liminal status, finally to be reintegrated into the village community as adults. However, as initiations go, it has some peculiar features as well. First and foremost, there is the close link between human and agricultural fertility, as exemplified in the many meanings of *wume*:

paying a bridewealth, ripening of grass, starting a new granary, and, indeed, initiating a boy. Here, maturity and fertility are essentially the same in all aspects—sexual, social, agricultural, and political. Though short on exegesis like most imagistic modes of religiosity, the ritual shows a continuous base-line exegesis in this respect, with the often voiced "wives, slaves, and sorghum." This becomes even clearer if we look at the whole agricultural cycle; our *gwela* triptych as such forms in itself the separation phase of the grand cycle, followed by a liminal period of a longer duration, that is, the entire growing season. The final rites of reintegration follow in the third phase, when the close link between agricultural and human fertility is in full view, as we will see in Chapter 11.

One other characteristic of both the *makwa* and the *gwela* initiations is gentleness. Nowhere are the rites violent, brutal, or dominant, neither in the boys' initiation nor in the bridal rituals of the *makwa*. Usually, as Turner points out,[13] it is the liminal period that is elaborate, both in rites and length, but here the seclusion period is short and does not entail any real tests or ordeals, neither genital operations nor ordeals of pain—one just has to eat well. This means that the flash bulb memory Whitehouse comments on—the deep impression a severe ritual can imprint on an initiate—is less applicable here.[14] It is not the deep impression of hardship or pain that remains in the *gwela*'s mind, but the collective guidance of a series of elders. For the correct implementation of the ritual, the *gwela* is always surrounded by others: an initiation father or mother, a helper and older or younger brothers, smith, *mnzefɛ* or the village chief, who all reinforce the episodic memory of the boys in the various phases of the ritual.

This gentle initiation is situated in a society with a violent past full of war, where slavery was rampant and life itself was insecure. Indeed, references to slaves and war are made throughout, but quite playfully. The main rituals reside in the reintegration phase, usually the shortest of the three episodes, but for the Kapsiki by far the most elaborate one. Theirs is an individualistic segmented society in which the hold of the lineage over the individual is fairly limited, a situation that resonates with the cultural ideal of individual male self-sufficiency. Since the transfer of rights and loyalties from house to village and from mother to patrilineage is not very large, this transfer can clothe itself in gentle symbolism, resulting in a playful performance of mature masculinity completely in tune with the gentle rhythm of ripening grain.

Initiation and Village Identity

In the *gwela*, ritual becomes a force on its own. Cognitively costly and definitely imagistic, it is great to watch and wonderful to experience. In the ritual passage, liminal time with its many symbols dominates, including the symbolic tests, the presentation to history, with finally the very subtle response of the "other world" when a dragonfly sets on a lance. Like the *makwa*, the choices within the ritual are limited, but the very moment the ritual offers some minor alternatives, divination steps in. In fact, any event during these large-scale rituals is imbued with meaning: someone becoming ill, sneezing on the road, falling, a dream at night—all minor daily events are transformed into messages. They are dealt with, again, with divination; in liminal times there are no neutral events. The liturgy is crucial so details stand out—the narcissism of the small difference, as Freud called it—and small variations accrue a great significance, both inside the village and as varieties of *gwela* ritual in other villages. So, let us now look at these differences.

The *gwela* are the new men of the village, for each village. A village not only produces its own men through the *gwela* initiation, it also produces its own identity as a village through the specific recombination of ritual elements. The new adult men are the emblems of the village that embody its permanence, and the rites express the village's particular identity and immortality. Even though initiation rites differ from village to village, no stranger coming from another village has any problem recognizing the rites for what they are: initiation, just like at home. Though the general structure remains constant, the elements can be freely interchanged, sprinkled with particulars, resulting in a tapestry of recognizable rites. This unity in variation is facilitated by a shared symbolic reservoir in which the signs and symbols used in the *gwela* are easy to interpret.[15] One of them is fertility. Fertility issues shine through but in varying ways, most directly in the anointed penis in Wula, more veiled in the form of getting a selection of the best meat cooked in a goat's omasum (in Sirakuti), or having to be silent in case birds eat the harvest. But fertility in Kapsiki is always nonhuman as well, as the tests and the many exchanges of food during and after the initiation testify.

The first parameters of intervillage variation are in the outfit. The goatskin is central, with a cord, mahogany oil, and sesame, but it is tied on by a variety of persons from older brother to *yitiyagwela*. Variation is found in the bracelets, the bronze objects, the little bells, and the cowry bands, but the common element is extensive decoration. Weapons are essential: shields (even if small), lances, clubs, and bows and arrows—the focus is on the quiver—but the role of the shield, the lance, and the club vary from village to village.

The differences, though very obvious to any Kapsiki, are after all variations upon a limited number of themes. One of them is history, of the villages and of their translocal roots. For instance, Sirak, a village northeast of the Kapsiki area, is considered "Kapsiki" by my informants, as they "do their *gwela* here in Mogode." In fact, as Sterner points out,[16] some families in Sirak do indeed send their boys south for initiation but the majority do not, since the provenance of Sirak families is varied. Initiation is reliving the past and highlighting the provenance of the village within the larger area, but only up to a point.

Some of the specificities of initiation depend on local histories, like the man who "fell out of the sky," a tale not found in most villages even if they all wear cowry shells as decoration. As in many African rituals and shrines,[17] the distinction between autochthony and newcomers is stressed at crucial points. So the *gwela* is a repository of several layers of history, of the old movements of people toward and inside the mountains but also of the migrations between neighboring villages and within the village. Each village has its own constellation of stories attached to initiation and thereby highlights its own identity through the specifics of the *gwela*, thus rendering the *gwela* rituals a welcome way of expressing village identity, the specific ritual constellation forming the identity focus of the whole village. Also each village has its internal history reflected in these variations; for instance, one lineage traces its origin from one of the Higi villages and shows that link in initiation: their *gwela* have a girl as *mehteshi* and not a boy (Figure 10.1), and they participate in the village proceedings every other year.

I first researched these various rituals in 1973, then again in 1988 and 2008, and throughout this period the initiation rites were remarkably stable, much more so than the *makwa* rites. But the development of ethnicity in Kapsiki/Higi is a recent phenomenon as well, and the importance of the village as a major parameter of identity has increased during the last decades. This dynamic might well account for the stability of the initiation rites: they reflect the identity of the village, its historic links and importance.

The older migration histories of the villages join the villages together in several clusters of initiation. One has already been mentioned, namely the cluster of villages around Mogode that wait for each other's *gwela*. Sir, Sirakuti, and Rufta form the Kakama subgroup; another group is Rumsiki, Sena, Garta, and Kamale. Each cluster has a different set of rituals, as we saw in the description of *huntere* initiation of Rumsiki. It is through similarities in liturgy that historical links between villages are stressed, with the links between clusters of villages shining through in comparable aspects of liturgy, while within each cluster subtle differences stress the ultimate individuality of the village. In the spectrum of *gwela* initiations, Kapsiki/Higi history is portrayed as being many stranded and with complex relations, and these rituals not only form a "machine à supprimer le temps" but also offer a way of remembering history. Thus the notion of "dwelling" again surfaces, as the history that is emphasized is very much the military one, referring to the vagaries of life in the past, and rituals of dwelling and of belonging in the end do not contrast but complement each other, a basic element in Kapsiki religion that will be stressed in the next chapter.

11

Harvesting Crops, Harvesting People

The Rhythm of Beer

In the smoky air of the brewing hut, Vandu Hake rubs his eyes, which are red from smoke and lack of sleep. The firewood burns slowly, just hot enough to keep the beer vat heated, and he has to tend to the burning logs every half hour or so. This is a night of continuous cooking, the crucial night of brewing, and he has to stay up all night, dozing between his duties. His new wife Kwanyè is fast asleep in her hut, but it is for her that Vandu is brewing because she is his *kwatewume* (his "stolen bride"). Some three months ago she appeared in the village, having come to Mogode from neighboring Kamale. He knew her from the Kamale market where he sold medicine: as a local healer, he travels around and knows the other villages quite well. She had struck up his acquaintance, and two weeks later she appeared in Mogode to get married. Usually a number of candidate grooms present themselves for such a runaway woman, but in this case she had already chosen him, so her mother's brother, in whose hut she was staying, sent for Vandu. He arrived and she went with him, settling in the empty hut he had in his compound. From then on he had, in Kapsiki terms, "stolen a woman," a kind of heroic deed seen as a coup, at least by men. Of course this particular woman had come under her own steam, had made her own choices and exerted all possible agency, and in fact this usually is the case. In any, event he is now a *zakwatewume*, "someone who still has to pay bridewealth." As a result the next annual festival in which all the new people in the village will be fêted, the large ritual called *la*, is crucial for him. When the village chief Wushwahwele announced the date for the *la* festival, about a week ago, Vandu and the other grooms started the complicated process of brewing, a day after the families who had a *gwela* to celebrate had done the same.

Vandu brews red beer, *tɛ*, which is the ritual beer and probably the oldest sort. A white variety called *mpedli* is brewed by women for market use and immediate consumption, and its brewing procedure is relatively simple. In recent years the red *tɛ* beer has increasingly become a sales commodity for women at village markets and in the cities. Men prefer it to *mpedli*, and the women have speeded up the traditional brewing process of *te* somewhat. But Vandu has to follow the long recipe and he, not his wife, has to do the brewing. Brewing *te* is traditionally a man's job, as part of the ritual for which the beer is destined. Therefore he has to heed some taboos; for instance, sexual intercourse is forbidden on brewing days, lest the beer become gluey and unfit to drink.[1]

Vandu started some time ago by soaking two measures of sorghum grain in water for 24 hours and then putting them in the dark under a cloth for four days. On the fifth day he uncovered the sprouts, untangled them, dried them in the sun, and ground them up. Using his wife's large bowls, he measured out 200 liters of water into the old oil drum he uses as a vat, put in the ground sprouts, now called *te njinu*, and let then soak for three hours. The secret of good brewing is the "separation of the waters," Vandu explained to me, while he decanted the upper layer of water from the vat for later use. He then lit a fire under the drum and began the first cooking, which would last some six hours, until early evening, tending the fire and stirring the mixture continuously to avoid coagulation. Later in the evening, when the liquid was a little cooler, he poured it into the *wuta*, the large earthen vat dug into the ground that is the central object in Kapsiki brewing. After a short sleep—alone—Vandu returned to the brewing hut and scooped away the *te njinu* that had risen to the surface. He then relit the fire, and that is where he is now. He puts some *lerhwa*,[2] a plant used in tobacco preparation as well, into the boiling mixture, which makes the cooked remains of the sprouts rise to the surface. He has learned this step from his wife, who uses it for her commercial *te*, a technique that the Kapsiki have borrowed from their Mafa neighbors. During the cooking some white froth appears, which he carefully wipes off with a broom, continuing to cook the broth over a slow fire. In the early evening Vandu will once more separate the liquids and pour the clear upper broth into the *wuta*, leaving the dark heavy stuff in the vat for the moment. That evening he will clean the beer jars with water and pebbles. After a good night's sleep, Vandu will pour the cooled clear upper broth into the jars, carefully, since the narrow-necked jars are not easy to fill. For commercial *te* the women add yeast, but for his ritual beer Vandu will just let the beer ferment slowly inside the jars.

Red beer is an important symbol in Kapsiki/Higi religion, always in contrast with the female-brewed *mpedli*. Used in sacrifices and all rites of passage, red beer purveys the general message of sociality, of linking the various parties involved. During the rain rites it serves as a reminder for *shala* to send rain, forging a link between this and the "other world." In sacrifices it relates the family to the larger community, tying individual rites to larger social units. Similarly, in the rites of passage beer conveys the blessings and power of the group over the individual; for instance, in marriage the beer-based blessing given by a father or his initiation representative is directed at fertility for the male patriline. One of the ways the *gwela* proves his mature masculinity is through brewing *te*. Funeral rites stage beer in various roles, such as the link between the deceased and his children in the farewell through the smith, and the continuity of the patriline when the beer is transferred from the old to the new *mele*. So in general *te* is male and stipulates harmony of the lineage structure and cooperation between the genders in procuring progeny. Thus continuity, fertility, and links with sacred places in villages are all expressed through beer.[3]

The Year Festival: Preparation

The *zakwatewume* just brew but the *gwela* have more obligations between the initiation and the annual festival. They not only brew a huge amount of red beer, but some special crops—sesame and couch grass—demand their attention as well. In the past all initiands walked in their special clothes, the *gwela* in their goatskins, wearing also a pouch of antelope skin with some tobacco to present to the elders, since the youngsters are real men now. But this custom has changed significantly: boys and girls now all wear normal, everyday clothes, though their behavior remains that of a liminal as they should not talk too much or laugh too loudly. The villages that perform the *la* festival wait for each other and follow an established order: Rufta, Sirakuti, Sir, Mogode, Guria, and Rumsu. Rufta starts at the fourth moon of the wet season (end of September), just after the end of the rains. In Mogode the *la* used to be at the end of October, just four months after the start of the *gwela* and on the first day of the first rain moon, but now it is in December.

The liturgy of the festival is punctuated by the rhythm of beer brewing. The general program is as follows:

Day	Activity
1	The village chief and the chief smith announce the start of the *la* in the village.
2	The *gwela* and *makwa* families begin brewing.
3	The *zakwatewume* start brewing.
4	Brewing continues.
5	The *lamehegeze* (lean-to structures) are dug. The *gwela* finish their outfits and the groom constructs a lean-to near the hut of the *makwa*, who leaves for her father's compound.
6	*Dzirhwa* (crossing the river): the *makwa* returns home with her trousseau and all the *gwela* perform the main rituals, concluding with the first dance.
7	*Tletegwecɛ* (close the quiver): the day of the big dance; the *gwela* start their round of the "big men" of the village.
8–10	Festivities by the youth (*gwemba*).
11	The end of the festivities, with dancing and the playing of flutes in the fields.

The first day nothing much happens. The *gwela* meet as soon as they have heard the village leaders announce the date, and they stroll together through the village after sunset. On day 2 the *gwela*, the bride's fathers, and the *zamakwa* (grooms) start their brewing, followed the next day by people like Vandu, men who have married a runaway wife in the past year. Day 4 is taken up by the various phases of the beer-brewing process.

The first day of real feasting is day 5, with the *lamehegeze* (digging the poles of the lean-to). The *tɛ* is in the jars now, fermenting slowly. In the morning the *makwa*, wearing a cache sexe and a bracelet with a cowry shell, set out for their father's home, where they will stay the night. Their husbands invite friends to help dig the holes for the lean-to poles near their bride's hut, paying them in jars of beer. Four jars of beer are given to the father-in-law as well.

Since a lot of strangers will visit the village the next day, the village chief consults a crab diviner to avoid potential problems and, depending on its instructions, he may perform a sacrifice at the spot of the following day's dance (*lamehegeze*). At the *la* festival for which Vandu brewed Chief Wusuhwahwele instructed smith Cewuve to ask the crab how to avoid trouble between Mogode and its neighbors. When arriving at the smith's, he noticed that Gwarda had already performed a sacrifice with a *rhwɛ* (medicine) he had inherited from his father. Gwarda cut pieces of *rhwɛ metetebu* (a specimen of *Cissus quadrangularis* that is thought to make people "soft") to prevent trouble and quarrels at the village's main dancing spots. Nobody was allowed to see him. The crab also instructed the smith to gather some sorghum grains from each ward in the village, grind it, and sacrifice it on his own *melɛ*, at the entrance to his house, at the spot where the *gwela* will gather, on the rocks where the first three clans will dance, and finally at the large dancing area. In the past when there was some tension between the villages, the chief had to slaughter a goat. Regardless of what the crab suggests, when the guests arrive, the chief cannot offer them anything before the *gwela* have crossed the river bed, which is the high point of the initiation.

This evening belongs to the *zakwatewume*, the men who have "stolen" a wife from another village: it is their moment of pride. And indeed their attire is spectacular, resplendent in a large boubou, with big woolen sashes, sword in hand, and bells around their ankles. When a *zakwatewume* dresses up, his neighbors flock to have some beer and give their comments while he warms up for the festival, dancing a few steps and singing a few lines. When he is deemed ready, they all go together, with a group of children trailing along, looking for a compound where the smiths have already arrived because one has to have music in order to dance properly. So the village sees groups of *zakwatewume* gather at several spots in the various wards, dancing until 11 pm (Figure 11.1). The grooms of the *makwa* are busy brewing beer, so they are absent during this pre-festival.

Figure 11.1 A *zakwatewume*. Rufta 1996.

Deep into the night, at about 3 am, some ward elders gather in the *gwela*'s hut and decorate the boy's spear with the dewlap hairs of a ram—the *mnta* we mentioned at the twin's coming out—which they fasten in a special way with a strip of indigenous cloth that has been coloured deep red with ocher, plus a piece of sorghum stalk.

The Final Journey

This festival day is called *dzirhwa* (crossing the river). It unfolds slowly, the *zakwatewume* looking for an additional cap or scarf to finish their attire. At first, people gather in the grooms' compounds with large supplies of beer, and some smiths are always present to provide music. The *zakwatewume* dress up—their ostrich feathers and tresses will be added later—and dance with their visitors. Gradually the visitors move on as a new attraction presents itself and they are curious, so they head for the compound of a *makwa*'s father. All the brides' fathers will send their daughters away with their trousseaus now, and everyone wants to see what the girls get. So this *berhe makwa* (accompanying the bride) is a popular event and forecourts are crammed with guests, the women from the ward in front. Now the *makwa* is going to the home of her new husband in full glory and with all her belongings, as a fully established married woman.

The visitors watch the women of the house bring out baskets and basins full of grain, as well as household utensils and lots of pots. One special item is a piece of soda that should be included in each trousseau and has to be carried by a boy. Another symbolic item is honey, since each trousseau has to contain two pots of wild honey. A goat is also brought along. All the gifts are displayed in front of the house for everybody to see and admire, to count and to calculate. Finally the bride comes out, dressed in her *livu* and a cache sexe, and organizes her belongings. Her father and mother take great pride in providing her with everything, but she will always insist on getting more. Pride in one's trousseau is important and is related to the wealth of the family and the amount of the bridewealth.[4]

The size of the trousseau has increased significantly over time. During my first fieldwork in 1972 it was mainly food—sorghum, millet, peanuts, and other food stuffs—with a few household utensils, such as pots, bowls, a cooking stick, and mats (Figures 11.2a and b). During the 1980s iron beds came to be part of the collection, an item much appreciated by brides. After the end of the Biafran war (and remembering that half of the Kapsiki/Higi live in Nigeria), Nigerian products such as enamel basins and plastic buckets came to dominate a trousseau. Since 2000 these conspicuous gifts have grown so large that it is difficult to provide the number of porters required to carry everything, and wealthier households now transport their trousseaus by truck. The proudly proceeding party is full of ululating women, drumming smiths and, today, a loudly hooting truck.

A long string of people follows the bride, who has just had her *livu* tied by one of her mother's co-wives or the wife of a clan brother. Just before her husband's compound, the bride makes a stop at the compound of her *yitiyaberhe* (her second father) for a sip of beer for all those carrying her possessions. He gives her a blessing and adds some things to the trousseau, such as salt and flour, while his wife gives some bowls and pots before sending her on her way to her husband's home. Later the groom will honor them with a few jars of beer.

The last leg of the route is short, and without any hesitation the bride enters her husband's compound and goes into her own hut. The women from her clan follow her into the house and shout: "Get those dregs from your granaries, here comes the real stuff. We will fill the granaries with good sorghum!" They bring all the food into the *makwa*'s hut and then the women of the house, principally the *makwa*'s co-wives, try to extinguish all the fires in the compound. A joking mock battle ensues in complete silence, with neither party speaking or yelling, a friendly scuffle usually won by the party of the *makwa* that should prevail and easily does so by sheer numbers. Then they relight the fires so that the cooking can be done on proper fire, theirs. Meanwhile the *makwa* has all her things transported to her personal hut: they are for her to keep and use, and eventually to dispose of as she sees fit. Nowadays with such huge showy trousseaus, she will have to return much of the stuff anyway. In 2003 one trousseau consisted of over 100 enamel vessels, and when I commented that there was no way that the

Figure 11.2a A trousseau in Mogode, 1973.

Figure 11.2b ... and one in 2003, Rumsu.

bride could use all of these—most were exactly the same (Figure 11.2b)—people pointed out that the majority would soon go back to her mother because she had borrowed them and they would be used again for another *berhe makwa*. So there are a limited number of "trousseaus" in circulation, helped by the fact that the villages have their rituals one after the other.

One little boy, assigned by the bride's father, comes with the bearers. While the bride is settling into her hut, she pretends to want to run back to her father's, and it is the boy's job to stop her from doing so by pulling gently at her cache sexe. He stays the night in her hut and is sent home the next day with a gift of some mush and a sauce of ground couch seeds and peanuts plus some vinegar. Later the next day he will repeat his "pulling" when the *makwa* have seen the *gwela* crossing the stream.

All those carrying the bride's possessions get a lick of the honey they have brought along[5] and a good swig of red beer and, around noon, when the *makwa* has really settled, the groom arrives. He has not been present during this whole episode, hiding in a neighbor's hut. He is of course very pleased that his *makwa* has arrived with a huge trousseau. Even if he has no command over the actual objects—that is for his bride to handle, work with, or sell—they are an asset for his compound and a positive reflection on the bridewealth he paid. Yet he should not be there for his bride's arrival, nor should he show too much pride in her trousseau.

That afternoon a son of the *makwa*'s father's sister slaughters the goat they have brought with them from her father and has its head and two legs brought to the bride's father—at least if she wants to express her gratitude. The back and the two other legs go to her mother and are transported courtesy of the women who came with the trousseau. Two pieces of natron are also divided among these women. Finally, one of her father's wives brings the bride a jar of water, dips the *makwa*'s right hand into it, and says, "Now you have everything you need to cook mush, now cook for your husband." The *makwa* will join the festivities in the village later, though their part in the collective rituals will be small since the main ritual attention will be first on the *gwela* and then on the men who have "stolen a woman." But as new women of the village, the *makwa* do have to greet the *gwela* of their year for the next phase of the festival.

That very afternoon features the ritual that gives the whole day its name: *dzirhwa* or crossing the river.[6] In their homes the *gwela* assemble for the final rites of their initiation. Everyone is in full dress now: antelope skin, brass objects, cowry shells, carrying a lance decorated with the only addition to their outfit, the dewlap hairs of a ram. Their fathers give them a blessing when they leave the door: "You have to work hard, marry women, get children, have respect for your father. Avoid the lazy people, do not follow a bad example."

Before the *gwela* leave their compound, their *kweperhuli* throw sesame seeds over their well-oiled backs. These women accompany them, carrying sorghum stalks, and so do the older brothers who first tied their goatskins, loudly banging on the shields they carry. The *mehteshi* (young helpers) go along too. At the gathering place called Kwanjakwanja the smith chief waits for them. Each time a *gwela* arrives, amid the loud shouts of his troupe, he joins the smith and dances in a small circle, singing: *a kwanja, kwanja, a kwanja, kwanja* (little calabash). Gradually the line of *gwela* gets longer, while a few hundred meters up the hill the village gathers, waiting for the big moment. The *mnzefɛ*, the ritual elder of the *ŋacɛ* clan, warns the boys not to stay in the river too long, because they have to finish before sunset—and if anyone stops them, they should stab him with their lance. In fact the brothers of the *gwela* will help their own brothers but sometimes try to trip up other boys. Those *gwela* who are not "real Mogode," the descendants of immigrants, skirt the crossing and go straight to the chief on the hill; it is not "their" brook, even if that immigration may have happened many generations ago. The autochthonous boys bend over and walk behind the smith to the rivulet, crouching as a sign of humility, according to the smith. Silently and cautiously the boys approach the river bed, which is just a trickle of water, while their helpers wait for them on the other side, flanked by this year's *makwa*, who watch the proceedings of their *mandala* (year-mates) with great interest. This is the boys' last ritual, when they leave behind their youth, just as the girls did when they returned to their grooms.

Quickly the *gwela* cross the river, the water hardly coming up to their knees. Their ritual mothers scrape the sesame off their backs, and the *gwela's* brothers untie the small sorghum stalks and bands of cloth, loosely arranging the ram's hairs on their lance points. The *gwela* put the cloths around their neck, and the *kweperhuli* run home to put the small stalk used in tying the skin away in their huts. The ritual high point over, the little boy again "forces" the bride to go home to her husband by pulling the back of her cache sexe; at least that is what he used to do in the past. Nowadays she wears a skirt, so he takes her by the hand. Only now is the *makwa* truly settled in her new home, though she joins the party immediately afterwards.

That night the bride will cook a lot of meat, mush, and peanut sauce, choose her best pots and bowls, filter the honey, and take it all to her husband's hut. Her boy and girl *mehteshi* will sleep in her own hut, while she spends the night in her husband's hut for the first time. The next morning the two children will be sent home with bowls of honey.

Meanwhile the main dancing area sees the start of a grooms' dance. All the grooms of either a *makwa* or a *kwatewume* climb up onto two large boulders in preparation for the next day, one rock for the first three clans, the other for the second three clans. After an hour everyone has seen who has married a "wife" or a "girl" this year and the people slowly move up the hill to the main dancing place. There they dance a few rounds, but dancing is limited this afternoon, just small groups around the grooms, and all head home when darkness falls.

Closing the Quiver

The next day the drinking and dancing continue in that order during a day called *tletegwecɛ* ("closing the quiver"), the quiver to be closed serving as a major decorative item in the *zakwatewume* dance. Starting at various places in the wards, the dancing groups slowly assemble in the main dancing area, all the *zamakwa* wearing huge gowns and carrying large cow tails as standard festive attire, the odd smith groom brandishing the tail of a horse or donkey. All the men who married a *kwatewume* this year, provided she is still with him, are now in full dress: woolen scarves with great tresses crossing their breast, back, and shoulders, decorated with ostrich feathers, felt caps, sword in hand, and iron bells around the ankles. Smith drummers zoom in on them, drumming ferociously, women shriek and ululate, and the men try to sing over the noise.

The *zakwatewume* are at the very center of the dance, the grooms from one ward dancing in a line beside each other, their newly acquired women directly behind them. All the faces are completely expressionless: no emotion is allowed to show, though they sweat profusely during the energetic dancing. Other women wipe their men's foreheads and the smith drummers, which have been hired by the grooms, stay right in front of them, since the grooms are the center of attention. The *kwatewume* brides are dressed in their very best: in the past in ocher and cowry shells, nowadays in dresses, with sunglasses, generous makeup, and shoes with heels. Co-wives dance behind them, holding huge umbrellas and wiping their foreheads, while on the outer fringe the *makwa* dance, in a wide circle, not with their husbands but with their year-mates. From all the neighboring villages people have come to watch this spectacle; since the *la* festivals are scheduled to follow each other, they have just had their own festival or will have it soon, and they like to compare who dances best. With harvest time still to come, they have the time to attend this festival today. The village chief now mounts his horse and for one short moment silences the drums and the songs. He gives a stern admonition that everyone should remain calm and not provoke a fight because he will have any culprits judged immediately. Later he takes his horse home and rejoins the party on foot.

The parents of both *makwa* and *gewela* have every reason to proudly show off in this dance, since they have managed to bring their children to maturity. For a *gwela* they dance and chant:

> Ah, the son of Deli Kwanyaba [it is the mother singing, naming the father]
> who speaks, who sings.
> his father is happy, I can take care of him
> He stays calm at the *keluɲu*, all are quiet
> Nobody should feel ashamed to hand me presents.

And the mother of a *makwa* sings:

> The feast, these people did not feast well
> the others feast like cattle herders [Fulbe, who cannot throw a party]
> Look at our feast, the feast of our grandfathers
> Daughter of Kwada Meha, we are happy,
> may *shala* keep our *makwa* and *gwela*.

The *gwela* themselves are spectators here, dancing if and when they want to but not for long, and the *makwa* also dance for a short while only. The festival is *about* them, not *for* them. The dancing continues until well after dark, and gradually people disperse. The compounds of the newlyweds are crammed with guests relying on beer for a meal, for "what woman will cook when there is so much beer around?" The little girls from the village, still dressed up, tour the village during the night, singing the songs of the *makwa* outside every compound, getting gifts of beer, sesame, or money.

> During my first year in Mogode the girls came to my house as well, since I was considered a *zamakwa* albeit one marriage was never celebrated in the proper fashion. Yet, I dutifully gave my wife's *yitiyaberhe* four jars of beer. I thought I had done my duty, but this night the girls came to my door: "*Nasara, nasara* who is in the water? *Nasara* who did not pay for his wife, red *nasara* who still owes the *wume*."

Though most guests will leave now, the youngsters remain because the next day is theirs, the *saferela* (the end of the *la*). The morning is for drinking with friends, and anyone can invite good friends to join in the beer drinking and insult strangers, those weird people from other villages. The afternoon is for dancing but this time in the market place, a dance "to find a girl." They start with the *gwemba*, a dance for the unmarried in which lines of young boys and lines of young girls circle the market singing to each other, the tallest at the front and the tiny ones at the back. Older boys direct the dancing, and the children at first hardly look at each other. Then the first daring boy presents the girl of his choice with perfume, which is available at local stalls. He douses her with it and puts some sweets in her dress while she sings and dances without showing any expression. Gradually others follow. Some boys throw coins on the ground for the smith drummers, and after this bout of conspicuous giving they rejoin their dancing ranks.

The next day may see a sequel to this dance but gradually the festival winds down and people resume their work. If all is well, the harvest is due and the fields are waiting to be cut. The dances change continually and new styles in dress and dancing can be seen each year, often coming from the Nigerian side.

The songs too follow their own fashions, frequently being sung in Nkafa, the western dialect of the Higi.

In 2001 the Lamido of Mogode stopped this part of the festivities, at least for Mogode. During the many protracted discussions about bridewealth, all these small presents given during the *gwemba* and other dances were increasingly being counted as part of the bridewealth, something that had never been done before. The problem was that the presents were given to the girl but when the marriage broke down, the husband reclaimed it from his father-in-law, who knew nothing about the gifts. So the dances were stopped and the smiths were not too unhappy, since these youngsters could not pay them properly in any case.

The End of Initiation

This *gwemba* is dancing for the kids, and as such is lost on the *gwela*. After all, they are adults now and the *saferela* is for the young ones. On the day they crossed the river, they all went to visit Kweji Kwala, the member of the chiefly clan who is the hereditary initiation head. His function is just to have all the boys come to drink, at his house, and he then receives the largest gifts of beer. The boys place their lances in his house, and some of them stay the night while others sleep at friends' houses. The village chief comes over to this compound, since Kweji Kwala is a clan member, and he blesses the lances by spraying beer them. The following nights they leave their lances at the houses of representatives of the other clans. For all of these, except for the village chief, this is what their position is about. It does not involve much more but they still feel honored to be the guardians of the lances and, of course, their owners will not depart without leaving behind some beer. Always the lances remain in the house, in the two groups according to the clans. The next morning the boys come to collect their lances and the clan representative blows some of the beer he has received on the lances to bless them in hunting, war, and fertility, and to avoid misfortune (Figure 11.3).

When they leave the last clan representative on the tenth day, he loosens their antelope skin. After leaving their lances at the home of the last clan representative, they head for the well where their *mehteshi* are waiting for them. They wash the strip of cloth (that tied the ram's hairs) and the *gwela* wash themselves, wearing their skins, and then head home to untie them.

On the eleventh day, the boys dress up in standard festive clothing with a red bonnet and gather at Rhwememinɛa, an outcropping close to Rhemetla, where they play their antelope-horn flutes, eat with their friends, and dance, thus concluding their initiation period, which has now made them *mɛpehweta*, those who tied the skin. They shave their heads except for a tuft in the middle, but take care to put their bonnet over it to hide it from view.[7]

Figure 11.3 The *gwela* at the *la* festival in Rumsu, 1995.

Some months later, usually during the wet season though it may be a year later, the *gwela* feast themselves and their *mehteshi*. Two *gwela*, each with his *mehteshi*, are involved in two kinds of parties. The first, *kantsu beza gwela* ("shaving the tuft"), sees two *gwela* friends arrange to brew red beer together and eat mush and a special sauce with meat. This meal is cooked and beer brewed by the girls of their lineage, who received meat from the initiation goat earlier, though the *mehteshi* also brings along food. The day before the party they shave their heads completely. Each of them in turn holds his feast, separated by a week, inviting both initiation fathers and some of their friends as well as ward elders, in a way that closely resembles the ceremonial way of marking friendship in Kapsiki: slaughtering a goat, eating and drinking for most of a day.[8] As is the case throughout the initiation, the *yitiyagwela* is essential and is invited ceremoniously: the *gwela* send him a jar of beer the evening before, and some sauce made of mice, a ceremonial dish used in the initiation of a granary too (Chapter 7). The food is served early in the morning and the initiation father makes a speech praising his pupil—sometimes mixing in some criticism—and then publicly shows his generosity with large gifts for his *gwela*: clothing, gowns, and other large gifts for which he needs the help of his friends. Historically the standard gift was a goatskin to be worn over the shoulder, but the crucial feature now is the bonnet. At the close of the proceedings the *yitiyagwela* puts the bonnet on the initiate's head.

The second type of *beza*, the *beza mehteshi*, is held later. Here the father of the young helper brews white beer and invites the *gwela*, his friend, and the other *mehteshi*. The *beza mehteshi* I witnessed had a more somber tone because the village just had experienced a number of deaths. The old men came to drink beer in the forecourt, and the ward chief complained that he got too little of the beef that was distributed. But when the food and beer arrived, the problems evaporated. The oldest in the ward took a morsel, said: "Let them all be healthy," and started eating. The two *gwela* and two *mehteshi* ate together in one corner and the following week the same thing would happen at the compound of the second *mehteshi*.

The relationship between *mehteshi* and *gwela* is permanent. Just as the mentor is like a father to the *gwela*, so too is the initiate like a ritual father to his helper. When the latter undergoes his own initiation, the *gwela* provides meat and beer and after the crossing of the river, will house his helper for the night. If the younger boy "steals a woman," he will hide her at his older friend's house. And when the *gwela* marries after his initiation, the *mehteshi* will help him with red beer if he marries a *makwa*, or with two jars of white beer in the case of a *kwatewume*, which they will drink with a group of friends in the *gwela*'s hut. If the new wife has already left, they will drink in the hut of the helper. The relationship between a *makwa* and her *mehteshi* is less intense and less structured. The *makwa* will just give mush when her *mehteshi* gets married, and a calabash of sorghum flour and white natron on the day the trousseau is presented. But their relationship ends there.

The *La* Festival: Defining Kapsiki

The *la* is first of all a feast, a celebration of life, production, and fecundity. As feasts go—and have gone since the dawn of man[9]—they have their own rhyme and reason. For the "modes" theory, they form the epitome of imagistics, and as far as the Kapsiki are concerned, rightly so, even optimally imagistic, one could say. The complexities of the boys' and girls' initiation give way to a more straightforward feast, where the outfit now is more important than the ritual act, and the performance at the dance overshadows meticulous liturgy. The "other world" seems to have receded somewhat, as in the large display of the bride's parents who sent their daughter to her husband with a magnificent trousseau. Divination is just for a few, like the village chief who wants to avoid fights or brawls. The homely humility of sacrifice is wiped out by the exuberant display of the *zakwatewume*, the proud husbands who proclaim to have stolen a wife from another village.

So this is for the whole village, and as such to some extent against the other villages. Chapter 10 discussed how initiation serves as an identity marker for the individual villages, at the same time linking them in historical tales of origin and isolating them in separate ritual constructions. The *la* festival, which is in essence the final part of both the *makwa* and *gwela* initiation ceremonies and a harvest festival at the same time, joins the villages in a series of similar and recognizable festivals that not only use similar items from their symbolic repertoire but also follow one another in a regular pattern. They attract considerable numbers of "foreigners" (visitors from other villages), so the Kapsiki/Higi are well aware of each other's annual rites. Whereas liturgies for the *gwela* rituals vary considerably, ritual sequences at the *la* festival are much more homogeneous. Over the years, the ethnicity focus of the Kapsiki increasingly tends to be the *la* festival, as a cultural nexus. In the 1980s some villages in the Kapsiki area that had never paid much attention to *la* rituals started organizing their own. One of them was Rumsiki, a village with a different local history which never fêted *la*.

On the initiative of a major player in the Rumsiki tourist arena, the *la* festival was introduced in Rumsiki and the people of that village started to celebrate the annual rite just as their neighboring villages have always done. However, it was held there less frequently, because its organization depends on the influence of some major persons. Thus the dynamics of the annual ritual underscore the "reluctant ethnicity" described in Chapter 3: the postcolonial situation unites the formerly autarchic villages on the one hand, while on the other it divides them because of the international border. The fact that this border is disputed does not diminish its efficacy in separating the two halves; on the contrary, the Kapsiki and the Higi are more conscious than ever of the border and its implications.

Within the ritual systems of the Kapsiki/Higi, the *la* festival is still a definition of identity in another sense. These are annual festivals at harvest time and this holds true for the year feast in all villages, some in a different series. My informants repeatedly told me that they performed the *makwa* rites just as the *gwela* did and that they were essentially the same. Though rituals for *gwela* and *makwa* are indeed intertwined, the descriptions in Chapters 9, and 10 would not directly lead one to this view. At first glance they appear different but, on closer inspection, they are in systematic opposition.[10] We already saw the opposition of iron and brass between *makwa* and *gwela*, but the same opposition holds for the role of the smiths, the place of the cowry shells on the outfit, the way they shave their heads, the importance of the village boundaries, the tests of "virginity," and the opposition between sun and rain. A host of details of the rituals stand in clear and consistent opposition to each other, even including some numerical symbolism. Thus both initiations seem to be each other's structural opposites, à la Lévi-Strauss, set within the general framework of the rites of passage. Such a systematic opposition indicates unity and is probably the rationale of my informants. *Makwa* and *gwela* progress through comparable stages, as shown in Figure 11.4, albeit in their different ways.

I have hinted several times at the Kapsiki equation between mature individuals and agricultural fertility. This will be our final emic analysis. The *gwela* has

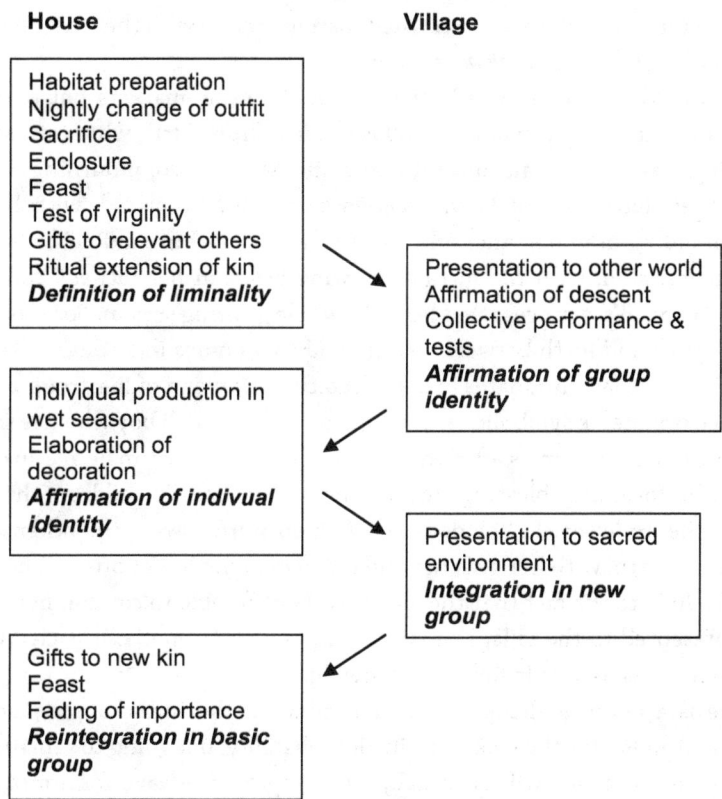

Figure 11.4 Structure of the initiation complex.

become a man, the bride a woman. Van Gennep stresses the transition toward a "monde sexué," but it is more a domestication of sexuality than the social acceptance of sexual activity. The purely sexual part is downplayed by the informants, as is shown by the refusal of the *kwalkwala* to have anything to do with the penis. The clearest symbol was in the Wula initiation, when the boy's penis is anointed by a lineage sister, thus by someone with whom he cannot have sexual relations but who signifies the importance of his fertility for the lineage. Most mentions of fertility are more veiled and verbal, always in conjunction with agriculture, as in the crucial and often-repeated blessing: "sorghum, wives, and children." The central symbol of the initiate is the goatskin that singles him out as a man, a warrior with his own place in the village community, well established before the village shrines and sacred history. Now he has ritually relived village history and has become a major representative among its neighbors. He has significantly expanded his network of kinsmen beyond the confines of his own lineage and is ready to widen it again with a network of in-laws, which is of supreme importance in Kapsiki society. Of course, he still has to establish himself as a major player in the village arena and at the end of the *la* festival has to make way for those adults who crowned their manhood with the "theft of a wife" from another village, the *zakwatewume*.

The symbols of the *makwa* initiation use the same markers but point in a different direction. Her major symbol is the *livu* (iron skirt), which stresses her belonging to the village, although it is also an instrument of mourning. Her network of relations has not been widened so much as replaced, with her own kinsmen fading in importance and substituted by her husband's. The liturgy is quite complicated, with the girl's see-sawing between her father's compound and her husband's, a process that lasts the whole growing season. For six months she goes back and forth between her old and new homes in a complex series of gift exchanges that culminates in the spectacular showing of her trousseau. Her definitive transfer is symbolically represented by the small boy who has to bring her home to her husband's after the last performance of her male age-mates. All people who formulate blessings for her mention primarily children, the repayment of the bridewealth. She does not look outward toward the other villages but to the hearth, with her own fire and her own utensils. Yet often in her songs she will allude to the fact that the village will not be able to contain her. Even if she is presented to the village's major mountain, Rhwemetla, it is clearly indicated that she is here only for the time being.

There is a definite element of communitas in the initiation sequences of *makwa* and *gwela*, for the *makwa* is, in all probability, not going to remain in the village all her life; she will eventually—or even soon—leave for another husband, who has to be in another village. Though all the ritual symbolism might be aimed at tying her to her place, like the iron, the fire, or her new kinsmen just around the corner, this is wishful thinking. For the boys it is similar: during their ritual they stress the unity between them as age-mates, the unity of the village, and the harmony within the village. As men among men, their symbolism aims at identifying their interests with those of the village as a whole. Here too, social reality is different. Kapsiki society can be seen as segmented, organized by rules that limit conflict, and guided by a definite ethos of individual autarchy. The harmony orientation of the ritual is to some extent indeed wishful thinking, and the ritual overstatement of male bonding and unity can be viewed as a counterbalance to social reality. Feasts, after all, are not meant to celebrate harmony but to produce it, and society will become what we think it is.

To return to the *la* festival, it not only ends the initiation of both boys and girls but also celebrates anyone else who helped increase the village's population, such as the *zakwatewume*, the men who "lured" women into the village. The central notion is *wume*, a word we encountered in many settings: bridewealth, boys' initiation, grasses ripening, and the new granary. So the term has a host of meanings centering on maturity, fertility, and reproduction, both human and non-human. The *la* festival is the culmination of this *wume* and illustrates the strong link between agricultural production and human reproduction, reinforcing the fundamental unity of all types of fertility and the supreme value of growth as the means for survival. The ritual calendar can be considered an agricultural one with all relevant rites of passage fitted in, or a human development calendar within which the agricultural activities have found their place. Either way they are one (Figure 11.5). Of course not all human passages can be "calendarized"—birth and death in particular cannot be—but we saw in the birth rituals, and most spectacularly in the twin rites, that the link between birth and initiation is strong, and thus maturity is crucial. Death is another matter, but the second funeral has found its way into the ritual calendar.

The Kapsiki calendar counts ten moons *hevɛ* ("wet") and three *rhele* ("dry"), optimistic names since the reality is the reverse: it rains for three months. The last three of the "wet" moons are called *heferhwe*, and form te the season of harvest, that more or less starts with the *la* festival. The *rhele* moons—about April, May, and June—are destined for the initiation and wedding rituals and end with a transition period called *hɛcimu*, until the actual onset of the rains. So the names for the moons are not so much about temperature and rain, but rather indicate the ritual seasons cultivation, harvest, and initiation. For example, making a *tame* is strictly reserved for *heferhwe* and *rhele*, where it does make ritual sense.

In the end, the two sets of rituals for dwelling and belonging that we distinguished in Chapter 2 are experienced in the Kapsiki case as essentially the same, both hinging on the notion of increase in the face of a harsh political and ecological environment. Survival is an effort, a feat, an accomplishment. Ritual is for the living, for this world, and this life is what counts. Nowhere is this point as clear as in the rituals surrounding death. It is often said that in Africa one's funeral is the most beautiful day of one's life, and this notion holds very true for

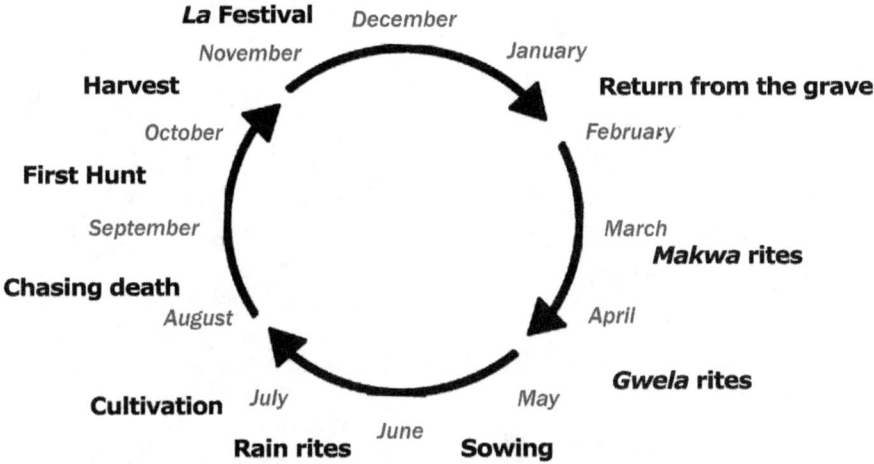

Figure 11.5 The ritual year cycle.

the Kapsiki. In the rites of death the vagaries of life shine through when these rituals highlight the way life should be but almost never is. For the Kapsiki a deceased kinsman is not really gone but is still with us as long as he dances on the shoulders of the smith, before us, with us, and towering over us. And that concept will occupy us in the next chapter, the one on the final dance.

12

The Dancing Dead

In Chapter 1 we left Zra Teri Kwada at the high point of his funeral dance on the smith's shoulders, gloriously decorated in his final statement of identity. Now we continue the tale of his final—and also finest!—hours in a more general way. Funerals in Africa are among the most spectacular rituals performed, and Kapsiki funerals are no exception, with their plethora of symbols and the sheer spectacle of the magnificently adorned corpse dancing high above the excited crowd. The dancing with the dead is the high point of the funeral and is characteristic of the Kapsiki. Yet they are not the only group that carries their dead in a final dance: the Sukur and the Gudur do so too.[1] These two groups have the same distant ancestral roots as the Kapsiki, and although the details may vary, the basic elements in the funeral ritual are comparable among the three groups, including the role of the smiths as undertakers. David and Sterner call this the "full transformational" model of the smith,[2] who in all three groups combines his metal work with his ritual tasks, such as divination and medicine, but above all else he is responsible for burials. The smiths are the village undertakers. On a visit to the village of Mabas, people told us that the last smith had left, and my assistant's immediate reaction was, "How, then, do you bury your dead?" The liminal time of the funeral is an important time for smiths: they are in charge of all the proceedings from the first dance to the decoration of the corpse, to the actual burial, and finally they perform the concluding rites at the burial mound (Figure 12.1).

The liturgy of the funeral varies according to the deceased and the season. The wet season sees a different set of funeral dances and musical instruments from those of the dry season, but most of the variations stem from the deceased himself or herself. Zra's is a "normal" kind of funeral even though he died young. Differences in status, gender, wealth, number of children, and special exploits in the deceased's life are all expressed in the proceedings, so variations abound between funerals for women, smiths, the village chief and priest, the leader of the hunt, victims of smallpox (even if it has now been eradicated) and leprosy, war victims, twins, rain makers, people killed by black magic, and the blacksmiths. Many of

Figure 12.1 Zra Teri Kwada, resting during the dance.

these differences are just details, variations on a few themes, the main theme being the identity of the deceased shining through in ritual and attire.

We focus again on Zra, an important "normal" person in the village, and then add details on possible variations as they are relevant. Funeral rites in general follow a definite pattern: they start out small with just a few groups involved, and over the three days of the funeral they increase in size as more and more groups join in. At the end the ritual tapers off, ending with a series of small rituals just for the next of kin. The usual format is as follows:

Day	Activity
1	Death, limited mourning and the announcement of the death.
2	The corpse is decorated for the first major dance for his or her own villagers.
3	The corpse is fully decorated; the big dance for the other villages. The tomb is dug. The burial.
4	Sacrifice and meal; return of clothing, the first phase of the burial mound.
5	Rest day.
6	The closing sacrifice at the burial mound. Additional work at the mound.
7	Rituals on the mound, the settling of inheritance and the finishing of the mound.

In the following months various groups of relatives perform a series of farewell rituals, and in the first month of the dry season in March the final rites at the mound conclude the funerals with the return of the sacrificial jar.

The rites of the first two or three weeks comprise the first part of the funeral, whereas the rituals at the burial mound in January or February can be considered as the "second funeral," the end of the mourning period. However, since the Kapsiki religion is not an ancestral religion (see Chapter 6), the second funeral is a restricted affair. Because of the cyclical nature of Kapsiki rituals, the last rites are part of the annual cycle of ritual, as we saw in the last chapter.

Preparation

When an adult man or woman dies, the family starts the mourning with cryptic, half-sung lines punctuated with loud shrieks. One of the family members informs the chief smith, and, on hearing the mournful cries, neighbors gradually flock into the compound: "*Amaa, amaa*, where am I now? What shall become of us? Son of the sun, you have left us." Soon the chief smith arrives with his son, who is usually a drummer; the former will take care of the corpse, his son of the first dance. The people present immediately start dancing, because to dance is to mourn, rhythmic moving to the beat of the drum but without specific steps. The women of the house put on their *livu*—the wives, daughters, and co-wives—and together they accentuate the drum beat with their rhythmic scraping of calabashes over their iron skirts. This first day, which may not start until the evening, is filled with just that, dancing and mourning by immediate kin and neighbors. If there is some time, two younger smiths will come with their *shila* flutes, the one type of flute that is strictly reserved for smiths. Their presence is greatly appreciated and the kinsmen of the deceased give them money during the dance. The flute accompaniment depends on the season, but a funeral without drums is unthinkable.

The chief smith puts the corpse on the place of honor, covered by a large blue shroud. One woman, a daughter or the wife of a neighbor, chases away the first flies with a cow's tail whisk while a broom is used if the deceased is a woman. The women of the house put a pot at the corpse's feet with sorghum grains (or couch grass seeds and indigenous Bambara ground nuts (*Voandzeia subterranea*) if it is a woman), a calabash with arrow shafts (a broom for a woman), and/or a cow's tail (if the deceased has owned cattle during his life) to identify him as a cultivator, a warrior, a hunter, and/or a rich man, the very themes that will reverberate throughout the whole ritual. People are very careful with these grains, because death is contagious in Kapsiki: if they fall on the ground and germinate, the deceased's male or female descendants will die very soon, so they are later carefully collected by the chief smith.

All the sons and sister's sons of the deceased have been alerted by now and start to take the news of the death to neighboring villages, calling upon all the in-laws and descendants of the deceased. Since the Kapsiki marriage system usually results in a large number of dispersed in-laws and matrilateral kinsmen, this can take some time and means a long drawn-out funeral. At Zra's home, the mourning dances continue until well into the night, as grief is deep, and the women in particular keep singing and dancing, slowly shuffling to their own beat and the rhythm of the drum.

Zra, our deceased, is a "real" Mogodian, a descendant in a straight patrilineal line from the founders of the village, and so a ritual has to be performed at night to mark this fact. At midnight a young sister calls upon the mountains, the outcroppings that dot the Kapsiki Plateau, asking where her brother is. She starts at the southeast, then works her way toward the northwest. A neighbor plays the part of each mountain, answering that Zra has gone on toward the next one. At the last one, Mcirghe, the highest peak of Mogode, he says: "I have taken him." Then the daughter bursts into mourning.

During the night the family is busy looking for women in the village who have brewed white beer to feed the smiths. Their kinsmen have to provide a goat for each day the corpse is above the ground, usually three days in total. One of the goats is used for the funeral proceedings, the others are for the smiths. If the deceased was very rich, his son will slaughter a cow and the smiths will be very happy, but that is not the case with Zra. However, keeping smiths content during the liminal time of the funeral is extremely important because this group, which normally has a lower status in the village, is suddenly quite dominant.

The First Farewell

Day 2 starts early, when the other smiths come to Zra's house at sunrise. The chief smith has slept in the compound under the small, low hangar that the family has constructed for the corpse to rest on during the night, and to keep the clothes that the lineage members will bring. This morning one of his sisters has washed his body, to clean him but also—if possible—to wash off his epidermis. Though this practice has become rare, people used to be buried "white," without their epidermis, but often the corpse is too well preserved to wash off the black skin easily, so people leave it on.[3]

The whole village is now aware of the death, if not by word of mouth then from the drumming. The youngsters get themselves ready to head for the bush. Armed with clubs, a dozen of them go off in the direction of their eastern neighbors in Sirakuti to collect the *safa* and *haze* plants we have encountered many times now. These are central symbols in several rituals but they are crucial in funerals. The plants have to be collected from far afield, if possible from the bush near another village, hence the clubs. In fact, the young men may try to provoke their neighbors into fighting: the greater the grief, the greater the inclination to fight.

In the past, many a war started this way.[4] If the deceased is a woman, the plants are collected from another ward, for a man they are from another village, and in any case with these plants luck will disappear from the ward or village, so people resent the intrusion. The Kapsiki notion of luck is a kind of personal good fortune that is in limited supply: if the others get more, we will get less, so one has to guard one's local luck. The old custom of catching someone from a village, shaving his head, smearing him with ocher, and then letting him go did not contribute to friendly feelings either, but this practice was abandoned in the 1950s. Kapsiki funerals do generate violent behavior, if not with other villages, then among the mourners, and no funeral is complete without a serious quarrel, usually verbal but sometimes escalating to a fight. The dances, at least on the second and third days, show something of this violence, with their fierce displays of swords, lances, throwing knives, and clubs, with their mock attacks and shows of anger.

The *safa* and *haze* plants are important symbols in any endeavor related to the bush: when a hunter catches a duiker in the bush, he will wear *safa* and *haze* on his head, and in the old days when someone caught a slave in the bush, the slave held *safa* and *haze* in his hands while singing the praise of his captor, with the latter being seated in the place of honor in the forecourt. If the slave was killed, his killer would cut off his genitals and hold these, plus his skin trousers, in his hand with, again, *safa* and *haze*. Anyone who has cultivated a lot will dance with *safa* and *haze* as a central symbol.

Most of the second day is spent in dancing and mourning, almost synonymous in Kapsiki funerals. The next-of-kin start early; in fact they have hardly stopped during the night, quietly mourning through the small hours, accompanied by the *shila* flutes and the ever-present drum. Inside the house the smiths start to clothe the body. Old Gwarda, the chief of the smiths, and his son Kwada direct the proceedings, while the third smith is the chief smith of neighboring Kamale, where Zra's family stems from.[5] Kwada shuts the opening of the compound with a cloth; no non-smith will dare to enter now, only the nephews who "are almost like smiths" at a funeral. The younger smith washes the body and himself, and splashes some perfume around to mask the smell.[6]

Setting Zra up on a stone under the lean-to, Gwarda fills his mouth and nose with cloth and ties a piece of the same white cloth around his face to keep his mouth shut; for a woman he uses bean fibers. Kwada meanwhile picks up a piece of cardboard and fills out the neck of the corpse in order to stabilize the head. The three smiths pad the body, which is dressed in long pants, with a blanket and then cover the whole with the large blue-black gown, the clothing of the dead. With care, Gwarda cuts out the pockets and gives them to the nephews because a death gown has no pockets. He also cuts off the sleeves; which he will keep himself: smiths make their own gowns out of the combined sleeves of the death gowns. He tears off two strips of cloth from the underside of the gown and turns it into an improvised pair of trousers, using a special knife that he keeps for this purpose. Two small holes are cut in which to hook the big toes and a large hole between the legs through which to pass decorating bands. This first gown is called *rhamca*—literally: skin of the bull—though in the past some rich people may have been buried dressed in a bull's skin; usually it was just a goatskin, and today it is a gown.[7]

Kwada wraps two blankets around the body and puts a second gown over the first one, which leaves large sleeves on the corpse. Now the smiths start with the decoration. Early this morning Zra's clan brothers brought bands of cloth, sashes, towels, and blankets in a variety of colors to adorn their brother, the more the better and the more colorful, the prettier. Starting with the broadest band, the smiths cross Zra's chest and back, each band being folded a bit narrower so that all the bands are visible as one multicolored decoration, crossing at the chest and the back, plus a similar band around the waist (Figure 12.2). Then the sashes and woolen cords are added, with their tresses in gaudy colors dangling in pairs over the corpse's shoulders. This is all strictly for decoration, for the glory of Zra and the clan.

The many layers of cloth, plus the blankets, make for an impressive final appearance by Zra. All the clothing and paraphernalia are brought by his clan brothers. One of them comes with the main symbols for the head, while the closest kin bring the gown, which these days has already been bought by the deceased himself, though not in this case. The clothes are for decoration, but the head will be fitted out with symbols to celebrate his identity. Sometimes the smiths use ostrich feathers, but only if he has stolen a wife in his life, and then only on the third day when the in-laws arrive. The smiths take their time and occasionally one of the brothers takes a peek into the house, where the final touches are being applied: porcupine quills, arrow shafts, cow's tails, woolen sashes, all for the head.

The last phase concentrates on Zra's head and is heavy with symbolism. A red felt cap, courtesy of his mother's brother, adorns Zra's head. Carefully, with his teeth, Gwarda removes its little end-cord; it would be bad luck to have it sticking out on the corpse. This cap, now a symbol of riches, was taken from the Fulbe, but these days the traditional blue and white cotton cap is used only by old men. Personal caps are inherited by the youngest son on his father's death, to dance with at the funeral, but Zra is too young to have a "last-born." Gwarda puts two similar caps at the side of the head (Figure 12.2), keeping them in place with some wrappings. Because Zra was a young man, Gwarda gives him a pair of glasses: Zra has to be able to see! Now for his specific identity. *Jimu*, porcupine quills, are a core symbol in burials. The smiths themselves bring the quills, the arrow shafts, and the black rooster's tail feathers.

The first few *jimu* should pierce the bonnet, as decoration; then two crossed quills are placed horizontally through the mouth, like cat's—or leopard's!—whiskers as an indication of fierce masculinity, and if the deceased had killed

Figure 12.2a,b Adorning the head with red caps.

someone, two more would have to be added. Quills are stuck in various places: on the head, often in a row, and in a triangle on the chest with sashes wrapped around them.[8] The decoration of the head is especially crucial and signals who the deceased really is. Gwarda attaches two bundles of *safa* and *haze* and two arrow shafts to the side of the head, again with wrappings to hold them in place and to make the head larger. If Zra had been rich, cattle horns would have been added to his head decoration, but he worked for "Eaux et Forets,"[9] so the smiths add some acacia branches. A cow's tail is attached to the back of his head, with its hair waving just in front of his face. On his chest two crossed arrow shafts sport the black feathers of a rooster, while bird feathers, though not black, adorn the other arrow shafts. All the decorations should be strictly symmetrical on every corpse.

Zra's importance is in full view now. First, one cow's tail indicates a well-to-do person, more tails would have indicated that he owned—or had stolen, which is considered the same—more than one cow; the *jimu* signal work and performance and, just before the dance, his colleagues from "Eaux et Forets" will put their own quills on his shoulder to indicate shared work, or as the Kapsiki call it, shared secrets.[10] The two plants *safa* and *haze* are associated with fields and the bush: he was a cultivator and a warrior, diligent at work and valiant in battle. The feathers in the shafts are very personal, especially the rooster's feathers, since they indicate ferocity and the feathers stem from his *ŋulu rhɛ*, the rooster of the house, signaling his status as the master of the house, with a wife and children. His oldest son should take these feathers to inherit his father's qualities and strength, but in the case of Zra, it will be his father's younger brother's son, a more distant relative. An untimely death calls for creative solutions.

All the decorations are tied on without pins or other iron objects: iron holds people in place and the dead person will have to move freely between the people of the village, in fact he has to dance. The smiths work almost silently, not even looking at the people dropping in. Everything should stay in place during the dance and it will be their fault if something comes loose. In fact, I have never seen that happen. Distant relatives, in-laws, and others who have just arrived come into the house to see Zra, then wail and dance a little and join the mourners outside the house. Dressing the corpse takes all morning, and a large dancing crowd gradually gathers outside the compound, where the younger smiths have joined in with drums and flutes to direct the dancing.

People are waiting outside, each adorned according to his or her own relationship with Zra. Clansmen and women wear a cloth tied around their waists. Zra's personal belongings—his quiver, shield, and cow-tail whisker—are carried by his brother's sons and younger (lineage) brothers. Grandsons would have danced with the special dance quiver but Zra was too young to have grandchildren, so a young *mekwe*, a younger brother of his wife, dances with it. All his lineage children dance with a porcupine quill in their hair, the first-born among them (and for older deceased, the children of those first-born), sporting the same red felt cap that Zra wears (a present from their mother's brother), with a quill piercing it. Zra's in-laws, important guests at the funeral, wear their finest and best: swords, grand gowns, dancing quivers, and sashes with tresses; of all the dancers their outfit most resembles that of the corpse. At an older man's funeral, his daughter's husband or his grandson will wear his quiver and arrows, and at an older woman's funeral, her daughter will wear her cache sexe.

In the dance not only the men show their relationship with Zra, there are fine distinctions between the women too. Nobody should dance empty-handed. The wives of the clan, those who married one of Zra's brothers, dance with a large hoe in their hands, a reminder of the work they did together in the fields. The daughters in Zra's lineage, that is, all the women born from the lineage, have tied on their iron skirts and so have all this year's new brides, the women of the ward, and close friends, and with their *livu* all these women express a close bond with the deceased. Following the rhythm of the drums, the girls and women scrape a calabash over iron rings, generating a characteristic harsh beat amid the tumultuous noise of the dance. Because Zra has died young, the women at this funeral stick closely to tradition; when someone older dies, they may feel freer to choose what to wear. The women of Zra's *hwelefwe* (bilateral kin) wave a large calabash to proclaim their kinship with him,[11] the finer points of kinship expressed by the strings of bean fibers they wear on their buttocks: the members of his matrilineage (*helefwe te ma*) on the left, the others (*hwelefwe te za*) on their right. Finally, almost forgotten sometimes in the crowd, Zra's widow and young daughter dance with cow-tails, a sign of marriage in a wealthy house. During a funeral for a woman, her sisters' daughters or her sisters-in-law would dance with a calabash. All the kinswomen have tied a string of indigo cloth around their left wrists, the *shiŋli* or mourning band, which they will wear until the end of the mourning period, next January. Zra's young daughter has tied some beads around a piece of rope and uses that as *shiŋli*; at the end of the mourning period she will burn the rope and keep the beads.

These days the stage is set for the smiths. While they are adorning the corpse, the smiths are well aware of their importance and make the most of the moment. When they have finished dressing it, they are allowed to drink their beer and proceed at ease, sipping from their calabashes and even taking time to drink "à deux" by putting their mouths together to empty it (Figure 12.3). Zra's brothers and sons exhort the smiths to greater speed as the throng of mourners is getting impatient, but the "black people of death" simply take their time, relishing the moment.

The dance itself is an expression of deep mourning. In Chapter 1 we saw the dance with Zra's corpse on the second day; the dance of the first day is similar, but smaller. It is just the home village that honors its dead, without the in-laws from other villages, but the charges, the wailing, the scraping of the *livu*, the yelling and the shouting are the same. How long the dance lasts depends on age and grief: with a young corpse and when people grieve deeply, the dance may last for hours, but if the deceased is very old with a full life behind him, half an hour will suffice. So with Zra the smiths dance for a long time, but many people will be too upset to dance at all, just sitting and grieving instead. Dancing is a common expression of mourning but a deep loss will inhibit the cultural ways of showing one's emotions; people just "sit and look with the eyes."

Figure 12.3a Drinking together from one calabash: 12.3*b* Inside the calabash.

After the dance, Zra is put in the place of honor in his forecourt while the dance continues. One of his sisters stays with him, chasing away flies with her cow's tail, singing softly: "I am the slave of the people here. You have left without saying goodbye. The people are here to greet you. If you are over there, tell my people that I suffer here." When the deceased is old, the dance loses its solemnity and amusement creeps in. The drummers zoom in on the village notables, on the sons and in-laws of the deceased, on his daughters and sons. Meanwhile at the house some of the old smiths gently undress Zra, putting all the cloths, tresses, and bands in the wooden boxes that used to belong to him. They do so very carefully, since people distrust each other with clothes and do not trust smiths at all. So some brothers look on and quickly put the full boxes on top of the granary in full view of everybody.

> At Teri Ngwene's funeral, a dispute breaks out about a missing piece of cloth. People then remember that the same thing happened at a previous funeral, some years ago, of Kweji Meha, and that it was the same smith, Deli Kwanyerhu! It was this very Teri Ngwene who had voiced the accusations, so that very smith must have now stolen the cloth in revenge. The smith vehemently denies the accusation: he had only taken the small piece used to fasten the ram's hair to the lance of the *gwela* (see Chapter 10). The dispute ends when the widow arrives and tells the smith that he should not be bothered as long as Teri's sons do not accuse him of anything. Deli, relieved and gathering up his courage, says that anyone who wants to accuse him of stealing something should do so in front of Rhwemetla (the ordeal mountain).

The smiths let the deceased sit in his forecourt until late in the evening as visitors are still coming, and they have to see and to greet him. As Tlimu Vandu explains:

> When you hear the news of a death, your meal does not taste good any longer. You have to go and see for yourself. So you go to the house, surround it with your group, and then go in. And yes, there he is, sitting in his black gown; now you know he is truly dead. Then you can go out and dance. That is why we do not like the Marghi (their western neighbors in Nigeria), who bury their dead quickly and make a straw puppet which they clothe and treat like a corpse. No, we dance with the corpse, as people used to say in the past that the body walks and dances by itself.

After most mourners have left, the smiths return the corpse to the house, and undress him. They fold the cloths and symbols in the chest, and then put the body on top of the small hangar built for burial purposes only, next to the chest with clothes, that will be used again tomorrow. The chest remains in full display, which should be a guarantee against theft.

The Moment of Glory

Well, the dead is not finished dancing yet, as day 3 is the big day, the main dance. The whole day people come from the surrounding villages to honor their in-law, their brother, *ksugwe*, their father or grandfather, sometimes their old enemy. In Zra's case, women from his clan who married into other villages show up in large numbers. These women have brewed beer, prepared mush with meat, slaughtered a goat if they are in-laws, and hired at least one smith with a drum. Before setting out for Mogode, they eat and drink first, have a short dance to warm up, and then in a long line head for the house of the deceased. The women carry their food and the men have dressed up in their best gowns, with a quiver over their shoulders, a woolen cap on their heads, and splendidly adorned with cords, tresses, and ostrich feathers if they have them, a band of cloth around their waist; indeed, they resemble both the outfit of the *zakwatewume* during the *la* festival, and to some extent the corpse itself. All the men take something to carry while they dance—a sword, a spear, or a throwing knife. A troupe bringing this *dafa zhaŋe* usually numbers between 30 and 100 persons,

At the house of the deceased, the women have been busy since sunrise cooking and brewing white beer, assisted by the nephews, who supply the smiths with food and beer; one of them helps the smiths to wash the body; some nephews even stayed the night inside Zra's compound. During the morning more small *ksugwe*, nephews, gather in the house and, led by the *maze kwele* (an old smith who is in charge of digging tombs), head out to a field where the tomb has to be dug. This is where we started in Chapter 1, with the nephews digging Zra's tomb under the watchful eye of Zhinerhu, the smith in charge of tombs, at the same time that the other smiths inside the house again clothe and decorate Zra. And it is for this dance that the *rerhɛ* add ostrich feathers to the glorious dancing dead[12] to proclaim his wealth, matching any feathers that the in-laws may sport. So, when the smiths finish with decorating Zra for the big dance, he is even more resplendent than on the previous day.

Before the "coming out" of the corpse, the *dafa zhaŋe* groups keep arriving from all neighboring villages. They do not visit Zra's house straightaway but enter a neighboring compound where the women of the group put down their food and beer, first for the smiths and then for themselves. With great gusto the arriving men of the group mount a mock attack on Zra's house, shouting, brandishing their spears and swords, and yelling, while the women ululate. Zra's kinsmen are more than ready to meet this challenge in the same vein and the two groups mingle in a frenzy of happy sham fighting.

As all the *mekwe* (in-laws) arrive today, this is the largest dance by far and also the most varied as each village has its own mourning song and all want to be heard. The central figures are the sons-in-law because they have to shine, showing that Zra's lineage has given them their daughters for a very good reason. Tlimu Vandu explains:

> People dance as *mekwe* in full attire so the women can see you dance. If the son-in-law does not dance well, who will know that his daughter is with you? So the *mekwe* puts on the quiver, puts a band around his waist close to his heart, takes the bow and a large knife. He should dance on the granary, above all the others, with the daughter of the deceased, his wife, or her sister. Then people say: "He has mourned well, he has danced well, and he is a real *mekwe*. I will give him my daughter as well."

The sons-in-law and daughters do indeed dance on the granary, which is tricky because they dance on the rim of the opening and could fall in it, which would make them the laughing stock of the whole village. From his high dancing point, the *mekwe* throws coins into the dancing throng for the smiths. For the *mekwe* this burial of his father-in-law or mother-in-law is expensive. He has to furnish at least a large gown, several goats, a red bonnet, some other clothes, a sizable amount of sorghum plus, if possible, money.

This afternoon the decorated corpse is brought out again through the gap in wall for the final farewell, and the smiths have exerted themselves to make Zra look resplendent, even adding quite a few ostrich feathers to counter the outfit of his in-laws. Some of his sisters' sons want to impress the audience and take turns with the smiths in dancing with the body, but usually the smiths are not too keen on losing their monopoly position. So only when the smiths complain about a lack of beer or demand too much, will the nephews ostentatiously take their place as corpse carriers.

If the deceased is older and had a good long life—definitely not the case with Zra—the dancing soon gets festive and, if the season allows it, the *kwaberhewuzha* is held, the "ladies-excuse-me" dance. In such a case the last wife of the deceased is important, since she has stayed with her ailing husband until the end and is honored for it; the drummers will zoom in on her before moving to the *kwaberhewuzha* proper. The corpse is put back in its place in the forecourt, and the drums begin with a new rhythm, calling especially the young people into the dance. Two large circles are formed, with the men outside and the women inside, dancing in opposite directions, and with everyone singing. This dance demands special steps to synchronize the dancers. After dancing half an hour, the women and girls stop, take a long sorghum stalk, and tap it on the head of one of the dancing men. He then leaves his fellow dancers and stands next to the woman, and this continues until everyone has found a partner. The song continues, the women singing to the men and vice versa. The texts of this *kad'e male* (to love a woman) quickly move from acquaintance to proposal: at first the two sexes playfully insult each other, but when they have found their partner, it evolves into a more inviting text.

> W: Give me money, where have you been today?
> M: The house of Kwada [the deceased] is lost,
> W: I want to be with you,
> M: The women from Yola are great [there are women from the Nigerian side],
> W: I do with you like I want,
> M: Why do you insult me?
> W: I want to be with you.
> M: Woman who cannot die,
> W: Let us leave together.
> M. What can I do with you?
> W. Let us spend the day together.
> M: Beautiful long-necked woman.
> W: My brother.
> M: Lightning has to kill you if you do not pray for me.
> W: I want to be with you!

No husband or wife can interfere or even object to what is happening during this dance, and many a runaway marriage has resulted from this *kwaberhewuzha* dance. The name indicates this: "The dance to be with the girl" and the more people from other villages there are present, the greater the gusto for the dance. Sometimes the hosting elders try to shorten the dance, afraid of losing women to those wonderful sons-in-law who are flaunting their wealth.

Burial

The dance winds down as the crowd starts going home about 5 pm. Just a few are left to watch the final proceedings, the burial itself. Formerly a body was clothed in a *rhamca* (literally: bull's skin), actually a fresh goatskin with, if possible, its leg strings fastened over the shoulder of the deceased or around his waist. In the 1980s and 1990s the *rhamca* was replaced by cloth because, the people claimed, a corpse decomposes too quickly with a goatskin. This particular goat was not slaughtered with a knife but was strangled, or its neck was broken, because it should die without spilling blood and in silence lest other people die, so its mouth was kept shut. If, very rarely, a bull is sacrificed, then it is stoned to death. The goat, in principle, should be from the deceased's flock. If it has to be bought, it will be very expensive, since people are reluctant to be linked with the death. While the other goats are just for the smiths, from this goat just one leg is for the smiths to eat the next day, with the head of the goat being for the chief smith and the chest being for the smith who measured the tomb.

When the corpse is prepared for burial, all decoration is removed, also from the head. For this last trip of the dead, the smiths fasten the bonnet with a strip of skin from the *kwe remɓenkema*, a goat normally given by a married daughter, now by a lineage daughter, given to her by her husband for the occasion. She had it slaughtered by Zra's nephews, who in turn will take home all the meat except two legs and the skin. These legs are for the sacrificial meal the next day, but now the skin is wrapped around the head of the deceased, covered with a piece of cloth, and then adorned with just two arrow shafts with black tail feathers from a rooster that was provided by the chief smith. Here the chief smith works alone, though the other smiths offer a running commentary.

When Gwarda has finished, all the smiths get some more beer and the farewell can start. One of the daughters gets some mush, and the chief smith puts it on the head of the deceased and eats it, with the other smiths. Then Zra's next-of-kin assemble before him and the chief smith presents a calabash of white beer to the deceased, saying: "Drink this, we have mourned you well; do not bother us and keep us from harm." He takes a mouthful and sprays it over the children: "Here, be healthy, very healthy. Have many children, I am not jealous." Gwarda's son hoists the body onto his shoulders and, for the first time, he exits the house through the normal entrance, not through the gap in the wall. Some of the dancers are still waiting, so he dances a few steps with them and then is quickly on his way, hurrying toward the tomb. There he puts the corpse upright with its feet in the hole and looks to see who has followed him, the family and the older smiths. Silence reigns now. No one may mourn out loud because the mourning will follow the deceased into the tomb and will never stop.

What happens now depends on the purported cause of death. If an internal abscess is suspected to have caused death, the corpse will be operated on at the tomb side by the chief smith. He cuts open the body and removes the suspect organ, since otherwise the whole clan dies from the same disease.

> An old woman, Kuve Meha, was operated on in this fashion. Her corpse had burst after two days, which is a sign of adultery with a smith. The officiating smith had forgotten his knife and tore her body open with his bare hands, an action the next-of-kin did not appreciate at all, but against which they could do very little. For protection, the smith touched first his own forehead, then that of Kuve, and again his own with an iron bar, put his foot on the bar and then proceeded to remove her organs, including her lungs and heart. After this grisly work, he

found a small spot on one lung and surmised that he had found the culprit. The corpse was buried but the organs remained above ground, next to the opening, and were later covered by the tomb itself. The iron bar was his protection against any possible infection.

Gwarda cuts strips of the black gown to hand to the next-of-kin, counting usually about a dozen people, possibly some brothers but mostly children. No wives or in-laws come to the tomb; they stay behind in the compound. These strips will serve as *shiŋli* (mourning bands around the arm) and will later eventually be joined by a belt of baobab fibers. Gwarda and another smith let the corpse down into the tomb, crossing its arms above its head. The smith then cuts some of the fibers that are holding the corpse's mouth shut and hands them to Zra's daughter, who will join them to her mourning band. The chief smith lowers the corpse until only the hands stick out above the ground. Then a son or daughter of the deceased strokes the right thumb of the dead, turns around, and walks home without looking back, a rite called *kased'e gweŋu*. In Zra's case, it is his young brother who in this way takes Zra's *ŋki*, his individual properties such as wealth, luck, and success. With a closed fist, he heads straight for his older brother's hut, "empties" his fist into the dark hut, and shuts the door.

Gwarda lets the body slide further into the burial chamber and joins the corpse in the chamber to arrange it properly, for a dead man should lie on his right-hand side with his head toward the south, facing east. A woman lies on her left-hand side, her head to the north, also facing the rising sun. Small babies are buried sitting upright, facing east as well, and their hands are placed on their head, to "pray *shala* for another child." The smith climbs out of the tomb carrying two hands full of earth and throws them at both sides of the chamber, while everybody checks to see whether the smith has done it well. (If not, bad luck will fall on the deceased's descendants.) The smith, with the fibers and a bracelet he got from a maternal kinsman of the deceased, touches the left shoulder or breast of all the descendants present, and in turn they throw earth into the tomb, first with the left hand and then with the right. The next day the daughter will retrieve the bracelet from the smith in exchange for a small gift of food. While the kin leave, the smiths shut the opening to the tomb with a large flat stone and shovel earth over it, leaving the handles of the adzes and digging stick in the earth.

Throughout, the smiths exude a businesslike attitude, just doing their job. They are at ease and make jokes: "Do not fill the tomb yet," says the chief smith while in the chamber; others comment on the heavy stone: "I want a lighter one on me, this will crush my ribs." Young smiths try to impress the others by carrying the corpse without any hands and pretend that the smell of the corpse does not bother them. And if they feel they have been badly paid, they will let their dissatisfaction show:

At the burial of Vandu Zra, a poor man, the smiths were not given a goat. They bury him very fast, tear the cloths off his head and throw them on the ground. For a split second, they give the son the chance to take the ŋki, but he refuses: "He was so poor; nobody wants that, better that his poverty enters the tomb with him." The smiths quickly finish the job and do not show up the next day for the concluding rituals.

Variations in Funeral

Within the general liturgy of the funeral, the rites express the specific identity of the deceased and sometimes the conditions of death. A woman who has worked hard and contributed to the bridewealth for her sons' *makwa* is adorned as a man, with *haze* plus a porcupine quill for each son and his *makwa*. Her personal riches will be symbolized on her head with cows' tails, and occasionally a broom. In that case, on the morning of day 3 a dozen women will go into the bush, disguised as men, to gather *safa* and *haze* to adorn her and to dig termites to put in front of her. The ward where they collect the termites will try to prevent them since, with the termites, "the luck of their chicken" will disappear as well.[13] The group of women will have to venture far afield. For example:

> At the funeral of Kwanyè Made, the wife of Gwarda leads a group of eight women clothed in large male gowns, with swords at their side and caps on their heads. The smith woman wears a headdress of cat skins as a sign of status and carries his hour-glass drum. After a few hours, they return in glory with the *safa* and *haze*, plus some termites and crickets, while singing war songs. At Kwanyè's compound, they sing the male mourning songs (*nhwene za*) and dance like men, aggressively charging against the "other" men and putting the stuff they collected at the dead one's feet. They take some of the termites back home to bring luck to their chicken. Everybody enjoys the travesty but a quarrel nevertheless ensues, as one of the women who should have gone did not show up. She defends herself by saying that her baby started sneezing on the way to the compound. As sneezing in whatever circumstances is a clear indication that a Kapsiki should change his/her plans, she decided not to go and went home.

In general, the rites for a woman are slightly different from those for a man. A woman is buried with a calabash which has been smeared with ocher on her head, her jaw is shut with bean fibers, and her head is not wrapped. If a boy dies before initiation, he will be decorated as a *gwela* so that he can be "initiated" during the funeral. His age-mates will not show up and he will be buried on day

2 as "people cry too much to keep him at home." He is buried sitting up and, like girls who die just before marriage, is buried quickly, and in neither case is a mound built over the chamber. Small children are also buried sitting up, with their arms crossed over their head, to "pray *shala* for another pregnancy." Young boys who have not yet performed their *gwela* rites should never see such a dead child, lest they go crazy. A former slave gets a normal burial but with a rope around one of his legs.

The issue is more complex when sorcery is the suspected cause of death. Then the brother of the deceased will make a small tomb behind his compound and put some mush on it. No kin will wear bean (*rhweme*) fibers during the funeral, since they are a kinship symbol, and no mourning bands will be worn after the funeral either. The brother comes to the real tomb later and puts a cross in the sand: "I will pay my brother." He then gathers some remains of the corpse at the washing place, including the epidermis if it has been washed off, to take to the place of the vengance ritual, thus avoiding the culprit protecting himself against revenge. The recipe would be to take the bean fibers and some earth from the washing place, burn the fibers, put the ash on one's temples, and drink some of the earth in water, thus preventing one's shadow from being summoned in the ritual.

Smiths are buried surprisingly quickly, since nobody will provide the other smiths with beer and food. A smith's burial is not so much a village affair as a smiths' affair in which non-smiths do not dare to mingle. At such a funeral all the young smiths vie to dance with the body, proud to show off their strength. The dance is completely dominated by smiths, because smiths say that "Non-smiths *melu* do not have the power even to beat their *livu* or to dance, let them just chase the flies away." Many smiths proudly show their medicine vials in cow or antelope horns and no *melu* dares to dance with them. The smith funeral I witnessed was particularly special since the deceased was a twin; all the kinsmen wore palm strips around their heads and their colleagues put some slag from the smithy in the tomb.

Though a funeral might be routine work for smiths, it is always a serious occasion. When there are two deaths at the same time, as happened once when I was on fieldwork, people take great care that the two corpses do not "meet," because such a meeting would risk an epidemic in the village and pairs of people would die instead of deaths occurring one at a time. The most special type of burial is that of the village chief.[14] A village chief is buried secretly in the middle of the night. His tomb is dug under his own granary or somewhere else in his compound, and there the chief smith puts a wooden bed and a jar with meat in it: the chief should be comfortable. He is not hoisted up on a smith's shoulders but is "walked" toward the prepared hole in the ground. The notables, that is, those who made sacrifices with him on the mountain, put a stick in his hand, keep him upright, and push him gently toward the tomb: *Hana merhe, hana*

Figure 12.4 Chief Wusahwahwele of Mogode in 2008.

merhe (thank you, chief). *Safa* and *haze* are taken from the bush from a distant village and put in the place of honor. There is no dancing outside, and any stranger is chased out of the village. The smiths beat the hour-glass drum and people in the compound sing war songs (*geza*) while the *maze* "walks." He is buried seated, the tomb is shut with a stone, and the earth that has been dug up is spread all over the village. Then people dance for six days, and the concluding rites are performed also at night. His stick will be given to the person he has indicated as his possible successor, though the final choice will be made later, but within a year, by the clan elders headed by the *mnzefɛ* (Figure 12.4).

This *mnzefɛ*, who is both the "chief maker" and the ritual war leader—someone we encountered repeatedly in the *gwela* rituals—is buried secretly at night without any dancing, but in a normal tomb outside the village perimeter. Another special burial is for the smith who heads the iron workers (*maze gedla*): he gets a narrow chamber and is also buried sitting up. All the men from the village bring some charcoal and fill the chamber with coal. He is buried on day 4, after his body has rested inside the forge. This funeral has special dirges, called the mourning of the sorghum: "Here, my hoe is broken, can you repair it? There is the man who fills the granary!" Old hoe handles, iron bars, and charcoal will adorn the tomb. The rainmaker has a similar type of funeral. Lepers are buried in a sheepskin and a white gown, and peanuts are put at their feet. Their *ŋki* will never be taken. They will be buried at night (lest the peanuts rot in the fields) and their corpse will not be danced with unless they have mentioned in their last words that they will not be "bothersome." White burial gowns have become standard among Christians, who nowadays bury in rectangular graves.

Completing the Tomb

The rites in the next phase show less variation, since the focus is on the mound that will be constructed on top of the chamber. We return to Zra's funeral, on the morning of day 4. His nephews repair the wall in his compound, and his daughters cook the food for today's sacrifice and put it in the calabash used to measure the tomb opening. The special sauce is the same ritual sauce used at weddings, *gwela* rituals, and granary initiation as well as at funerals, this time with a large chunk of meat from the *kwe rembeŋkema* the goat Zra's daughter is also using for the upcoming ritual. This rite at the tomb is called *nerha ɗafa* (throw the mush). With a few brothers and a smith, the family walks to the tomb. The women sing the *nhwene gela* (dirge of the rock) while walking: "I am like a dog now. Where can I go? The house is for whom now? I thought I was someone, but now that you have died, I have become a thing. Who will help us with our troubles?" Together they build the tomb by piling the excavated earth on the tomb, first with a few handfuls each and then they start building the low circular stone wall that makes up the structure of the tomb. When they are halfway through, the smith puts a broken pot in the sand, all the descendants hold their hands over the pot palms downward, and the smith puts some pieces of mush on the back of their hands, which they let roll onto the sand. All the women participate except for those who are pregnant, because they are too vulnerable. The smith closes the pot with some leaves and everyone sits down to eat the rest of the mush and the sauce. They leave the hoe handles crossed on the mound when this ritual of the *nerhe ɗafa* is finished.

At the compound, clan members who provided the strips of cloth for Zra's adornment arrive to retrieve their possessions, but first Zra's *hwelefwe* (bilateral kin) has to eat. Theirs is the ritual meal of *zhazha*, in this case the *zhazha hwelefwe*, a mix of cooked beans, and sorghum grains. *Zhazha* is not ground, and thus is an expression of poverty, since only celibates—the ultimate poor!—eat without grinding. They start eating with their left hand, then their right, making sure they eat several of each grain in each bite. The *hwelefwe te ma*, Zra's matrilineage, eats inside the compound, his *hwelefwe te za*, his cognatic stock, outside. They then have their heads shaved by the smith, who carefully burns all their hair.

The second part of the meal is the *ɗafa hwelefwe* (mush of the family), white mush with chicken that is eaten by clan members and their wives, while the *hwelefwe* members stay on their two spots in the compound. The lineage members wait for their strips of cloth, and the tension of the funeral has clearly been released. They sit and chat, relieved that everything went well. A distant kinsman of Zra's joins them: he is late for the funeral and starts a real mourning wail, which dampens the serene atmosphere. Nobody says anything, although they remark afterwards: "If somebody comes suddenly with his wailing, the others will be sad again as well."

The widow (or widows) does not eat the *zhazha* but does have her head shaved. She will not go to the tomb but will cook the meat of the *kwe rembeŋkɛma* (the goat "to wrap the face") that her daughter has brought. At nightfall, with a few of the wives of her brothers-in-law, she will walk the road that leads halfway toward the cemetery, eat the meal from her husband's personal eating calabash, and break it when she has finished. She then returns to the compound.

Meanwhile, a sister's son busies himself with the strips of cloth the clansmen have come for. He dips a sorghum stalk in sauce, rubs it over the chests with the cloth, and then hands the men their cloths. Each then dips his fingers in the sauce, rubs the clothes with it to "cleanse the bad luck," then packs them away. This is all the attention the cloths get; they will not be washed, because "washing would reduce the brightness of the colors." This is the moment when anybody who happens to have special knowledge about the circumstances leading to the death should speak up: if anyone suspects sorcery, now is the time to declare it.

This series of sacrifices on the burial mound, *d'afa kwele*, continues two days later: people build up the tomb and leave some *safa* and *haze*. About two weeks later the last and central ritual of this series will be held, called *tɛ kwele* (the beer of the tomb) or *tɛ ncimu* (the beer of the tears). One of the daughters cooks mush and chicken sauce, and everyone eats at home. The son of one of Zra's sisters has brewed red beer and takes a jar to the tomb side. Wailing loudly their dirge, *nhwene gela*, the little cortege winds up to the grave: "I am like a dog now," "Why did you leave us alone?," "Please tell my father that his daughter is suffering here." At the tomb the sons take away the hoe handles, and finish the tomb. The smith pours beer into his bowl and pours it over the descendants' hands: "Let everyone be healthy." Another measure of beer is poured onto the mound itself, and then they all drink from the smith's bowl, a crucial sign of liminality, for in "normal" times a smith's bowl is out of bounds for non-smiths.

This is the moment to settle the deceased's debts. Any debtor should claim his dues: they will get the first beer from the bowl, and since it is a smith's cap at a tomb side, if they lie they will surely die. The sons also discuss any outstanding loans Zra may have had in order to claim those.

> At Tizhè Kwebe's funeral, his two brothers discuss the debts of their brothers-in-law, part of the bridewealth evidently. One has not given a goat for the funeral, while the other has just paid eight goats as bridewealth, which is not nearly enough. They are unsure how to approach the first case, but the second is clear. Their sister will not return to the man before he pays up! If he makes any comments, he will lose his wife plus his eight goats.

At Zra's funeral there are no debts to be claimed, and they put the hoe handle, personal property of Zra, back on the finished tomb with some *safa* and *haze* and return with the digging stick. The clan and ward members await them in the compound, drinking beer, since any red beer sacrifice has a public end. The sisters' sons then repair the roofs of Zra's personal hut and his beer hut as a signal that the funeral has ended; it was his daughter who took off the roof tops when the funeral started. Now all the descendants will have their heads shaved again except for a small tuft at the crown of the head like the *gwela*, which will be removed during the closing rites, at the "second funeral" in February.

Before the yellow-sorghum harvest, the final ritual of the series is held, called *tɛ kwambu gɛŋa*, (beer to pour on the stone). The son of the deceased brews beer, and makes an appointment with the chief smith. From its place in the forecourt he takes the *gɛŋa*, the oblong stone that the deceased had kept there to adorn his grave. For a man this is the stone that will be stand on his tomb; a woman's grave may be finished with her mill stone or several smaller stones. The chief smith leads the little group to the tomb, the son and some other members of the family with beer, while the sister's son carries the *gɛŋa*. The smith places the stone upright on the tomb, pours the beer over it and says something like: "Take good care of your children." Toward me, the chief smith insists that the gravestone represents the children of the deceased. Someone with a lot of children will have more *gɛŋa* on his grave, but Zra has only one. The rest of the family are waiting at home to drink on their return.

If the funeral takes place in the dry season, one more ritual may be added. A son-in-law who could not attend the funeral hires a few smiths and gathers friends to come and dance at the deceased's home. This ritual is called *bukata*, a Hausa term that implies doing something out of the proper time because it has been forgotten. At that time, usually three weeks after the funeral, the married daughters come to their parents' home to cook *d'afa kwele mɛ cɛ*, "mush for the entrance to the chamber." Family and friends join them to eat this white mush and goat meat.

Return from the Tomb

By now the tomb has been finished and people wait for the harvest in order to hold the concluding rites of *tɛ shiŋli* (the beer of the mourning bands). In what is for the Kapsiki the first month of the dry season, namely January/February, these rites that end the mourning period are held and symbolically bring the deceased back home. Though it is part of the ritual cycle, this is an individual ritual done separately for each person who has died, but always during this moon. The next of kin consult the crab for an appropriate date and prepare beer. The evening before this *tɛ shiŋli*, the kinsmen and the chief smith take Zra's former *melɛ*, full of beer and representing his dead father of old, to the tomb. The smith pours a calabash of beer on the *geŋa* and another on the rest of the tomb: "May your children be healthy and have many kids." A third calabash is drunk by the sons, daughters, and the *hwelefwe* present at the tomb. The jar with the rest of the beer is left on the tomb.

The next morning the compound's forecourt fills up with old men, ward members, friends who have helped with the *dafa zhaŋe*, in-laws and the inevitable sisters' sons of the deceased, some mothers' brothers, plus quite a few neighbors. The smith has come early and is busy shaving everyone's heads, while a nephew cuts their mourning bands with an axe and burns the *shiŋli* with the hair. I use as an example here the *tɛ shiŋli* of Mbeleve, a member of the *zeremba* clan, but now definitely a dead member. The atmosphere is relaxed because the rains have been good, though some guests comment on the new *melɛ*, which is too black for their taste. Most people chat about the following month, when the *makwa* will start their preparations. The old men complain that too many boys now marry girls from another village, and indeed quite a few marry girls from Guria. The girls' parents are not happy about it either, so they demand a higher bridewealth. While commenting, an old man crushes the empty jar on which he is sitting, eliciting a lot of jokes but a sour face from the son of the deceased, Deli Mbeleve, since the jar is someone else's and he will have to pay for it. However, the culprit is an older clan brother, so nothing can be said. Deli gives Kwandu, the sister's son of Mbeleve, that is, his own cousin, a jar of beer and two lumps of tobacco. Kwandu starts pouring the beer, distributing it with great care. This is the *tɛ kwarha dzeve durwhu* (beer to put the hand into the pot) and also presents the last chance for anyone with whom Mbeleve had taken out a loan to reclaim it from the inheritance. The oldest member of his clan goes first and starts his discourse: "Let the son be healthy, and find a wife" (Deli is still single). Then the others drink in strict order: first the son, then the elders from other clans, and finally everyone else. The many guests require more jars of beer, while the smith puts his cap on the ground and gets a little bit out of every calabash. When the first jar has been finished, the oldest clan elder signals the sister's son to get the tobacco, which they divide among the clan members present.

Chief smith Gwarda then leads the immediate kin to the cemetery. He takes along another jar of beer and some ground couch seeds, which he got from Mbeleve's daughter. Two other lots of couch seeds were distributed earlier between the smith himself and the mother's brother. At the burial mound, the smith puts the new *melɛ* on the mound, pours some beer from the jar on the mound into a calabash, mixes it with some of the ground couch seeds, and hands everyone present a piece of couch seed mush. He then shuts the opening of each *melɛ* with mush and decorates them with *safa* and *haze*, taking care not to spill anything: if these grains germinate on the tomb, children will die.

The chief smith then pours the mixture of beer and couch mush over the backs of the hands of the children who are stretching out over the mound. His son Kwada, who has assisted, asks his father to do the same, since both smiths are part of the *zeremba* clan and thus considered to be kinsmen. When pouring, Gwarda admonishes the deceased: "You have to be good now. You have been well mourned, do not be jealous, and take care of your children. They have to have children themselves, and you should not prevent them." Mbeleve's children take mahogany oil and ocher from their bags and rub the *geŋa* until it is a fiery red, then they rub their own heads and legs. Together, the smiths and children drink the rest of the mix (Figure 12.5), and when it is finished, Kwada gives a long speech to the dead along the lines that: "Mbeleve should not be naughty, and finally let his son marry, and also let his youngest daughter marry and have children. Then his wife will not leave again."

One by one the children now climb on the burial mound. Gwarda takes a mouthful of beer with couch seed paste, sprays it over them, and, in the name of the deceased, blesses each of them. One daughter gets the following blessing: "Stay healthy and God will give you a child" and her brother: "Your father will protect you and not be jealous any longer, and you can father a child like he fathered you."[15]

Then, in a gesture that mirrors the arrival of the corpse, each of the children is taken on the shoulders of a mother's brother, carried a short distance, and put down, just as half a year before, the smith carried the corpse to the tomb so that "good luck can come back." Gwarda hands the new sacrificial jar to Mbeleve's

Figure 12.5 Tɛ *shiŋli* (beer of mourning bands) of Mbeleve, his daughter receiving the beer.

oldest son, Deli, who suggests taking his father's *melɛ*, since his own is too black and badly fired. Gwarda is adamant: Mbeleve was a mean person when he was alive, and it is better that he disappear completely, so he punches a hole in the old *melɛ*. (Gwarda is dead right; about two years later Deli will die.) But it is indeed the normal procedure. Indeed, a son has the choice of *melɛ* to smash and will usually do away with his father's *gumeze* or *veci*, the other types of sacrificial jars, because they may be dangerous for pregnant women. If he smashes either of them, he will have some shards ground to use for the new *melɛ*. Usually the old *melɛ* is left at the tomb, with a hole proclaiming the end of the deceased's father. In the case of a woman the old and the new *melɛ* are small, undecorated jars or pieces of quartz.

All the children head for their homes, where their friends who helped during the funeral await them. Each of the children will have brewed beer since this is an important occasion; after all, it is their coming of age as independent persons, with their own sacrificial jar. Right after this *tɛ shiŋli*, the widow (or widows) visits the burial site for the first time. She takes along another jar of *tɛ* and at the burial mound she tells her late husband that she has been faithful to him but that this period has now ended. If she remarries, he should not begrudge her that. She is now free to remarry either a brother or a clan brother of her husband's—a levirate marriage—or she will look elsewhere for a new husband, who will then have to pay a new bridewealth.

That afternoon clan members bring along a goat, chicken, or rooster for the first sacrifice on the new *melɛ*, the *melɛ kapsa kwufurhu*, the hidden sacrifice. This is done on the following day for a woman, and two days later for a man, and it proceeds as a normal *melɛ*, only the jar itself is still shut with a ground couch seed paste and decorated with the *safa* and *haze*. Deli Mbeleve has dutifully invited a smith woman, the potter who made his new *melɛ*, and now performs the sacrifice very early: "Here, I cut the rooster, give me health, give me a woman and let me have children so I can sacrifice again." He then roasts the bird and waits for his brothers to drink the *tɛ* together. The smith woman softly claps her hands and eats and drinks last. Deli has inherited his father's house, which is now truly his own. He has given tobacco to his clan sisters' sons, and his dead father now has to take care of him in order to have a good house. This *melɛ* will remain the son's sacrificial jar until his death.

The Granary of Life and Death

The new *melɛ* concludes the funeral proceedings from the first dirges to the final return of the jar, also ending a liminal time when normal relations are turned upside down. The smiths, normally a socially inferior group, set the tone at this time; women may dress as men, the body leaves the house through the wall, non-smiths drink from smiths' bowls, goats are slaughtered without a knife, and grain should not germinate. On the other hand, the corpse itself is in its full personal glory, radiating the status he had during life, and the deceased's relationships with the various clans, with in-laws and with mother's kin and sister's kin, are in full focus. In general, the deceased is portrayed as in real life, but relations between the living and the dead are subject to reversal.

The three days of dancing with the dead are in many ways a symbolic denial of death: the deceased is not yet truly dead. The story that formerly the dead truly danced themselves, is illustrative, as is the chief who at his funeral 'walks' to his grave. Any deceased is dressed, he does not really leave his house but sneaks out through the wall, and he has to see the mourners and surely has to be seen by everybody. But he is even more than a living being, larger than life, dressed as never before, and even flying on the shoulders of the smith. He grows in stature during the funeral as does the ritual itself: the first day sitting between kinsmen, the second day looking out over the village, and on the final day the ritual unites villages that are traditionally enemies, featuring in-laws and transcending debt relations. Metcalfe and Huntington[16] stress the body as a natural symbol for symbolic statements, and in Kapsiki this holds for the outfit of the corpse, his impressive decorations.

This magnificent stature hides the fact that living beings are gradually transformed into objects of loathing. Kapsiki funerals last for three days because of the long-time political and social relations within the village as well as between villages, as everybody—friend and foe, kin and affine—have to see the deceased in person. A three-day-old body stinks, and smell is important in Kapsiki,[17] which is one reason why the "caste of undertakers," the smiths, has a lower status. So the deceased is elevated to an ambivalent status in his final dance, the center of all attention while giving off a vile smell.

The deceased's stature is underscored by a central part of the mythical corpus of Hwempetla. The culture hero of the village is portrayed on the shoulders of the smith during a funeral, wrapped in his burial shroud and with his *makwa* swinging the tail behind him. Every dead person is in some sense a Hwempetla who flies on a smith's shoulders to his tomb, and indeed at the final farewell when the corpse leaves the house through the proper entrance, the smith runs to the tomb with the long sleeves of the dead man's gown flapping in the wind. But the funeral as such cannot really be seen as the enactment of the myth, as Hwempetla is following the rules of burial in the myth. Death rites are older than the culture hero, though he did add some extra details.

After that climax, the closing scene of the funeral is relatively simple and no longer features the deceased: he has quickly lost most of his identity and is really dead. Gradually the groups around the dead person regroup. First his bilateral family does so, then the clan, and finally the women of his clan. The first group eats *zhazha*, a meal of cooked sowing grains, and the other groups eat more traditionally ground and cooked food. The clan members have expressed their link with the dead through the clothes he wore during the dance. He was "them" on the shoulders of the smith and so it is proper that the clothes "eat" with him when they are being returned.

After the mound is finished, the deceased can still be annoying, be jealous of the living, or be a ghost about which people may dream, no longer living but liminal between the realm of the living and that of the dead. When the burial mound is completed, this situation has to change and the deceased has to leave. His children now walk in his footsteps, inheriting his possessions and settling his debts. Consequently they are, more than the man himself represented on the mound by the *geŋa*, the red-painted upright phallic stone. Typically, this phase is characterized by red beer, the ritual brew; white beer was used for the first part of the funeral.

So after the last rites, the deceased's son takes his *mele* home from his father's mound, carrying the beer that was inside his father's *mele*, thus illustrating the continuity of the house. The wall is repaired and the new *za* pours his beer in his *mele*, so his business is now in order. During the final ritual, the children gave their father beer in an inverted fashion, letting it stream over the back of their hands, the same way the women gave him mush earlier. The father will remain associated with the *mele*, often addressed as "father," not so much as an intermediary between the son and his *shala* but more of a companion to *shala*. Henceforth sacrifices are done in private, the public phases are over. The father is back in the house and the grandfather has been smashed to pieces. This particular African society has no religious niche for ancestors, and even though his name will not be forgotten quickly, the father's father has gone down *tlidi* (a grass), descending another step in the long ladder of life and death.

Three symbolic complexes are relevant in the funeral. The first is iron, the second is head outfit, in particular the *safa* and *haze*, and the third is the shape of the tomb itself. Iron, as we have seen, was a symbol of belonging, of lineage, and of village continuity in the bride's attire, and the *makwa* was decked out in iron. What is the place of iron in a burial? Generally speaking iron is where the corpse is not. The corpse is clothed in an elaborate and complicated attire, but no pins are used. Though the heads of kinsmen are shaved with a razor, iron never touches the corpse, the only exception being a tomb-side operation (and the one we saw was even done without any instruments). There the iron bar is used to ward off any contagion. The chamber has to be dug with the usual iron implements, but when the diggers leave the tomb, the iron tips of the digging sticks and the hoes are carefully removed and only the wooden handles remain at the mound. The goat killed for the deceased has to be strangled, not cut—again no iron! Iron is antithetical to death. In the *livu* the metal signals the permanence of patriline, in short iron is the dwelling of a fleeting population. Brass is nowhere in sight in funerals, associated as it is with wildness and transient riches. The metals are for life, not death.

The second pair of symbols, *safa* and *haze*, have a range of applications. They are almost always used as a pair, in decorating the corpse, in the communal hunt, and formerly also to mark newly captured slaves. These slaves were adorned with *safa* and *haze* as well as arrow shafts and rooster tail feathers, and they had to sing the praises of their captors. The Kapsiki recognize the association between a slave and a corpse and *safa* and *haze*, both of which have to be collected from well outside a village and are thus associated with the bush, war, victory, and wealth. The *tame* initiation shows the *haze* half of the pair in its most agricultural setting, stipulating grain and animal fertility and tying the granary to the rites of becoming. The *safa* features on its own in the closing of the village sacrifice, *haze* is crucial in the *tame* initiation. Together, *safa* and *haze* are the symbols of male productivity par excellence and, in their array of meanings, define masculinity in the broad array that characterizes Kapsiki culture: a real *za*, man, should be fierce and fertile, productive and proactive, a man of the bush.

The other symbols of the head gear are more direct but evoke a similar image. The arrow shafts, the rooster feathers and the cow tails point at a more domesticated identity, masculinity, home ownership, and riches; for a woman the arrows-plus-feathers give way to a pair of brooms. Wealth, according to my informants, is seen in the sashes and ostrich feathers, and with these kinds of symbols the smiths have some leeway; for instance, they can use the horns of cattle. Crucial are the *jimu*, the quills, which, according to my informants, are loaded with various meanings. Inserted through the upper lip, they signal someone killed by the deceased, especially if the quill is red, the *jimu shala*. Crossed across the breast, they signify the work done by the deceased, notably cultivation done in the bush. If the deceased used to work with colleagues, they will put quills on his shoulder, at that moment when the corpse is hidden both from the inside and the outside. The general notion, then, is "his secrets," that is, the representation of the work, accomplishments, and achievements of the deceased, and it is this element which has remained very strong; at a very recent death, a woman was abundantly honored in sashes, with for the rest just the *jimu* (see cover picture).

To round off the funeral symbols, I want to look into the structure of a Kapsiki tomb, so the third symbolic element is the *kwele* itself (Figure 12.6). A cross-section of a tomb (left) and a *tame* (right) immediately suggests their symbolic identity. The underground chamber is dug out in a peculiar fashion, and the narrow, round aperture widens into a round, bell-shaped room. The *tame* is built communally by the kinsmen and the sisters' sons and rests on a stone structure in the center of the house. Under the *tame*, the Kapsiki keep their *mele* that will eventually end up on top of the burial mound of the house owner.

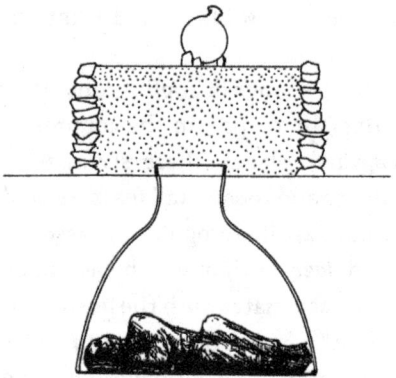 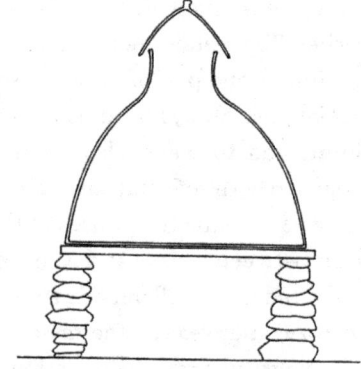

Figure 12.6 Tomb with corpse and *melε*.   A *tame* on its pedestal.

The *tame* is dedicated in a way strongly resembling both a *gwela* initiation and a burial, decorated once again with *safa* and *haze*. So a Kapsiki is buried in his *tame*, at the center of his agricultural life, in a symbolic granary that resembles his own initiation, his adulthood, and his social position within the village. After life he rests in his *tame*, under the sacrificial jar that was kept under the same *tame* while he was alive. A chief never even leaves his house but is buried right under his own *tame*. So when in rituals death is confronted with an assertion of life, here life is largely agricultural fertility. I am usually careful about suggesting symbolic meanings, because of my theoretical views about the openness of ritual and symbolic interpretation, but since my informants never stated anything about the identity between tomb and granary, I dared to suggest this association to them. Their reaction: "At last you are getting to the crux of the matter. But why did it take you so many years to see it?"

A Theory of Kapsiki Death

Death is a continuous presence in Kapsiki life, "la mort apprivoisée," as Philippe Ariès put it when talking about the Middle Ages in Europe.[18] Death is neither a taboo nor an infraction in life but a familiar apparition, the sudden arrival of a distant relative, unexpected and quite unwelcome. *Mte* (death) is a being, if only with one leg,[19] thus more than human and yet not fully human, a person with whom one can strike a deal but from whom in the end no one ever escapes. In the Hwempetla myth, he is the fastest, but in the squirrel tales he is dumb, like the hyena, dumb but strong. Human cleverness can hold him at bay for a short time only but then succumbs anyway.

A good death for a Kapsiki man is to live to see his children move away and prosper, have his youngest son live in the house with a wife and with his grandchildren, and have one last faithful wife at his side when all his other spouses have left. Then death can come, but not too suddenly. It has to leave enough time for him to settle his affairs, to proclaim his last words, telling people where his tomb is to be, where hidden possessions are stacked away, who guards his cattle and how many there are, where the smaller of the two *gumeze* jars is hidden, and what debts are still outstanding. In these quite formalized last words, he will also indicate what robe to use as his burial shroud and where the cloth is to close his mouth. The final countdown takes time. If death arrives gently, the funeral will be the feast it should be, with the young ones enjoying the "ladies-excuse-me" dance with the smiths paid well in goats and the mourning songs well sung. Finally, before entering the chamber, his son will take his *ŋki* to continue his father's life. Later, on returning from the tomb, the father will be represented by the jar and thus be able to guard over his sons' families. That is as far as it goes, since becoming an ancestor is not the issue in Kapsiki/Higi religion.

But many deaths are not good deaths: they are too sudden, too early, or not from old age; in fact most deaths are bad. The differences will show in the ritual, since it is the better kind of deaths that the main liturgies aim at, and the worse kinds that the variations and changes in ritual are geared for. But like all the other rituals described above, death rituals are about life, only in this case life means death. Rituals are an abstraction of life, a way to deal with it, to live it, to attribute meaning and to relate to the "alien inside us," the prevailing sense of and fear for our own mortality. Death, indeed, is the alien inside us and we need rituals to speak to him.

Metcalfe and Huntington, in their comparative work on death rites,[20] have analyzed three dynamics in mortuary ritual, elaborating on the much older one of Robert Hertz. Their threefold scheme, diagrammed in Figure 12.7, offers us a theoretical perspective on Kapsiki death rituals.[21]

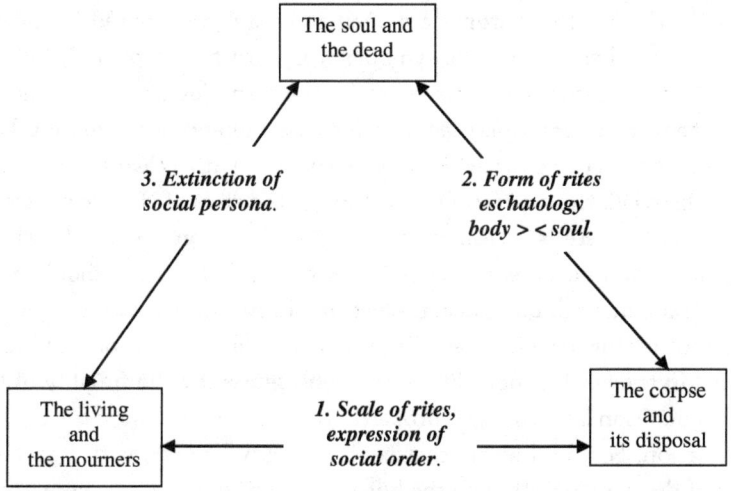

Figure 12.7

In this scheme each of the dyadic relationships has its own theoretical angle. In the description I have elaborated upon the way social relations were expressed in ritual, the first dynamic in the figure, and indeed in the variations of burial the various social categories of the Kapsiki do shine through.

Metcalfe and Huntington show a connection between the elaboration of the second dynamic, the rites and the conceptions of the afterlife. In an inverted sense, this holds for the Kapsiki, since their lack of concern for a constructed immortality rhymes with the relative ease of the last rites. As we saw, the absence of ancestors resonates with cosmology and eschatology, since the Kapsiki are not overly interested in the fate of the soul, nor in the details of the afterlife of the *shinaŋkwe*, a shadowy existence by any standards. Yet, I have some doubts here, since also in African cultures with massive second burials the actual notions of the afterlife are just as vague and noncommittal as in Kapsiki,[22] even if in those cases the transition of the deceased's soul does give rise to elaborate rituals. I think other issues are at play here, residing not so much in the cognitive aspects of religion, but in the dynamic of ritual itself and in the general tendency toward performance in a culture. Large second funerals often include other imagistic elements to embellish the rituals, such as masks.[23] In Kapsiki the second burial is limited to finishing the burial mound and returning the *mele*, and the relative soberness of these secondary rites reflects, indeed, the restricted eschatological expectations of the Kapsiki.

In fact, Kapsiki second burial addresses more the third dynamic, between the dead and the living. One major symbol, the *geŋa*, may serve as an example. One for a man, several for a woman, these upright stones represent the enduring social persona of the deceased, through one of the few overt sexual symbols in Kapsiki mortuary rites. For most of his life a man has his *geŋa* at the seat of honor in his forecourt, and the association is clearly one of fertility and progeny. When during the final death rites these stones are oiled and made a shiny red with generous application of ocher; the phallic symbolism is hard to escape and, indeed, my informants do recognize its connection with the man's fertility but stress also the relation of a woman's multiple *geŋa* with her sons. Funeral rituals in Kapsiki, as we have seen, are structured in the classic three phases, with a clear focus on the first phase of the triad, the separation. But, though the rites of the second burial are more laid back, there is a clear inversion: the corpse on the smith's shoulders during the second burial is mirrored in his son carried on the shoulders of his uncle from the mound. But the main feature of reversal is feasting the return of the jar, another inverted journey. From that moment on, not only is the father addressed in the jar, his mortality is also represented by the fragility of the jar. When a generation later the jar is broken at the son's funeral, so too is the father's representation. For the Kapsiki that is immortality enough, with a gradual "extinction of the persona"; though the lineage should continue, the deceased's own individuality does not stretch into future generations.

As Nigel Barley remarks, a burial is also about "de-conceiving the deceased,"[24] when the father "returns home" he has in fact lost his position in the home. In this sense the first funeral is about "over-conceiving the deceased" by overstressing his value and importance, which renders the demise of the deceased easier to bear. So during the liminal phase not only is the deceased liminal, but also his immediate kin and spouse(s), and they are the ones to adjust to their new situation in life. That time is relatively short in Kapsiki, one cultivation season only, sometimes just the harvest, and the family that is mourning simply shows it by carrying mourning bands without too many social and ritual restrictions. The deceased should not be out of the house for too long, and though the tomb houses his remains and his discarded jar, eventually he has to be brought home after a short delay, and then again he is a relative. But also the family has to be quite quick in adjusting to the new situation, and does so when the father is back at home in a different form and function.

Death rituals are complicated in Kapsiki/Higi culture and, like the *la* feast, completely imagistic. The most technical issues, how to adorn the corpse and dance with it, are in the hands of specialists, the smiths. It is their contribution that guarantees a smooth performance of the ritual; like the true undertakers they are, the smiths lighten the organizational load for the grieving family, facilitate the expression of emotions through dance, and take care of the most awkward transition of all, that of a beloved one into a decaying corpse. For the family this is an infrequent ritual, with all the load of emotion involved, and with the exuberance belonging to a culturally accepted expression of high emotions. For them exegesis stops here, halted by the very emotions involved. For the smiths, however, it is a frequent ritual, which is much less emotional, more professional, and thus invites exegesis. And being specialists in death—as well as in other transformations—they are the ones who feel free to speculate about the counterintuitive concepts that these rituals address and bring forth, and thus generate their own authority on the matter.

There is, however, a clear limit on exegesis, by smiths or others, and that is grief. The final word on death rituals is about emotion and its relationship with ritual. The mere presence of deep emotions precludes the kind of exegetical reflection that frequent—and calm!—ritual often generates. The ritual itself is the answer to grief: the dancing, the wailing, the plethora of cultural forms, especially the symbols that adorn the head of the dancing dead. That holds for a "good death" but is in fact clearer for a "bad" one. Following a "bad death," ritual may no longer be sufficient to calm people's emotions, and people cannot really perform any longer. Ritual deals with emotions through a balancing act. On the one hand, participating in the ritual increases grief among more marginal participants at a funeral; after all, people cry when attending the funeral, more than before or afterwards.[25] On the other hand, their sharing in grief does help the principal mourners. Through the ritual the emotions are somewhat equalized, the close family scaling down their emotions to a communicable degree while outsiders raise their emotional pitch to a level comfortable for the bereaved. Ritual and emotions are in a "cybernetic relationship,"[26] which in mourning means that ritual is the emotional equalizer, one crucial key to interpret the death rituals.

Christianization brought a major change in funeral rituals in the 1990s, the most important being at the tomb itself. Dancing, outfits, the role of the various kin, and especially of the smiths have remained virtually unchanged, but what has changed with conversion is the tomb itself. Christians and Muslims are no longer buried as was described above but in a square hole dug with a digging iron, and so a grave, and the hole is filled afterward. Anyone who has left the traditional religion (defined as *kadzerhe mele*, sacrifice on the jar) has left his granary in the earth as well, that is, he will have another type of burial. The burial mounds over the graves are often still in the shape of a circle but the main change is that they are made of cement. The dances have remained very similar, only with the burial should in white (like the cover picture), and most of the Christians still follow the ritual distribution of food. Provided no chicken is sacrificed on the jar, they feel comfortable following the funeral liturgy. The position of the smiths remains unchallenged in burials.

What has changed most is the tomb itself. The old burial mounds were built of loosely piled stones that blended naturally into the landscape as a small hill with some peaks, eventually disintegrating, sometimes with the headstone falling into the chamber and the mound collapsing. So with the passing of two generations, when the grandfather's *mele* turned into an old jar, the burial mound itself slowly disappeared as well. Today grave mounds are made of cement and built to last, and they are sometimes whitewashed, thus becoming conspicuous in the landscape as permanent features, even carrying inscriptions naming the deceased and the burial date. They have been personalized and made eternal, a definite inversion of the traditional tomb. And increasingly people are choosing their own special spot for their tomb, leaving the communal cemeteries as places of the past, so the recently dead are becoming landmarks on the Kapsiki landscape. After their dance of glory they dot the hillsides with shining white mounds that no longer blend into the environment.

13

Dynamics of Kapsiki Ritual

The Smell of Ritual

My first ritual in Kapsiki was a funeral, so I got my anthropological baptism during the most spectacular of all the Kapsiki rites, and looking back I can still remember the intense excitement I felt at that time. I walked behind the smith who was carrying the corpse on his shoulders through the throng of dancing people, with the drums going full blast and the shrill sounds of the *shila* flutes just audible above the din of the mourning masses and their songs of war. I had a great time. Participating in a strange and unknown ritual is exhilarating, and the burial with the dancing dead is an intoxicating one, a shot of adrenalin for a researcher: "This is the 'real' thing, now I am truly doing fieldwork, now I will be a 'real' anthropologist," I told myself. An anthropologist defines himself through the strangeness of his environment, appreciating that he has ventured into a parallel universe. I was entering a world where nothing was what it seemed and where meanings floated around to be captured at a later stage.

Reflections and analysis come later as the first experience of a strange ritual is more gut-felt and existential than reflective, especially such a captivating one. My first memory, thinking back, is the smell, that unmistakable sweetish smell of death, and I remember thinking that I could almost follow smith and corpse with my eyes closed. In our culture of sanitized death we hardly ever smell death, but it does have a distinct smell of its own, one that evokes instant recognition. It smelled strangely familiar, and I knew I was following a corpse, and one some days old. Actually, the smell was not too bad, more an odor than a stench, and it became for me the odor of the other, the smell of the field, the smell of ritual. It is not a smell we have learned to abhor in our culture, more one to avoid, and I expected the Kapsiki not to mind too much either, being used to it. But to my intense astonishment, the opposite proved to be the case: they detested the smell of death. I learned later that smiths were considered dirty mainly because they had to carry smelly corpses, and still later when I researched the Kapsiki terms for odors, the notion of *ndaleke* stood out, the smell of a corpse. For the Kapsiki this is the most abhorrent of all their fourteen named smells.[1] Then, inevitably, one of the first paradoxes of this culture surfaced: if they loathe the smell of a three-day-old corpse so much, why do they take so long to bury it? Having a separate group of undertakers, the smiths, solves part of this riddle, since they are the ones who bear the brunt of the malodorous burial practice. But still, why do they do it so late that a separate caste is needed, which in many respects is a rather costly social solution?

This was actually one of the few questions on ritual to which informants had a ready answer, one we already touched upon. Everyone has to see for himself that the deceased is really dead, they told me, and the only way to really be sure is to see him, see him on the shoulders of the smith, dressed in his finery, his eyes somewhere behind the wrapper, high above the crowd. Then one knows, and then one can mourn, lament, dance, and pay appropriate homage. This lack of trust in the acceptance of death ties in with the general gist of this society, with its notions of privacy, autarchy, self-sufficiency, and a general distrust of the other, a society that has long been splintering under the relentless pressures of slave raiding and war. As we saw in the previous chapters, Kapsiki society has tried to define itself as being fully harmonious in its rites of belonging, but as a counterpoint, not as a factual description.

Indeed, the notion of "see for yourself" does fit, but it is still couched in terms of the ritual itself: one sees the dead on the shoulders of the smith, dancing by proxy. Given the tensions between Kapsiki villages with their long history of internal strife, war, and tension due to runaway marriages,[2] it becomes almost inevitable that the final Kapsiki ritual should last three days. Anyway, whatever the explanation, it is the funeral itself, the dancing dead, that is the real expression of death. And thus, notwithstanding the abhorrence of *ndalεke*, the smell of ritual is inescapable, generating the need for smiths but also obfuscating the fact that a loved one is being transformed into a loathsome, smelly object through the very ritual that defines its new status. The same ritual that directs mourning and makes the loss bearable produces a terrible stench. The dancing dead is the real dead, but also the dancing dead is really dead. And the nose knows for sure.

"This is Ritual!" Minimal and Maximal Rites

Most languages, like the Kapsiki one, have no generic term for either "ritual" or "religion." Each ritual is called by a specific term: *melε rhε* is the sacrifice of the house, with its named parts, *batle melε*, *ŋa melε*, and so on, forming together the *dzerhe melε* (sacrificing). The latter term is also used as a general lexeme for the whole complex of Kapsiki indigenous religion, as against Christianity and Islam (*sansana*, the Fulbe religion). But when they perform a ritual, they know that they are performing, and so do the spectators. This awareness does not call for a reverential attitude, nor for special outfits or special linguistic performances, since Kapsiki ritual shows itself often to be quite homely, part of everyday life, without specific formulas or attitudes. The prayers and blessings during a sacrifice or initiation are straightforward and in everyday language. The transition from a common act to a ritual is usually not clearly marked and is gradual and smooth, though there is a recognizable core to the ritual, a symbolic focus that defines the high point of the proceedings. In sacrifice this is the killing of the chicken, in initiation it is the passing through the river, and in the *makwa* it is the crouching and crawling toward the mountain and running together with their male year-mates. Only in rituals for the whole village, such as the village sacrifice, is the whole day marked off as a day-out-of-time, as a ritual day on which nobody should cultivate.

Social transactions accompany this gradual progress toward the apogee of a rite. As we have seen, Kapsiki rituals are replete with exchanges of food. For instance, marriage is dominated by both major and minor exchanges between a host of participants from the groom's side and even more so from the bride's family. In the coming-of-age rituals of boys and girls, the accent is on an extension of kin in the form of initiation parents, and on their younger brothers and sisters, with the liturgy focusing on their roles and all the compulsory exchanges. From the Kapsiki perspective, there is no major distinction between the payment of the bridewealth itself and gifts to the bride's ritual father, even if these latter are clearly part of the ritual transfer of the bride.

So ritual times arrive gradually, with a slow recognition that something special is at hand. There is no clear border between the so-called "sacred" and "secular." For instance, the *la* festival starts very slowly, gradually building up each day to a high point that terminates on the seventh day and is the culmination of the year. But the interaction with daily life goes deeper than just a gradual buildup of the feast. Not only do most of the rituals fall into the slots assigned to everyday life, but the core of some rituals is also closely linked to daily interaction. Sacrificial killing of a goat or chicken is usually done in the same way as for a normal meal, the only differences being in the people sitting around, the beer and the jar, the occasion, and the division of the meat. Only a very special sacrifice, such as the village one, calls for a specific method of killing, but usually the occasion and relations define the ritual even more than the act. Thus, the ritual reinforces the self-evident structures in which the ritual is embedded, homing in on the various parties involved by highlighting the rights and duties, the privileges and costs of all routinized social positions. Sacrifice is not so much a timeless act as a heightened relationship within time. I have called this a cognitively optimal ritual, easy to think about, easy to do, and difficult to forget; the term "minimal ritual" is also apt, not to diminish the importance of these rites but in order to indicate their small distance from everyday life. Characteristically, rites of dwelling tend toward optimal rituals. Just as the frequency of ritual is an important characteristic in the distinction between imagistic and doctrinal religion, so too the frequency of the "model act" in daily life is crucial for the distinction between optimal and costly rituals, or minimal and maximal rites. Optimal rites model themselves on acts that happen frequently. The paradigm of sacrifice is the meal, daily, ordinary, normal, and impossible to forget. Gift-giving is another example, especially gifts of food, but so are building a wall and cultivating a field.

This characteristic makes their exegesis, the attribution of their meaning, quite straightforward, since the closeness of the model act precludes any flights of interpretive fancy. A sacrifice, such as the Kapsiki one, is a meal within a family, with some special guests who are invisible. The latter are human to a large extent, addressed yes, fed definitely, personally known without a doubt, but they are not seen and they digest nothing. There is no problem of liturgy, because everybody does almost the same every day, and thus the exegesis remains close to home: eating with the "other." The bull sacrifice differs mainly in the flashiness of parading the bull before the admiring eyes of the ward, but showing off is not unusual in Kapsiki society; in fact it happens every market day just as the level of "sacrificial violence," as Girard would have it, is higher at market time. Thus, dwelling rites have a sort of homeliness; even when the epidemic is chased away, it is dealt with as would be any unwelcome stranger, throwing refuse at him while yelling at him to leave.

The rites of belonging demonstrate a greater contrast with daily life. Their models are acts in daily life that occur less frequently. The *gwela* find their model in history but in a rarified part of history, like war and hunting, and their ritual realizes a maximal separation between the ritual world and the daily one. Their main symbol is the journey, through a river, over an old trajectory, or between historic spots, and journeys are not common. The *makwa* engage in a contest, which is also out of the ordinary, and also make a journey, short and crawling. And of course the funeral transforms an immobile corpse into a dancing dead, the model being the notion of feast itself, a fundamental category of human action and by definition not a daily one. The *la* festival that unites the rites of dwelling with the rites of belonging is evidently a special part of the whole ritual cycle, a welcoming party for visitors, zooming in on the new adults in a society. Its model is again the feast, including the inevitable showing off. We have seen birth rituals bridging this divide; for single births the rites follow daily activities—such as tying a child on its mother's back—but the rites surrounding twins are based on a much less frequent happening, namely the arrival of nonkin strangers.

So these cognitively costly rites, the maximal ones, seem to heighten the differences from everyday life by overplaying strangeness in outfit, acts, and symbols. For the *gwela* this means a distinctive outfit, ornamentation, and behavior: he walks at night and has to shun the sun, he has to cross a riverbed and perform tests, and he accosts foreigners. In short, he has to behave as differently as possible.

The *makwa* is decked out with a skirt that relates to death, to the future funeral of her kinsmen and in-laws, the iron binding her at the very moment she gains mobility, and in order to shine in her singing, she has to crouch and crawl first. The daily-life models of these acts are not frequent—war, conflict, subjugation, and the visits of strangers—and thus are situated in time, usually the past. For the *gwela* there is the warrior, the old board game the boys have to play, as well as the ancient type of roof they have to construct, all things referring to a past that is not to be revived. Throughout his initiation, the initiate refers back to the past in order to have a new future: he will become an adult by first becoming more rooted in the past, and with the *makwa* new life is generated by tying her to death and the village. So within the framework of history, these are maximal rituals that stress the distinctness of the participants and of time, and that highlight the virtual world of ritual, defining a world out of time that is linked to the normal world through a series of inverted, less obvious links. This inherent strangeness does call for exegetical reflection, which in their case is not easy, since the rites present a challenge for exegesis, starting as they do from a large semantic void.

Symbol and Meaning

Chapter 2 contained a tongue-in-cheek definition of rituals as symbols having sex. So, when we construct meaning for ritual, we have to interpret symbols first. We seem to recognize a special act easily and immediately as being a ritual. Though participating in an unknown ritual is like arriving in a foreign country where the signs and symbols are strange and incomprehensible, one thing is certain, and that is the fact of ritual itself. In another fieldwork setting I witnessed such an immediate recognition, but in a reverse fashion. Visitors to my fieldwork area in Mali started to implement a foreign ritual, Amerindian in fact, yet all Malians immediately recognized the strange acts—burning tobacco—as being a ritual and they just as instantly wanted to participate in it. We seem to have a sense for detecting ritual, probably related to our agent detection device, which goes into overdrive when a ritual is performed, that is, when people do things that seem to have no aim, serve no goal, and make no inherent sense.[3] As was mentioned in Chapter 2, this recognition is the first stage in the attribution of meaning. According to Rappaport's concept of self-referential meaning the first level of meaning in ritual is recognizing the act as special, not normal, and one's own position inside "a ritual," at a special time, in a special act.[4] Grimes begins his definition of ritual with "a special act"[5] and in fact that is sufficient. While performing rituals, people are very aware of the special nature of the act.

If self-reference were the only aspect, rituals would indeed be void and senseless, regardless of participants' insistence that they are highly meaningful, in fact Staal's much debated thesis.[6] As stated in Chapter 2, rituals create a semantic void through several processes, one being the counterintuitivity of actions that is filled at two levels. The first level is the notion that "this is a ritual," that is, self-reference. The second level starts from this fact and links the forms of the ritual to presumed effects, with a minimum of explanation. We see many strange acts and a multitude of symbols, but where is rhyme and where is reason? This "canonical" meaning (Rappaport's terminology) or exegetical reflection (in the "modes" theory) is constructed during and after the rituals at varying levels.[7] It is at this level that we construct meaning, and that is what we looked for in the Kapsiki ritual complex.

In the descriptive chapters I constructed this canonical meaning by listening to the informants and looking at the whole array of the symbols in rituals, Turner's exegetical and operational meaning. In the imagistic mode of religiosity infrequent rituals generate a high commitment but a low and spontaneous exegetical reflection. Usually the exegetical gist of the rituals is straightforward: to have food, women, progeny, and health. And yes, some misfortune for one's enemies is also welcome. For the dwelling rituals this is as far as it goes, with slightly more specific aims such as to have a nice rain and to chase the epidemic over the western horizon. Informants do not explain more, not because they are unable to do so but simply because that is enough, both cognitively and emotionally. A more complex discourse surfaces in the rites of belonging. Exegetical reflection on the rituals leads to some speculation about the supernatural actors, spearheaded either by those with a vested interest, like the smiths, or by people with a certain psychological profile that are apt to ponder the imponderable, like clairvoyants. They are the ones who have to try to make sense out of ritual. And as an anthropologist, I am partner to their exegesis.

Symbols speak to each other and derive some meaning from their internal arrangement as well, so we now look at the position of a symbol inside its own semantic field, Turner's third option. In principle the Kapsiki draw their symbols from many fields, but some fields are more symbolically productive than others. I shall touch here on four: food, animals, plants, and metal. First food. The sorghum varieties themselves—red, yellow, and white—are incidentally used as a symbolic vehicle, as when the *makwa* are served white mush by a content husband (who then takes no risk and uses rice for real whiteness). The yellow *magweda* stands for the "real Mogodian," considered the oldest strain and the longest to ripen, the very variant to which the ritual calendar is geared. Maize, as the first harvest, may indicate a close relationship, indicating someone close to one's heart.[8] More varied are the sauces or specific dishes. In the descriptions I indicated them simply as special sauce or dish, so here we can have a further look. The general icon of food, often used in public speech for life itself, is *d'afa*, mush, the everyday staple made from sorghum or millet. It is served at almost all functions, and many rituals are indicated through the relevant dish:

for example, "mush of the bride," "mush of the mentor," and so on. The finer distinctions stem from the specific sauces, such as the *mndɛ* (birth), the mice sauce (granary), or *luku* (couch seed) sauce for the second funeral. The prime marker of a feast is the *rhedle* sauce, made of ground peanuts and beans plus some spices, and this special sauce we encountered in marriage, *gwela*, and death rituals. The Kapsiki women consider it the "first sauce," and it dominates the food in the rituals of belonging.

Special dishes other than mush have specific symbolic content. Food at sacrifice is *rhwempe*, a mixture of grilled and ground peanuts and sorghum, considered a very old type of food. Demanding much work, it is the food of respect, a fitting gift for the *makwa* to her in-laws, and of course to *shala*. As a very nourishing dish it serves as a food for the road, thus good for the *gwela* ritual. Privately—very privately—a wife may serve such a dish to her husband if she thinks he "lacks in force." When the bilateral kinsmen of a deceased are served *zhazha* (beans and sorghum grains cooked whole), it "expresses poverty," an apt dish at the loss of a loved one. After all, *zhazha* is made by bachelors who, without a wife, indeed are the epitome of poverty (it is easy cooking).

These variations are understandable only if one knows the complete array of cooking, since most associations cannot be derived from the food itself. The point is that cooking is the link between ritual and specific food forms and informs the symbol. Rituals are a way to draw attention, so prescribing a specific dish in itself is a useful discourse of difference; what better way to mark an occasion than by specific food.

Animals often offer a discourse on one's own society. Though Kapsiki religion shows no totemism, the variety in fauna offers a ready expression of distinctions made in social life. The general distinction between smith and non-smith, shines through in food taboos. The smiths eat those animals that the *melu*, other Kapsiki, deem inedible, such as the monitor lizard, tortoise, and donkey; their meat is considered inedible because their position among animals is similar to that of smiths in Kapsiki society.[9] But these taboos seldom surface in rituals, since they are self-evident and do not draw attention. There are, however, individual animals with high symbolic content, stand-alone symbols with an identifiable meaning: the leopard belongs to the dangerous power of Gudur, the porcupine to death, the duiker to game animals in general and initiation in particular, plus of course the control of twins over scorpions. The curious equation of the sun with the ram is not particular to the Kapsiki area and bears an association with bush and liminality, but this link is not elaborated upon in the rituals, limited to rams' hairs as *mnta* on top of the lance or the millet stalk of the *gwela*, and the notion of the *veci* jar. The dragon fly seems to be an incidental apparition on the lance, not tied into any other ritual, while on the other hand the prime position of the ground squirrel in the folk tales does not translate into a symbolic position in rituals.

In this field the main symbols come from domesticated animals, since these are central not only in sacrifices but also in the clothing of the initiates. The goatskin for the *gwela* and his helper and the baby sling for the child testify to the crucial place of goat and sheep in Kapsiki culture, a close symbiosis of people and goats/sheep. The cattle hide in the *makwa* outfit and the abundant display of cows' tails on the head of the dancing dead, with the occasional horn stuck in the bands, speaking of riches and wealth, of success in life. This symbolic highlight of cattle is underscored by the insistence that the leather come from indigenous Kapsiki cattle, the small West African shorthorn.[10] For the Kapsiki the rooster symbolism is evident, as the fowl that is just as clearly polygynous as any owner of the house hopes to be, so the feathers on the corpse indicate success with women, with wives.

So wild animals are stand-alone symbols, their association with the wilds sufficient for the denotation of fierce masculinity and achievement in life. By contrast the domesticated ones are more deeply embedded in symbolism, reflecting the deep historical dwelling of this religion. Snakes seem to bridge the divide between wild animals and domesticated ones. On the one hand they have an extremely close association with the house, since they are deemed not only to live inside the house, but even to be the house *shala* itself. They are essentially wild but dwell definitely inside the compound, but while in the house they are not at all domesticated. These snakes, with the *mendereleke* as their prime representative, are a sign of approval by the wild of the domestic dwelling, but throughout are linked to the individual home owner and house, not to his larger family.

Probably plants form the largest semantic domain to be tapped for symbols, but only a small selection are actually used. *Safa* and *haze* have been commented upon at some length, but their choice has never been explained, in fact. "Just a choice," say my informants. But then, the small differences between grasses, well known in daily life, can well serve as indications of human differences: the small 'yaŋka grass for the initiates' and twins' bracelet, and the sturdy *wetle* grass for masculinity. A female symbol with an iconic relation to the outer world is the *rhweme* (bean fibers). During funerals the mother's side of the family wears them and the jaw of a dead woman is fastened with *rhweme*; in the past they also served as a cache sexe. The connection with femininity is hidden and constructed but was revealed when a female informant told me about its association with the placenta. On the surface of the placenta, the chorionic arteries are recognized as *rhweme*, which makes the notion very feminine indeed. But I am not sure that all women construct the meaning of *rhweme* in this way. In any event, in such a large semantic field the sheer number of botanic species[11] precludes a structural assignment of meaning, leaving room for an iconic one, or associations that really "stand alone," such the *peha* palm for twins and *gwela*.

A semantic field with limited options is metallurgy, as in the opposition between iron and brass that neatly symbolizes the opposition *makwa–gwela*. But metals form a hospitable field for the attribution of meaning, if only by the difficult manufacturing. Very few non-metallic objects are specifically made for ritual, since most of these are common utensils that accrue additional meaning, sometimes distinguished by minute details only. The sling, the rain cape, and the calabashes are daily objects, and even the *mele* differs only in details from a standard beer jar. The *duburu* bar is the epitome of a very common object accruing meaning, being in fact a tool blank; however, it forms a crucial symbol in itself, but also as the basis of many objects specifically made for ritual. Custom-made ritual artifacts are indeed made from either iron or brass. Examples are the *gwela* lance, his brass accoutrements, the whole of the bride's outfit, and the many special bracelets. When iron objects are not present, as in funerals, their complete absence is significant. This special position of metallurgy in symbolism highlights the role of the metals in dwelling in these mountains, and also on the position of the smiths as ritual specialists.

Following Mary Douglas,[12] one would expect the body to be a crucial symbolic discourse, but that is not really the case in Kapsiki. The head may be the object of symbolic attention in the dance of death, but the majority of the symbols are not overly corporeal. The tufts of hair of the *gwela*—and the village chief plus the chief smith—are hidden, and the remnants of births form a fleeting symbol, as we saw with the placenta, which became a feature of the house. Far more important is the home, with its clear structured division into higher–lower, male–female, wall–interior, entry–brewery, with the *tame* as the center, plus the grindstone at the edge of the forecourt. So the house is not divided into left–right, but into higher–lower,[13] the environment dominating the human side. So, despite the highly individualized cosmology, Kapsiki symbolism is one of collective dwelling, resonating more with environmental elements such as rivers, mountains, and special rocks than with the individual body. And house and bush are connected as well; in fact the dominant symbol of the wall does just that, separating inside from outside, and thus regulating the interaction between the two. Also the tomb is a simulacrum of the *tame* and thus connects the house with the bush; the cemetery, just like the snake, affords the same linkage.

We have distinguished between minimal and maximal rites, and symbols follow suit in such a distinction. The relation between symbol and model object appears in three ways: iconic (resemblance), metonymic (part-whole), and metaphoric (arbitrary linkage between disparate items). Many elements in the rituals are iconic, closely resembling objects in daily life. Especially the rituals of dwelling abound in very recognizable symbols, close to everyday life, with just a minor twist according to the occasion: the fact that a particular dish is prescribed at all, the children "eat" on top of their belly, and the wall is reinforced. Thus the symbols of dwelling have an iconic character, being more or less what they are, namely a meal, a drink, or a gift. In the symbols of belonging this is the case to some extent. The corpse is decked out in opulence, with ordinary means, and many symbols have to do with clothing. No informant hesitates when defining the meaning of the *gwela* outfit: the *gwela* are clothed as warriors of old. This iconic directness makes spontaneous exegesis easy but also restricts its scope, since informants will often "recognize" symbols more than they interpret them.

Metonymic symbols abound in the rituals of belonging. The surging crowd indicates its relationship with the dancing dead by the objects they dance with: a hoe represents joint work on the field and a cow's tail is part of larger wealth. The feathers of the rooster stand for the whole bird, which in turn represents the whole compound structure. The *makwa* cowhide girdle is a specific part of the whole cow served at the wedding. Many food symbols fall into this category. The *rhedle* sauce made of beans—a dish that demands a lot of time to prepare—is served at weddings and initiation ceremonies and is eaten by the family at funerals; *tame* initiations feature a sauce of mice, part of the bush. Some food is considered exclusively female, such as dishes with sorrel and couch grass, because these crops are cultivated only by women and are used by women to serve to their friends; so these grains are put at the feet of a deceased woman in the forecourt, a metonymic relationship mainly.

Many symbols are well into the realm of metaphor, and here the attribution of meaning is arbitrary, or as my informants say, "simply chosen." It is the linkage between meaning and form that is significant in itself, a mechanism that is well illustrated by the *safa* and *haze*. We encountered this symbolic couple in many places; the general signification is that of the bush, the wilderness, both cultivated and noncultivated, and liminality. In funerals this association is highlighted by the need to get them from afar—for a woman, from another ward; for a man, from an adjoining village; and for a chief, from a village far away. But they function also in the *tame* and in the second funeral,[14] and there signification becomes broader, as we saw, indicating masculine maturity. The two plants become important symbols first through the "choice" for whatever reason, but second mainly by virtue of popping up in various contexts. So their overall meaning is constructed from their linking position between several rituals, the plants themselves offering few clues for direct interpretation.

In all instances, icon, metonymy, and metaphor, symbols accrue their meaning by focusing attention. Jonathan Z. Smith described ritual as a way of giving attention,[15] and within the ritual setting the symbols do just that: they draw the attention to either specific features of the environment, pointing out the crucial spots in the house, the history of the village, and the new potential of the *gwela*. Few items are as effective in drawing attention as food, and we saw how the various dishes, simply by being different, focused our attention on the specificity of the ritual. This does not need to be complicated at all. During the dance of the dead the women signal their bond with the deceased through quite straightforward items, hoes and calabashes, plus the more complex *livu*. But also the metaphoric symbols focus the attention on the unity of ritual, the web of signification that unites the various ritual expressions.

The ultimate way of giving attention is performance, and even for the quite privacy-oriented Kapsiki performance during ritual is crucial. The rituals of belonging concern the whole community, and when community does show up, it expects a show in return, for to perform is not simply to do an act, but to show the doing of it. These rites of belonging are performances that not only have to be done correctly, but also have to look good, so the audience is crucial. A ritual may be seen while being done, but many rituals have to be seen in order to be done well; and then they should be seen to be well done. Even if the Kapsiki culture is not overly theatrical,[16] a major ritual is at the same time a happening, a feast, and a way to distinguish oneself as a youngster, a dancer, a son-in-law, a grandson, or for that matter a dutiful wife, a mourning daughter, or a smitten friend. Dancing, Kapsiki youngsters stipulate, is useless when no women or girls are watching; that would be a dance for nothing. And when the *makwa* puts on her *livu*, she may clothe herself symbolically in the deep history of iron production and clan stability, but she also is part of a swirling performance and simply likes the rasp of the calabash on the iron rings.

Attention implies attention to feelings as well. In performances emotions have to be seen, albeit in their ritualized and circumscribed expressive form, and are to some extent judged. Expressing emotions, as stressed in the opening chapters, is crucial in rituals; that is what rituals are there for. Ritual is a party where a show of feeling is welcome. But emotions are never fully individual and are never formless: they do receive form and approbation through the culture in question. Furthermore, showing emotions generates them, seeing emotions multiplies them, while witnessing emotions being performed well extends gratification and closure. So the performance of the ritual generates, channels and molds the cultural ways of handling emotions; indeed, ritual and feelings steer each other in a cybernetic relationship.

Ritual and Time

The rituals of belonging are more of a performance than are rituals of dwelling, and here we find specific symbolic acts, such as crossing a river, crawling toward a mountain, and dancing above a crowd. These rituals point two ways. One is toward the future, to the new life that awaits the young men and women, so divination is always part of the proceedings, here a kind of divination with a longer span of control than is usually the case. It is also a type of divination that points toward the future and not to the past as divination usually does.[17] The other ritual reference is to the past, such as war or—in the outfit of the dancing dead—the glory that was his past life, in an exuberant overstatement that no one could possibly match in life. So the main issue here is time. Belonging is dwelling inside a group in a linear time frame, marked by a past and a future that are linked by rituals. Whereas the dwelling rites exude a sense of timelessness, the rites of belonging are very much punctuated by the passage of time and changes in life. They generate joy in the first passages of mankind and resignation in the last: gratitude in a new birth, excitement in the case of twins, excitement and apprehension at a first marriage, pride in the *gwela*, glory in the increase in the number of people in the *la* festival, and of course finally grief and resignation at a funeral. Emotion, in the end, is what human life is about, and so is ritual. One emotion generated by ritual is a feeling of togetherness, the most classic of all Durkheimian theses. A subtext of the symbolism in the rituals of belonging is the overstatement of social cohesion, the production of communitas, and the performance of ritual portraying an ideal of society that is unattainable anyway. So in this context, ritual portrays a society out-of-time, a society that has not been ravaged by time, nor by all the afflictions that flesh is heir to.

One core characteristic in Kapsiki ritual is the ultimate link between dwelling and belonging through the cycle of rituals. More than anything else, the calendar unites the various expressions of religiosity. Sacrifices follow the seasons of agriculture, and hunts and harvest rites have their place in the yearly rhythm, but the same holds for weddings, initiations, and even the second part of a funeral. In the end, fertility and productivity are linked, closely linked even, as we noticed in the notion of *wume* and in the general symbolism of the *la* festival, celebrating the harvest of crops and humans in a general display of fertility and wealth. The cycle of life is the cycle of the harvest, of any harvest: grain, women, and men.

Despite this cyclical aspect, history is part of both kinds of ritual in two contrasting ways. The first tendency is to stay out of history.[18] The general insecurity of life, with its risks of drought, locusts, and epidemics, but also the threats of slavery and war as constant reminders of precarious existence, have generated an awareness of the fragility of existence that shows in the defensive posture of all sacrifices. History is what one should avoid. In the rites of belonging, history operates at another level. Here the environment is seen not so much as a threat and human opponents not as frightening slave raiders, but here the "other" is equal, like the other clan, the other village, and any threat that is coming from peers. History in the rites of belonging is the history of the village, performed with a certain amount of pride and self-confidence, with a deeper link in time working toward a collective identity. Dwelling in the physical environment means that human dwelling made changes on the landscape, as each village developed its footprint over the course of time. In the rites of belonging, the imprint is collective and confident. The village fêtes the fact that it has managed to survive against all the odds and, in doing so, has distinguished itself from other villages that are seen both as competitors and as models, hence expressions of ethnic and village identity. In their dwelling rites, the Kapsiki relate to the larger Mandara region, while belonging divides them into smaller units, even making a distinction between autochthony and immigrants within the village. Ritual as dwelling is what people share on a small scale, rituals of belonging tend to separate by drawing boundaries.

The imprint on the landscape made by a deeply rooted culture implies the construction of sacred places. The term "sacred" is little used by anthropologists, and with good reason, but shrines are important nevertheless. Kapsiki shrines, like those of many groups in the area, are usually manmade (Figure 13.1), with jars as the core type, though the house has other sacred spots as well: the sides of the opening in the wall, the place of honor, the space under the *tame*, supplemented by a string of old grindstones. And no object is as deeply historical as the grindstone; in this intensely dwelled environment, these stone hollows are the only prehistoric remnants more or less *in situ*, with a possible age stretching from the present all the way back to the Neolithic.[19]

Pots may be central in ritual, but they are in principle and in practice transient, lasting just one generation; so if any old human relic can serve as a model for a perennial sacred spot, it is not the pot but the grindstone.[20] Characteristically these vestiges of very old habitation are attributed more to *shala* than to people of old. Though people still use stone querns for milling, throughout the Mandara Mountains these remains are thought to be made by "giants," an emic appreciation of their age. But age alone is not enough to render an object sacred.

Figure 13.1 Creating a shrine: the *haze* on the new *mele*. Mogode 1973.

Some very old things, such as Neolithic axes, are used in rituals, but few people know about them and still fewer have seen them, because they are never used publicly in rituals. These Neolithic artifacts are associated with rain and *shala*, not with people and not with a house.[21] Kapsiki cosmology is not into ancestors, and a shrine has to be linked in principle with living people, dead kin mainly serving as a link between the living ones. Indeed, Kapsiki religion is very human, operating on a human scale, enmeshed with human history.

Rituals have changed over time. In all the descriptions in this volume, I first concentrated on the rituals as they were known by my informants at the time of my first fieldwork in 1972–1973, and then I indicated the dynamics of change. Many of the rituals, dwelling as well as belonging, have shown the influences of past changes, and these were well appreciated by my informants and are part and parcel of the present. Many of the rituals define themselves as a result of interactive history, as they exhibit the changes made in the past. Still, as was discussed in Chapter 2, the general discourse is on tradition, which is in fact a continuous process of incorporating changes. Thus the fragility of existence is matched by fragility of the rituals themselves, and if they disappear completely, initiatives to revive them are seldom taken. We saw the Mogode village sacrifice under threat: the village chief was piqued by the lack of respect from Muslims and used the non-performance of the ritual as a sanction against the new religion. If no misfortune results from the sanction, it will be difficult for him to resume the sacrifice unless others urge him to do so.

Rituals change also by accumulation, as they easily accrue new elements. The rain hunt offers a clear example of this process, where, despite the injunction by the village culture hero, remnants of earlier rainmaking practices are included in the liturgy. The low level of exegesis precludes any kind of conceptual orthodoxy, so the inherent contradictions do not pose a problem. In itself this dynamic of ritual enrichment and renewal works, but only if the major liturgy is in place and functions as a general framework into which to fit new elements. People are generally more aware of omissions than additions, so a notion of loss is more evident than one of enrichment.

Different rituals change in different ways and at different speeds. We saw the wedding rituals open to rapid change, easily gearing themselves toward modern variants and new expressions of wealth. The influence of the Christian churches, with their focus on the marriage ceremony as the principal rite of passage, is important here, just as is the increased focus on wedding rites and conspicuous giving. New technologies, the sound system, the mobile phone, and the many new status symbols that are the products of modernity encourage people to see the *amalea* as the central feature of the wedding ceremony. *Gwela* rituals, on the other hand, have been quite resistant to change, a resistance that coincides with the increased use of these rituals to define the village itself. *La* rituals show a more mixed course: some are disappearing, others are flourishing, and in yet other villages *la* festivals are even being introduced where they did not exist before, albeit with varying success.

However, the main change in Kapsiki/Higi rituals of belonging and dwelling will be disappearance, as the doctrinal modes of religiosity, Christianity and Islam will eventually take precedence over imagistic modes. Right now in a few villages the feast of Christmas is siphoning off some village festivals, such as the *la* festival. How quickly this process happens will depend on the Kapsiki definition of their own traditional feasts and on what they define as "religion," a Western concept. As Christianity and Islam are deemed to be "religions" and serve as models, they are seen to be in competition with similar aspects of Kapsiki/Higi culture, the rituals described in this volume, but only insofar as these are considered to be "religious." The question then arises: "What is religious in the rituals?" This is, in effect, a new question and in some way inverts the traditional order. For instance, when Christian and Muslim men consider whether or not they want their sons to experience the *gwela* rites, they balance the cultural elements against the religious ones, a distinction that has never been made before. Christian missions do the same, at least those missions interested in Kapsiki culture.[22] This view may well result in a truncated participation in the ritual whereby the "modern" boys participate in most rites, such as tying on the new skin, and ignore the sacrifices at home, since any kind of sacrifice or use of the word *mele* is anathema to them. Thus a definition by default of Kapsiki religion emerges as the use of the *mele*.

African religions do not, however, disappear as quickly as is often surmised, and they tend to raise their heads long after they have been given up as a lost cause. Ethnographies have sometimes been instrumental in revivals, but in the end it is people themselves who choose their own paths through history, and who fashion their own religious landscapes. Ritual and religion are about human creativity in the production of meaning, and as the ways of the past have always been an inspiration in setting a course for the future, so in all probability the wealth of ritual forms that the Kapsiki and Higi have created will continue to be a source of creativity to shape their future themselves.

APPENDIX

A Founding Myth of the Kapsiki

The first part of this story, *rhena ta Ngwed'u* (the story of Mogode), cited in full in Chapter 6, gives the prologue for the story of the main protagonist, the culture hero Hwempetla. So we pick up the story with the birth of our hero, the son of Teri Dingu or Puku.

Figure App. 1 Teri Puwe tells the story of Hwempetla. Mogode 2006.

Rhena ta Hwempetla (Story of Hwempetla)

Hwempetla's mother was not Puku's *makwa* but a *kwatewume*. All the children from her former marriage had died, so she had left her first husband. She went to Puku, who accepted her as his wife, but she was the unloved wife. He talked to her but not in the way a man normally speaks to a woman; he slept with her once but it was months before it happened again. When she conceived Hwempetla, it had been more than a year, people say, since her husband had slept with her.

She gave birth to Hwempetla when the other women were threshing sorghum. People sent her into the field to help and so she gave birth in the bush. All the women were busy taking their harvest to the threshing floor and nobody helped her to carry her sorghum after the delivery. So she sat down to give the baby some water and had to carry the infant in her arms, because Puku had not given her a sling in which to carry the child, like other women normally received. So she tied the baby in an old sack. After the threshing, she sat down and cried: "Why does *shala* not heed me? The sorghum is too heavy to carry." She did not know yet that she had given birth to a prodigy. Hwempetla then spoke up and said: "Put it on the top of your head and do not complain. I will help you." The woman put the basket on her head and it was very light so she could carry her child in her arms.

A little further she saw an antelope and asked who would skin it for her without touching the meat (so it could be used as a sling). Her son said, "Look at it from the corner of your eyes; then the animal will die and you can take it." She did so and it fell down dead. He told her to take the antelope and put it on her head. "I will help you," he told her. So she did and found that the grains and the antelope together were very light. She went home and showed Puku, her husband, what she had. He wanted to know who had done it for her, but she told him that she had found it dead on the ground and did not tell him that her son had arranged it, because he had forbidden her to speak about it.

At her request, Puku skinned the animal, gave her the skin but distributed all the meat among his other wives, and she did not get anything at all. She still had no grains for food and had to make her food from beer dregs. Hwempetla told his mother not to cry. When her husband handed over the skin, the other women told her that no one was going to help her to prepare the skin. The child helped to rub the skin to make it soft, but some hairs remained on it. All the same she used it as a sling while the child was small.

Several years later, when Hwempetla was a boy and old enough to tend animals, he told his mother that if he went on a journey, she should not leave her hut. "People will not ask you to do anything anyway, and if they ask, you should pretend to be ill. In no circumstance leave your hut. I know my father will not come for you either. I tell you this because the people will come and ask for me." And Hwempetla left for the field very early in the morning and went to Rufta. He wandered around for about three days. One morning, when the cattle were gathering in the cold to go into the fields, he stood between them. A few men on a hill saw that the cows assembled quickly at one point that morning. They told their children to make sure that the cattle did not leave for the field too soon, but when the children approached the animals, the cattle all sank into the ground. The children ran over to the spot and called the men. Together they tried to stop the cows, but in vain.

Hwempetla went home with the cows. It was night when he arrived at the mountain, but he climbed it with the animals, leaving them just outside the forecourt on the field near the compound wall. He had brought a lot of cattle. One can still see on the mountainside the place where he left them, since their hoof prints are still there. [And on the side of the mountain, hoof-like impressions in the volcanic rock are indeed visible.] He left the cows under the earth, however, with just their horns sticking out. He called his mother to tell her that he was back and that she should not go outside yet.

A co-wife came out to fetch water, stumbled over the horns, fell, and broke her jar. Another came out and the same thing happened. And with the third one, the same thing happened again. Then Hwempetla called his mother to come out to fetch water. She came out, fetched water, and went back with her jar full. When she got home with the water, Hwempetla told her to get his father to come out to see what had happened in his compound. His mother was worried about his reaction, but her son encouraged her. The woman called and got her husband to come and have a look at what had happened in his compound. He went out and Hwempetla got all the cattle to climb out of the earth, like a miracle. Puku came and saw his compound surrounded by cattle. He was flabbergasted and went into the woman's hut. "Who has done this thing, wife of mine?" he asked. "The child that is with me did it. Hwempetla. He had told me not to leave the hut, so I stayed inside," she said. From that moment on, Puku started to love his wife. "Whose cattle are these?" Puku asked Hwempetla. He answered: "Ours! *Shala* has given these to us." Puku stayed in that hut, gave his wife sorghum and meat again, and slept with her but not with his other wives.

After receiving the cattle from Hwempetla, Puku went over to Guria to tell the people what had happened. "Very good," the people of Guria said, "but be sure to give us the heads when you kill them." So every time a cow died, Puku took the head and a leg to Guria. Hwempetla grew angry, though, and saw that the people from Guria were getting fat. Hwempetla told his brothers that if a cow died, they would not give them the head any longer. Soon a large bull died and Puku told his children to take the head and a front leg to the people of Guria. They duly gave the meat to Guria but then Hwempetla said to his brothers: "Let us not give the meat to the people of Guria. Let us roast the meat and we will see how the war turns out. If there are too few of us, we will give them meat again." They sat down, made a fire, cut the meat in long strips, roasted it, and ate it all up. Then they went home.

"Did you give the meat to the people of Guria?" their father asked them. "Yes," they said. But the people of Guria did not see the head of the bull. "Where is the bull?" they asked the children. "At home in the stable," the children lied to them. The others came to Puku and asked where the bull was. "People told us it was ill in the stable." "Another bull? Did my children not bring you the head and the front leg I sent them with?" "You told them that you are strong enough to fight us. If not, they would not have eaten it on the road," the people from Guria said angrily.

When the children came back from the bush and had put the cattle into the pen, the father called them over and asked where they had left the meat. "We roasted it over there in the field." Their father told them that the people from Guria had come to fight. "How can we suffer a war? You are still small; what can we do against Guria, sons?" Hwempetla told them that they would fight and that they were big and strong enough. The father took a calabash and put it on Keluŋudehwetᵢ [a rock between Mogode and Guria, some 2 km further along the road]. He gave each of them five arrows. "If each of you can shoot all five arrows into the calabash, then and only then do I know that you are ready for battle." They shot all the arrows into the calabash. Puku saw that all the arrows were inside; none lay on the ground.

The following day the people from Guria came and the fighting began. They shot at the people of Guria but did not kill them and yet none of the arrows fell on the ground. Hwempetla and his brothers shot their arrows at the people from Guria but no one was killed. Then Gwenji, a stranger, came, since he had heard of the war with Guria and had come to help Hwempetla and his companions with a huge buffalo horn full of poison (*rhwɛ*), mixed with thorns. They covered the battlefield with it, and when the people from Guria stepped on it, they started to die. From that day on, people called the newcomer Gwenji Rhwɛ. Guria was decimated and Mogode freed.

[Long] after the battle, Gwenji came to the house of Hwempetla, who sent his sons to meet the newcomer in the forecourt. Maze, the oldest son was too busy with his calabash, the second had urgent business with his quiver, only the third took the time to meet the stranger. Since then Gwenji has been part of the *makwamte* clan. On a certain day, Hwempetla's children crossed the river at Teki and found someone on the bank under an acacia. Nobody knew him and they asked who he was. He answered, "*Mava kwasewe*" [slave of the acacia], and that is how his clan came to be named *mava* (slave), since nobody knew where he came from.

The next episode of Hwempetla's life is his wager with Rain, as told at the end of Chapter 6,[1] which resulted in Mogode not "buying rain." The final episode, the one of Hwempetla's death, has been told on pages 122 and 123, relating how the hero flew to his grave, with his wife.

Since then, the people of Mogode, who have been dancing with their dead since the start of time and were freed from Guria domination by their hero, have not paid for rain but ask Hwempetla, at his and his wife's grave, to implore the *shala* of the heaven for rain (Figure App. 1[4]).

The Kortchi variant

I mentioned in Chapter 6 the counterpart of this tale in Kortchi, a village at the eastern end of the Cameroonian Kapsiki area, in fact one reason to count them as Kapsiki. Their story goes as follows:

Nikukuɗ (the Kortchi equivalent of Nayekwakeɗɛ, the other name for Hwempetla) was the first to arrive in Kortchi from Gwava, an area that was empty when he arrived. He could do miracles. When he was a little boy, he told his mother "Fetch that antelope," and the animal stood stock still. During a drought his mother searched for water. He told her where to dig. She did and water came up that turned into a great river.

He became chief. He could be in several places at the same time and stole cows and goats without getting caught. During a long drought, the people from Sir (the neighboring village to the west) came with a smith to ask for rain. Nikukuɗ transformed into an animal by growing large teeth and a tail, so the people addressed his brother. Nikukuɗ told the smith to dance with the people in front of his brother, since he himself was not good at rain making. The smith retorted: "But we came for you!" Nikukuɗ went into his hut and came out looking like a white man. So the people of Sir said: "There is the chief, he was still in his hut." Nikukuɗ gave the people strips of dried meat and told them to walk home behind the smith drummer, and no matter what noise they might hear behind them, they should not turn around to look. There they went, and the smith heard strange noises but dared not turn. Nikukuɗ, with his powers, made all the people from Sir sink into the ground, with only their hands visible. When the smith arrived in Sir, people asked him where their people were. "Maybe they will come later; they were behind me," the smith answered. The next morning the people from Sir went out to look for them and discovered the hands, but when they tried to pull them out, everyone sank deeper and disappeared.

When he was about to die, Nikukuɗ tried to hide before Death. He walked straight through a mountain (the place is shown in Kortchi), but Death followed him. He tried to hide in the seeds of the sorrel but Death saw his toe sticking out. Nikukuɗ then told his people: "I am going to die. Nobody can hide before Death. I could have done it in the seeds of the sorrel, but there was not enough of it. If there was a place to hide for Death, I would have found it, but there is none. When I am dead, please wrap me in my bull's skin and do not cut off its tail." And so it happened. The smith hoisted him on his shoulders and all Nikikuɗ's 26 wives held onto the tail. Suddenly Nikukuɗ flew from the smith's shoulders to the top of the mountain of Kortchi with all his wives. There he shed the skin and disappeared. People say that he became a white man.

Birth Order Names

A birth order name follows ("counts") the pregnancies of the mother. Such names are not an exception in the area and can be found through much of the western and southern Mandara Mountains.[5] For the Kapsiki the complete list of names is shown in Table App. 1, using the orthography of the administration.

After nine pregnancies the names start again, with the affix *meha* ("grand, old"), *Tizhèmeha* (usually rendered as *Tshimeha*), *Kuvemeha*, and so on. The birth order names do carry some additional associations, that is, presumed character. *Tizhè* usually is considered a bit odd, "weak in the head" and not very bright. After all, he had to open his mother's birth canal, which does bring damage. Yet a parent's relationship with one's first born should be very close, as *Tizhè* or *Kuve* may represent the family after the death of the father or mother; also they inherit more than the next siblings, including the *mele*. *Zra* too is associated with dumbness, slow and not very quick-witted, but reliable, someone who "plods through." On the other hand, *Deli* and *Kwarumba* are deemed smart, quick, clever, and full of ruses. In the many traditional stories the squirrel is called *Deli* or *Temba* (in the Higi dialect), who has only his quick wits to cope with the dumb but persevering leopard answering to the name of *Zra* (or *Zeremba* in the Higi form). One special occasion that has to enter the name is a birth in the fifth month, *Terimcè* (after *mcife*, five). A son born in that month has to be called *Terimcè*, a girl *Kwaterimcè*. That month brings bad luck, and the only way to avoid it is to name the child after the month.

Table App. 1. **Birth Order Names Table**

	(son)	(daughter)
1st	Tizhè	Kuve
2nd	Zra	Masi
3rd	Deli	Kwarumba
4th	Vandu	Kwanyè
5th	Kweji	Kweji
6th	Teri	Kwateri
7th	Sunu	Kwasunu
8th	Kwada	Kwada
9th	'Yèŋu	Kwayèŋu

Glossary of Kapsiki Terms

Table App. 2. **Glossary of Kapsiki terms**

amalɛa	gift-giving feast
ba	epidemic
berhe makwa	accompany the bride
berhe mte/ berhe ba	ritual to chase death
beshɛŋu	black magic
beza	closing rite *gwela*
cɛ	hut
dabala	entrance hut
damara	smallpox
dɛdimu	woman's granary
derha	forecourt
dlave	band of cloth
dlera	crab, divination
duburu	tool blank
dzakwa	smith cap
dzirwha	rite in *la* feast
ɗafa	mush
ɗafa kwele	ritual on the tomb
ɗafa zhaŋe	food gift at funeral
fete	fault
gedla	smithy
geza	war song
gɛŋa	grave stone
ghi	child conceived without prior menstruation

(continued)

Table App. 2. (continued)

gumeze	type of sacrificial jar with trifid neck
gutuli	"spirit"
gwela	boy initiate
gwemba	dance in *la* feast
gwenji	clan
gweru	small crops storage
gɛŋa	upright stone
heferhwe	harvest season
hegi	locust
henetla	bull sacrifice
heshi	ancestor
hɛcimu	in-between season
hɛd'i	earth
hɛvɛ	rainy season
hirdɛ	party at wedding
huntere	boy initiation Rumsiki
hwelefwe	bilateral family
Hwempetla	culture hero
hweta	skin
hweta zheda	bead skirt
hweteru	"evil eye"
hwutu	leather belt
jimu	porcupine
jivu	bad relationship
kapsekɛ	to germinate
katsala	warrior

Table App. 2. (continued)

kayita	clan, lineage
kelɛɲu	"clairvoyant," "nightwalker"
keluɲu	resting place
kwaberhewuzha	"ladies-excuse-me" dance
kwageze rhena	start of sexual relations
kwalerha	twin
kwalkwala	piece of sorghum in outfit *gwela*
kwatewume	previously married wife
Kwatladerevɛ	place in initiation
kwatlahutu	official in initiation
kwatlazewe	mentrix of the initiate
kwele	tomb
kweperhuli	initiation mother of *gwela* or *makwa*
ksugwe	mother's brother, sister's son
la	year ritual
lamehegeze	fifth day of *la*
leke	rain cape
livu	iron bridal skirt
makwa	bride, previously unmarried
mandala	initiation year-mate
makwamtɛ	clan
makwajɛ	clan
makwiyɛ	
margi	black
matini	child with too close sibling
matlaba	*gwela* adornment, brass plague

(continued)

Table App. 2. (continued)

mazavɛ	harrier hawk
maze	chief, chiefly clan
maze rerhɛ	chief smith
mbeli kwa hɛdi	"people in the earth," the dead
mblama	ward headman
Mcirgue	highest peak of Mogode
meha rhwu	to judge
mehele	character
mehtembu	man's granary
mehteshi	young helper of *gwela* or *makwa*
mekwe	father-in-law, son-in-law
meleme	village
melɛ	sacrificial jar, sacrifice
melu	non-smith, "farmer"
mendereleke	mythic house-snake
Mentsehe	initiation rock
merhe	agency, chief
mete	witch
midʼimte	last words
mnta	ram's hairs
mnzefɛ	priest, warleader
mpa	war
mpedli	white beer
mpi	breath, life
mpisu hwu	spit on belly, ritual
Mte	Death

Table App. 2. (continued)

mɛpulu	wall entrance
mɛpehweta	just initiated
nasara	European
Nayekwakeɗɛ	Hwempetla
ndalɛke	smell of the corpse
ndemeva	rain maker
ndirhwu	part of ritual chasing of death
ndrimike	evil
nhwene	dirge
Nikikuɗ	Kortchi version of Hwempetla
ntsehwele	cleverness
ntsu	eye
Nzambe	peak between Mogode and Sir
ŋa	build
ŋacɛ	clan
ŋki	personal characteristics
ŋulu	rooster
peli va	ritual hunt for rain
psa pulu	inaugurating a house
pulu ŋeza	place of honor in forecourt
rerhɛ	smith
rhamca	burial shroud
rhedle	peanut sauce
rhele	dry season
rhena heca	folk story
rhuli	cache sexe, pubic apron

(continued)

Table App. 2. (**continued**)

rhwa	brook, watery place
Rhwamerhe	initiation brook
rhweme	mountain, sky, fibers (tonal difference)
Rhwemetla	judging and initiation mountain
rhwempe	dish of sorghum and peanuts
rhwɛ	medicine
Rhuŋgeɗu	place of old Mogode
rhɛ	compound
safarela	last day of *la*
shala	god
shasha	measles
shave	going-out rite
shi	grandparent / grandchild
shila	flute
shinaŋkwe	shadow, spirit
shiɲli	mourning band
tame	plaited granary
takase	bracelet
tereme	horn
tletegwecɛ	second day of *la*
tlidʼi	grass
tɛ	red beer
tɛnjinu	dried sorghum sprouts
Va	Rain
veci	sun, sacrificial jar
verhe	food party

Table App. 2. (continued)

wume	bridewealth, maturing
wuta	beer vat
yindlu	wall
yitiyaberhe	bride's mentor
yitiyagwela	mentor of *gwela*
zakwatewume	groom of secondary wife
zamakwa	groom of young bride
zeremba	clan
zhazha	bean dish
zuvu	reed flute

Kapsiki Plant Names

Table App. 3. **Kapsiki plant names**

berumu	Andropogon gayanus Kunth. Var. bisquamulatus (Hochst) Hack
cenɛ	Khaya senegalensis (mahogany)
haŋgedle	Cissus quadrangularis L. (veldt grape, devil's backbone
haze	Cymbopogon giganteus Chiov.
hazhaze	Diheteropogon amplectans
heyintsu	Diospyros mespiliformis Hochst & A.D.C.
hwemeke	Boswellia sp.
hwɛɓɛ	Crinum sp.
keyitu	Grewia cissoides Hutch. & Dalz. (grewia)
kwakweme	Strychnos inocua
kwantereza	Cassia singuena Del.
kwelemed'e	Tapinanthus globiferus (A. Rich) van Tiegh

(continued)

Table App. 3. **(continued)**

lekeleke	Isoberlinia doka Craib & Stapf (doka)
luku	Elytrigia repens (L.) Desv. ex Nevski (couch grass)
magwed'a	Sorghum bicolor, sorghum, yellow
mazala	Ficus populifolia Vahl (a fig)
meŋkwed'a	Ficus populifolia (see mazala)
mndɛ	Mollera angolensis O. Hoffm.
ŋwene	Grachis hypogea (peanut)
ŋwene wuve	Voandzeia subterranea (Bambaza groundnut)
peha	Phoenix reclinata (wild or Senegal date palm)
pesekene	Philosligma thonningii (Schum) Milne Redh.
rhweme	fibers of Vigna unguiculata, (bean, tonal difference with *rhweme*, mountain)
safa	Combretum glutinosum Perr ex D.C.
sesele	Indigofera tinctoria L. (indigo)
sewe	Acacia albida Del.
tere	Vetiveria zizanioïdes L. Nash. (Vetiver grass)
vɛmɛ	Erythrina stanoidea
wetle	Saccharum spontaneum L. (wild sugar cane, kans grass)
wumbela	Cassia nigricans Vahl
yaŋka	a grass, no determination available
zuvu ha	Steganotaenia araliacea Hochst.

END NOTES

Chapter 1

1. Through much of the Mandara Mountains, smiths form an endogamous group within each of the ethnic groups, also in Kapsiki/Higi culture. We will encounter them throughout the book, serving in many functions: as funerary directors, musicians, iron blacksmiths, brass casters, diviners, and healers, while their wives are potters. I will use the term "smith" in Kapsiki to indicate the whole group, with "blacksmith" only for those who work with iron.
2. Kinship terms are notoriously hard to translate. *Ksugwe* means both sister's son and mother's brother, in a restricted Omaha kinship terminology, so the proper translation would run "close male relative in the female line." For the small *ksugwe* I will sometimes use the—not overly inaccurate—"nephew," for the big one occasionally the—even more inaccurate—"uncle."
3. The date is January 18, 1988, the place Mogode in northern Cameroon.
4. I follow here the terminology established by Nicholas David: a grave is a square hole fitting a coffin; a tomb has a round or bell-shaped burial chamber and some superstructure, the burial mound. Nicholas David, "Mortuary Practices, Ideology and Society in the Central Mandara Highlands, North Cameroon," in *Mort et rites funéraires dans le basin du Lac Tchad*, ed. Catherine Baroin, Daniel Barreteau, and Charlotte von Graffenried, (Paris: ORSTOM, 1995), 75–101.
5. *Zra Teri Kwada*
   Tema Zeraɗa gɛwa?
   Rhwene gamba hwa za
   Tema Zraɗa beshiwa?
   Kasa tɛ ŋwale mbelishi na
   Wa same ɗa ŋgaɗa gɛwa
   Kamnze kɛma wale va mbeli nci nyi
   Wa mnza ta ɗa gɛwa
   Zra Teri Kwada
   Tema Zraɗa gɛwa
   Tema cewudale beshiwa
   Za kedasa taŋga
   Tema Zra Kuveɗa gɛwa
   Felehwe ta duzale
   Butu Zraɗa gɛ
   Zra ŋgwamena ti
   Tema Zraɗa beshiwa
   Ware derhwava zhili
   Tema sa ŋkɛma 'ya gɛ
   Tema sa rhu tɛ 'ya gɛ

6. *Khaya senegalensis*. All botanical determinations have been done by the Wageningen Institute for Plant Systematics and Botanic Geography, thanks to the cooperation of Dr. A. J. M. Leeuwenberg.
7. The maps were made by Nel de Vink, London; the relevant information for the map stemming from the 1:25.000 maps of both the Nigerian and the Cameroonian side of the border, and Christian Seignobos and Olivier Iyébi Mandjek, *Atlas de la province de l'Extrême Nord du Cameroun* (Minrest Cameroun, Paris: IRD, 2000).

Chapter 2

1. For instance, Jean Boutrais, *Le Nord du Cameroun, des hommes, une region*. (Collection Mémoires 102; Paris: ORSTOM 1984).
2. Walter van Beek, "African Tourist Encounters; Effects of Tourism in Two West-African Societies," *Africa*, 73, 3 (2002): 251–289.
3. The 2003 Cameroonian census indicates 96,00 Kapsiki; Nigerian figures are less reliable, but the Higi tend to be twice as many as the Cameroonian Kapsiki. So I use a conservative estimate of 200,000, allowing for some over-reporting by censuses.
4. Tim Ingold, *The Perception of the Environment. Essays in Livelihood, Dwelling and Skill* (London: Routledge, 2000).
5. Ingold, *Perception*, 153.
6. Ingold, *Perception*, 172.
7. Ingold, *Perception*, 179.
8. Ingold, *Perception*, 186.
9. Maurice Merleau-Ponty, *Phenomonology of Perception* (London: Routledge, 1962), 24.
10. Ronald Grimes *Deeply into the Bone: Re-inventing Rites of Passage* (Berkeley: University of California Press, 2000); Jonathan Smith, *To Take Place: Toward Theory in Ritual* (Chicago: University of Chicago Press, 1987).
11. Judith Sterner and Nicholas David, "Pots, Stones and Potsherds: Shrines in the Mandara Mountains (North Cameroon and Northeastern Nigeria)," in *Shrines in Africa: History, Politics and Society*, ed. Alan C. Dawson (Calgary: University of Calgary Press, 2009), 1–40.
12. The crucial synopsis of the theory is Harvey Whitehouse, *Modes of Religiosity. A Cognitive Theory of Religious Transmission* (Oxford: Altamira Press, 2004), followed by many edited volumes in the same series, "Cognitive Science of Religion." See also Pascal Boyer, *Religion Explained: The Human Instincts that Fashion Gods, Spirits, and Ancestors* (London: Vintage Books, 2002).
13. Whitehouse, *Modes of Religiosity*, 76.
14. Boyer, *Religion Explained*.
15. Robert McCauley and Eric Lawson, *Bringing Ritual to Mind: Psychological Foundations of Cultural Forms* (Cambridge: Cambridge University Press, 2002).
16. Frits Staal, "The Meaninglessness of Ritual," *Numen* 26, 1 (1975): 2–22; Frits Staal, *Agni, the Vedic Ritual of the Fire Altar*, (Berkeley: Asian Humanities Press, 1983).
17. Catherine Bell, *Ritual, Perspectives and Dimensions* (New York: Oxford University Press, 1997).
18. Roy Rappaport, *Ritual and Religion in the Making of Humanity* (Cambridge: Cambridge University Press, 1999). Boyer, *Religion Explained*. Anthony Wallace, *Religion, an Anthropological View*, (New York: Random House, 1966).
19. Walter van Beek, *De rite is rond. Betekenis en boodschap van het ongewone* (Tilburg: Tilburg University Press. 2007).
20. Victor Turner, *The Forest of Symbols: Aspects of Ndembu Ritual* (Ithaca, N.Y., Cornell University Press, 1967), 19.
21. Respectively Combretum *giganteus* Chiov. and *Cymbopogon glutinosum* Perr ex D.c.
22. Cf. *Phoenix reclinata*. In earlier publications this plant has erroneously been identified as *Albuca sudanica*.
23. Grimes, *Deeply into the Bone*, 162.

24. Grimes, *Deeply into the Bone*, 246.
25. Walter van Beek, "The Innocent Sorcerer: Coping with Evil in Two African Societies, Kapsiki and Dogon," in *African Religion: Experience and Expression*, ed. Thomas D. Blakely, Walter van Beek, and Dennis L. Thompson (London: James Currey, 1994), 196–228; Walter van Beek "Medicinal Knowledge and Healing Practices among the Kapsiki/Higi of Northern Cameroon and Northeastern Nigeria, in *Markets of Well-being. Navigating Health and Healing in Africa*, ed. Marleen Dekker and Rijk van Dijk, (Leiden: Brill, 2011), 173–200.
26. Walter van Beek, "The Dirty Smith; Smell as a Social Frontier among the Kapsiki/Higi of North Cameroon and Northeastern Nigeria," *Africa* 2, 1 (1992): 38–58; "Iron, Brass and Burial: the Kapsiki Blacksmith and His Many Crafts," in *La forge et le forgeron*, ed. Yves Monino, (Paris: CNRS/ORSTOM, 1991), 281–310; "Eating Like a Blacksmith: Symbols in Kapsiki Ethnozoölogy," In *Anthropology in the Netherlands*, ed. Patrick Josselin de Jong and Eric Schwimmer (Den Haag: Verhandelingen Koninklijk Instituut voor Taal-, Land- en Volkenkunde 95, 1982), 114–125.

Chapter 3

1. The actual expression was cruder: *mpa kala neha, kahale neha we*, war is like a vagina, it never grows old.
2. Bawuro Barkindo, *The Sultanate of Mandara to 1902. History of the Evolution, Development and Collapse of a Central Sudanese Kingdom*, (Stuttgart: Franz Steiner Verlag, 1989).
3. A TL dating done in 1974 on a shard-plus-environment gave—350 years (± 50 y). The sample was taken on Rhuŋged'u, the original settlement and sacrificial mountain; the dating was done by what is now called the Curt-Engelhorn-Zentrum Archäometrie of the University of Tübingen.
4. Nicholas David, "The Ethnoarchaeology, and Field Archaeology of Grinding at Sukur, Adamawa State, Nigeria," *African Archaeological Review*, 15, 1 (1998): 13–63.
5. Walter van Beek, "Les Kapsiki" in *Contribution de la recherche ethnologique à l'histoire des civilisations du Cameroun*, vol. I, ed. Claude Tardits, map p. 114 (Paris: CNRS, 1982).
6. This holds not only for the northern part of the Mandara mountains, about which more is published, but also for the southern one: Ryszard Vorbrich, "Ethnic and Settlement Processes in a Refuge Territory and Forms of Social and Political Organization," *Hemispheres* 5 (1988): 165–192; Ryszard Vorbrich. *Daba—Górale Północnego Kamerunu* (Wrocław: Polskie Towarzystwo Ludoznawce, 1989).
7. The Arab word for peacemaker, used for Europeans.
8. Dixon Denham, *Narrative of Travels and Discoveries in Northern and Central Africa in the Years 1822–1823* (London: Hackluyt, 1826), 195. The number of slaves Denham mentions seems inflated; see Jeanne-Françoise Vincent, "Sur les traces du major Denham: le Nord-Cameroun il y a cent cinquante ans. Mandara, 'Kirdi' et Peul," *Cahiers d'Études Africaines* 72, 18-4 (1978): 575–606.
9. In principle the Muslim Emirate of Wandala or Mandara bears the same name as the mountain range where the Kapsiki/Higi live. Conforming to general usage, I use Wandala for the Muslim emirate, and Mandara for the mountains.
10. Scott MacEachern, *Du Kunde. Processes of Montagnard Ethnogenesis in Northern Cameroon* (Calgary: University of Calgary 1990), 93.
11. The term *Kirdi* means "pagan" and stems probably from Baghirmi; see Judy Sterner, *The Ways of the Mandara Mountains: A Comparative Regional Approach* (Köln: Köppe, 2003) n 2, and Jacques Lestringant, *Le Pays des Guider au Cameroun: Essai d'une histoire régionale* (Paris: private printing, 1964), 42. The term is widely used throughout the region for all non-Muslim groups but it never specifies the group.
12. Denham, *Narrative of Travels*, 313.
13. Barkindo, *The Sultanate of Mandara*, 150.
14. Scott MacEachern, *Du Kunde Ethnogenesis*, 91. Scott MacEachern, "Selling Iron for Their Shackles: Wandala-'Montagnard' Interactions in Northern Cameroon" *Journal of African History* 43 (1993): 256.

15. Denham, *Narrative of Travels*, 197.
16. Vincent, who has traced Denham's itinerary in convincing detail, is clear in this identification, Vincent, "Sur les traces," 575–606.
17. MacEachern, *Du Kunde Ethnogenesis*, 91.
18. Heinrich Barth, *Reisen und Entdeckungen in Nord- und Central-Afrika in den Jahren 1849 bis 1855: Tagebuch seiner im Auftrag der Brittischen Regierung unternommenen Reise II* (Berlin: Perthes, 1857), 316–424.
19. Barth's mention of holding cockfights to resolve conflicts, though questioned by MacEachern, (*Du Kunde Ethnogenesis*, 100), is correct, if one surmises Marghi as including Kapsiki/Higi. The villages of Kamale and Mogode both apply the "rooster ordeal," while the place "Koptchi" (Barth, *Reisen*, 218) refers to the Kapsiki village on the eastern side, Kortchi, where the custom is known as well; see Charles K. Meek, *Tribal Studies in Northern Nigeria*, 2 vols. (London: Kegan Paul, Trench, Trubner & Co, 1931), Chapter 4.
20. Probably due to trade routes which skirted the mountains. MacEachern, *Du Kunde Ethnogenesis*, 77.
21. Walter van Beek, *The Kapsiki of the Mandara Mountains* (Prospect Heights, Ill.: Waveland Press 1987).
22. For a detailed description, see Walter van Beek, *Bierbrouwers in de bergen; de Kapsiki en Higi van Noord-Kameroen en Noordoost Nigeria* (Utrecht, 1978), 153–178.
23. Some informants, especially from Sirakuti, thought that the people from Mogode had come to hunt monkeys but the consensus was that they were out to collect plants for the funeral.
24. See van Beek *The Kapsiki*, 1989, and for an early overview of this phenomenon, M. G. Smith, "Secondary Marriage in Northern Nigeria," *Africa* 23, 4, (1953): 298–323.
25. Les structures coloniales à l'arrivée du colonisateur allemand ne furent guère modifiés. Les rapports entre les Habé [pagans] et les Foulbé restèrent ceux de vassaux payant tribut à leur féodaux, avec ce correctif que la puissance militaire européenne était mise au service des autorités authochthones instituées et jouait donc en faveur des chefs peuls. En effet, ces officiers allemands prirent appui sur les lamibés; aussi furent-ils enclins à confirmer officiellement l'autorité peule sur les groupements païens qui avaient rejeté celle-ci, qui étaient depuis toujours hors de son obedience. De Lestringant, Le Pays des Guider, 162.
26. "Es ist traurig zu sehen, wie unser deutsches Hinterland durch diese Sklavenjachten entvölkert wird. Alle Gefangenen gehen über den Benuë hinweg nach Norden, sie werden als Sklaven nach Jola und von hier nach Sokoto als Tribut gezahlt oder an die Hausahändler verkauft, welche sie ebenfalls nach Sokoto, sowie Kuka oder Kano auf den Markt bringen. Es wäre hier an der Zeit im Verein mit den Engländern, speziell der Royal Niger Company, diesem Unwesen zu steuern." Johannes Morgen, "Reisen im Hinterland von Kamerun 1889/91," Verhandlungen der Gesellschaft für Erdkunde zu Berlin, 1 (1891): 382; see also Berlin Archives R 1001/3300, R 1001/3325, R 175F FA 1/73, 38–54.
27. The story of Hamman Yaji was told to me in Mogode in 1989.
28. *Behu* and *praw praw* are Kapsiki idiophones for slitting a throat and tearing flesh from a carcass, respectively. Kapsiki language is extremely rich with these descriptive sounds, which are used to enliven the tales of terror and passion about the past.
29. Sa'ad Abubakar, *The Lamibe of Fombina: A Political History of Adamawa, 1809–1901* (New York: Oxford University Press 1977).
30. A. H. M. Kirk-Greene, *Adamawa Past and Present: An Historical Approach to the Development of a Northern Cameroons Province* (London, 1969), 63. Of the elite troops of Zubeiru 424 were reportedly killed by machine gun, but Zubeiru escaped.
31. Berlin Archives R 175F FA 1/75 p. 267–374, ibid. 72, pp. 142–143. Zubeiru became a cult figure almost instantly: "There are, however, still Fulani in Yola who are convinced that ... Zubeiru himself was mysteriously lifted to the skies in a thick protective mist sent by the guarding hand of Allah." Kirk-Greene, *Adamawa*, 63.
32. Oberleutnant Dominik, a central personage in the early history; H. Dominik, *Von Atlantik zum Tchadsee. Kriegs und Forschungsfahrten in Kamerun* (Berlin: Ernst Siegfried Mitler und Sohn, 1905).

33. James H. Vaughan Jr. and A .H. M. Kirk-Greene (eds.), *The Diary of Hamman Yaji. Chronicle of an African Ruler* (Bloomington: Indiana University Press, 1995), 9.
34. Kirk-Greene, *Adamawa*, 4.
35. Dominik, *Atlantik*, 208–210.
36. Dominik spells his name as "Hamandjadji."
37. "Nach Fullahart war der Yerima (Prinz) gar nicht traurig über den Tod seines Vaters. Denn er war nun Lamido und lange genug habe er erwarten müssen, meinte er. Im Hof der Lamidoseste erhob sich lautes Wehklagen. Die Weiber umstanden den Toten, wälsten sich in Asche, rangen die Hände gegen Himmel und kreischten vol wilden Weh." Dominik, Atlantik, 210.
38. ". . . denn unbeirrt um alle Sentamentalitäten galt es, die deutsche Herrschaft hier auszurichten, wie einer Rocher de bronze." Dominik, Atlantik, 210.
39. Kirk-Greene, *Adamawa*, 4.
40. Eldridge Mohammadou, *Les Lamidats du Diamaré et du Mayo Louti au XIXe siècle (Nord-Cameroun)*, (Tokyo, 1988), 282. Though brutal, this story does fit in with the general picture of Dominik.
41. Mohammadou, *Lamidats*, 211.
42. Vaughan and Kirk-Greene, *Diary*.
43. All entries are from the 1995 edition of the diary.
44. After the end of World War I the former colony of Kamerun was partitioned under the authority of the League of Nations as Mandated Territories between Britain and France until 1946.
45. "Nach einem Ruhetag verabschiedete ich mich am Morgen des 5/1 [1906] von Hama Jádi, der mich ein Wegestück begleitet hatte, mit dem von herzen kommenden Wünsch; Allah möge ihm ein langes Leben bescheeren. Sein in Bungel, nahe Demea, sitzender etwa 12 jähriger Sohn scheint glüchlicherweise nach dem Vater zu schlagen," Berlin Archives 81966–120, 199.
46. Kanuri Archives, SNP 10/2 95p/1914, cited also in Vaughan and Kirk-Greene, *Diary*, 14.
47. Vaughan and Kirk-Greene, *Diary*, 13.
48. Judy Sterner, *The Ways of the Mandara*, 2003.
49. Kirk-Greene, *Adamawa*, 75.
50. Vaughan "Culture History", 1078–1095.
51. Vaughan and Kirk-Greene, *Diary*, xiv.
52. But not nearly in the same numbers. Van Beek, *The Kapsiki*.
53. Probably someone caught in performing *beshɛŋu*, harmful magic. Kamale is a Higi village.
54. This must have been Haman Belo, who ruled until 1922, well remembered in Mogode.
55. Gawar is just on the eastern side of Kapsiki territory in Cameroon. It owed allegiance to the Emir of Marua, so for Yaji Mogode belonged to Marua (Vaughan and Kirk-Greene, *Diary*, 70). If respect for the Emir of Marua was the main reason for Yaji's forebearance toward Mogode, that did not protect Sena and Kamale, which also were in the fief of Gawar (Mohammadou, *Lamidats*, 264). But then, border issues were common also between Lamibe, as the diary repeatedly shows. And Kamale and Sena did not house a minor Fulani chief, as Mogode did.
56. Duriez, *Zamane. Tradition et modernité dans la montagne du Nord-Cameroun* (Paris: Harmattan, 2009).
57. Harrier hawks, probably *Polyboroides radiatus*.
58. Also important were his contacts with the daughter of Rabeh. She contacted Yaji and gave him presents (entry 28-10-1918). Rabeh was a war lord who had come from Mahdist Sudan, had wanted to establish a new Bornu by the force of the new guns, destroyed the Wandala emirate, and was killed by the French in 1900. An earlier Mahdist rebellion inside the Adamawa emirate by Hayat Sa'id had already shown the anti-establishment and anti-colonial force of such a movement (Abubakar, *Fombina*, 131 ff). The British, weary from their Sudan experiences, had already been confronted with a Mahdist rebellion in Nigeria as well, that of Sabiru, Paul Lovejoy, *Slavery, Commerce and Production in the Sokoto Caliphate of West Africa* (Trenton, 2005), 323–326. The Germans had already been alarmed by these contacts. Berlin Archives R 175F FA/75 pp. 267–324.
59. Kirk-Greene in Vaughan and Kirk-Green, *Diary*, 151.

60. Vaughan and Kirk-Greene, *Diary*, 32, 33.
61. Vaughan and Kirk-Greene, *Diary*, 34, 35, 41.
62. José van Santen, *They Leave their Jars behind: The Conversion of Mafa Women to Islam* (Leiden: VENA, 1993), 84.
63. Thus one of the Kapsiki clans in most villages is called the *mava* (slaves, people of slave descent), and some of the ethnic names in the region, such as the Matakam of Mafa, reminisce about a slave past in general. See James Vaughan Jr., "Mafakur: a Limbic Institution of the Marghi (Nigeria)," in *Slavery in Africa; Historical and Anthropological Perspectives*, ed. Igor Kopytoff and Suzanne Miers (Madison: University of Wisconsin Press, 1977), 85–104.
64. See Sterner, *The Ways of the Mandara*, 29 n. 5.
65. Van Beek, "Les Kapsiki."
66. For an overview of the groups in the mountains see Renate Lukas, *Nicht-islamische Ethnien im Südlichen Tchadraum* (Wiesbaden: Franz Steiner Verlag, 1973), as well as Renate Lukas, *Die materielle Kultur der nicht-islamische Ethnien von Nordkamerun und Nordostnigeria* (Wiesbaden: Franz Steiner Verlag, 1977).
67. "Ihre Farmen sind Musterleistungen, ihre Wohnsitze richtige Schmuckkästchen, auf Schritt und Tritt begegnet man der Liebe zur eigenen Heim und zur Ordnung, dem Sinne für Gemütlichkeit und schöne Form; in diesem Bienenkorb ähnlichen Wohnsitzen haust tatsächlich ein Bienenvölkchen." Berlin Archives, B R175FA 1/120, p. 204.
68. Jeanne-Francoise Vincent, *Princes montagnards du Nord-Cameroun. Les Mofou-Diamaré et le pouvoir politique* (Paris: Harmattan, 1991), 71.
69. Kirk-Greene, *Adamawa*, 84.
70. Alain Beauvilain, *Nord-Cameroun, crises et peuplement* (Alain Beauvilain, 1989), 247.
71. The British and French Mandates became the British and French Trust Territories under the UN in 1946. Because the British part was defined as undecided in its colonial attribution (Kirk-Greene, *Adamawa*), a plebiscite was held in December 1959. The population of the British Cameroons chose to remain with the British Cameroons. Cameroon gained independence in October 1960 and a second plebiscite was held to resolve the question to which nation it wanted to belong. The northern territories, where the Higi reside, chose Nigeria, the southern territories (now North West and South West Provinces of Cameroon) chose Cameroon. The recent (2005) settlement of the border dispute between Nigeria and Cameroon by the The Hague International Court of Justice, ended in redrawing the border again, a few kilometers to the east. The village of Mogode became divided, some wards moving with the border; but for 700 meters my own house would have become Nigerian. For the effect of these partitionings on the Mandara, see Bawuro M. Barkindo, "The Mandara Astride the Nigeria-Cameroon Boundary," in *Partitioned Africans*, ed. A. I. Asiwaju (London: Hurst, 1985), 29–49; as well as Vaughan, "Culture History", 1078–1095.
72. See also Marcel Roupsard, *Nord-Cameroun. Overture et developpement d'une région enclavée*, (Paris: EHESS, 1987).
73. Later, in the much more imposing presence of the chief of Gudur, I was well instructed, taking my shoes off and seating myself on the corner of the mat, well below the chair the chief was using. However, considering my height, the chief stood up and remained standing during much of the encounter (see Chapter 7 and Fig. 7.4a).
74. Similar instances are reported in other places in the mountains. Sterner (*Ways of the Mandara*, 39) was "embarrassed to find them thanking me for saving them from the Fulbe," and Müller-Kossack reports that people thank him that "his brothers" had finally arrested Hamman Yaji (Gerhard Müller-Kosack, *The Way of the Beer: Ritual Reenactment of History among the Mafa* (London: Mandaras, 2003), 43.
75. The question is whether the village Kortchi, deemed to have a separate langage and also divergent customs, should be counted Kapsiki. As is noted in the language and orthography preface, I have done so, following my Kapsiki informants, with the shared Nayekwakeɗɛ myth as a major argument (Chapter 6).
76. James Vaughan Jr., "The Religion and the World View of the Marghi," *Ethnology* 3, 4 (1964): 389–397, and Vaughan, "Culture History."

77. Such as Sukur, Mabas, Bulahay Shugule, Mefele, Sirak, Muhur, and Cuvok. See Müller-Kosack, *The Way of the Beer*, 349.
78. In fact the reverse held for the Mofu, whose two parts, Mofu Gudur and Mofu Diamare, had been joined by the administration but on closer inspection were found to be two ethnic groups. Vincent, *Princes montagnards*.
79. Van Beek, *The Kapsiki*.
80. Roger Morhlang, *Higi Phonology*, Studies in Nigerian Languages 2 (Zaria, 1982).
81. Mohrlang, *Higi Phonology*.
82. Walter van Beek, "The Innocent Sorcerer: Coping with Evil in Two African Societies, Kapsiki and Dogon," in *African Religion: Experience and Expression*, ed. Thomas Blakely, Walter van Beek, and Dennis Thompson (London: James Currey, 1994): 196–228.
Van Santen, *They Leave their Jars*, 140.

Chapter 4

1. A. H. M. Kirk-Greene, *Adamawa Past and Present: An Historical Approach to the Development of a Northern Cameroons Province (London, 1969)*, 219.
2. Walter van Beek, *The Kapsiki of the Mandara Mountains* (Prospect Heights, Ill.:Waveland Press 1987).
3. The smiths in the Mandara area are being studied extensively: Judy Sterner and Nicholas David, "Smith and Society: Patterns of Articulation in the Northern Mandara Mountains," in *Metals in Mandara Mountains' Society and Culture*, ed. Nicholas David (Trenton, N.J.: Red Sea Press, 2012, 87–113, in press); James H. Vaughan Jr., "Eŋkyagu as Artists in Marghi Society," in *The Traditional Artist in African Societies* ed. W. L. d'Azevedo, (Bloomington: Indiana University Press, 1973), 162–193.
4. A Kanuri term for "headman."
5. Walter van Beek, "The Ideology of Building: The Interpretation of Compound Patterns among the Kapsiki of North Cameroon," in *Op zoek naar mens en materiële cultuur*, ed. H. Fokkens, P. Banga, T. Constandse, and M. Bierma (Groningen: Groningen University Press, 1986), 147–162.
6. *Hana, wuzege, hana a shala tada keyaŋa ndedeke ki rhɛ da.*
7. For an analysis of the various marriage careers see van Beek, *The Kapsiki*.
8. *shala ta da, nde wusu kezeme ashɛ gɛ.*
9. *hana shala, hana shala.*
10. *yita, ndeke da leŋeleŋe pe 'ya. Pelu teŋwela jive 'ya kafa rhena. Mpelɛ ya ŋkede wundu nya kedema ntsu tada mbe hwu seda.*
11. *Nde ŋaŋa wusu kezeme, yita. Ndeke da leŋeleŋe, kelemte zererhwe nya kiku.*
12. Walter van Beek, "Kapsiki Beer Dynamics," in *Ressources vivrières et choix alimentaires dans le bassin du lac Chad*, ed. Eric de Garine, Olivier Langlois, and Claude Raimond (IRD, 2006), 477–500.
13. Van Beek, "Kapsiki Beer Dynamics," 490.
14. The crux of the brewing process, viz. sprouting the sorghum, in effect is the very reason these people are called Kapsiki: *psekɛ* means "to sprout," see Preface.
15. The Kapsiki also have a white beer variant that is brewed exclusively by women, for immediate consumption or for the market. Recently the women have taken up brewing the red *tɛ* for the market, developing a quicker process, and in the process enhancing the taste.
16. Richard Werbner, *Ritual Passage, Sacred Journey: The Process and Organization of Religious Movement* (Manchester: Manchester University Press, 1989), 4.
17. Jeanne-Francoise Vincent, "Divination et possession chez les Mofu montagnards du Nord-Cameroun," *Journal de la Société des Africanistes* 51, 1 (1971): 71–132. James Vaughan Jr., "Mafakur: a Limbic Institution of the Marghi (Nigeria)," in *Slavery in Africa; Historical and Anthropological Perspectives*, ed. Igor Kopytoff and Suzanne Miers (Madison: University of Wisconsin Press, 1977), 85–104; Alfred Adler, *Le baton d'aveugle; divination et royauté chez les Moundang* (Paris: PUF, 1971). For a more elaborate account of crab divination, see Walter van Beek, "Crab Divination among the Kapsiki of North Cameroon," in

Reviewing Reality. Dynamics of African Divination, ed. Phil Peek and Walter van Beek (2012). For the historical orientation of divination: Walter van Beek and Phil Peek "Divination: du bon sens dans le chaos", in *Arts d'Afrique. Voir l'invisible*, ed. Paul Matharan, (Bordeaux, Musée de l'Occitanie, 2011), 149–154, 225–228.

18. The verb *kaŋa* has a wider meaning and is also used for making pottery and performing a sacrifice. The latter connotation is the closest in this case.
19. Walter van Beek, "The Innocent Sorcerer: Coping with Evil in Two African Societies, Kapsiki and Dogon," in *African Religion: Experience and Expression*, ed. Thomas Blakely, Walter van Beek, and Dennis Thompson (London: James Currey, 1994), 196–228.
20. The notion that pots *are* people, as argued for the Bulahay and Mafa to the north of the Kapsiki, does not hold for the Kapsiki, at least not nearly so strongly: Nicholas David, Judy Sterner, and Kondji Gavua, "Why Pots Are Decorated," *Current Anthropology* 29 (3), 1988, 365–289. Compare also the Mofu situation, Jeanne Vincent, "Le prince et le sacrifice: Pouvoir, religion et magie dans les montagnes du Nord-Cameroun," *Journal de la Société des africanistes* 2 (1987): 89–121.
21. For a treatise on the cognitive weight of the various senses in Kapsiki, see Walter van Beek, "Eyes on Top: Culture and the Weight of the Senses," in *Invisible Africa; Sprache und Geschichte in Afrika*, 21, ed. Anne Storch (Köln: Koppe, 2010), 245–270.

Chapter 5

1. Walter van Beek, "The Innocent Sorcerer: Coping with Evil in Two African Societies, Kapsiki and Dogon," in *African Religion: Experience and Expression*, ed. Thomas Blakely, Walter van Beek, and Dennis Thompson (London: James Currey, 1994), 196–228.
2. He also used to be the war leader in the past
3. With thanks to Judy Sterner.
4. pa hale ta da paya meleme ganye kama kempa mbeli kaya mbeli dzakwa nyɛ, mba mbeli kadzemte.
5. Charlotte von Graffenried, *Das Jahr des Stieres: ein Opferritual der Zulgo und Gemjek in Nordkamerun*. Studia Ethnographica Friburgensia 2 (Freiburg: Universitäts Verlag Freiburg. 1984).
6. Judy Sterner, *The Ways of the Mandara Mountains: A Comparative Regional Approach* (Köln: Köppe, 2003).
7. Gwagwa wutse, gwagwa tla, kahene tla Kafte we, gerede wusu a Kafte; tehwu tehwu Rhukele 'ya ŋeda yita.
8. Sukur is the old center of iron production and probably from that position has gained a large reputation; see Adam Smith and Nicholas David, "The Production of Space and the House of Xidi Sukur," *Current Anthropology* 36, 3 (1995): 441–471. Also this is one reason why Dumas-Champion could relate this whole bull slaughter complex to a cycle of regicide and initiation. Françoise Dumas-Champion, "Regicide et initiation. Limitation des règnes et le cycle initiatique dans les monts Mandara (Cameroun et Nigeria)," *Journal des Africanistes*, 65, 1 (1995): 5–34. However, most of the cultures in the mountains are more acephalous than centralized, and surely for the Kapsiki this relationship does not hold. If anything, the year cycle is relevant, as in the Kapsiki villages with bull sacrifices these alternate with the chasing away of death.
9. The description and analysis of Gerhard Müller-Kosack, *The Way of the Beer: Ritual Reenactment of History among the Mafa* (London: Mandaras, 2003) is very convincing in this respect.
10. Alan Dawson (ed.), *Shrines in Africa: History, politics and society*, ed. (Calgary: University of Calgary Press, 2009).
11. Ronald Grimes *Deeply into the Bone: Re-inventing Rites of Passage* (Berkeley: University of California Press, 2000).
12. Judy Sterner and Nicholas David, "Pots, Stones and Potsherds: Shrines in the Mandara Mountains (North Cameroon and Northeastern Nigeria)," in Dawson, *Shrines in Africa*. 1–40. (Calgary: University of Calgary Press, 2009).
13. Nicholas David, Judy Sterner, and Kondji Gavua, "Why Pots Are Decorated," *Current Anthropology* 29 (3), 1988, 1–14. For an analysis of ancient grinding equipment in the region, see Nicholas David, "The Ethnoarchaeology", 13–63.

14. Peter Geschiere, *The Modernity of Witchcraft: Politics and the Occult in Postcolonial Africa* (Charlottesville: University of Virginia Press, 1997).
15. David, "The Ethnoarchaeology," 54.
16. René Girard, *Violence and the Sacred* (Baltimore: Johns Hopkins University Press, 1977).
17. Walter van Beek, "De zondebok en het kwaad: een etnografische kritiek," in *Mimese en geweld: beschouwingen over het werk van R. Girard*, ed. Walter van Beek (Kampen: Kok Agora, 1988), 126–145. For the meat central in feasting, see Martin Jones, *Feast. Why Humans Share Food* (Cambridge: Cambridge University Press), 2007.
18. David Parkin, *The Anthropology of Evil* (Oxford: Blackwell, 1985). See also Walter van Beek, "The Escalation of Witchcraft Accusations," in *Imagining Evil: Witchcraft Beliefs and Accusations in Contemporary Africa*, ed. Gerrie ter Haar (Trenton, N.J.: Africa World Press, 2007), 293–316.
19. Dawson, "Introduction," *Shrines*, 2009.
20. Igor Kopytoff and Suzanne Miers, "Introduction," in *Slavery in Africa; Historical and Anthropological Perspectives*, ed. Igor Kopytoff and Suzanne Miers (Madison: University of Wisconsin Press, 1977), 3–84.

Chapter 6

1. *Shala* has honorific titles that are sometimes used: *Mehete tehwu rhweme, Jigelafte, Kwamaduwe*. These are not so much names as but titles with no specific meaning, and they resemble the terms neighboring groups use for their world of the gods. Christians prefer *Jigelafte pele Rhweme* (God in heaven) to distinguish themselves from a *shala* with its personal connotations, though the Bible translation freely uses the word *shala*. The similarity of *jigelafte* to the Mafa word for god, *Jigile*, by no means implies that the concept of god in Mafa is the same. In the latter culture *Jigile* seems to be more of a high god, without the dominant personal aspect of the Kapsiki: Gerhard Müller-Kosack, *The Way of the Beer: Ritual Reenactment of History among the Mafa* (London: Mandaras, 2003), 74; but on the other hand, *Jigile* has also been called "guardian spirit" (Godula Kossack, personal communication) and the combination of the two is closer to the Kapsiki notion of *shala*.
2. Both singular and plural forms are acceptable so it can be "my *shala*" or "our *shala*." The Kapsiki language has an inclusive "we" form, which includes the listener, and an exclusive one, which distinguishes the speaker's group from the listener. When talking about *shala*, this form makes a big difference: our *shala* with you as a member, or our *shala* in opposition to yours.
3. The case of twins is illustrative. There is some discussion as to whether they have one or two *shala*, but they are in some way their own *shala* (see chapter 8).
4. Harvey Whitehouse, *Modes of Religiosity. A Cognitive Theory of Religious Transmission* (Oxford: Altamira Press, 2004), 105.
5. *Tapinanthus globiferus* (A. Rich) van Tiegh.
6. Cf. Richard Fardon, *Between God, the Dead and the Wild: Chamba Interpretations of Ritual and Religion* (Washington, D.C.: Smithsonian Institution Press, 1990).
7. I have been unable to identify this species.
8. I have been unable to identify it.
9. *Pesekene, Piliostigma thonningii* (Schum) Milne Redh.
10. Matthew Schoffeleers, "Twins and Unilateral Figures in Central and Southern Africa: Symmetry and Asymmetry in the Symbolization of the Sacred," *Journal of Religion in Africa*, 21, 4 (1991): 345–372. See also Walter van Beek "Forever Liminal: Twins among the Kapsiki/Higi of North Cameroon and Northeastern Nigeria", in *Twins in African and Diaspora Cultures; Double Trouble or Twice Blessed*, ed. Ph. Peek, (Bloomington, Indiana University Press, 2011), 163–182.
11. Judy Sterner, *The Ways of the Mandara Mountains: A Comparative Regional Approach* (Köln: Köppe, 2003).
12. Walter van Beek, "The Healer and His Phone. Medicinal Dynamics among the Kapsiki of North Cameroon." in eds. Mirjam de Bruijn, Francis Nyamnyoh, and Inge Brinkman, *Mobile Phones: The New Talking Drums of Everyday Africa* (Leiden,:Langaa & African Studies Centre, 2009), 125–134.

13. Walter van Beek, "Les savoirs Kapsiki," in *La quête du savoir: Essais pour une anthropologie de l'education au Cameroun*, ed. Renaud Santerre and C. Mercier-Tremblay (Montreal, Presses Universitaire Laval, 1982), 180–207.
14. Peter Geschiere, *The Modernity of Witchcraft: Politics and the Occult in Postcolonial Africa* (London: University of Virginia Press, 1997).
15. Walter van Beek, "The Escalation of Witchcraft Accusations," in *Imagining evil: Witchcraft beliefs and Accusations in Contemporary Africa*, ed. Gerrie ter Haar (Trenton, N.J.: Africa World Press, 2007), 297.
16. René Jauoen, *L'eucharistie du mil: Languages d'un people, expressions de la foi*, (Paris: Karthala. 1995), 18; Jeanne-Francoise Vincent, "Statut et puissance du 'Dieu-du-ciel' en Afrique de sahel," in *"Dieu seul! Le Dieu du ciel chez les montagnards du nord des Monts Mandara*, ed. J. Fedry et al. (Yaoundé: Presses UCAC, 2008), 140; T. Sundermeier, *The Individual and Community in African Traditional Religions* (Hamburg: LIT Verlag. 1998), 161. See also Bernard Juillerat, *Les bases de lorganisation sociale chez les Mouktélé (Nord Cameroun)*, (University of Paris: Mémoires de l'Institut de l'Ethnologie VIII, 1971), 160; H .E. Scheub, *A Dictionary of African Mythology: The Mythmaker as Storyteller* (Oxford: Oxford University Press, 2000).
17. Müller-Kosack, *The Way of the Beer*, 66. Good examples are also to be found in Judy Sterner, *The Ways of the Mandara Mountains: A Comparative Regional Approach* (Köln: Köppe, 2003), 215–218, and Juillerat, *Les bases*, 63.
18. I collected over 120 folk tales in 1972–1973, a selection of which is in the process of being published. In 2010 a new batch of stories was collected, to be compared with the first.
19. This tale recounts the traditional way of buying a cow; usually a cow was not bought outright, but piecemeal in a lasting relationship with the seller, who at the death of the cow received its head.
20. This particular mountain has caves, proof of Hwempetla's flight through the air. One of them is used for girls' initiation ceremonies at the time of their first marriage. See Chapter 9.
21. Recorded in 2005.
22. Other themes are linked as well, like a struggle with a *gutuli* who can pierce a mountain, but the themes of rain, cattle rustling, and of course flying away at death are always there, see also Christian Duriez, *Zamane. Tradition et modernité dans la montagne du Nord-Cameroun*, (Paris: Harmattan, 2009), 67–70.
23. When Vincent argues that these mountain societies showed a definite monotheism, she is convincing regarding many of the religions but misses the distinctions such as this one, a personal god. Vincent, "Statut et puissance," 2008.
24. Nigel Barley, cogently I think, argues that this stereotype of ancestors as a separate reality distorts African thinking on this issue, because in many cultures there is no vernacular term for ancestors, since they are simply kinsmen, part of the group, even if dead: Nigel Barley, *Dancing on the Grave. Encounters with Death* (London: Abacus, 1995), 92.
25. Christian Duriez, the Roman Catholic missionary in Sir, who through his pastoral work of over 20 years knows the Kapsiki very well, recognizes these short relations but does not disencumber himself completely of the "ancestor orientation" of African religions: Duriez. *Zamane*, but also in Christian Duriez *À la rencontre des Kapsiki du Nord-Cameroun. Regards d'un missionaire d'après Vatican II*, (Paris: Karthala, 2002).
26. Rita Astuti, "Ancestors and Afterlife," in *Religion, Anthropology and Cognitive Science*, ed. Harvey Whitehouse and James Laidlaw (Durham: Carolina Academic Press, 2007), 161–178.
27. Vincent, "Statut et puissance ," 147–178.
28. Possibly also the Marghi concept of *iju*, being both "supernatural" and personalized. Vaughan, "The Religion and the World View", 390.

Chapter 7

1. I have not been able to identify this bird. It has become rare; possibly a sunbird.
2. On the position of Gudur see Catherine Jouaux, "Gudur: chefferie ou royaume?" *Cahiers d'Études Africaines* 114, 29-2 (1991): 193–224.

3. Flutes, of various kinds, are important symbols signifying wind and thus are tied in with the agricultural cycle.
4. Shala ta rhweme, menehwete zhewu ta ndere 'ya, nahe ndeke wusu kazeme kaŋa, mpi dzeve va rha: ndeke mu yemu kawuza ha; mba na kepetleke wundu le hwa, kade dle 'ya we.
5. Shala a 'ya ndere 'ya, nde ŋaŋa kezeme kweleŋu pe 'ya, ndeke d'a yemu ha.
6. For a detailed account of village provenance, see Walter van Beek, "Les Kapsiki" in *Contribution de la recherche ethnologique à l'histoire des civilisations du Cameroun*, vol. I, ed. Claude Tardits (Paris: CNRS, 1982).
7. Judy Sterner, *The Ways of the Mandara Mountains. A Comparative Regional Approach*, (Köln: Köppe, 2003).
8. For a full description see Wallter van Beek, *Bierbrouwers in de bergen; de Kapsiki en Higi van Noord-Kameroen en Noordoost Nigeria*, (Utrecht: ICAU, 1978): 153–178.
9. Judy Sterner and Nicholas David. "Pots, Stones and Potsherds: Shrines in the Mandara Mountains (North Cameroon and Northeastern Nigeria)." In *Shrines in Africa; History, Politics and Society*, ed. Allan Dawson, (Calgary: University of Calgary Press, 2009), 1–40.
10. Catherine Jouaux, "La chefferie de Gudur et sa politique expansioniste," *Du politique à l'économie: études historiques dans le bassin du lac Tchad*, ed. Jean Boutrais (Paris: ORSTOM, 1991), 193–224. Catherine Jouaux, "Premières et secondes obsèques en "pays" mofu-gudur: symbolique et enjeux sociaux," in *Mort et Rites Funéraires dans le Bassin du Lac Tchad*, ed. Catherine Baroin, Daniel Barreteau, and Charlotte von Graffenried (Paris: ORSTOM, 1995), 115–136. For the relation between symbol and power in Africa, see Walter van Beek "Cultural Models of Power in Africa," in *Land, Law and Politics in Africa, Mediating Conflict and Reshaping the State*, ed. Jan Abbink and Mirjam de Bruijn, (Leiden: Brill, 2011), 25–48.
11. Probably *Phoenix reclinata*.
12. Catharine Bell, *Ritual, Perspectives and Dimensions*. (New York: Oxford University Press, 1997).
13. Roy Rappaport, *Ritual and Religion in the Making of Humanity*. (Cambridge: Cambridge University Press, 1999); Walter van Beek, *De rite is rond. Betekenis en boodschap van het ongewone*, (Tilburg: Tilburg University Press, 2007).
14. Alfred Gell, *The Anthropology of Time. Cultural Constructions of Temporal Maps and Images* (Oxford: Berg, 1992), 151–154.

Chapter 8

1. Probably *Phoenix reclinata*.
2. This traditional method of caring for the umbilical cord seems to be responsible for quite a number of tetanus infections and was one of the major reasons for the high child mortality rate that has characterized Kapsiki demography for so long: André-Michel Podlewski, *La dynamique des principales populations du Nord-Cameroun* (Cahier ORSTOM, série Sci. Hum. III, 1966 no 4, 1966).
3. A similar system exists among the Guidar, though with a total number of ten names. Chantal Collard, "Les noms numéro chez les Guidar," *L'Homme* 11, 4 (1973): 91–95.
4. Figure 8.1 is a photo of a twin, which is why the child is older.
5. Walter van Beek, "The Innocent Sorcerer; Coping with Evil in Two African Societies, Kapsiki and Dogon." In *African Religion: Experience and Expression*, ed. Thomas Blakely, Walter van Beek, and Dennis Thomson, (Oxford: Currey, 1994), 200–202.
6. The Kapsiki have a four-lexeme basic color terminology which includes red. Anything beautiful is easily associated with the color red: Walter van Beek, "Color Terms in Kapsiki," in *Papers in Chadic Linguistics*, ed. Paul Newman and Roxana Ma (Leiden: 1977), 13–20.
7. Clairvoyants whose spirits roam the bush at night, see Chapter 6.

8. Kwalerha taŋayɛ, mbeli nyi kesa ta rhweme
   mberishi ŋelɛ, Kwandɛ ta rhweme
   Kwalerha tewutse, Kwalerha rhɛŋ'yɛ
   Mberishi rhweme, sayɛ te rhweme
   Kwawutsu, tawa sana?
   Mberishi ŋelɛ wushi shiabu
   Rhɛŋkɛ nde rhate we.
   Zhahale tekumbu na Kwandɛ
   Nakɛ rhu tehwulu dehwu matsehwa Kwandɛ
9. *Saccharum spontaneum*, L.
10. Another term for God, probably related to *jigile* or *Zigile*, the Mafa term for God. See also José van Santen, José. *They leave their jars behind: The conversion of Mafa women to Islam*, (Leiden: VENA, 1993), 119–121; and Jeanne-Françoise Vincent, "Statut et puissance du 'Dieu-du-ciel' en Afrique de sahel." in *'Dieu seul! Le Dieu du ciel chez les montagnards du nord des Monts Mandara*, ed. J. Fedry et al., (Yaoundé: Presses UCAC, 2008), 147–178.
11. *Ficus populifolia* Vahl, Moraceae.
12. The mother's milk, in the form of her breast, may be used as a powerful symbol in cursing. When a mother chews on a nipple and speaks bad words, or even thinks "bad thoughts," the results for her child will be immediate. This *bedla* of the mother is the most potent curse of all and, quite characteristically, operates through direct bodily contact between mother and child (van Beek, "Innocent sorcerer," 215).
13. Catherine Gros, "Inclassables jumeaux, et pourtant . . . Place et signification des jumeaux et anthropologie sociale," in *Des Jumeaux et des Autres*, ed. Claude Savary and Catherine Gros (Genève: Museum of Ethnography, 1995), 25–50.
14. The clans are more pronounced in identity construction in daily life than in the major sacrifices and rites of passage.
15. Walter van Beek, *Bierbrouwers in de bergen; de Kapsiki en Higi van Noord-Kameroen en Noordoost Nigeria*, (Utrecht: ICAU 1978), 154ff.

Chapter 9

1. See Walter van Beek, "Les Kapsiki et leurs bovins," in *Des taurins et des hommes*; Cameroun, Nigéria, ed. Christian Seignobos and Eric Thys (Paris: ORSTOM 1998), 15–39.
2. Walter van Beek, "The Iron Bride", in *Metals in Mandara Mountains' Society and Culture*, ed. Nicholas David, (Trenton, N.J.: Africa World Press & The Red Sea Press, 2012, 285–301, in press).
3. Cattle are routinely given into the custody of a close friend to avoid eventual claims of brothers.
4. For a comprehensive treatment of marriage proceedings, including bridewealth, see Walter van Beek, *The Kapsiki of the Mandara Mountains*, (Prospect Heights, Miss.: Waveland Press, 1987).
5. These *wudu makwa*, small iron points, have become rare, and nowadays the *kweperhuli* gets money, FCFA 5,000, so it has become more expensive.
6. Van Beek, *The Kapsiki*.
7. For the impact of tourism, see Walter van Beek, "African Tourist Encounters; Effects of Tourism in Two West-African Societies." *Africa*, 73, 3 (2002), 280–289.
8. See Van Beek, *The Kapsiki*, 130
9. For the importance and symbolism of cattle, see Van Beek, "Les Kapsiki et leurs bovins."

Chapter 10

1. In earlier publications I used the spelling *gewela*, but I have brought my orthography in line with the now standard one, *gwela*.
2. Walter van Beek, "A Touch of Wildness. Brass and Brass Casting in Kapsiki," in *Metals in Mandara Mountains' Society and Culture*, ed. Nicholas David (Trenton, N.J.: Africa World Press, 2012, 303–323, in press).
3. *Elytrigia reprens* (L.) Desv. ex Nevski.
4. Determination uncertain
5. Paul Biya is president of Cameroon.

6. From *mndɛ* (*Mollera angolensis* O. Hoffm.)
7. These bead skirts are quite popular with tourists and usually sold as cache sexe, which they are not.
8. Judy Sterner, *The Ways of the Mandara mountains. A Comparative Regional Approach*, (Köln: Köppe, 2003).
9. Victor Turner, *The Ritual Process: Structure and Anti-structure* (London: Routledge, 1969).
10. Arnold van Gennep, *Les rites de passage, étude systématique des rites: de la porte et du seuil* (Paris: Picard 1981 [1904]).
11. Catharine Bell, *Ritual, Perspectives and Dimensions*, (New York: Oxford University Press, 1997).
12. For an analysis of this model see Walter van Beek, "Les savoirs Kapsiki." In *La quête du savoir. Essais pour une anthropologie de l'éducation au Cameroun*, ed. Renaud Santerre and C. Mercier-Tremblay, (Montréal: Presse Universitaire Laval, 1982), 180–207.
13. Turner, *The Ritual Process*, 67.
14. Harvey Whitehouse, *Modes of religiosity. A Cognitive Theory of Religious Transmission*, (Oxford: Altamira Press, 2004), 156.
15. The concept is from Scott MacEachern and a felicitous one: Scott MacEachern, "'Symbolic Reservoirs' and Inter-group Relations: West African Examples," *The African Archeological Review*, 12 (1994): 205–224.
16. Sterner, *The Ways of the Mandara Mountains*.
17. Alan Dawson, "Introduction", in *Shrines in Africa. History, politics and society*, ed. Allan Dawson, (Calgary: University of Calgary Press, 2009), vii-xvii.

Chapter 11

1. In the early 1980s, women in the cities of northern Cameroon started to brew red beer for commercial purposes; Kapsiki women now also brew red beer, since it can get a better price at the market than other brews. They brew at home and, depending on their relationship with their husband, will either use the brewery or install their equipment outside. Grain for commercial beer production, as is the case for *mpedli*, is kept separate. The women keep their own stocks and do not use the main granary for their grain supply.
2. Species unknown.
3. For a full analysis see Walter van Beek, "The Gender of Beer: Beer Symbolism among the Kapsiki/Higi and the Dogon," in *Liquid Bread. Beer and Brewing in Cross-Cultural Perspective*, ed. Wolf Schiefenhövel and Helen Macbeth, (New York: Berghahn, 2011), 147–158, as well as Walter van Beek "Kapsiki Beer Dynamics," in *Ressources vivrières et choix alimentaires dans le bassin du lac Chad*, ed. E. Garine, O. Langlois and C. Raimond, (Paris: IRD, 2006), 477–500.
4. For a detailed description of the trousseau, see Walter van Beek, *The Kapsiki of the Mandara Mountains*, (Prospect Heights, Miss.: Waveland Press), 1987.
5. In the last few decades, honey has become scarce and half of it is normally redistributed immediately.
6. *Rhwa* in Kapsiki means any size of river or stream, with or without water in it.
7. Such a tuft of hair is standard for the chief but will be shaved off with all others.
8. Walter van Beek, *Bierbrouwers in de bergen; de Kapsiki en Higi van Noord-Kameroen en Noordoost Nigeria*, (Utrecht: ICAU 1978), 156.
9. Martin Jones, *Feast. Why Humans Share Food* (Cambridge: Cambridge University Press), 2007.
10. Van Beek, *Bierbrouwers*, 345–349.

Chapter 12

1. Judy Sterner and Nicholas David, "Pots, Stones and Potsherds: Shrines in the Mandara Mountains (North Cameroon and Northeastern Nigeria)." In *Shrines in Africa; History, Politics and Society*, ed. Allan C. Dawson, (Calgary: University of Calgary Press, 2009), 1–40;

Catherine Jouaux, "Premières et secondes obsequies en 'pays' mofu-gudur: symbolique et enjeux sociaux." In *Mort et Rites Funéraires dans le Bassin du Lac Tchad*, ed. Catherine Baroin, Daniel Barreteau, and Charlotte von Graffenried, (Paris: ORSTOM, 1995), 115–136.

2. Nicholas David and Judy Sterner, "Smith and society: Patterns of Articulation in the Northern Mandara Mountains", in *Metals in Mandara Mountains' Society and Culture*, ed. Nicholas David, (Trenton, N.J.: Red Sea Press, 2012, 84–113, in press).
3. This occasionally happens with the Marghi as well. Vaughan personal communication.
4. See the opening example in Walter van Beek, *The Kapsiki of the Mandara Mountains*, (Prospect Heights, Miss.: Waveland Press, 1987).
5. Zra is a descendant of immigrants in Mogode, as, in fact, are most people in the village. However, his village of origin, Kamale, is just an hour's walk, downhill, in Nigeria.
6. Zra has been dead for 2½ days at the moment described, and even in the relatively cool winter season, decomposition has already set in.
7. See Chapter 1.
8. The quills of a rare variety of red porcupine are used for the burial of men known as great warriors—or thieves. Red porcupines have a reputation for ferocity, and catching one is tricky since they are clever and evade capture easily.
9. The Cameroonian government's forestry service.
10. *Kamɓe malema* in Kapsiki.
11. In the case of a female death, her sister's daughter, the husband's brother's wife, the direct descendants of the mother of the deceased woman as well as the wives of her husband's clan, that is, her classificatory co-wives.
12. The first picture in Chapter 1 is from the second day of Zra's funeral.
13. If there are termites in the tomb, the women have to pay the smiths to collect the termite earth as food for their chickens.
14. As was already mentioned in earlier descriptions: Charles Meek, *Tribal studies in Northern Nigeria*, (London: Kegan Paul, Trench, Trubner & Co, 1931); Keith Otterbein, "Mortuary Practices in Northeastern Nigeria," *Bulletin of the West Bengal Cultural Research Institute* 6, 1/2 (1967): 10–18; and "Higi armed combat," *Southwestern Journal of Anthropology*, 24 (1968): 195–213.
15. "Kweleŋu nza na shala ndeke wuzege, and 'A yityiyda tlete rhu ne rha, mba nkɛ kedlu ŋa rha a na kewuve kayake ŋaŋa, kala 'ya yake ŋaŋkɛ.
16. Peter Metcalfe and Richard Huntington, *Celebrations of Death: The Anthropology of Mortuary Ritual*, 2nd ed. (Cambridge: Cambridge University Press, 1991), 182–184.
17. Walter van Beek, "The Innocent Sorcerer; Coping with Evil in Two African Societies, Kapsiki and Dogon." In *African Religion: Experience and Expression*, ed. Thomas Blakely, Walter E. A. van Beek, and Dennis L. Thomson, (Oxford: Currey, 1994), 196–228.
18. Philippe Ariès, *The Hour of our Death* (Hammondsworth: Penguin, 1983).
19. Matthieu Schoffeleers, "Twins and Unilateral Figures in Central and Southern Africa: Symmetry and Asymmetry in the Symbolization of the Sacred." *Journal of Religion in Africa*, 21, 4 (1991): 345–372.
20. Metcalfe and Huntington, *Celebrations of Death*, 34.
21. See Nicholas David, "Mortuary Practices, Ideology and Society in the Central Mandara Highlands, North Cameroon." In *Mort et rites funéraires dans le basin du Lac Tchad*, ed. Catherine Baroin, Daniel Barreteau, and Charlotte von Graffenried, (Paris: ORSTOM 1995), 75–101. In general see Ariès, *The Hour of our Death*.
22. One example I do have firsthand knowledge of is Dogon culture of Mali. The Dogon have a definite abhorrence of the corpse yet have massive second funerals, centering on their famous mask dances. See also Nigel Barley, *Dancing on the Grave. Encounters with Death*, (London: Abacus, 1995), 101.
23. Among the Dogon, see note 22; this is the mask cult, which is also an initiation.
24. Barley, *Dancing on the Grave*, 103.
25. Barley, *Dancing on the Grave*, 27.
26. Metcalfe and Huntington, *Celebrations of Death*, 78.

Chapter 13

1. Walter van Beek, The Dirty Smith; Smell as a Social Frontier among the Kapsiki/Higi of North Cameroon and Northeastern Nigeria." *Africa* 2, 1 (1992): 38–58
2. This is the main theme of Walter van Beek *The Kapsiki of the Mandara Mountains*, (Prospect Heights, Miss.: Waveland Press, 1987).
3. Pascal Boyer, *Religion explained: the Human Instincts that fashion Gods, Spirits and Ancestors* (London: Vintage Books, 2002),45.
4. Roy Rappaport, *Ritual and Religion in the making of Humanity*, (Cambridge: Cambridge University Press, 1999).
5. Ronald Grimes, *Deeply into the Bone. Re-inventing Rites of Passage*, (Berkeley: University of California Press, 2000), 25.
6. Frits Staal, "The Meaninglessness of Ritual." *Numen* 26, 1 (1975): 2–22.
7. Rappaport, *Ritual and Religion*.
8. Color symbolism is not dominant, showing mainly in food, plus the twin's preference for red. Kapsiki color terminology has four basic terms, yet symbolism follows the classic African tripartite system, white, red, and black: Walter van Beek, "Color Terms in Kapsiki." In *Papers in Chadic Linguistics*, ed. Paul Newman and Roxana Ma. (Leiden: 1977) 13–20.
9. See Walter van Beek, "Eating Like a Blacksmith, Symbols in Kapsiki Ethnozoölogy." In *Anthropology in the Netherlands*, ed. Patrick Josselin de Jong and Eric Schwimmer, (Den Haag: Verhandelingen Koninklijk Instituut Taal-, Land- en Volkenkunde nr. 95, 1982), 114–125.
10. Walter van Beek, "Les Kapsiki et leurs bovins." In *Des taurins et des hommes*, ed. Christian Seignobos and Eric Thys, 15–39 (Paris: ORSTOM, 1998).
11. My ethnobotanic sampling resulted in an estimated 1,200 botanic species recognized and named by the Kapsiki, albeit by specialists.
12. Mary Douglas, *Natural Symbols. Explorations in Cosmology* (London: Cresset Press, 1970). Jan van Baal and Walter van Beek. *Symbols for Communication. An Introduction to the Anthropological Study of Religion* (Assen, van Gorcum, 1985).
13. In Mofu, lateralization is more important, and inverted, left being associated with the male side, right with female. Though Vincent suggests that it is similar in Kapsiki, this is not the case: Jeanne-Françoise Vincent, "Main gauche, main de l'homme; essai sur le symbolisme de la gauche et de la droite chez les Mofu (Cameroun du Nord)," in *Système des signes. Hommages à G. Dieterlen* (Paris: Hermann, 1978), 485–509.
14. A mythical story which one informant told me links haze with Hwempetla's mother, but this was categorically denied by others.
15. Jonathan Smith, *To Take Place: Toward Theory in Ritual*, (Chicago: University of Chicago Press, 1987), 98.
16. For instance compared to Dogon culture in Mali, my other field area.
17. Walter van Beek, "Crab divination among the Kapsiki of North Cameroon." In *Reviewing reality. Dynamics of African Divination*, ed. Walter E. A. van Beek and Philip M. Peek. 2012, in press.
18. Walter van Beek, Slave Raiders and Their People without History," in *History and Culture; Essays on the Work of Eric R. Wolf*, ed. Jan Abbink and Henk Vermeulen (Amsterdam: Het Spinhuis, 1982), 53–71.
19. Nicholas David, "The Ethnoarchaeology and Field Archaeology of Grinding at Sukur, Adamawa State, Nigeria." *African Archaeological Review*, 15, 1 (1998), 53.
20. Judy Sterner and Nicholas David, "Pots, Stones and Potsherds: Shrines in the Mandara Mountains (North Cameroon and Northeastern Nigeria)." in *Shrines in Africa; History, Politics and Society*, ed. Allan G. Dawson, (Calgary: University of Calgary Press, 2009), 1–40.
21. The volume on smiths will dwell extensively on these Neolithic remains.
22. Christian Duriez, *Zamane. Tradition et modernité dans la montagne du Nord-Cameroun*, (Paris: Harmattan, 2009).

Appendix

1. This particular story is told more widely with the ground squirrel in the role of Hwempetla. The squirrel is the standard protagonist in traditional Kapsiki stories (*rhena heca*). In the squirrel version, the ending is different: the squirrel marries Rain's daughter and gives an elephant as bride wealth. To trick his father-in-law, he eats the elephant from the inside, helped by the leopard, and then arranges it that the angry Rain catches the leopard *in flagrante delicto*, that is, with its mouth full of meat.
2. This particular mountain has caves, one of which is used for girls' initiation at their first marriage.
3. During the annual rain hunt, these tombs are repaired and covered with leaves to ask Hwempetla for rain, a message he will purvey to Rain.
4. Teri Puwe died in March 2010.
5. This system of number-names is not uncommon in the area and is also found among the Guidar, albeit with small but significant differences: Chantal Collard, "Les noms numéro chez les Guidar." *L'Homme* 11, 4 (1973), 91–95, and Chantal Collard, *Organisation sociale des Guidar ou Baynawa* (Paris: EHESS 1977).

REFERENCES

Abubakar, Sa'ad. *The Lamibe of Fombina. A Political History of Adamawa, 1809–1901*. Zaria: Ahmado Bello University Press, 1977.
Adler, Alfred. *Le baton d'aveugle; divination et royauté chez les Moundang*. Paris: PUF, 1971.
Ariès, Philippe. *The Hour of Our Death*. Hammondsworth, UK: Penguin, 1983.
Astuti, Rita. "Ancestors and Afterlife." In *Religion, Anthropology and Cognitive Science*, edited by Harvey Whitehouse and James Laidlaw, 161–178. Durham, N.C.: Carolina Academic Press, 2007.
Barkindo, Bwaro Mubi. *The Sultanate of Mandara to 1902. History of the Evolution, Development and Collapse of a Central Sudanese Kingdom*. Stuttgart: Franz Steiner Verlag, 1989.
———. "The Mandara astride the Nigeria-Cameroon Boundary." In *Partitioned Africans*, edited by A. I. Asiwaju, 29–49. Londen: Hurst, 1985.
Barley, Nigel. *Dancing on the Grave. Encounters with Death*. London: Abacus, 1995.
Barth, Heinrich. M. *Reisen und Entdeckungen in Nord- und Central-Afrika in den Jahren 1849 bis 1855: Tagebuch seiner im Auftrag der Brittischen Regierung unternommenen Reise*. Berlin: Perthes 1857.
Beauvilain, Alain. *Nord-Cameroun, crises et peuplement*. Alain Beauvilain, 1989.
Bell, Catharine. *Ritual, Perspectives and Dimensions*. New York: Oxford University Press, 1997.
Boutrais, Jean (et al.). *Le nord du Cameroun, des hommes, une région*. Collection Mémoires 102 Paris: ORSTOM 1984.
Boyer, Pascal. *Religion Explained: the Human Instincts that Fashion Gods, Spirits and Ancestors*. London: Vintage Books, 2002.
Collard, Chantal. "Les noms numéro chez les Guidar." *L'Homme* 11, 4 (1973), 91–95.
———. *Organisation sociale des Guidar ou Baynawa*. Paris: EHESS, 1977.
David, Nicholas. "The Ethnoarchaeology and Field Archaeology of Grinding at Sukur, Adamawa State, Nigeria." *African Archaeological Review*, 15, 1 (1998): 13–63.
———. "Mortuary Practices, Ideology and Society in the Central Mandara Highlands, North Cameroon." In *Mort et rites funéraires dans le basin du Lac Tchad*, edited by. Catherine Baroin, Daniel Barreteau, and Charlotte von Graffenried, 75–101, Paris: ORSTOM 1995.
David, Sterner "Smith and Society: Patterns of Articulation in the Northern Mandara Mountains." In *Metals in Mandara Mountains' society and culture*, edited by Nicholas David, 87-113. Trenton, N.J.: Red Sea Press, 2012, 87–113, in press.
David, Nicholas, Judy Sterner and Kodzo Gavua, "Why Pots are Decorated." *Current Anthropology* 29, 3 (1988): 265–289.
Dawson, Alan C. "Introduction." In *Shrines in Africa. History, Politics and Society*, edited by Allan C. Dawson, vii–xvii. Calgary: University of Calgary Press, 2009.
Denham, Dixon. *Narrative of Travels and Discoveries in Northern and Central Africa in the Years 1822–1823*. London: Hackluyt, 1826.
Dominik, Hans. *Von Atlantik zum Tchadsee. Kriegs und Forschungsfahrten in Kamerun*. Berlin: Ernst Siegfried Mitler und Sohn, 1905.
Douglas, Mary T. *Natural Symbols. Explorations in Cosmology*. London: Cresset Press, 1970.

Dumas-Champion, Françoise. "Regicide et initiation. Limitation des règnes et le cycle initiatique dans les monts Mandara (Cameroun et Nigeria)." *Journal des Africanistes*, 65, 1 (1995): 5–34.

Duriez, Christian. *Zamane. Tradition et modernité dans la montagne du Nord-Cameroun*. Paris: Harmattan, 2009.

———. *À la rencontre des Kapsiki du Nord-Cameroun. Regards d'un missionaire d'après Vatican II*. Paris: Karthala, 2002.

Fardon, Richard. *Between God, the Dead and the Wild: Chamba Interpretations of Ritual and Religion*. Washington, D.C.: Smithsonian Institution Press, 1990.

Gell, Alfred. *The Anthropology of Time. Cultural Constructions of Temporal Maps and Images*. Oxford: Berg, 1992.

Geschiere, Peter. *The Modernity of Witchcraft; Politics and the Occult in Postcolonial Africa*. Charlottesville: University of Virginia Press, 1997.

Girard, René. *Violence and the Sacred*. Baltimore: Johns Hopkins University Press, 1977.

Grimes, Ronald L. *Deeply into the Bone. Re-inventing Rites of Passage*. Berkeley: University of California Press, 2000.

Gros, Catherine. "Inclassables jumeaux, et pourtant . . . Place et signification des jumeaux et anthropologie sociale." In *Des jumeaux et des autres*, edited by Claude Savary and Catherine Gros, 25–50. Genève: Museum of Ethnography, 1995.

Ingold, Tim. *The Perception of the Environment. Essays in Livelihood, Dwelling and Skill*. London: Routledge, 2000.

Jauoen, René. *L'eucharistie du mil: Languages d'un people, expressions de la foi*. Paris: Karthala, 1995.

Jones, Martin. *Feast. Why Humans Share Food*. Cambridge: Cambridge University Press, 2007.

Jouaux, Catherine. "Gudur: chefferie ou royaume?" *Cahiers d'Études Africaines* 114, 29-2 (1991): 193–224.

———. "La chefferie de Gudur et sa politique expansioniste." In *Du politique à l'économie: études historiques dans le bassin du lac Tchad*, ed. Jean Boutrais, 193–224. Paris: ORSTOM, 1991.

———. "Premières et secondes obsequies en 'pays' mofu-gudur: symbolique et enjeux sociaux." In *Mort et Rites Funéraires dans le Bassin du Lac Tchad*, edited by Catherine Baroin, Daniel Barreteau, and Charlotte von Graffenried, 115–136. Paris: ORSTOM, 1995.

Juillerat, Bernard. *Les bases de l'organisation sociale chez les Mouktélé (Nord Cameroun)*. University of Paris, Mémoires de l'Institut de l'Ethnologie VIII, 1971.

Kirk-Greene, A. H. *Adamawa Past and Present. An Historical Approach to the Development of a Northern Cameroons Province*. London: IAI, 1969.

Kopytoff, Igor, and Suzanne Miers. "Introduction." In *Slavery in Africa; Historical and Anthropological Perspectives*, edited by Igor Kopytoff and Suzanne Miers, 1–35. Madison: University of Wisconsin Press, 1977.

Lestringant, Jacques de, *Le Pays des Guider au Cameroun: Essaye d'une histoire régionale*. Paris: private printing 1964.

Lovejoy, Paul. *Slavery, Commerce and Production in the Sokoto Caliphate of West Africa*. Trenton, N.J.: Africa World Press, 2005.

Lukas, Renate. *Nicht-islamische Ethnien im Südlichen Tchadraum*. Wiesbaden: Franz Steiner Verlag, 1973.

———, *Die materielle Kultur der nicht-islamische Ethnien von Nordkamerun und Nordostnigeria*. Wiesbaden: Franz Steiner Verlag, 1977.

McCauley, Robet N., and E. Thomas Lawson. *Bringing Ritual to Mind. Psychological Foundations of Cultural Forms*. New York: Cambridge University Press, 2002.

MacEachern, Scott. *Du Kunde. Processes of Montagnard Ethnogenesis in Northern Cameroon*. Calgary: University of Calgary, 1990.

———. "Selling Iron for their Shackles: 'Wandala-Montagnard' Interactions in Northern Cameroon." *Journal of African history* 34 (1993): 247–270.

———. "'Symbolic Reservoirs' and Inter-group Relations: West African Examples." *The African archeological review*, 12 (1994): 205–224.

Meek, Charles K. *Tribal studies in Northern Nigeria*, 2 vols. London: Kegan Paul, Trench, Trubner & Co, 1931.

Merleau-Ponty, Maurice. *Phenomonology of Perception*. London: Routledge, 1962.

Metcalfe, Peter, and Richard Huntington. *Celebrations of Death. The Anthropology of Mortuary Ritual*, 2nd ed. Cambridge: Cambridge University Press, 1991.
Mohammadou, Eldridge. *Les Lamidats du Diamare et du Mayo Louti au XIXe sciècle (Nord-Cameroun)*. Kyoto: Kyoto University Press, 1988.
Morgen, Johannes. "Reisen im Hinterland von Kamerun 1889/91." *Verhandlungen der Gesellschaft für Erdkunde zu Berlin*, 1 (1891): 124–198.
Morhlang, Roger. *Higi Phonology*. Studies in Nigerian Languages 2. Zaria: SIL 1982.
Müller-Kosack, Gerhard. *The Way of the Beer: Ritual Re-enactment of History among the Mafa*. London: Mandaras, 2003.
Otterbein, Keith. "Mortuary Practices in Northeastern Nigeria." *Bulletin of the West Bengal Cultural Research Institute* 6, 1 (1967): 2–17.
———. "Higi Armed Combat." *Southwestern Journal of Anthropology*, 24 (1968): 95–213.
Parkin, David, ed. *The Anthropology of Evil*. Oxford: Blackwell, 1985.
Podlewski, André-M. *La dynamique des principales populations du Nord-Cameroun*. Cahier ORSTOM, série Sciences Humaines III, no 4, 1966.
Rappaport, Roy A. *Ritual and Religion in the Making of Humanity*. Cambridge: Cambridge University Press, 1999.
Roupsard, Marcel Nord-Cameroun. *Overture et developpement d'une région enclavé*. Paris: EHESS, 1987.
Scheub, Harold E. *A Dictionary of African Mythology: The Mythmaker as Storyteller*. Oxford: Oxford University Press, 2000.
Schoffeleers, Matthieu. "Twins and Unilateral Figures in Central and Southern Africa: Symmetry and Asymmetry in the Symbolization of the Sacred." *Journal of Religion in Africa*, 21, 4 (1991): 345–372.
Seignobos, Christian, and Olivier Iyébi Mandjek. *Atlas de la province de l'Extrême Nord du Cameroun*. Paris: Minrest Cameroun Paris IRD, 2000.
Smith, Adam, and Nicholas David. The Production of Space and the House of Xidi Sukur. *Current Anthropology* 36, 3 (1995): 441–471.
Smith, Jonathan Z. *To Take Place: Toward Theory in Ritual*. Chicago: University of Chicago Press, 1987.
Smith, M. G. "Secondary Marriage in Northern Nigeria." *Africa* 23, 4 (1953): 298–323.
Staal, Frits. "The Meaninglessness of Ritual." *Numen* 26, 1 (1975): 2–22.
———. *Agni, the Vedic Ritual of the Fire Altar*, 2 vols. Berkeley: Asian Humanities Press, 1983.
Sterner, Judy. *The Ways of the Mandara Mountains. A Comparative Regional Approach*. Köln: Köppe, 2003.
Sterner, Judy, and Nicholas David. "Pots, Stones and Potsherds: Shrines in the Mandara Mountains (North Cameroon and Northeastern Nigeria)." In *Shrines in Africa; History, Politics and Society*, edited by Allan C. Dawson, 1–40. Calgary: University of Calgary Press, 2009.
Sundermeier, T. *The Individual and Community in African Traditional Religions*. Hamburg: LIT Verlag, 1998.
Turner, Victor. *The Forest of Symbols: Aspects of Ndembu Ritual*. Ithaca, N.Y.: Cornell University Press, 1967.
———. *The Ritual Process: Structure and Anti-structure*. London: Routledge, 1969.
Van Baal, Jan, and Walter E.A. van Beek. *Symbols for Communication. An Introduction to the Anthropological Study of Religion*. Assen: van Gorcum, 1985.
Van Beek, Walter E. A. "Color Terms in Kapsiki." In *Papers in Chadic Linguistics*, eds. Paul Newman and Roxana Ma, 13–20. Leiden: 1977.
———. *Bierbrouwers in de bergen; de Kapsiki en Higi van Noord-Kameroen en Noordoost Nigeria*. Utrecht: ICAU 1978.
———. "Les Kapsiki." In *Contribution de la recherche ethnologique à l'histoire des civilisations du Cameroun*, vol. I ed. Claude Tardits, 113–119. Paris: CNRS, 1982.
———. "Les savoirs Kapsiki." In *La quête du savoir. Essais pour une anthropologie de l'éducation au Cameroun*, edited by Renaud Santerre and C. Mercier-Tremblay, 180–207. Montréal: Press Universitaire Laval, 1982.

——. "Eating Like a Blacksmith, Symbols in Kapsiki Ethnozoölogy." In *Anthropology in the Netherlands*, edited by Patrick E. Josselin de Jong and Eric Schwimmer, 114–125. Den Haag: Verhandelingen Koninklijk Instituut Taal-, Land- en Volkenkunde nr. 95, 1982.

——. "The Ideology of Building. The Interpretation of Compound Patterns among the Kapsiki of North Cameroon." In *Op zoek naar mens en materiële cultuur*, edited by H. Fokkens, P. Banga, T. Constandse, and M. Bierma, 147–162. Groningen: Groningen University Press, 1986.

——. *The Kapsiki of the Mandara Mountains*. Prospect Heights, Miss.: Waveland Press, 1987.

——. "De zondebok en het kwaad: een ethnografische kritiek." In *Mimese en geweld: beschouwingen over het werk van R. Girard*, edited by Walter E. A. van Beek, 126–145. Kampen (Netherlands): Kok Agora, 1988.

——. "Iron, Brass and Burial: the Kapsiki Blacksmith and His Many Crafts." In *La Forge et le forgeron*, edited by Yves Monino, 281–310. Paris: CNRS/ORSTOM, 1991.

——. "Slave Raiders and Their People without History." In *History and Culture; Essays on the Work of Eric R. Wolf*, edited by Jan Abbink and Henk Vermeulen, 53–71. Amsterdam: Het Spinhuis, 1992.

——. "The Dirty Smith; Smell as a Social Frontier among the Kapsiki/Higi of North Cameroon and Northeastern Nigeria." *Africa* 2, 1 (1992): 38–58.

——. "The Innocent Sorcerer; Coping with Evil in Two African Societies, Kapsiki and Dogon." In *African Religion: Experience and Expression*, edited by Thomas Blakely, Walter E. A. van Beek, and Dennis L. Thomson, 196–228. Oxford: Currey, 1994.

——. "Les Kapsiki et leurs bovins." In *Des taurins et des hommes*, edited by Christian Seignobos and Eric Thys, 15–39. Paris: ORSTOM, 1998.

——. "African Tourist Encounters; Effects of Tourism in Two West-African Societies." *Africa*, 73, 3 (2002), 251–289.

——. "Kapsiki Beer Dynamics." In *Ressources vivrières et choix alimentaires dans le bassin du lac Chad*, edited by E. Garine, O. Langlois and C. Raimond, 477–500. Paris: IRD, 2006.

——. "The Escalation of Witchcraft Accusations." In *Imagining evil. Witchcraft Beliefs and Accusations in Contemporary Africa*, edited by Gerrie ter Haar, 293–316. Trenton N.J.: Africa World Press, 2007.

——. *De rite is rond. Betekenis en boodschap van het ongewone*. Tilburg: Tilburg University Press 2007.

——. "The Healer and his Phone. Medicinal Dynamics among the Kapsiki of North Cameroon." In *Mobile Phones: The New Talking Drums of Everyday Africa*, edited by Mirjam de Bruijn, Francis Nyamnyoh, and Inge Brinkman, 125–134. Leiden: Langaa & African Studies Centre, 2009.

——. "Eyes on top. Culture and the Weight of the Senses." In *Invisible Africa; Sprache und Geschichte in Afrika* 21, edited by Anne Storch, Koppe, Köln (2010) 245–270.

——. "Forever Liminal: Twins among the Kapsiki/Higi of North Cameroon and Northeastern Nigeria." In *Twins in African and Diaspora Cultures; Double trouble or twice blessed*, edited by Ph. Peek, 163–182. Bloomington: Indiana University Press, 2011.

—— "The Gender of Beer: Beer Symbolism among the Kapsiki/Higi and the Dogon." In *Liquid Bread. Beer and Brewing in Cross-Cultural Perspective*, edited by Wolf Schiefenhövel and Helen Macbeth, 147–158. New York: Berghahn, 2011.

——. "Medicinal Knowledge and Healing Practices among the Kapsiki/Higi of northern Cameroon and northeastern Nigeria." In *Markets of Well-being. Navigating Health and Healing in Africa*, edited by Marleen Dekker & Rijk van Dijk, 173–200. Leiden, Brill, 2011.

——. "Cultural Models of Power in Africa." In *Land, Law and Politics in Africa, Mediating Conflict and Reshaping the State*, edited by Jan Abbink &Mirjam de Bruijn, 25–48. Leiden: Brill, 2011.

——. "The Iron Bride." In *Metals in Mandara Mountains' Society and Culture*, edited by Nicholas David, 173–200. Trenton, N.J.: Africa World Press & The Red Sea Press, 2012, 285–301 (in press).

——. "A Touch of Wildness. Brass and Brass Casting in Kapsiki." In *Metals in Mandara Mountains' Society and Culture*, edited by Nicholas David, 303–323. Trenton, N.J.: Africa World Press & The Red Sea Press, 2012 (in press).

———. "Crab Divination among the Kapsiki of North Cameroon." In *Reviewing reality. Dynamics of African Divination*, edited by Walter E. A. van Beek and Philip M. Peek. 2012 (forthcoming)
Beek, Walter E.A. van, and Phil Peek. "Divination: du bon sens dans le chaos." *Arts d'Afrique. Voir l'invisible* edited by Paul Matharan, 149–154, 225–228. Bordeaux, Musée de l'Occitanie, 2011.
Van Gennep, Arnold. *The Rites of Passage*. London: Routledge and Kegan Paul.
Van Santen, José. *They Leave their Jars behind: The Conversion of Mafa Women to Islam*. Leiden: VENA, 1993.
Vaughan, James H. Jr. "Culture History and grass roots politics in a Northern Cameroon kingdom." *American Anthropologist* 66, 1964: 1078–1095.
———. "The Religion and the World View of the Marghi." *Ethnology* 3, 4, (1964): 389–397.
———. "ɛŋkyagu as Artists in Marghi Society." In *The Traditional Artist in African Societies*, edited by Warren L. d'Azevedo, 162–193. Bloomington: Indiana University Press, 1973.
———. "Mafakur: a Limbic Institution of the Marghi (Nigeria)." In *Slavery in Africa; Historical and Anthropological Perspectives*, edited by Igor Kopytoff and Suzanne Miers, 85–104. Madison: University of Wisconsin Press, 1977.
Vaughan, James H., Jr., and A. H. M. Kirk-Greene (eds.). *The Diary of Hamman Yaji. Chronicle of an African ruler*. Bloomington, Ind.:Indiana University Press, 1995.
Vincent, Jeanne-Françoise. "Divination et possession chez les Mofu montagnards du Nord-Cameroun." *Journal de la Société des africanistes* 51, 1 (1971): 71–132.
———. "Conception et déroulement du sacrifice chez les Mofu." *Systèmes de pensée en Afrique Noire*,2 (1976): 177–203.
———. "Main gauche, main de l'homme; essai sur le symbolisme de la gauche et de la droite chez les Mofu (Cameroun du Nord). "In *Système des signes. Hommages à G. Dieterlen*, edited by G. Dieterlen, 485–509. Paris: Hermann, 1978.
———. "Sur les traces du major Denham: Le Nord-Cameroun il y a cent cinquante ans. Mandara, 'Kirdi' et Peul'." *Cahiers d'Études Africaines* 72, 18–4 (1978): 575–606.
———. "Le prince et le sacrifice: pouvoir, religion et magie dans les montagnes du Nord-Cameroun." *Journal de la Société des africanistes* 2 (1987): 89–121.
———. *Princes montagnards du Nord-Cameroun. Les Mofou-Diamaré et le pouvoir politique*. Paris: Harmattan, 1991.
———. "Statut et puissance du 'Dieu-du-ciel' en Afrique de sahel." Repr. in *'Dieu seul! Le Dieu du ciel chez les montagnards du nord des Monts Mandara*, edited by J. Fedry et al. 147–178. Yaoundé: Presses UCAC, 2008,.
Von Graffenried, Charlotte. *Das Jahr des Stieres: Ein Opferritual der Zulgo und Gemjek in Nordkamerun*. Studia Ethnographica Friburgensia 2. Freibrg: Freiburg Universitäts Verlag, 1984.
Vorbrich, Ryszard. *Daba—Górale Północnego Kamerunu*. Wrocław: Polskie Towarzystwo Ludoznawce, 1989.
Wallace, Anthony F. C. *Religion, an Anthropological View*. New York: Random House, 1966.
Werbner, Richard. P. *Ritual Passage, Sacred Journey. The Process and Organization of Religious Movement*. Manchester, Manchester University Press, 1989.
Whitehouse, Harvey. *Modes of Religiosity. A Cognitive Theory of Religious Transmission*. Oxford: Altamira Press, 2004.

INDEX

African Traditional Religion, 22–23
afterlife, conception, 278
agriculture
   cycle, 226f, 227
   harvest, 132
   Kapsiki, 11
   Kapsiki calendar, 247f
   locust threat, 138, 143–144
   preparation for season, 131–132
amalɛa
   girls lining up behind groom, 197f
   husband, 195–197
   wedding custom, 196
ancient grindstone, shrine, 21, 96, 134
animals, symbols of, 287–288
antelope, skin, 207, 217
Arab-Kanuri expedition, Denham, 27
argumentum ad autoritatem, 23

ba (death). *See also* Mte (Death)
   ritual, 87, 92–93
   scapegoat story, 98
Bana neighbors, 41
Barley, Nigel, 279
Barth, Heinrich, slave trading, 27–28
batle melɛ, 60, 61f, 63, 64
battles, village conflicts, 28–29
beer. *See* tɛ
   brewing process, 317n14
   burial mound, 268–269
   gwela brewing, 214, 242
   recipe for, 64
   rhythm of, 230–232
   sacrificial jar at cemetery, 270–272
   separation of the waters, 231
   smiths, 257
   sorghum, 149–150
   tɛ shiŋli, mourning bands, 269–272
   white, for smiths, 252, 262
   white beer by women, 317n15
   women brewing red beer, 323n1

berhe makwa, 234
berhe mte, chasing death, 139–142
besheŋu, black magic, 76–77, 163
Biafra War, 42
birth order names, children, 165–166, 302–303
birth rituals, 160–163, 168, 180, 284, 321n2
black magic
   besheŋu, 76–77, 163
   ward sacrifice, 76–77
blood, first, of bull sacrifice, 90
Boyer, Pascal, 16, 17, 71
boys. *See* initiation rites
brass. *See also* initiation rites
   boy initiation, 20, 93, 181, 207–209, 212
   manhood, 212–215
   symbolism, 208, 244, 288–289
breech births, 164, 169
brewing, beer for ritual, 140, 317n14
bride. *See also* wedding
   blessings, 191–192
   bridal iron skirt, 182–185
   bridesmaid (*mehteshi*), 183, 185, 188, 193, 194
   calling party, 185–189
   integration into new family, 197–203
   iron, 204–206
   marriage transactions, 193–194
   married, 188
   sexual intercourse, 192–193
   stolen bride, 230
   symbols of belonging, 204–206
   trousseau, 235, 236f, 237
   virginity, 189
   yitiyaberhe (initiation father), 187–188
bridewealth
   marriage transactions, 193–194
   trousseau, 235, 236f, 237

Britain
  Cameroon, 316n71
  colonial force, 31, 34, 35, 37–38
  World War I, 315n44
building, term, 14
Bulahay culture, pots as icons, 95
bull sacrifice
  dancing, 89, 90, 93
  division of meat, 90–91
  first blood, 90
  hangar for meat, 88
  Kapsiki culture, 87–94
  showing bull to village, 92f, 93
burial mound, term, 311n4
burial rituals. *See also* funeral
  completing the tomb, 267–269
  corpse, 261–264
  Kapsiki, 123
  return from tomb, 269–272
bush, *gutuli*, 108–109
buying rain, 132, 136–139

cache sexe, 323n7
  bride, 235
  hazhaze, 211
  rhuli, 182, 187–188
calabash
  decoration, 215, 220, 222
  funeral, 251, 256–257
calendar
  Kapsiki, 247f
  ritual and time, 292
calendar rituals, 153, 155
calling party, bride, 185–189
Cameroon
  border dispute, 316n71
  British, 316n71
  census, 312n3
  Kapsiki and Higi, 10–11, 12, 24
  maps, 12, 13
  tourist attraction, 9, 10
  women brewing red beer, 323n1
candidate grooms, 230. *See also* wedding
cascade of life, Kapsiki, 105–106
Catholics, missions, 43–44
cenε, suicide, 7
cεva, objects for rain, 136
cemetery. *See* corpse; funeral; tomb
chanting day, ritual, 216
chasing Death, 139–142, 247f
chicken
  sacrifice, 65, 111
  ward sacrifice, 75–77
children
  beer after funeral, 272
  birth order names, 165–166, 302–303
Christianity, 45, 282, 295
  bull sacrifices, 91

dwelling, 51
Christians, 24, 74
  changing funeral rituals, 280
  dropping rituals, 211
  missions, 43–44, 295
  shala, 103
clairvoyants, 101
clans
  child linking, 180
  maze, 52
closing the quiver, drinking and dancing, 239–241
colonial rule, Mandara area, 11
colonization, Kapsiki and Higi, 30–34, 39–42
color red, twins, 170, 321n6
Combretum, safa leaves, 83
compound, mountainside Kapsiki, 54–56
cooking, wedding, 190
coping rituals, 153–154
corpse. *See also* funeral
  burial, 261–264
  burial chamber, 263
  coming out, 259–261
  Dogon culture of Mali, 324n22
  dressing and adorning, 4–5, 253–256
  funeral preparation, 251–252
  placement in forecourt, 258–259
  purported causes of death, 262–263
  rhamca, 254
  smell, 273, 281–282
  symbolism of head, 254, 255f, 274
cosmology, Kapsiki, 101–108, 127
co-wives, 235, 239, 251, 324n11
crab
  birth of baby, 162–163
  bull sacrifice, 89
  calling the bride, 186
  divination, 66, 67f, 69, 83, 118, 233
  first hunt ritual, 151
  harvest ritual, 147, 149
  twins, 173
  wedding, 193
crops. *See also* agriculture
  harvest rituals, 147–150
  Kapsiki, 11
  locust threat, 138, 143–144
cultivation, agricultural season, 131–132, 247f
culture
  religion, 14–15
  symbolic images, 19–21
curse, twins, 170
cyclical rituals, 154–155

dafa, food icon, 286–287
dafa kapsa pulu, sorghum mush, 58, 62
dafa mndε ceremony
  birth, 163–165
  twins, 173–178
dafa zhaŋe, funeral, 259
dabala, entrance hut, 55, 56f, 60, 88, 164

Index

Damara, smallpox, 112, 113
dance
  announcing amalɛa, 196–197
  bull sacrifice, 89, 90, 93
  chasing Death, 140
  closing the quiver, 239–241
  end of initiation, 241–243
  first appearance of baby, 160
  funeral, 5, 6–7, 249, 250, 253, 256–257
  initiation, 224–225
  kwaberhewuzha, 260–261
  "ladies-excuse-me," 260–261, 277
  la festival, 234
  rain ritual, 133–134
  three days with dead, 273
  twins, 170, 173–174, 175, 176
dedímu, granary, 58, 59f
death
  good, and bad, 276–277, 279
  granary of life and, 272–276
  symbolism, 214
  theory of Kapsiki, 276–280
Death (*Mte*), 276
  chasing, 139–142, 247f
  folk tale, 122–123
  unseen being, 112–113
decoration
  brass in initiation, 208
  burial of corpse, 262
  calabash, 215, 220, 222
  corpse, 254–256
  dung on granary, 129f, 130
  haze, 20–21
  intervillage variation, 228–229
Denham, Major, Arab-Kanuri expedition, 26–27
derha, forecourt, 54–55, 56f, 57, 88
diggers, funeral, 3–4
divination
  birth of baby, 162–163
  crab, 66, 67f, 69, 83, 118, 233
  gwela, 222
  initiation, 228
  interpretations, 107–108
  optimal ritual, 72–73
  sacrifice, 64, 66–69
  witchcraft, 116
dlera, divination, 66, 67f
Dominik, Oberleutenant, 32, 33
Douglas, Mary, 289
dreams, *keleŋu*, 106, 172
dung decoration, *tame*, 129f, 130
Duriez, Christian, missionary, 320n25
dwelling. *See also* rituals of dwelling
  environment, 25
  Mandara Mountains, 14–16
  notion, 14, 16, 22, 50–51
  rituals and, 69–71, 291–292
dzakwa, 81
dzirhwa, crossing the river, 234, 237

emotions, death rituals and, 279–280
environment
  culture and physical, 15
  ecology, 14
  Kapsiki's way of dwelling, 25
epidemics, 120, 131, 153, 155, 292
  smallpox and measles, 112, 113
  wind and, 141–142
episodic memory, rituals, 17, 227
ethnicity
  Kapsiki/Higi, 229
  reluctant, 244
European colonizers, Kapsiki/Higi, 30–31
exegesis, authority, 97

family, revenge for death, 7
fatherhood, symbols, 179–180
feast, 8, 23, 58
  bull sacrifice, 88–90, 92, 98–99
  Christmas, 295
  death ritual, 279
  divination, 68
  gwela, 242, 284
  initiation, 245
  Kapsiki death, 277
  la festival, 204, 218, 221, 233, 243
  lineage sacrifice, 78–79
  manhood, 210
  personhood, 161
  return of the jar, 278
  ritual, 283–284, 287, 291
  twin, 173–178
  village sacrifice, 84
  wedding day, 183, 185, 188, 189–194
fertility
  gwela, 214, 228
  red beer, 231–232
  twins, 162, 178
  wume, 246–247
fete, fault, 114
fieldwork, visiting Gudur, 145–146
flash bulb memory, 227
folk tales
  Hwempetla, 121–124
  Rain, 122–124
  rhena heca, 118, 120
  story of Mogode, 297–301
food. *See also* feast
  birth rituals, 180
  color symbolism, 325n8
  exchanges at rituals, 283
  sacrifice, 287
  symbols, 286–287
fortress, compound, 54–56
France
  colonial force, 31, 34
  World War I, 40, 315n44

Fulbe
  chiefs, 30–32, 35–37
  culture, 45, 131, 254
  enemies, 15, 40–42, 208
  jihads, 26–28
  religion, 89, 282
funeral. *See also* corpse
  burial, 261–264
  burial mound, 267–269
  completing the tomb, 267–269
  corpse dressing, 4–5, 253–256
  dance, 6–7, 249, 253, 256–257
  dance on day 3, 259–261
  first farewell, 252–259
  granary of life and death, 272–276
  "ladies-excuse-me" dance, 260–261
  moment of glory, 259–261
  mourning, 251–252, 253
  preparation, 251–252
  red beer, 231
  return from the tomb, 269–272
  safa and *haze* collection, 252–253, 264, 266
  symbolism of *safa* and *haze*, 253
  symbols, 249, 253
  usual format, 250–251
  variations, 249–250, 264–266
  war song, 5–6
  Zra Teri Kwada, 3–8

Garta, 28, 36, 40, 42, 132, 229
geŋa
  personal stone, 134
  stone for grave, 269, 274
  symbol at burial, 278
gedla, maze, burial, 266
genealogy, *jewu* lineage, 77, 78f
gentleness, *gwela* initiation, 227
geography, Mandara Plateau and hillsides, 11, 14
German colonizers, Kapsiki/Higi, 30–34, 39–42
Girard, R., 71, 97–98
goat
  price of black, 74–75
  village sacrifice, 80–83, 86
  symbolism, 96
goatskin
  burial, 261
  gwela, 93, 207
  intervillage variation, 228
  symbol, 245
God, terms for, 322n10
good and evil, Kapsiki life, 111
granary
  compound, 55, 56f
  dung decoration, 129f, 130
  harvest, 148
  initiating, 128–132
  life and death, 272–276
  plaiting process, 128–129
  tame, 56f, 58, 59f

grindstone, ancient, 21, 96, 134
grooms. *See also la* festival
  makwa, 233
  zakwatewume, 232–234
ground squirrel, Hwempetla, 326n1
Gudur
  chasing Death, 140–142
  coping rituals, 153–155
  fieldwork, 145–146
  locusts, leopards and, 143–145
  rain ritual, 136–139
  visiting, 145–146
gumeze, jar, 61, 82, 82f
Guria, 121
  buying rain, 132, 136–139
  initiation, 210
  la festival, 232
  spirit walkers, 100
  village, 39
gutuli
  concept, 108–109
  organization, 109–110
  shala, 126, 178
  spirits, 101, 119, 141
  trees, 110–113
  twins, 169
Gwava, buying rain, 132
gwela
  boys and brass in initiation, 207–209
  brewing beer without supervision, 214
  chanting day, 216
  closing the quiver, 239–241
  coming out, 215–221
  day of sweet revenge, 216
  end of initiation, 241–243
  fertility, 214
  final rites of initiation, 237–238
  gentleness, 227
  initiation and village identity, 227–229
  Kapsiki calendar, 247f
  Mogode, 210, 212, 221, 228–229
  parties, 242–243
  picture, 209f
  plaiting tame, 129, 130
  preparation for manhood, 209–215
  rites of belonging, 284–285
  seclusion, 213–215, 226f
  showing bull to village, 92f, 93
  songs for coming out, 218–219
  structure of initiation, 225–227
  twins, 181
gwela rites, 25
gwemba, dancing, 241
gwenji, clan, 74, 79–82, 85
gweru, granary, 58, 59f

haŋgedle, medicinal plants, 117–119, 137
harvest

Index

agriculture, 132
  grain, 147–148
  Kapsiki calendar, 247f
  maize, 148
  rituals, 147–150
  sorghum, 147, 149–150
  wume, 155
haze
  adoring corpse, 29
  burial mound, 268
  collection for funeral, 252–253, 266
  creating shrines, 293
  decorating, 20–21
  first hunt, 151
  funeral symbolism, 253, 255, 264, 274–276
  granary, 148
  grasses, 82–83
  Hwempetla's mother, 325n14
  initiation, 210
  plaiting, 128, 130
  symbols, 288, 290
hɛd'i aŋgelɛ, 40
hɛd'i feransɛ, 40
hegi, enemy, 39
"Heidenexcesse," military mission, 34
henetla, bull sacrifice, 87–94
Higi. See Kapsiki/Higi
Hina, 143
hirdɛ, wedding party, 195–197
home sacrifice, 59–66, 96–97
Homo sapiens, 18
Homo significans, 18
honey
  distribution, 323n5
  festival, 237, 238
  symbol, 235
human life, leopard threat, 138–139
human sacrifice, 144
hunting
  first, of season, 150–152
  initiation rites, 219–220
  Kapsiki calendar, 247f
  rain ritual, 132–136
hwɛβɛ, 113, 117–118
Hwempetla
  coping risks, 153
  dead person, 273
  myths, 124–127
  story of, and rain, 135
  story of Mogode, 297–301
  story with ground squirrel, 326n1
  village hero, 83, 121–124
hweteru, "evil eye," 118–119

identity
  ethnic and village, 292–293
  initiation and village, 227–229
  sacrifice, 97
  symbols for twins, 180–181

indigenous religion, 23
individual, relationship with shala, 105–108, 114
Ingold, Tim, 14
initiation rites. *See also gwela*
  boys and brass, 207–209
  bride integrating into new family, 197–203
  coming out, 215–221, 226f
  complex *gwela* ritual, 210–213
  day of sweet revenge, 216
  end of, 241–243
  gwela rites, 210
  gwela with lances and shields, 217f
  hunting, 219–220
  sacrifice, 224–225
  seclusion of boys, 213–215, 226
  structure of, 225–227
  testing of boy initiates, 217–221
  toward manhood, 209–215
  variations by village, 221–225
  village identity and, 227–229
  Wulu initiation, 222–224
iron, funeral symbolism, 274–275
Islam, 45, 282, 295
Islamization, 45, 91

jealousy, mete, 118
jihads, Fulbe, 26
jimu, head gear symbols, 275

Kamale, 4, 27, 36, 39, 40, 42, 50, 82, 229, 230, 253
kamava, slaves, 76
kaŋa, verb, 318n18
Kanuri force, Musfeia, 27
Kapsiki
  calendar, 247f
  Cameroon and Nigeria, 10–11, 12
  cascade of life, 105–106
  census, 312n3
  coping with risk and time, 152–155
  death rituals, 276–280
  divination, 66–69, 72–73
  emotion, 8
  funerals, 249–251, 273
  glossary of terms, 303–309
  la festival, 243–248
  language, 314n28, 319n2
  life and personhood, 160–163, 169–170
  marriage, 52
  mythical tales, 121–124
  oral history by Yaji, 30–39
  personhood, 160–163
  plant names, 309–310
  religion, 17, 22–24
  rituals, 16, 72
  sacrifice identity, 97

Kapsiki (*continued*)
  theory of death, 276–280
  tourism, 9
  village politics and rituals, 98–99
  wedding, 189–194
Kapsiki cosmology, *shala*, 101–108, 127
Kapsiki/Higi
  administration of villages, 33
  belonging and dwelling, 295
  colonization, 30–31
  decorating calabash, 215
  ethnicity development, 229
  external threat, 28–29
  history, 43
  initiation, 225–227
  intercolonial rivalry, 31
  la festival, 244
  Mandara Mountains, 11, 12, 13, 51
  map of, and neighbors, 12
  personal *shala*, 126
  population, 11
  property debate, 50
  religion, 22–24
  rituals and symbols, 19
  shrines, 95–96
  symbol of red beer, 231–232
  wedding à la mode, 195–197
katsala, real warrior, 28–29, 208
kawume gwela, 211
kayita, 77
keleŋu
  dreams, 106, 172
  sacrifice, 118–119
  spirit walkers, 100–101, 142
keluŋu
  harvest ritual, 149
  ward sacrifice, 75–76
kinship terms, 311n2
Kirdi, pagan, 27, 313n11
Kortchi
  buying rain, 132
  story of Nikukud', 301–302
  trait inheritance, 118
ksugwe, 3, 58, 65
  kinsmen at wedding, 191
  wedding, 189–190
kwaberhewuzha, dance, 260–261
Kwada, Zra Teri, funeral, 3–8
kwakwere, fruit, 68
kwalerha, twins, 169–173, 178–179
kwatewume
  marriage in Mogode, 195
  stolen brides, 230, 238, 239
kwatlahutu, initiation, 211

kwatlazewe, 214
kwele, 259, 268, 275
kweperhuli
  gwela coming out, 215
  initiations, 210, 213–215, 237–238
  wedding proceedings, 186, 188, 191, 194

lactation, newborns, 167
ladies-excuse-me dance, 260–261, 277
la festival
  daily activity, 232–233
  defining Kapsiki, 243–248
  end of initiation, 241–243
  final journey, 234–238
  Kapsiki calendar, 247f
  preparation, 232–234
  ritual cycle, 284
  ritual times, 283–284
  saferela, 240
Lamido of Mogode, 38, 45, 50, 241
lances
  coming out, 218–219, 220
  gwela with, 217f
  Kapsiki, 208
land conflict, rooster ordeal, 49–50
landscape, environment, 15
language
  Gudur, 145
  Kapsiki, 314n28, 319n2
  orthography and translations, 44
leopards
  Gudur, 144–145
  howling and mourning, 142
  threat to humans, 138–139
life
  feasting a twin, 173–178
  first appearance of newborns, 159–160, 161f
  Kapsiki personhood, 160–163
  number names, 163–168
  symbols of personhood, 178–181
  twins, 169–173
liminality, 181, 208, 245f, 268, 287, 290
lineage
  child linking two, 180
  makwajɛ clan, 77, 78f
  Rufta, 99
  sacrifice, 77–79, 97
livu
  bride's iron skirt, 182–185, 202, 235
  calling the bride, 185–189
  description, 183f
  funeral, 251
  makwa initiation symbol, 246
  makwa wearing, 184f
  symbols of belonging, 204–206
lizards, rain hunt, 133f, 134

locusts
  coping with risk and time, 152–155
  threat to crops, 138, 143–144
loinskin, goat and antelope, 207

Madagali, 35, 38
Mafa, 9, 143, 222, 231
  bull sacrifice, 87, 91, 94
  ethnic group, 42
  Fulbeization, 45
  mythological imagination, 120
  pots as icons, 95
Mafa Jigile, concept, 126
magistic religion, dynamics, 21–24
maize, harvest, 148, 286
makajɛ, clan, 85
makwajɛ clan, 77, 78f
makwa, 63
  closing the quiver, 239–241
  first-time brides, 183, 185–189, 234–235, 237–238
  harvest, 148
  integration into new family, 197–203
  Kapsiki calendar, 247f
  marriage, 195–196
  rites of belonging, 284–285
  role in death ritual, 140
  songs admonishing, 190–191
  symbols of initiation, 246
  twins, 177, 181
  wearing *livu*, 184f
makwajɛ, clan, 79, 85
makwamte, clan, 79–80
makwiyɛ, clan, 79
Mandara Mountains
  bull sacrifice, 87
  divination in sacrifices, 66–69
  dwelling in the, 14–16
  German column, 39
  Kapsiki/Higi, 11, 12, 13, 51–53
  Mandara Plateau and hillsides, 11, 14
  prehistory, 25–26
  rain maker, 136
  smiths, 311n1
  tourism, 9–10
manhood
  definition, 226
  initiation toward, 209–215
maps, Kapsiki/Higi and area, 12, 13
Marghi, 11, 28, 35, 41, 93, 215, 222, 258
margi, 41
marriage. *See also* bride; wedding
  bridal skirt, 182–185
  calling the bride, 185–189
  stability, 195–196
matini, child without milk, 167
matriline, *mete*, 115
Mauss, M., 71
mawka, rites of belonging, 284

maze, village chief, 52, 79, 86
maze gedla, burial, 266
maze rerhɛ, 306
maze Wula, 41
mblama, ward headman, 53
Mbororo mission, 44
Mcirgue, 306
mɛ pulu, 57, 70
meaning, term, 18
measles, Shasha, 112, 113
meat division, bull sacrifice, 90–91
meha rhwu, 114
mehelegu, 306
mehtembu, granary, 58, 59f
mehteshi
  bridesmaid, 183, 185, 188, 193, 195
  coming out, 216–221
  end of initiation, 241–243
  gwela initiation, 238
  initiation rites, 198–203, 213–214
mekwe, 3, 256, 260
melɛ, 59, 74
  concluding funeral proceedings, 272–276
  hidden sacrifice, 272
  melɛ keluɲu, 64, 75–76
  melɛ keshi, 60, 64, 78
  melɛ meleme, 64, 79–87, 97
  melɛ peli, hunting beer, 151
  melɛ rhɛ, 59, 60, 69
  melɛ Rhuŋgedu, sacrifice, 79–87
  melɛ va, jar of rain, 136
  sacrificial jar, 49, 57, 59–66, 71–72, 105f, 108
  shrine in Kapsiki, 95–96
  village sacrifice, 64, 79–87, 97
  ward sacrifice, 64, 75–76
meleme, villages of Kapsiki/Higi, 51–53
melu, non-smith, 3, 53, 132, 265
memory, rituals, 17, 227
Mentsehe, 202, 203, 210, 211, 217, 218, 306
message, term, 18
metal, funeral symbolism, 274–275, 288–289
mete
  jealousy, 118
  reputation, 116
  witchcraft, 115–118, 224
mice, delicacy, 130–131
Michika, 27, 42, 43, 44, 126
midimte, last words, 3, 62
midwife, birth, 162–163
missions
  Catholic, 43–44, 320n25
  Christian, 43–44
mnzefɛ
  bull sacrifices, 91–92
  burial, 266
  initiation, 227
  priest, 80–81, 83–84, 86
  rain ritual, 136

modes theory, rituals, 16–18
Mofu Diamare, 40
Mogode, 7, 15, 230
  animal raids, 36
  berhe mte, 139
  Chief Wusahwahwele, 266f
  closing the quiver, 239–241
  gwela, 228–229
  initiation, 210, 212, 221, 228–229
  Kapsiki village, 9, 10, 13
  kwatewume marriage, 195
  la festival, 232
  locusts, 143
  neighbors, 28
  rain ritual, 132–135
  sacred mountain, 25
  sacrifice for village, 74
  spirit walkers, 100
  story of Hwempetla, 297–301
  tame initiation, 128
  village, 39
  village sacrifice, 80, 98
  wards, 53
Mokolo, Mandara Mountains, 9
Mora, slave markets, 27, 28
mother, daughter of clan, 167
motherhood, symbols, 179
mother's milk, symbol in cursing, 322n12
mourning. *See also* funeral
  beer of mourning bands, 269–272
  collective, at funeral, 7
  corpse placement, 258–259
  dance at funeral, 256–257
  funeral, 251–252, 253
  war song, 5–6
mpa te mpa, real war, 28
mpedli, 230, 231, 307, 323n1
mpisu hwu, rite, 60, 64
Mte (Death), 307
  chasing death, 139–142
  theory of, 276–277
  unseen being, 112–113
Muslims, 24, 74, 212, 295
  bull sacrifice, 89
  brutality, 40
  emirates, 26
  Hamman Yaji, 37
  shala, 103
  urban life, 45
Muzuku, buying rain, 132
myths
  Hwempetla, 121–124
  Kapsiki rituals, 121–122
  Nayekwakedɛ, 121, 301, 307

ŋacɛ, 79, 80, 81, 82, 85
ŋa melɛ, 64
names
  birth order, for children, 165–166, 302–303
  ceremony for children, 165–166
  number, of newborns, 163–168
  secondary, 165–166
nasara, 4, 26, 41
Nayekwakedɛ myth, 121, 301, 307
ndalɛke, smell of corpse, 281–282
ndemeva, rain maker, 132
ndrimike, bad things, 98
neighbors, Kapsiki/Higi, 12
newborns, first appearance, 159–160, 161f
nhwene, 5, 264, 267, 268, 307
Nigeria
  border dispute, 316n71
  census, 312n3
  Kapsiki and Higi, 10–11, 12, 24
  maps, 12, 13
Nikukud, Kortchi story of, 301–302
ntsehwele, 107, 114, 307
ntsu, 118, 307
number names
  starting life, 163–168
  system, 326n5
Nzambe, 121, 133, 307

objects, *shala*, 104
odors, terms, 281–282
orthography, language, 44
other side
  exegetical reflection, agency and invisibility, 124–127
  good and evil, 111
  psychic disturbance, 109
  seen and unseen sides of personhood, 114–119
  shala and individual, 101–108
  spirit walkers, 100–101
  stealing sorghum, 119
  unseen beings, 108–113
  Va, 111–112
  Veci, 111

pacification, Germans, 39–40
pagan, Kirdi, 27, 313n11
parenthood, symbols, 179
parents
  first appearance of newborns, 159–160, 161f
  number names for children, 163–168
  parenthood, 179
  twins, 176–178
Parkin, David, 98
patrilineal society, mete, 115
pax colonialis, 11, 39, 75
peha, 310
  child birth, 160, 177
  initiation, 147, 207–208
  rituals, 288
  symbol, 21, 181
peli va, 132, 139, 307

personhood
    shadow, 114–115
    slow dawn of Kapsiki, 160–163
    symbols, 178–181
places, *shala*, 104
plant names, Kapsiki, 309–310
plants, symbols of, 288
population, Kapsiki/Higi, 312n3
pots are people, notion, 71, 318n20
power, rain and, 136–139
pregnancy
    Kapsiki, 161
    order, 163, 165, 167, 171
    shala, 104–105, 265
property debate, rooster ordeal, 49–50
Protestants, orthography, 44
Psikyè, *xi*, *xii*
psa pulu, 57
pulu, 58
pulu ŋeza, 55, 57

quills
    burial of men, 324n8
    corpse decoration, 254–256, 264, 275

raiding
    abolition, 38–39
    slavery, 27–29, 30, 33, 35
Rain. *See also Va*
    calendar rituals, 153–154
    folk tales, 122–124
    twins, 172
rain
    agricultural season, 131–132
    coping with risk and time, 152–155
    crops, 143
    Kapsiki calendar, 247
rain rituals
    buying, 136–139
    hunting, 132–136, 150–152
    Kapsiki calendar, 247f
    rain and power, 136–139
    red beer, 231
rebellion, rain makers, 138–139
red beer. *See* tɛ
relationship
    individual and shala, 105–108, 114
    Mensch and Umwelt, 14
religion. *See also* Christianity; Christians; Muslims
    African Traditional Religion, 22–23
    cascade of life, 105–106
    culture and society, 14–15
    dynamics of imagistic, 21–24
    Kapsiki, 17, 22–24, 287
    meaning of ritual, 16–18
    rain ritual, 134
    relationship of individual and *shala*, 105–108
    shala as supernatural double, 125–126
rerhɛ, 53, 259, 307

revenge, family, for death, 7
revenge, ritual, 216
rhamca, 254, 261, 307
rhɛ
    Kapsiki compound, 54–56, 77, 96
    starting a house, 56–58
rhena heca, folk tales, 118, 120
rhena ta Hwempetla
    story of Mogode, 297–301
rhuli, cache sexe, 182, 187–188, 205
Rhuŋgeɗu, 15
    initiation, 219
    sacrifice on mountain, 79–80, 84, 121
Rhuŋweɗu, singing at, 201–202
Rhu Rumsu, holy mountain of Rumsu, 9
rhwa, 308, 323n6
Rhwamerhe, stream, 83, 121
Rhwazhake, birth-order name, 167
rhwɛ, medicine, 68, 104, 233, 300, 308
rhweme, 87, 103, 126
    female symbol, 288
    funeral, 265
Rhwemetemale, woman mountain, 50
Rhwemetla, 246
    day of coming out, 215, 216
    initiation ritual, 198–199, 203
    makwa in *livu*, 184f
    rooster ordeal, 49–50, 138
rhwempe, ritual food, 62
rituals. *See also* funeral; *gwela*; initiation rites
    African village politics, 98–99
    birth, 160–163, 168
    burial, 123
    burial mound, 267–269
    buying rain, 136–139
    calendar, 153, 155
    calling the bride, 185–189
    changing, 294–295
    chasing Death, 139–142
    chasing death (*ba*), 87, 92–93
    closing the quiver, 239–241
    coping with risk and time, 152–155
    cyclical, 154–155
    death, 277–280
    dwelling, 69–71
    first hunt of season, 150–152
    first rites for twins, 173–178
    food exchanges, 283
    funeral, 249–251
    harvest, 147–150
    hunting rain, 132–136
    initiation, 209–215, 229
    initiation at singing rock, 197–203
    meaning of, 16–18
    memory, 17, 227
    minimal and maximal rites, 282–285
    personhood, 179
    rites of passage, 16,

rituals (*continued*)
  single vs. double births, 178
  smell of, 281–282
  starting a house, 56–58
  symbol and meaning, 285–291
  symbols having sex, 19–21
  and time, 291–295
  twins, 169–173
  wedding, 189–194
  wedding à la mode, 195–197
rituals of belonging, 14, 16, 22, 284
  inclusion, 99
  ritual and time, 291–295
  symbols, 290–291
rituals of dwelling. *See also* dwelling
  collective identity of village, 292–293
  compound, 54–56
  divination, 66–69
  home sacrifice, 59–66
  lineage sacrifice, 77–79
  myth, history and Hwempetla, 121–124
  price of black goat, 74–75
  rooster ordeal, 49–50
  starting a house, 56–58
  ward sacrifice, 75–77
rooster, symbolism, 288
rooster ordeal
  conflict resolution, 314n19
  legitimacy, 138
  property debate, 49–50
Rufta
  initiation, 210
  la festival, 232
  lineages, 99
Rumsiki
  initiation rituals, 221, 229
  la festival, 244
  scapegoat ritual, 97–98
  settlement, 51, 86
Rumsu
  chasing Death, 140, 142
  initiation, 210
  Kapsiki village, 9
  kinship system, 52
  la festival, 232
  sacrificing a bull, 87–94

sacred, 16, 95, 293
sacrifices
  addressing *shala*, 102
  bull, 87–94, 318n8
  burial mound, 268
  chicken, 65, 111
  divination, 64, 66–69
  elements, 64
  food at, 287
  hidden, after funeral, 272
  house, 59–66, 96–97
  human, 144
  initiation, 224–225
  Kapsiki/Higi rituals, 94–95
  la festival, 233
  lineage, 77–79, 97
  new life, 159–160
  "optimal" rite, 71–73
  price of black goat, 74–75
  red beer, 231
  rituals of dwelling, 59–66
  scapegoat ritual, 97–98
  symbolism of *safa* and *haze*, 275
  village, 79–87, 283
  ward, 75–77, 97
  wedding, 183
sacrificial jar. *See also* melɛ
  cemetery, 270–272
safa
  adoring corpse, 29
  burial mound, 268
  collection for funeral, 252–253, 266
  decorating, 20–21
  first hunt, 151
  funeral symbolism, 253, 255, 264, 274–276
  granary, 148
  leaves, 83
  symbols, 288, 290
saferela, end of *la*, 240, 241
scapegoat
  Kapsiki ritual, 97–98
  New Testament, 87
scorpions, twins, 171
semantic memory, rituals, 17
sexual activity, 215, 245
sexual intercourse, bride and groom, 192–193
shala, 59, 61, 63, 65
  birth and personhood, 162–163
  chasing Death, 142
  first hunt ritual, 151
  first-person usage, 103
  honorific titles, 319n1
  individual with own, 101–108
  last rites, 274
  new life, 159–160
  notion, 103–104, 125
  personal, 126
  places and objects, 104
  pregnancy, 104–105
  rain ritual, 137–138
  relationship of individual and, 105–108, 114
  Rhwemetla, 49
  sacrifice as optimal rite, 71–73
  translation, 102
  twins, 169–170, 172
Shasha, measles, 112, 113
shave
  parents coming out, 159–160, 164, 166
  shave mbe cɛ, ritual, 216
  twins, 173, 176

shi, 199, 308
shila, 251, 253, 281, 308
shinaŋkwe
  "evil eye" *hweteru*, 118–119
  evil types, 115
  mete, 115–118
  shadow, 100–101, 114–115, 278
shrines
  ancient grindstone, 96
  creation, 293f
  initiation, 229
  Kapsiki/Higi rituals, 95–96
  places of sacrifice, 95
singing rock, initiation at, 198–203
Sir
  gwela rites in, 222, 223f
  initiation, 210
  la festival, 232
Sirakuti, 29, 82
  buying rain, 132
  death, 252
  initiation, 210, 229
  la festival, 232
  war, 37, 40, 42, 119
slavery
  abolition of raiding and trading, 38–39
  early travelers and, 26–29
  Kapsiki history, 25
  Mora, 27, 28
  raiding and trading, 27–29, 30, 33, 35
  witchcraft or theft accusations, 36
smallpox, *Damara*, 112, 113
smell
  corpse, 273, 281–282
  ritual, 281–282
Smith, Jonathan Z., 290
Smith, William Robertson, 71
smith-cum-corpse, funeral, 6
smiths
  adorning corpse, 4–5, 253–256
  caste of undertakers, 273
  corpse burial, 261–264
  digging a tomb, 3
  funeral preparation, 251–252
  Kapsiki society, 287
  Mandara Mountains, 311n1
  ritual tasks, 249
  smell of death, 273, 281–282
  term, 53
  white beer, 252, 257, 262
snakes, *shala* or *gutuli*, 110–111
society
  Kapsiki, 287
  religion, 14–15, 24
Sokoto Caliphate, 31
song contest, initiation ritual, 199–203
songs
  closing the quiver, 239–241
  coming out, 218–219

sorghum
  harvest, 147, 149–150
  spirit stealing, 119
  symbolism of varieties, 286
  sowing, agricultural season, 131–132
spider, *tamtamba gwecɛ*, 111
spirit walkers
  keleŋu, 100–101, 106
  stereotype, 119
  twins, 179
Staal, Frits, 18
Strümpell, "Hauptmann" Karl, 39
Sukur, bull sacrifice, 94, 318n8
supernatural
  notion of, 102
  shala and individual, 101–108
  term, 101
symbolic images
  goatskin, 245
  honey, 235
  initiation and village identity, 227–229
  metals at funeral, 274–275
  mother's milk, 322n12
  plants for decorating, 20–21
  rituals, 19–21
symbolism
  adorning corpse, 4–5
  animals, 287–288
  brass, 208, 288–289
  color, 325n8
  death, 214
  funeral, 253, 255, 264, 274–276
  head of corpse, 254, 255f, 274
  rituals, 285–291
  rooster, 288
symbols
  ancient grindstone, 21
  belonging, 204–206
  funeral, 249
  iron bride, 204–206
  personhood, 178–181
  relation with model object, 289–290
  safa and *haze* plants at funeral, 253
  war, 25
symbols having sex, rituals, 19–21, 204–206

tame, See also granary
  capacity, 130
  communal meal after making, 130–131
  compound, 56f, 58, 59f, 70–71
  decoration, 129f, 130
  harvest, 148
  initiating a granary, 128–132, 154, 290
  tomb, 275–276, 276f
tɛ, 64
  red beer, 230–232
  ritual beer, 57, 59
  tɛ ba, 84

tɛ (continued)
  tɛ derha, social beer, 68
  tɛ dlema, jars of stable, 88
  tɛ ksugwe, drinking bout, 98
  tɛ kwantedˆe rhɛ, beer, 57
  tɛ njinu, 64, 231
  tɛ shiŋli, mourning bands, 269–272
  white beer, 252, 262, 317n15
tereme, instrument, 82
theft accusations, slave market, 36
threshing, women, 147–148
time, ritual and, 291–295
Tizhɛ, first-born son, 63
Tlukwu
  buying rain, 132
  trait inheritance, 118
tomb. See also burial rituals; funeral
  completing the, 267–269
  conversing with nephew in, 4f
  digging, 3–4
  Kapsiki, 4, 275–276, 276f
  return from the, 269–272
  term, 311n4
  termite collection, 324n13
tourism
  Kapsiki culture, 9–11
  Mandara Mountains, 9–11
trading
  abolition of slave, 38–39
  slavery, 27–29
tradition, notion of, 23
translation, language, 44
tripartite structure, gwela initiation, 225–227, 226f
trousseau, bride, 235, 236f, 237
tsu, 308
Turner, Victor, 19
twins
  birth order, 164
  color red, 170, 325n8
  first appearance, 159–160
  first rites for, 173–178
  parents of, 176–178
  scorpions, 171
  special babies, 169–173
  symbols, 180–181
Tylor, E. B., 71

Va, 111–112, 308
veci, 62, 63, 111, 272, 287, 309
verhe
  initiation, 215, 218, 220
  wedding day, 189–194
village
  chasing Death from village to, 140–142, 141f
  collective identity, 292–293
  sacrifice, 79–87, 283
village hero, Hwempetla, 121–124, 297–301
village identity, initiation, 227–229

village politics, Kapsiki rituals, 98–99
virginity
  tests, 214, 244
  wedding, 189
visit, Gudur, 145–146

Wandala, 26, 27
war
  Biafra War, 42
  kwarhweredlɛahweredlɛa, 39
  symbols, 25
  threat from neighbors, 28–29, 40–41
ward sacrifice, 75–77, 97
war of the women, terms, 52
warriors
  katsala, 208
  preparation and protection, 28–29
war song, mourning, 5–6
wealth, brass, 208–209
wedding. See also bride
  à la mode, 195–197
  bridal attire, 193–194
  bridal skirt, 182–185
  bull slaughter and meat division, 183–184
  calling the bride, 185–189
  closing the quiver, 239–241
  feast, 189–194
  first-time brides, 183
  guests, 190
  initiation at singing rock, 197–203
  iron bride, 204–206
  marriage stability, 195–196
  proceedings by kweperhuli, 186, 188, 191, 194
  songs admonishing makwa, 190–191
West Africa, Fulbe jihads, 26
white beer, 252, 262, 317n15
Whitehouse, Harvey, 16, 71, 227
wind
  chasing Death village to village, 140–142
  epidemics, 141–142
witchcraft
  mete, 115–118
  slave market, 36
women. See also bride
  burial, 264–265
  death of female, 324n11
  "ladies-excuse-me" dance, 260–261, 277
  singing nhwene gela, 267
  threshing, 147–148
  white beer brewing, 317n15
Wula
  bull sacrifice, 87, 91, 94
  buying rain, 132
  gwela initiation, 222–224
wume, 155, 226–227, 246–247
wuta, 231, 309

Yaji, Hamman, 41
  colonial powers, 34
  history of Kapsiki, 30–39
yindlu, stone wall, 54, 56f, 70
yitiyaberhe, initiation, 187–188, 205, 235
yitiyagwela, initiation, 210, 212, 224–225, 228, 242
yitiyamakwa, 309

zakwatewume
  closing the quiver, 239
  dance and festivities, 234, 239
  festival preparations, 232–234
  la festival, 243, 246
  paying bride wealth, 230
zamakwa, 239
zeremba, clan, 79–82
zhazha, ritual meal at mound, 267–268, 274, 287
Zimmerman, Captain, 34, 39
Zra Tè, Vandu
  arrest, 38
  Kapsiki lore, 37
  Mogode resident, 31
  oral history, 34, 34f
  sacrifice, 59, 61–62